HEALTH POLICY

Application for Nurses and
Other Healthcare Professionals

Demetrius J. Porche,
DNS, PhD, FNP, ANEF, FACHE,
FAANP, FAAN

Dean and Professor
School of Nursing
Louisiana State University Health Sciences Center, New Orleans
New Orleans, Louisiana

JONES & BARTLETT
L E A R N I N G

World Headquarters
Jones & Bartlett Learning
5 Wall Street
Burlington, MA 01803
978-443-5000
info@jblearning.com
www.jblearning.com

Jones & Bartlett Learning books and products are available through most bookstores and online booksellers. To contact Jones & Bartlett Learning directly, call 800-832-0034, fax 978-443-8000, or visit our website, www.jblearning.com.

Substantial discounts on bulk quantities of Jones & Bartlett Learning publications are available to corporations, professional associations, and other qualified organizations. For details and specific discount information, contact the special sales department at Jones & Bartlett Learning via the above contact information or send an email to specialsales@jblearning.com.

Production Credits
VP, Product Management: David D. Cella
Director of Product Management: Amanda Martin
Product Manager: Rebecca Stephenson
Product Assistant: Anna-Maria Forger
Production Assistant: Brooke Haley
Director of Vendor Management: Amy Rose
Senior Marketing Manager: Jennifer Scherzay
Product Fulfillment Manager: Wendy Kilborn
Project Management and Composition: S4Carlisle Publishing Services

Cover Design: Scott Moden
Director of Rights & Media: Joanna Gallant
Rights & Media Specialist: Wes DeShano
Media Development Editor: Troy Liston
Cover Image (Title Page, Part Opener, Chapter Opener):
    © Orhan Cam/Shutterstock
Printing and Binding: Edwards Brothers Malloy
Cover Printing: Edwards Brothers Malloy

Library of Congress Cataloging-in-Publication Data
Names: Porche, Demetrius James, author.
Title: Health policy : application for nurses and other healthcare professionals / Dr. Demetrius J. Porche.
Description: Second edition. | Burlington, Massachusetts : Jones & Bartlett Learning, [2019] | Includes bibliographical references and index.
Identifiers: LCCN 2017042558 | ISBN 9781284130386 (pbk.)
Subjects: | MESH: Health Policy | Delivery of Health Care | United States | Nurses' Instruction
Classification: LCC RA394 | NLM WA 540 AA1 | DDC 362.1--dc23 LC record available at https://lccn.loc.gov/2017042558

6048

Printed in the United States of America
21 20 19 18 17   10 9 8 7 6 5 4 3 2 1

Dedication

This book is dedicated to my parents, Hayes James Porche, Jr. and Diane Lirette Porche; my two sisters, Anastasia Porche Arceneaux and Chelsealea Porche Lovell; my brothers-in-law, Rory Lovell and Jason Arceneaux, Sr.; and my nephews and nieces, Seth Thomas Porche, Sebastian James Porche, Jason Arceneaux, Jr., Jasmine Arceneaux, and Madeline Lovell. A special dedication goes to my lifetime partner Dr. James Michael DelPrince—thanks for your love and daily support.

Demetrius J. Porche

In Memoriam

This book is in memory of Reverend Dr. James Arnold Ertl, my best friend and partner, for a life of friendship, smiles, laughter, travel, and love that ended too soon. In memory with my love, until we meet again.

Demetrius J. Porche

Contents

Acknowledgments

The ability to write a textbook on policy originates from my life experiences and knowledge that has been facilitated by multiple mentors throughout my career. This book is the result of critical feedback from my graduate students regarding policy courses taught in schools of nursing and schools of public health. To all my students, thanks for challenging and transforming my thinking regarding policy and politics.

Preface

The policymaking process is a dynamic and complex process that occurs within a political context. The political context of policymaking comprises multiple constituents and stakeholders with varying needs, wants, and desires. In addition, the constituents, stakeholders, and policymakers each have varying paradigms that influence and shape their perspective of the societal needs, wants, and desires. The unique paradigm of all individuals involved in the policymaking process influences the potential solutions and policy alternatives identified during the policy formulation and implementation phases.

Nurses as primary healthcare providers have a wealth of knowledge regarding healthcare systems, clinical practice, academia, and diverse populations that can be maximized with the knowledge of policymaking and politics to influence policy. Nurses and other healthcare professionals have an underutilized potential to impact policymaking processes. This book provides the foundational knowledge regarding the governance structures of our country and the multiple processes that influence and impact policymaking.

To effectively influence policy and politics, nurses and other healthcare professionals must attain civic competence. Civic competence requires nurses and other health care professionals to have a knowledge base about the structure and processes of governance and government.

Chapter 1 provides an overview of policy. The various types of policy are described along with several policy models. This chapter introduces the reader to policymakers and policy networks that influence the policymaking process. The concept of civic competence is introduced. It concludes with foundational policy concepts that serve as a foundation for understanding and developing policy.

Chapter 2 presents the governmental structure in the United States. The U.S. government structure at the federal, state, and local levels is presented. The founding laws and principles for other policymaking decisions are reviewed, including the Constitution and the federalism perspective of governmental structure. The branches of government are presented along with an explanation of the federal budgeting process. Government structure at the nonfederal level is discussed with content on state constitutions and city charters.

Chapter 3 presents the various positions and departments within the executive branch of government. The role of the respective executive-level positions and departments in the policymaking process are reviewed.

Chapter 4 reviews the structure of the legislative branch of government. The two chambers of the U.S. legislature (House and Senate) are presented with a discussion of the policy agendas of the primary political parties in the United States. The legislative process of developing laws is presented, along with the roles and responsibilities of legislative members and staff.

Chapter 5 considers the role of the judicial system in policymaking, interpretation, and implementation. The structure of the federal, state, and special court systems is presented with a review of the stages of the litigation process. The adjudication role of the U.S. Supreme Court is discussed. The nurse's role within the judicial system as a legal nurse consultant or expert witness is reviewed.

Chapter 6 is a new chapter providing an overview of the healthcare systems. The healthcare systems in the United States are instrumental in the policymaking process and responding to federal, state, and local policy. This chapter introduces four basic models that form the structure of our healthcare system. The social determinants of health are introduced as a framework for our healthcare system.

Chapter 7 is a new chapter introducing global, international, and planetary health policy. The interrelationship and differentiation of global, international, and planetary health are presented. An overview is presented of several global health organizations. Planetary health is linked to other healthcare policy.

Chapter 8 focuses on public health policy. Public health policy is directed to preserve the health and welfare of the population. Various types of public health policy measures are presented to ensure the preservation of health in normal and emergency situations. This chapter focuses on policy designed to protect the populace as an entity, not only individuals.

Chapter 9 considers the complex policy formulation and implementation process. This chapter has expanded the policy models that are process oriented and describes the policymaking process from drafting policy proposals to drafting rules and regulations. The nurse's role as a policymaker is presented. Policy instruments are introduced as policy measures. This chapter presents the policy implementation process and concludes with policy termination as a means to end current policy or to advance new policy.

Chapter 10 expands the policy analysis models and processes. This chapter presents the readers with multiple processes that can inform the manner in which they engage in analyzing policy. An essential element of policy analysis is included—bill or law analysis.

Chapter 11 presents the research process, research utilization, and evidence-based regulation as possible means to influence policymaking. The utilization of research as a policy measure should be considered in the planning phases of the research process. The need for and impact of policy is analyzed through the process of policy research and policy evaluation. This chapter presents various policy evaluation models and processes that can be utilized to ensure that policy achieves what was intended.

Chapter 12 focuses on the utilization of evidence to influence quality improvement processes. The integration of evidence into quality improvement processes as a means of policy formulation or modification is introduced. This chapter presents several quality improvement models.

Chapter 13 is a new chapter on board governance and policy leadership. The role of governance in policymaking is explored. The role of nurses and other healthcare professionals as policymakers through governance on boards is presented. Bylaws are reviewed as the critical board governance documents.

Chapter 14 is a new chapter that focuses on institutional and association policy. Institutional and association policy processes are explored. Diagnosis of organizational politics is presented as a strategy to influence policy.

Chapter 15 focuses on politics, an often forbidden word in nursing and other healthcare professions; however, it is a process that every nurse uses daily. Chapter 15 focuses on presenting both the theoretical and practical aspects of politics. New content on stakeholders and constituents is presented. This chapter describes many skills that can be used in the political process to influence policy. These skills are presented to provide the nurse with a political toolkit to engage in the policymaking process. New content is presented on conflict resolution and negotiation, two important skills of politics.

Chapter 16 focuses on ethical policymaking. The practice of policymaking and the political activities that influence policy formulation and implementation must occur within an ethical framework. Chapter 16 presents the ethical perspective to ensure that constituents and policymakers engage in an ethical manner consistent with their personal and professional values and accepted ethical codes.

The concluding chapter, Chapter 17, presents the multiple institutes that engage in the policymaking and political process. These policy institutes fund evaluation and research that influence policy or may actively engage in composing positions that influence the thoughts regarding the policy agenda or policy solutions. In addition, many of these institutes and foundations engage in active policy analysis.

The intent of this book is to provide nurses in academia, practice, community settings, and various healthcare systems with an overview of the policymaking process to build their civic competence. This book seeks to provide the knowledge necessary to engage in the policymaking process as an influential nurse or healthcare provider.

Demetrius James Porche

Policy Overview

Policy and political processes are strategies that nurses and other healthcare professionals can use to implement community- and societal-level change. Policy development and formulation are considered population-based interventions useful in impacting the nation's health. There are various levels and types of policy. Therefore, policy development and formulation can occur at an individual, group, or institutional level. Policy is not random but purpose and goal driven. Policy and politics are interrelated concepts. Policy determines politics and politics determines policy.

Nurses and other healthcare professionals at all educational levels and in all practice settings should strive to become politically knowledgeable and actively participate in policy decision making. An individual who possesses the knowledge, skills, and ability to engage in policy formulation, implementation, analysis, evaluation, termination, and political processes is considered to have civic competence. Civic competence is a measure of active engagement in policy and political decision making. A basic prerequisite to civic competence is a knowledge base about the structure and processes of governance and government. Mason, Gardner, Outlaw, and O'Grady (2016) identified four spheres in which nurses can influence policy: government, workplace, organizations, and community. These four spheres can be applied to other healthcare professionals. These spheres of influence are based on the situational and organizational context in which nurses and healthcare professionals engage in practice. Nurses and some healthcare professionals are employed in government offices and the executive branch. Nurses and other healthcare professionals engage in policy development and formulation through their work environment. As professionals, healthcare providers are members of several clinical specialty organizations in addition to organizations of personal interest. As citizens, healthcare professionals are members of communities and in some situations the healthcare professional's workplace is encompassed within the community setting. This sphere

1

of influence model emphasizes the healthcare professional's role in impacting policy based on the multiple contextual situations in which these individuals live and practice. In addition, the healthcare professionals are powerful both in numbers and in the intensity of their commitment to impact policy decision making and policy outcomes. Nurses and other healthcare professionals are encouraged to capitalize on their collective potential to influence policy.

Policy Defined

An understanding of the word *policy* requires comprehension of multiple definitions and the various manners in which the term is used to convey different meanings. The term *policy* can be used to refer to standing decisions or principles that serve as guidelines for actions. Policy used in this manner may not actually be written but more a practice that provides precedence for future activities. It has also been used to refer to proposals, goals, programs, position statements, or opinions of organizations. Therefore, policy has numerous definitions depending on the culture, context, and manner of use. Definitions vary from very simple to complex contextual meanings. The following is a brief summary of multiple definitions of *policy*:

- The principles that govern an action directed toward a given outcome
- A way and means of doing things
- A stated position on an issue
- A plan or course of action selected by any branch of the government or organization
- Authoritative statements, decisions, or guidelines that direct individual behavior toward a specific goal
- Authoritative decisions rendered by any branch of government— legislative, judicial, or executive (Longest, 2015; McLean & McMillan, 2010; Titmuss, 1974)

The multiple definitions of policy indicate that policy is considered a discipline, an entity, or an outcome, and it is a process for achieving a desired outcome. Therefore, the context in which the term *policy* is used must be considered in order to understand the intended meaning. **Table 1-1** presents other policy-related terms.

Policy and Political Theory

Theory attempts to describe, explain, and predict behavior and processes. Theories are made up of concepts and constructs that define the theoretical paradigm that facilitates describing, explaining, and predicting behavior and

TABLE 1-1   POLICY-RELATED TERMS

TERMS	DEFINITION
Policy solution	The proposed answer that will resolve the expressed issue or problem.
Private policy	Policy not within the public domain that is typically produced by or governing nongovernmental agencies or organizations.
Policy intention	The expected or anticipated outcome. The policy intention represents what is meant to be achieved by the policy.
Unintended consequences	Sometimes known as policy blowback, these consequences are the unexpected effects that result from the politics surrounding a policy or the development and implementation of a policy.
Policy effect	The measurable impact of a policy; it can be intended or unintended.
Regulatory policy	Regulations or rules that impose restrictions on a target group.
Distributive policy	A type of allocative policy that spreads benefits throughout society.
Redistributive policy	A type of allocative policy that takes benefits, money, or power from one group and gives it to another group.

processes. These concepts are linked together through a theoretical framework that identifies propositional statements. These propositions explain the manner in which the theorist perceives the concepts as related. From a policy and political perspective, characteristics of good theory exhibit a valid representation of reality; economy of scale; testability; heuristic nature; prediction simulation; relevance and usefulness; powerful inferences; reliability through replication; objectivity; veracity; and logical organization (Smith & Larimer, 2016).

Types of Policy

There are multiple types of policy. Policy types are designated based on the intent and focus of the policy. Some policy is not mutually exclusive to one typology.

For example, some health policy may also be considered public health policy. In addition to the various definitions of policy, there are different types of policy that further contribute to the meaning of the term. The different types of policy are health, public, public health, social, institutional, organizational, and legal. The type and scope of policy that exist are determined by the governmental structure and political and economic systems. These various types of policy are not always mutually exclusive in their defining characteristics.

Health Policy

Health policy can be generated through governments, institutions, or professional associations. Each branch and level of government in the United States can influence health policy. Health policy can also be made through private sector organizations such as insurance companies. Health policy consists of policy that impacts the health of individuals, families, populations, or communities. Health policy includes policies that affect the production, provision, and financing of healthcare services; however, these policies are more appropriately known as health systems policy. Health policy integrates the definition of health and policy. Health is a concept that is accepted as important to individuals and communities. Some definitions of health are rather simplistic; other definitions define health along a continuum. A simplistic definition of health is the mere absence of disease. Other definitions of health recognize health as existing along a continuum that includes maximal states of positive health and recognizes that an illness or disease process may be present but the individual may experience a positive state of being that is interpreted as "healthy." A generally accepted definition of health at both the national and international level is the World Health Organization's (WHO) health definition. The WHO defines health as a state of complete physical, mental, and social well-being and not merely the absence of disease or infirmity (World Health Organization, 1998).

Health policy builds on this basic definition of health. Health policy, in general terms, is any policy that affects the health of individuals, communities, or society. Health policy is considered a broad type of policy that may include other types of policy such as public policy or public health policy.

Public Policy

Public policy is policy that impacts the general public or citizens. It generally serves the interest of the public. Public policies are authoritative statements generated from the three branches of government—executive, legislative, or judicial—that impact the general public. Defining attributes of public policy are made in the "public's" name, made or initiated by a branch of the government, and interpreted or implemented by the public sector. The definitions of public policy are numerous, without consensus on one definition. The following are some accepted public policy definitions:

- Whatever the government chooses to do or not to do to regulate behavior, organize bureaucracies, distribute benefits, or extract taxes (Dye, 2017)
- The sum of government activities that influences the life of citizens, whether the government acts directly or through other agents (Peters, 2015)
- A government statement about what it intends to do or not to do, such as a law, regulation, ruling, decision, order, or any combination of these (Birkland, 2016)
- Authoritative decisions made by the three branches of government— executive, legislative, or judicial—that are intended to direct or influence the actions, behaviors, or decisions of others (Longest, 2015)

The definitions of public policy vary by author. However, the definitions of public policy do have common elements or themes. These commonalities focus on governmental influence or regulation and governmental action directed toward individuals or communities.

The World Health Organization further defines what is considered healthy public policy. The WHO (1998) considers healthy public policy as any course of action adopted and pursued (by a government, business, or other organization) that can be anticipated to improve (or has improved) health and reduce inequities in health. Public policy is generally considered a product of some public demand that elicits a government-directed course of action aimed at resolving a problem, or in response to political pressure. The distinctive purposes of public policy are to resolve conflict over scarce resources and provide programs that meet public needs.

Public Health Policy

Public health policy intersects policy that is health related but impacts the general population. It may be defined as "the administrative decisions made by the legislative, executive, or judicial branches of government that define courses of action affecting the health of a population through influencing actions, behaviors, or resources" (Porche, 2003, p. 318). This is in contrast to health policies, which are considered applicable only within specific organizations or institutions, known as organizational or institutional health policy.

Social Policy

Social policy consists of policy that impacts the general welfare of the public. Policy that focuses on meeting the human needs of education, housing, and instrumental social support is typically considered a type of social policy. Some exemplars of social policy areas include:

- Well-being and welfare
- Poverty
- Justice
- Living conditions
- Animal rights
- Unemployment
- Social security
- Housing
- Education
- Food subsidy programs
- Family and child protection

Institutional Policy

Institutional policies are policies that are developed or implemented by an institution that affects the respective constituents of the institution. Institutional policies frequently govern the workplace environment. Typical institutional policies consist of policies and procedures outlined in operational manuals.

Organizational Policy

Organizational policies are administrative decisions typically made by a board of directors that outline the decisions, position, or official statements that represent the constituents of the organization. Organizational policies can be in the form of bylaws, policy and procedure manuals, articles of incorporation, resolutions, or position statements.

Legal Policy

Legal policy is generally policy founded upon laws or officially accepted rules promulgated through a legislative or executive governmental process. In addition, legal policy does include case law that is developed through judicial opinions and judgments. Legal policy includes policies that relate to the legal profession. Legal policy includes policy that conforms to the law. Most laws are considered policy but not all policy is considered law or legal policy. For example, institutional and organizational policies may or may not consist of laws or legal policy.

Health, public, public health, social, institutional, organizational, or legal types of policy assume many forms. These various types of policies can be in the form of law, rules or regulations, operational decisions, or judicial decisions. Laws can be enacted at all levels of government. Laws are generally considered freestanding legislative enactments that attempt to achieve a predetermined outcome. Laws enacted at the federal or state levels of government are implemented through the formation of rules and regulations by agencies within the executive branch of government. In addition to the formation of rules and regulations, executive branch agencies develop programmatic operational decisions that further implement the intent of the law. These operational decisions can be in the form of policies or procedures. Decisions rendered through the judicial branch can also formulate legal policy. Administrative decisions from the judicial branch are precedent setting in the formation of policy, such as with case law.

Another typology of policy is whether it is substantive or procedural. Substantive policy is policy that significantly changes or alters the current status of events. Procedural policy informs the manner or process in which the policymaking body implements changes.

Policy Intention

Policy is developed and formulated with a specific strategic intention. Two strategies that assist with the implementation of the policy intent are regulation and allocation. A policy with a regulatory intent is designed to prescribe and control the behavior of a particular population. A policy with an allocation intent focuses on providing resources in the form of income, services, or goods to ensure implementation of policy to individuals or institutions. Allocation policies can be distributive or redistributive. Distributive policy doles out resources in a planned manner consistent with the policy intent. In contrast, redistributive policy redirects existing resources from a current allocation mechanism to a new direction through a different allocation mechanism.

Legislative policy may be formulated, then delegated to an executive agency for the development of specific rules and regulations to operationalize the policy. In this manner, the policy intention should focus the promulgation of rules and regulations to ensure that policy implementation is consistent with the policy intention.

Policymakers

The policy process engages a variety of different individuals and organizations. Individuals who participate in the development and formulation of policy are referred to as policymakers. Policymakers consist of legislators, executive agency employees, and institutional and organizational administrators and leaders. Individuals who are in, or have privileged access to, the inner circle or upper echelon of Congress, the state legislature, executive agencies, or organizational and institutional leadership are referred to as policy elites. In addition, the policymakers themselves are also referred to as policy elites (Buse, Mays, & Walt, 2012).

Networks

Issue networks consist of individuals or coalitions with an active citizen base that is politically interconnected. These issue networks have specialized policy knowledge especially regarding their issue of interest. Issue networks are considered important to policymakers and the policymaking process. Issue networks generally are aligned with the sentiment of the citizens. In addition, issue networks are a resource that has the ability to apply political power and pressure on policymakers and to generate policy solutions (Smith & Larimer, 2016). Sabatier and Weible (2014) refer to policy networks that are similar to what Smith and Larimer describe and characterizes policy networks as stable patterns of social relations between interdependent constituents that form around a problem or policy. Network management provides the ability to impact these policy networks in the manner desired for collective action.

Network management may be considered a political strategy. Network management consists of controlling and organizing constituents with different goals or preferences in relation to a problem or policy alternative into the same existing relationship network or coordinating divergent efforts within an existing network to impact a specific policy. Network management is also the merging of multiple networks into one network for a common purpose or cause. The effectiveness of network management is dependent upon the number of constituents, the critical mass of constituents needed to exert political power, complexity of existing networks, extent of self-reliance of network, dominance of network, and the degree of conflict of interest between network members and the entire network (Sabatier & Weible, 2014).

Policy Decision Making: Influencing Factors

The policy decision-making process is influenced by multiple factors. A general systems model has been used to describe the forces that influence the policy decision-making process. Greipp (2002) identified three major forces that affect policy decision making: consumers, providers, and regulatory bodies. Motivating and inhibiting factors were identified that affect the decision-making process.

Consumers are considered clients, families, and communities. Consumer forces are represented by those who have a perceived need for healthcare services and products. Providers are healthcare professionals who render care to clients, and also scientists or researchers. Providers include family caregivers. The last driving force in health policy decision making is regulatory bodies. Regulatory bodies include governments, legal systems, third-party payers, political action committees, other special interest groups, and ethics and institutional review board committees. These three driving forces interact and influence each other during the health policy decision-making process. The factor with the greatest influence will shape the policy issue and policy adopted (Greipp, 2002).

Motivators and inhibitors are the intervening positive and negative variables that can influence the perspective of consumers, providers, or regulatory bodies. Motivators are the positive variables that influence the decision making in the direction of what is best for the common good. Inhibitors are negative variables that influence the perspective in the direction of self-interest rather than public interest (Greipp, 2002).

Agenda Setting

One of the first processes of policymaking is agenda setting. Many believe that agenda setting is the most critical aspect of policy development and formulation. The word "agenda" indicates that there is some type of prioritization of issues or some listing of issues that is defined as relevant or pertinent. Policymakers must be aware of competing and multiple agendas that influence the public and stakeholder opinion regarding policy. There are typically at least four agendas regarding each issue: media agenda, public agenda, political agenda, and the executive branch/government agenda.

Agenda setting is the process of determining what problems are deserving of policy solutions and resolution at the current time. Kingdon's policy development model proposes the interaction of three policy streams that create a window of opportunity when these respective streams align. These three streams are problem, policy, and political. An individual who ensures that the respective problem is brought to the policymaking arena is known as a *policy entrepreneur*. A policy entrepreneur seizes the opportunity within a favorable political climate to bring the policy problem to the forefront of the public agenda for policy development (Kingdon, 2011).

An agenda is a collection of problems, understandings of causes, symbols, solutions, and other elements of public concern that attract the attention of members of the public and/or policymakers. An agenda is also referred to as a coherent set of proposals, each related to the other and forming a series of potential enactments. As stated previously, agenda setting is the process by which problems and potential solutions gain or lose attention and potential for policy action.

There are multiple levels of agenda. Each agenda level brings the issue or policy closer to the action potential of policymaking. The agenda levels are agenda universe, systemic agenda, institutional agenda, and decision agenda. The agenda universe represents all the ideas that could potentially be brought up and discussed within a society or political system. Systemic agenda represent the issues that are commonly perceived by members of a political group or community as meriting some public attention and involving matters within their scope of authority or legitimate jurisdiction for action. Institutional agenda is a subset of the broader systemic agenda. The institutional agenda represents the items explicitly being given consideration for action by the policymakers. Lastly, the decision agenda contains those items that are actively on the table for policymaking action by policymakers. **Figure 1-1** presents a model of the policy agenda levels (Kingdon, 2011). The movement of issues through the various levels of an agenda is influenced by multiple variables.

Agenda setting is influenced by interpersonal social and political networks. These networks exert considerable influence on policy agenda setting. This process is sometimes referred to as interpersonal agenda setting. Interpersonal agenda setting uses social or political networks to mediate relationships among involved stakeholders and constituents such as policymakers, governmental representatives, elected officials, media, and the general public, to influence the agenda and ultimately policy.

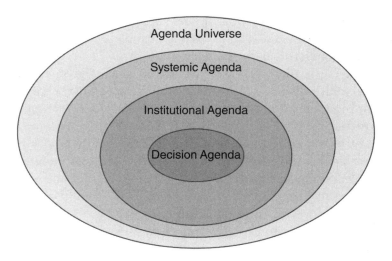

Figure 1-1   Agenda Levels Model

Other driving forces of agenda setting consist of the problem's magnitude, research, political forces, public opinion, and the government's executive official. Problems that are defined and placed on the policy agenda for policy formulation are generally broadly identified by policymakers as important or requiring urgent action to resolve a public health or safety issue. In addition, the perceived magnitude of a problem can be influenced by the amount of public salience and amount of conflict surrounding the respective problem or policy. Problems that have a broad or widespread implication are more likely to be placed on the policy agenda for policy development and formulation. The placement of a problem on the policy agenda is also dependent upon the social and political context of the circumstances surrounding the problem at the given time (Longest, 2015).

A *problem* represents an unsettled matter that demands a solution or decision. Two general requisites of a problem are a perplexing or vexing situation and an invitation for a solution. A problem is generally considered an area in which there is a discrepancy between what is wanted (desired situation) and what exists (current situation). Sabatier and Weible (2014) proposes that problem analysis consists of examining the participants, positions, outcomes, action-outcome linkages, level of control participant's exercise, information available, and the cost and benefits associated with developing a policy to resolve the problem.

Research data provide support for the policy agenda. Research data, such as epidemiological data, outline the determinants of a problem and suggest the impact of an issue, for example, through morbidity and mortality statistics. Research determines the extent and nature of a problem, clarifies the associative or related factors, and provides evaluative data regarding potential policy alternative solutions. Research data clarify the problem for placement on the policy agenda. In addition, research presents data that form the baseline foundation for future comparison and measurement of the policy impact and outcomes (Longest, 2015).

Political forces influence the likelihood of a problem being placed on the policy agenda. Problems or policies directly related to a political party's platform are more likely to be placed on their policy agenda. Chapter 15 provides more detail on the influence of politics on policy formulation.

Public opinion's interaction with media creates a cyclic agenda-setting process. The media informs public opinion, and public readership impacts the media's focus on problems or issues of public interest. Each informs the other within the policy agenda-setting process. Public opinion can be shared directly with elected officials, obtained through special interest polls, and communicated with the press through letters to the editor.

The governmental elected officer (e.g., president, governor, or mayor) commands the attention of the public and media. These elected officials frequently communicate to the public through the media. During this communication, they are informing the public using the media as a means to prime and frame the problems. These governmental officers have the ability to communicate in the public domain their expected direction for problem resolution and the proposed policy resolution. Formal forums used to communicate these issues are framed as "State of the State" or "State of the Union" speeches. These speeches frequently outline the respective governmental elected officer's policy agenda (Longest, 2015). The manner in which the problems are outlined and policy resolutions are presented frame our thinking regarding the viable policy options and expected outcomes.

Policy Models

A *model* is a description of a complex entity or processes in an understandable manner. A model is sometimes described as a complex program, process, or entity that is replicable within other similar situations. Models are designed to be summative in nature. A model may be composed of a narrative description with an associated figure detailing the relationships between the concepts, variables, or items represented in the model. A policy model is a description of the complex process of developing, implementing, and evaluating the policies and the policymaking processes within a political sphere of influence. Some policy models are presented in the following material and in Chapter 9. These policy models are used to explain the policymaking process but can also be used as a framework to conduct policy analysis (see Chapter 10).

Hall Agenda-Setting Model

The Hall agenda-setting model proposes that an issue or problem emerges on the policy agenda when three criteria are strongly met. These three criteria are legitimacy, feasibility, and support. Legitimacy of an issue or problem is established if the policymaking body believes they have an obligation to engage. Feasibility represents the potential ability to implement the policy solution. Feasibility is dependent upon the availability of necessary resources, such as knowledge, human, fiscal, and physical. Support refers to the amount of public support for the issue or problem (Buse et al., 2012).

Policy Triangle Model

The policy triangle model is a simplified approach to understanding the policymaking process using four interrelated factors. Buse et al., (2012) propose four factors that define the policy triangle as policy context, policy process, policy content, and actors. The policy context consists of the systemic factors that have an impact on the policy solution. Policy context also consists of situational factors (transient conditions that impact policy), structural factors (unchanging elements of society), cultural factors (value and belief systems), and exogenous factors (level of interdependence or level of sovereignty). The policy process is the systematic process of policymaking (problem identification, policy formulation, policy implementation, and policy evaluation). The policy content consists of the policy resolution. Actors are individuals who engage in the policymaking process such as constituents, interest groups, or legislators (Smith & Larimer, 2016).

Politics, Policy, and Values Model

Policymaking is considered a complex, multidimensional, dynamic process that is influenced by the values of those individuals who establish the policy agenda, determine the policy alternatives, and define the goals to be achieved by the policy, the implementation methods, and ultimately the manner in which the policy is evaluated. This model asserts that the value framework of everyone involved provides the large context in which decisions are rendered. Politics is the next contextual sphere that is within the espoused value system and also provides a comprehensive context in which the policymaking process occurs. At the core of the model exist the policymaking stages, which are circular and repetitive. These stages consist of agenda, goals, policy alternatives, policy selection, policy implementation, policy evaluation, then cycling back to agenda setting. Politics influences each step of the process (Mason, Gardner, Outlaw, & O'Grady, 2016).

"Garbage Can" Model

This model proposes that there are policy solutions that have been previously discarded as possible or applicable that remain circulating with the potential policy sphere. These discarded policy solutions might get attached to an identified policy issue or problem (Hanney, Gonzalez-Block, Buxton, & Kogan, 2003). This discarded policy solution may or may not be appropriate to the problem or issue but gets attached as a viable solution.

Contextual Model

Policy models provide the framework to understand policy and the policymaking process. The contextual policy model proposes at least five contextual dimensions to define the environment that influences policymaking. This contextual model of policy can also facilitate policy analysis. The five contextual dimensions are:

- Complexity and uncertainty of the decision-system environment
- Potential for constituent feedback

- Ability by constituents to control policy formulation
- Stability of constituents and policymakers over time
- Activation of the interested parties

Schneider and Ingram Social Construction Model

The social construction model emphasizes the role of the target population's influence in policymaking processes. Schneider and Ingram (1993) propose that the policymaking process can best be understood by knowing the legislative official's perception of target populations and their respective needs. They further propose that the target population can be categorized as advantaged, contenders, dependents, or deviants. The manner in which the respective target population is seen and categorized will determine the level of influence the respective group has over policymaking. The social construction model perceives target populations along two dimensions: (1) positive or negative and (2) powerful or powerless. The target populations are perceived in relation to their relative power base and ability to influence policy. For example, children and disabled persons can be categorized as dependent and are viewed very positively but may be perceived as having less power than other groups.

In addition, Schneider and Ingram propose five categories of tools used to influence the policymaking process. These tools are authority, incentive, capacity-building, symbolic and hortatory, and learning (Schneider & Ingram, 1990). Authority tools are statements substantiated by legitimate forms of governmental power that grant permission or prohibit specific actions in certain circumstances. Incentive tools are motivators that influence an individual to engage in volitional behavior to receive the motivator. Capacity-building tools provide needed education, training, or resources to empower individuals to make decisions or engage in activities. Symbolic and hortatory tools use the individual's internal motivation as a catalyst for action based on their beliefs and values. Learning tools use needs assessment data to identify the informational needs and inform the needed policy.

Political Influence Model

Political influence represents the ability of an individual or group to impact the policy agenda and policy development and formulation process. The political influence model proposes that nurses have the ability to significantly influence policy development, formulation, and implementation within four spheres. The four spheres of influence are government, workplace, organizations, and community. A nurse's active engagement in these environments provides the nurse with an opportunity to advocate for specific policy agendas and

Figure 1-2   Political Influence Model

influence policy development and formulation from a nursing perspective. Other healthcare professionals as well as nurses can engage in political influence within these four spheres. **Figure 1-2** presents visual representation of the political influence model.

6 Ps Model

The 6 Ps policy model provides a simplistic framework from which to understand the multiplicative factors that influence policy development. The 6 Ps policy model consists of policy, process, players, politics, press, and public polls. **Figure 1-3** depicts the aspects of the 6 Ps policy model.

Problem-Centered Public Policymaking Process Model

The problem-centered public policymaking process model presents a complex, dynamic, nonlinear, cyclical, and iterative process that can be used to understand policymaking and to analyze policy. The model is considered to revolve around a central core element, the problem. A premise of the model is that

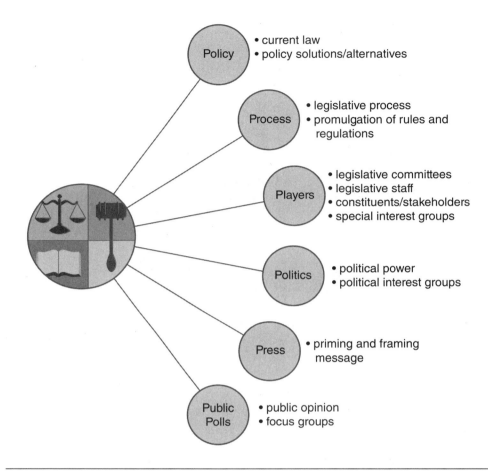

Figure 1-3   The 6 Ps Policy Model

problem recognition and correct identification of the "real" problem are necessary conditions for the policymaking process. This model considers the major players in the policymaking process to consist of legislators, members of the executive branch, and members of interest groups. This model recognizes that policymaking and policy analysis are two separate processes; however, these activities may occur concurrently as a means to formulate or modify policy. The six phases of the problem-centered public policymaking process are:

- Agenda setting—the initial and crucial phase that uses Kingdon's three streams—problems, policy, and politics—to determine the readiness of the window of opportunity to develop policy

- Policy formulation—identifying policy alternatives and developing or formulating the selected policy alternative
- Policy adoption—selection of the policy
- Policy implementation—mobilization of the physical, human, and fiscal resources to carry out the intended policy
- Policy assessment—determining the extent to which the policy implementation is in alignment with the intention, statutory requirements, and expected objectives
- Policy modification—using the policy assessment to modify, maintain, or eliminate the implemented policy (Dunn, 2016).

Punctuated Equilibrium (PE) Model

Punctuated equilibrium describes the process of achieving policy change. This model proposes that policymaking occurs through incremental changes that occur over an extended period of time. These extended periods of incremental policy changes are followed by brief periods of major or transformational policy change (Sabatier & Weible, 2014).

Policy Cycle–Process

The formation and implementation of policy experiences revision as findings from policy analysis, policy evaluation, and policy research informs policy-makers of needed changes in the current policy. This process is referred to as the policy cycle. The policy cycle is composed of 10 components: issue raising, agenda setting, policy drafting, public support building, policymaker support building, policy development and formulation, policy passage, policy implementation, policy evaluation, and policy revision. **Figure 1-4** depicts the policy cycle. *Policy* consists of the current laws and policies that are competitive and similar along with all potential policy solutions and alternatives. *Process* includes the legislative processes required to evolve from policy idea to draft policy. Depending on the level of policy development—federal, state, or within an executive agency—the policy process may include the promulgation of rules and regulations in accordance with administrative law and procedures. Players include all individuals and groups that have a vested interest in the problem or policy resolution. Politics consists of the processes utilized to influence the public, legislators, or other stakeholders regarding the desired course of policy action. Press represents the media message regarding the problem or policy resolution. Lastly, public polls provide a real-time assessment of public opinion regarding the proposed policy (Hall-Long, 2009).

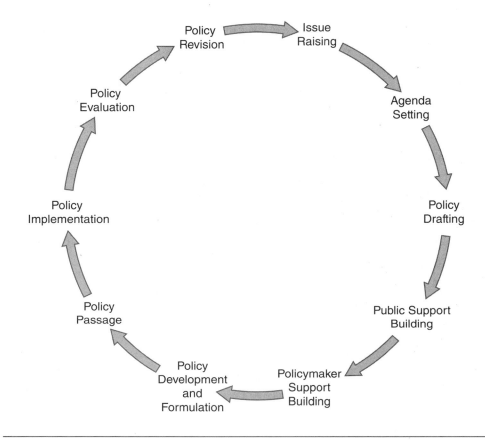

Figure 1-4   Policy Cycle

Policy on Policy

A policy on policy is a guidance document regarding several aspects of the policymaking process. Policy on policy implies that a policy is generated to outline the terminology used in the policymaking process, the manner in which policies are made, the policy approval process, the time interval for reviewing policies for modification and change, and frequently the policy model for the governmental body, organization, or institution.

Institutional policies frequently have a *policy on policies*. A policy on policies determines the process for the development, adoption/approval, and management of institutional policies in addition outlining the policy format and template. The policy on policies may also determine authoritative structure, accountability, and the types of policies within the institution.

Foundational Policy Concepts

Foundational policy concepts are thoughts, notions, or ideas that provide the supporting structure that is basic to the understanding of policy. Foundational policy concepts assist in the development, formulation, and interpretation of policy frameworks and implications. Some foundational concepts that will be relevant to the understanding of policy structure, analysis, and impact are authority, regulation, national security interest, supremacy, privacy, rights versus privileges, federalist structure, indemnification, balance of power, and democracy.

Authority

Authority is the power or right to give an order, make decisions, or enforce behaviors. Scope of authority is the amount of authority delegated to an individual, agent of an organization, or institutional body through some formal governance document, law, statute, or legally binding authoritative statement or under some agency agreement. Scope of authority is critical in policy to determine whether a principal is liable for the acts of his/her agent. It is critical to know, during policy formulation and approval processes, who or what body has the authority to approve or implement the policy under consideration. Scope of authority should always be a consideration in the political process of influencing policy.

Regulation

Regulation is a type of policy designed to carry out a specific type of legislation. Regulations are generally promulgated in accordance with the appropriate administrative law procedures at the local, state, or federal level. Regulations are rules designed to implement specific legislation that generally directs specific behaviors, actions, or procedures.

National Security Interest

National security interests are those interests that are relevant to the protection and maintenance of a nation's sovereignty and destiny. The concept of national security interest is based on the espoused perspective of supremacy of the nation-state. The several philosophical perspectives on the conceptual boundaries of national security interest vary from focusing on a single nation-state's interest over all other nations to a collective international perspective that considers the interrelationships among nation-states as essential to each nation's security and the collective security of all nations. Essentially, national security interest focuses on a nation's power structure to control the extent to which outside forces can harm a country or nation. In essence, it is the safekeeping of the nation as a whole. National security goals are to:

- Preserve the safety of the American homeland and protect our nation's domestic institutions and vital systems;
- Maintain a global balance of power for America and its allies;

- Guarantee freedom of the seas to promote world commerce and economic viability;
- Maintain a global economy based on economic freedom;
- Develop domestic resources and maintain international energy market free from political manipulation; and
- Ensure dedication to America's core values and universal freedom principles.

Nations use a variety of power instruments to protect national security interest such as the armed forces, law enforcement, intelligence agencies, diplomacy, foreign aid, and international financial controls.

The protection of national security interests consists of multiple types of securities. The prominent elements of national security interest are political security, economic security, energy and national resources security, technological security, and homeland security. Political security protects a nation's sovereignty of the government and political systems with the protection of society from unlawful threats and external pressures on the government or political infrastructure, systems, and processes. Economic security protects a nation's economic capacity to provide for the citizenry to include protection of the nation's wealth and economic freedoms to make financial decisions. Energy and national resource security is the protection of and access to a nation's natural resources such as oil, gas, water, food/vegetation, and minerals. Technological security is the process of implementing measures and systems to secure and protect a nation's communication systems and information. Homeland security focuses on domestic security. A nation's domestic security depends on securing a country's borders through airport and port security, border security, transportation security, and immigration enforcement.

National security interests are interconnected to collective defense, collective security, and global security. Collective defense is an official arrangement among or between nation states to offer support or defense to other member states if threatened or attacked. These collective defense policy agreements form the basic structure of national allies. Collective defense is considered as a form of collective security. Collective security is a regional or global concept of international institutions such as the United Nations, which uses international law, aid, and governance to maintain peace and protect member nations. Global security is the set of ideas developed by the United Nations on the premise that no single nation is secure unless all nations are secure. The focus of global security is on the elimination of conflict between all nations (Holmes, 2015; National Security Act of 1947).

Supremacy

Supremacy is a general state of being relatively superior to others in authority, power, or status. Supremacy establishes the power hierarchy to declare what policies have power over or authority over other policies. The concept of supremacy is critical in the policy formulation process to ensure that a policy being developed and then implemented is commensurate with and does not violate the policy that is superior to it. For example, state level policy has to be commensurate with and not violate federal policy.

Privacy versus Confidentiality

The concept of privacy provides for an individual to be free from public attention, being observed, interference, or intrusion. Privacy also refers to an individual's right to control access to his or her body. The concept of privacy is rooted in common law. Privacy is frequently confused with confidentiality. Confidentiality refers to personal information that is shared with another person but should not be divulged to a third party without the individual's expressed consent. Confidentiality implies that information provided by an individual will be protected from release or being divulged to a third party.

Rights versus Privileges

Rights and privileges are frequently confused and incorrectly used interchangeably. An individual's perception of something as being a right or privilege may also influence his or her political perspectives on policy. A right is generally accepted as something that is inherently an irrevocable entitlement provided from the moment of birth as a result of being a human, whereas a privilege is an entitlement granted by another person, state, or body on some conditional basis.

Federalist Structure

The federalist structure is the division of political authority and power among various levels of government. In the United States, our federalist structure divides power among the executive, legislative, and judicial branches of government but also delineates scope of authority among federal, state, and local governments. Broadly, federalism is a system of authority delineation and power structure division among various levels. Federalism is a concept that is also used in institutions and organizations as a framework to structure and distribute authority.

Indemnification

Indemnification is a policy clause used to allocate risk among individuals, groups, or parties. The purpose of an indemnification clause in a governing document, contract, or policy is to clearly state which individual, group, or party is responsible for what risk. Through an indemnification clause in the policy, an individual, group, or party is held harmless or secured against loss or damage (Byrnes, 2007; Garner, 2014).

Balance of Power

Balance of power is provided by our federalist structure. It is a system of checks and balances established through our U.S. Constitution to distribute power among the executive, legislative, and judicial branches of government. The expected outcome from a balance of power is stability.

Democracy

Democracy is governing by the people. Governing by the people entitles individuals to have a voice into their governmental processes and policy formulation. Democracy can be executed directly or indirectly through a representative democratic process. Direct democracy enables each individual to personally, without a mediator or representative, engage in the decision-making or policymaking process. In a representative democracy, individuals select or elect others to provide voice and participate in the decision-making or policymaking process on their behalf. It is expected in a representative democracy that representatives act after consulting with their constituency. The following are considered essential characteristics of a democracy:

- People govern themselves through direct or representative democracy.
- People have the right to vote.
- Citizens are active participatory members in politics, civic life, and voting.
- Human rights for all citizens are protected under the law.
- The rules of law and procedures apply equally to all citizens.

Summary Points

- Policy and political processes are strategies that nurses and other healthcare professionals can use to implement community- and societal-level change.
- Four spheres in which nurses and other healthcare professionals can influence policy are government, workplace, organizations, and community.
- The term *policy* has been used to refer to proposals, goals, programs, position statements, or opinions of organizations.
- The multiple definitions of policy indicate that policy is considered a discipline, an entity, or an outcome, and a process of achieving a desired outcome.
- The different types of policy are health, public, public health, social, institutional, organizational, and legal.

- Health policy consists of policy that impacts the health of individuals, families, special populations, or communities.
- Public policies are authoritative statements generated from the three branches of government—executive, legislative, or judicial—that impact the general public.
- Public health policy intersects policy that is health related but impacts the general population.
- Social policy consists of policy that impacts the general welfare of the public.
- Institutional policies are policies that are developed or implemented by an institution that affects the respective constituents of the institution.
- Organizational policies are administrative decisions typically made by a board of directors that outlines the decisions, position, or official statements that represent the constituents of the organization.
- Legal policy is generally policy that is founded upon laws or officially accepted rules promulgated through a legislative or executive governmental process.
- Most laws are considered policy but not all policy is considered law or legal policy.
- A policy with an allocation intent focuses on providing resources in the form of income, services, or goods to ensure implementation of policy to individuals or institutions.
- Distributive policies dole out resources in a planned manner consistent with the policy intent.
- Issue networks consist of individuals or coalitions with an active citizen base that is politically interconnected.
- Network management consists of controlling and organizing constituents with different goals or preferences in relation to a problem or policy alternative into the same existing relationship network or coordinating divergent efforts within an existing network to impact a specific policy.
- Individuals who are in, or have privileged access to, the inner circle or upper echelon of Congress, the state legislature, executive agencies, or organizational and institutional leadership are referred to as policy elites.
- Three major forces that affect policy decision making are consumers, providers, and regulatory bodies.
- There are typically at least four agendas regarding each issue: media agenda, public agenda, political agenda, and the executive branch/ government agenda.

- Agenda setting is the process of determining what problems are deserving of policy solutions and resolution at the current time.
- Kingdon's policy development model proposes the interaction of three policy streams that create a window of opportunity when these respective streams align. These three streams are problems, policy, and politics.
- Agenda setting is influenced by interpersonal social and political networks.
- Policymaking is considered a complex, multidimensional, dynamic process that is influenced by the values of those individuals who establish the policy agenda, determine the policy alternatives, and define the goals to be achieved by the policy, the implementation methods, and ultimately the manner in which the policy is evaluated.
- The six phases of the problem-centered public policy-making process are agenda setting, policy formulation, policy adoption, policy implementation, policy assessment, and policy modification.
- The policy cycle is composed of 10 components that are cyclic: issue raising, agenda setting, policy drafting, public support building, policymaker support building, policy development and formulation, policy passage, policy implementation, policy evaluation, and policy revision.
- Policy on policy is a guidance document to the entire policymaking process for a governmental body or organization.
- Policy concepts form the basis for understanding and developing policy.

References

Birkland, T. A. (2016). *An introduction to the policy process: Theories, concepts, and models of public policy making* (4th ed.). New York, NY: Routledge.

Buse, K., Mays, N., & Walt, G. (2012). *Making health policy* (2nd ed.). Berkshire, UK: Open University Press.

Byrnes, B. (2007, June). Why your contract should contain an indemnification clause. *The Journal of Light Construction*, 1–2.

Dunn, W. (2016). *Public policy analysis: An introduction* (5th ed.). New York, NY: Routledge.

Dye, T. (2017). *Understanding public policy* (15th ed.). Boston, MA: Pearson.

Garner, B. (2014). *Black's law dictionary* (10th ed.). St. Paul, MN: Thomson West.

Greipp, M. (2002). Forces driving health care policy decisions. *Policy, Politics and Nursing, 3*(1), 35–42.

Hall-Long, B. (2009). Nursing and public policy: A tool for excellence in education, practice, and research. *Nursing Outlook, 57*, 78–83.

Hanney, S., Gonzalez-Block, M., Buxton, M., & Kogan, M. (2003). The utilization of health research in policy-making: Concepts, examples and methods of assessment. *Health Research Policy and Systems, 1*(2), 1–28.

Holmes, K. (2015). *What is national security?* Retrieved from http://index.heritage.org/military/2015/important-essays-analysis/national-security/

Kingdon, J. (2011). *Agendas, alternatives, and public policies* (2nd ed.). Boston, MA: Longman.

Longest, B. (2015). *Health policymaking in the United States* (6th ed.). New York, NY: Health Administration Press.

Mason, D. J., Gardner, D. B., Outlaw, F. H., & O'Grady, E. (Eds.). (2016). *Policy & politics in nursing and health care* (7th ed.). St. Louis, MO: Elsevier.

McLean, I., & McMillan, A. (2010). *The concise Oxford dictionary of politics* (3rd ed.). Oxford, England: Oxford University Press.

National Security Act of 1947 (Public Law 80-253), Section 101(a), now codified at 50 U.S.C. § 3021.

Peters, B. G. (2015). *American public policy: Promise and performance* (10th ed.). Chatham, NJ: Chatham House Publishers.

Porche, D. (2003). *Public & community health nursing practice: A population-based approach*. Thousand Oaks, CA: Sage.

Sabatier, P. A., & Weible, C. M. (Eds.). (2014). *Theories of the policy process* (3rd ed.). Boulder, CO: Westview Press.

Schneider, A., & Ingram, H. (1990). Behavioral assumptions of policy tools. *Journal of Politics, 52*(2), 510–529.

Schneider, A., & Ingram, H. (1993). Social construction of target populations: Implications for politics and policy. *American Political Science Review, 87*(2), 334–347.

Smith, K. B., & Larimer, C. W. (Eds.). (2016). *The public policy theory primer* (3rd ed.). Boulder, CO: Westview Press.

Titmuss, R. (1974). *Social policy: An introduction*. New York, NY: Pantheon.

World Health Organization. (1998). *Health promotion glossary*. Retrieved from http://www.who.int/hpr/NPH/docs/hp_glossary_en.pdf

Governmental Structure

Government is an entity, organization, or institution that provides the structure of rule within a defined city, state, country, or nation. Government is also considered the act or process of governing, especially the development, implementation, and evaluation of public policy in a political unit. The purposes of government are multifaceted. The government provides the political and organizational structure to rule an entity (city, state, country, or nation); protects the interest of the state or sovereignty; develops policies; protects the interests of individuals; provides peace and stability; provides services; and promotes the general welfare of the citizens.

Governmental Structure

The U.S. Constitution forms the government and the legal basis of the U.S. legal system. The three primary functions of the U.S. Constitution are to allocate power between the federal government and the states (federalism), divide power among the three branches of government (separation of power), and limit the amount of government power (protection of individual liberties). **Figure 2-1** presents the branches of the U.S. government. **Figure 2-2** shows a comprehensive representation of the government structure (Longest, 2015).

Federal

The federal government of the United States is centered in Washington, DC. The federal government consists of 10 regional offices. **Box 2-1** outlines the states included within each of those regions. At the federal level, the government is composed of the executive, legislative, and judicial branches. These branches are briefly described in the following text, and respectively in Chapters 3, 4, and 5. This federal government structure forms the basis of our system of federalism in the United States.

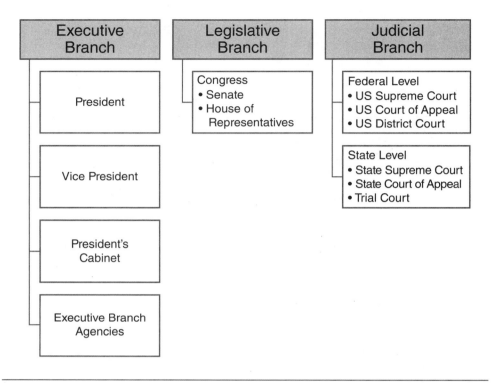

Figure 2-1   U.S. Branches of Government Structure

State

The state governments are organized and structured under state constitutions. The state constitutions are similar to the federal constitution. In a federalist system, each state government mirrors the federal government structure with three branches of government to ensure state-level distribution of power. Again, these branches are executive, legislative, and judicial. State-level laws or policies must not conflict with federal laws or policies.

Local

A state constitution outlines the local governmental structure for the respective state. The local government structure can consist of parishes, counties, cities, and villages. Local governments usually have a governance structure that is parallel to the federal and state government structure. A mayor typically leads the executive branch, which is composed of an elected city council or board. The function of government at the local level is described through either a city charter or city constitution. Laws or policies at the local level must not conflict with either state or federal laws or policies.

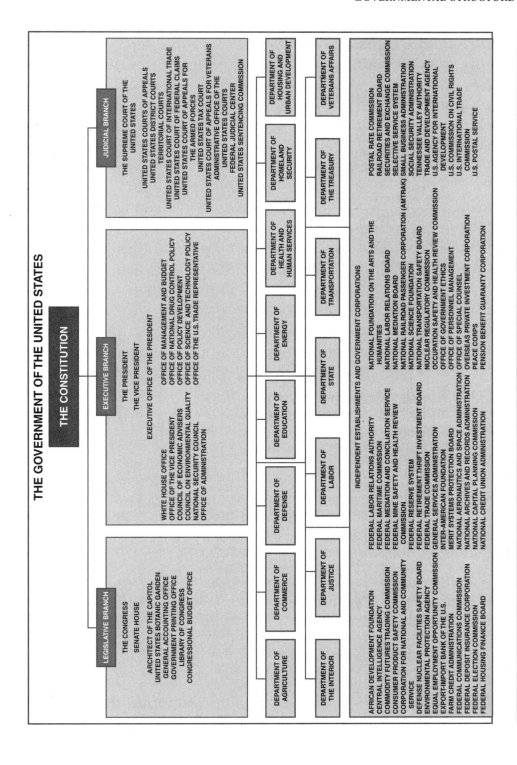

Figure 2-2 Comprehensive U.S. Government Structure

BOX 2-1 U.S. FEDERAL REGIONS

Region 1
- Connecticut
- Maine
- Massachusetts
- New Hampshire
- Rhode Island
- Vermont

Region 2
- New York
- New Jersey
- Puerto Rico
- Virgin Islands

Region 3
- Delaware
- Maryland
- Pennsylvania
- Virginia
- West Virginia
- District of Columbia

Region 4
- Alabama
- Florida
- Georgia
- Kentucky
- Mississippi
- North Carolina
- South Carolina
- Tennessee

Region 5
- Illinois
- Indiana
- Minnesota
- Ohio
- Wisconsin

Region 6
- Arkansas
- Louisiana
- New Mexico
- Oklahoma
- Texas

Region 7
- Iowa
- Kansas
- Missouri
- Nebraska

Region 8
- Colorado
- Montana
- North Dakota
- South Dakota
- Utah
- Wyoming

Region 9
- Arizona
- California
- Hawaii
- Nevada

Region 10
- Alaska
- Oregon
- Washington
- Idaho

U.S. Constitution

The Constitution of the United States is the supreme law of the land. It is the legal reference for the highest judicial decisions in the United States made by the Supreme Court. The Constitution serves as the foundation of and provides the legal structure for the U.S. government. It defines the structure, power, and responsibility of the branches of government and serves as a model document for state constitutions and city charters.

The Constitution consists of a preamble, seven original articles, and 33 amendments. **Box 2-2** presents the preamble. The seven original articles provide the legal foundation for legislative power, executive power, judicial power, state

---

BOX 2-2 U.S. CONSTITUTION PREAMBLE

"We the People of the United States, in Order to form a more perfect Union, establish Justice, insure domestic Tranquility, provide for the common defence, promote the general Welfare, and secure the Blessings of Liberty to ourselves and our Posterity, do ordain and establish this Constitution for the United States of America."

BOX 2-3 U.S. CONSTITUTION SEVEN ORIGINAL ARTICLES

---

1. Establishes congressional powers and limits.
2. Forms the executive branch of government.
3. Creates the judicial branch of government.
4. Provides the duties and responsibilities of the states.
5. Describes the U.S. Constitution amendment process.
6. Provides for retaining of country debts that were present before the Constitution was adopted.
7. Identifies the required number of states to ratify the Constitution.

---

powers and limits, amendment ratification methods, and ratification process of the Constitution itself. **Box 2-3** presents a summary of the seven original articles. Of the 33 amendments, 27 amendments have been ratified by the required number of states and are part of the Constitution. The first 10 represent what is known as the U.S. Bill of Rights, shown in **Box 2-4**. The remaining 17 amendments further provide guidance on legal rights and government structure. **Box 2-5** presents a summary of those remaining 17 amendments (11–27).

BOX 2-4 BILL OF RIGHTS OF THE U.S. CONSTITUTION

---

1. Congress shall make no law respecting an establishment of religion, or prohibiting the free exercise thereof; or abridging the freedom of speech, or of the press; or the right of the people to peaceably assemble, and to petition the Government for a redress of grievances.
2. A well regulated Militia, being necessary to the security of a free State, the right of the people to keep and bear Arms, shall not be infringed.

(continues)

BOX 2-4   BILL OF RIGHTS OF THE U.S. CONSTITUTION (CONTINUED)

3. No Soldier shall, in time of peace, be quartered in any house, without the consent of the Owner, nor in time of war, but in a manner to be prescribed by law.

4. The right of the people to be secure in their persons, houses, papers, and effects, against unreasonable searches and seizures, shall not be violated, and no warrants shall issue, but upon probable cause, supported by Oath or affirmation, and particularly describing the place to be searched, and the persons or things to be seized.

5. No person shall be held to answer for a capital, or otherwise infamous crime, unless on a presentment or indictment of a Grand Jury, except in cases arising in the land or naval forces, or in the Militia, when in actual service in time of War or public danger; nor shall any person be subject for the same offence to be twice put in jeopardy of life or limb; nor shall be compelled in any criminal case to be a witness against himself, nor be deprived of life, liberty, or property without due process of law, nor shall private property be taken for public use, without just compensation.

6. In all criminal prosecutions, the accused shall enjoy the right to a speedy and public trial, by an impartial jury of the State and district wherein the crime shall have been committed, which district shall have been previously ascertained by law, and to be informed of the nature and cause of the accusation; to be confronted with the witness against him; to have compulsory process for obtaining witnesses in his favor, and to have the Assistance of Counsel for his defense.

7. In suits at common law, where the value in controversy shall exceed twenty dollars, the right of trial by a jury shall be preserved, and no fact tried by a jury, shall be otherwise reexamined in any Court of the United States, than according to the rules of the common law.

8. Excessive bail shall not be required, nor excessive fines imposed, nor cruel and unusual punishments inflicted.

9. The enumeration in the Constitution, of certain rights, shall not be construed to deny or disparage others retained by the people.

10. The powers not delegated to the United States by the Constitution, nor prohibited by it to the States, are reserved to the States respectively, or to the people.

BOX 2-5   U.S. CONSTITUTION AMENDMENTS 11 TO 27

11. Provides the foundation for sovereign immunity—states are immune from out-of-state citizens and foreigners not living within the state borders.
12. Revises presidential election process.
13. Abolishes slavery and involuntary servitude.
14. Defines citizenship, provides due process clause, and describes privileges or immunity clauses.
15. Prohibits denial of voting rights on the basis of race, color, or previous servitude.
16. Permits Congress to levy income tax without apportioning it among the individual states.
17. Provides for the election of U.S. Senator by popular vote.
18. Prohibits manufacturing or sale of alcohol within the United States (repealed in 1933).
19. Prohibits denial of voting rights on the basis of sex.
20. Changes the president and vice president dates of term of office.
21. Repeals 18th Amendment.
22. Establishes term limits for president.
23. Grants Washington, DC, electors in the Electoral College.
24. Prohibits revocation of voting rights due to nonpayment of taxes.
25. Outlines the succession of the presidency and establishes the procedures to fill the vice president vacancy.
26. Prohibits denial of voting rights on the basis of age (18 years of age or older).
27. Delays implementation of congressional salaries until after the next election of representatives.

Federalism

Federalism separates the legal scope of authority into two governmental tiers, federal and state. Federalism grants the federal government limited authority but allows the state governments plenary powers to protect the public. The chief powers for public health purposes are the powers to regulate interstate commerce (Gostin & Wiley 2016). In addition to delegated powers, states maintain the powers that they had prior to the ratification of the U.S. Constitution. The "reserved powers" doctrine holds that states can exercise all powers inherent in government to protect the public through the formation of policies and political structures (Gostin & Wiley 2016; Grad, 2005).

Federalism is a government system that provides for shared sovereignty among multiple levels of government in which the national government retains supremacy. There are three essential characteristics that must be present under a federalism structure of governance: (1) There must be a provision for multiple levels of government to act simultaneously on the same territory or on the same citizens. (2) Each of the respective levels of government must have its own sphere of authority and power, which may overlap with the other levels of government. (3) In accordance with the U.S. Constitution, federal law is supreme over state law. Likewise, most state constitutions provide that state law is supreme over local laws and policies (Mueller, 2001).

In addition to being considered a government system, federalism is also considered a political system with a division of political units at the national, state, and local levels. The central purpose of federalism is to ensure protection against tyranny, encourage policy diversity, manage conflict between governmental levels, disperse power, and ensure representation of the people in a democracy. The U.S. Constitution provides for a federalist system; however, it provides protection only for national and state governments. Local governments have delegated powers generally derived from the state constitution. The federalism perspective has changed over time. **Box 2-6** presents the federalist perspective over time in the United States. The perspective can be used in policy analysis to examine the context in which national, state, or local policy was developed.

The structure under federalism sets up a hierarchy of powers. In a federalist structure that has a national- and state-level government, the federal government has preemption over state or local laws. This is permitted through the national supremacy clause in the U.S. Constitution. There are different types of preemption. *Total preemption* exists when the federal government assumes all powers over state laws. *Partial preemption* exists when a policy of the same or similar topic exists at the national and state level. In this situation, partial preemption permits state laws concerning the policy to be valid as long as the state law does not conflict with the federal law. The standard partial preemption permits state laws or regulatory agencies to regulate activities in a field regulated by the federal government as long as the state regulatory policy standards are at least as stringent as the federal policy standards. In contrast to preemption, a federalism structure permits federal mandates. Federal mandates are direct orders or regulations to the state government that require the

BOX 2-6 FEDERALISM CONTEXT IN THE U.S. FOR POLICY ANALYSIS

Pre-Federalism Period: 1775 to 1789

- This period was marked by the establishment of a national government under the Articles of Confederation.
- A new constitution was drafted and adopted that formed the federal system of government.
  - 1776—Declaration of Independence
  - 1777—Drafted Articles of Confederation
  - 1781—Articles of Confederation approved by states
  - 1786—Articles of Confederation reconsidered
  - 1787—New Constitution drafted

Dual Federalism Period: 1789 to 1865

- Dual federalism is established with national and state governments as equal partners with distinct scope of authority.
- Period is marked by tensions between the national and state governments.
  - 1789—Constitution approved by states.
  - 1789 to 1801—Period known as the Federalist Period—Leaders such as George Washington, Alexander Hamilton, and John Adams promoted the establishment of the federal government.
  - 1791—Ten Amendments added to the Constitution as the Bill of Rights. Congress also established the Bank of the United States.
  - 1798—Doctrine of Nullification passed to permit states to suspend federal laws within its boundaries that were determined unconstitutional.
  - 1815—States' Rights Doctrine urged states to protect citizens against acts of Congress that were not constitutional.
  - 1819—Doctrine of Implied Powers—Permitted federal government to pass laws that were determined to be "necessary and proper" to carry out constitutional duties.
  - 1820s to 1830s—States clash over tariffs.
  - 1824—Federal regulation of interstate commerce
  - 1842—Testing of Constitution's supremacy clause and States' Rights Doctrine
  - 1850—Fugitive Slave Act and prelude to Civil War
  - 1860—Civil War

(continues)

BOX 2-6   FEDERALISM CONTEXT IN THE U.S. FOR POLICY ANALYSIS (CONTINUED)

- 1862—Morrill Act—Provided land grants to states to support the expansion of higher education public institutions

Dual Federalism Period: 1865 to 1901

- There is increasing presence of national government in areas traditionally in the purview of the states.
  - 1868—Due process and equal protection clauses of the Constitution—Added 14th Amendment, which proposes due process and equal protection clauses. These clauses strengthened the federal government's judicial powers.
  - 1873—Doctrine of States' Rights revived—Ensured that state and national citizenship were distinct entities, restored some state powers.
  - 1887—Interstate Commerce Commission Act strengthened Congress' role in regulation.
  - 1890—Sherman Anti-trust Act—Permitted Congress to control the formation of monopolies.
  - 1896—Civil rights' Separate But Equal doctrine—Permitted segregation as long as accommodations were equal. This doctrine was overturned in 1954.

Cooperative Federalism Period: 1901 to 1960

- This era was marked by greater cooperation by multiple levels of government.
  - 1910—New Nationalism—Sought to expand the powers of the national government.
  - 1913—Sixteenth Amendment—Authorizes the federal income tax system and develops "grants-in-aid system."
  - 1933 to 1938—Period of New Deal—Expanded role of government in domestic affairs to include economic and social policy. This was an attempt to impact the economic situation.
  - 1944—McCarran Act—Delegates regulation of banking and insurance to the states.
  - 1954—Civil rights and states' rights reconsidered—The 14th Amendment of the U.S. Constitution was used to establish due process and equal protection with a final determination that segregated schools were inherently unequal.

BOX 2-6   FEDERALISM CONTEXT IN THE U.S. FOR POLICY ANALYSIS (CONTINUED)

Creative Federalism Period: 1960 to 1968

- The era of the Great Society further shifted powers to the national government level through the expansion of grant-in-aid programs. Grant-in-aid program regulations were used as a mechanism to induce control over state-level policy. A large number of grants were provided by the federal government during this period.

Contemporary Federalism Period: 1970 to 1997

- This era experienced an increase in unfunded federal mandates and continual disputes over the federal government systems' amount of regulation.
- Concerns emerged about duplication of services, fragmentation, overlap, and confusion of federal and state responsibilities.

New Federalism: 1970s to 2001

- This period focused on reducing national control over grant programs.
- Decentralization of national programs with revenue sharing
  - ◆ 1995 to 1997—Formation of the "Contract with America" and Health Insurance Portability and Accountability Act
  - ◆ 1993 to 2001—Presidency of Bill Clinton sought to end the era of government and focus on development and reformation of social programs such as health care, education, and environment.

21st-Century Federalism

- 2001 to 2009—President George W. Bush promoted a federalist centralization of power at the level of the federal government and executive branch. Federalism was depreciated during this period.
- 2009 to 2016—President Barack Obama proposed to return the country to the core principles of federalism. President Obama's roots in community organizing and empowerment proposes a potential paradigm that will support an agenda of shared power and collaboration at multiple levels of government that extends to individual empowerment.
- 2016 to Present—President Donald J. Trump's perspective on federalism appears to be in favor of returning power and decision making back to the state level.

conduct of specific state activities generally through the enactment of federal laws. If fiscal resources are not allocated to the states for the implementation of these federal mandates or to assist with offsetting the cost of implementation, it is considered an unfunded federal mandate. Some examples of unfunded federal mandates are the Age Discrimination Act, Safe Drinking Water Act, and Americans with Disabilities Act.

The federalist structure is deeply rooted in our American governance structure. The federalism framework of governance structure provides the basic framework that guides the development of organizational or institutional structures, delineation of authority and accountability, and policy processes.

The federalism perspective has changed over time in the United States. The federalist perspective should be considered as one engages in the policy analysis process. The federalist perspective provides the context within which policy was developed within the respective time period.

Under the federalist separation of the government into federal and state hierarchies, states are delegated police power. Police power provides the legal authority to ensure the health, safety, and welfare of society. In addition, states are granted *parens patriae* (patriarchal power) and taxation power.

Police Power

Police was the original term used to describe the powers that permitted the sovereign government the right to control its citizens. The purpose of this was to promote the general health, safety, comfort, morals, and prosperity of the public (Gostin & Wiley 2016). The three underlying principles of police power are to promote the greater public good, permit the restriction of private interest to promote public good, and permit pervasiveness of state powers.

Parens Patriae Power

Parens patriae means "parent of the country." *Parens patriae* power provides the state with inherent power through sovereignty to safeguard citizens of the state. This power basis provides states the legal authority to protect the interests of minors and incompetent persons: States may make decisions on behalf of individuals who are incapable of making decisions for themselves. *Parens patriae* allows states to assert their own general interest regarding communal health, safety, comfort, and welfare (Gostin & Wiley 2016).

Taxation Power

Taxation is a power that regulates individual private behaviors through economic penalties. The power to tax is frequently referred to as the power to govern people's individual behaviors (Gostin & Wiley 2016).

Centralism

In contrast to federalism, in which sovereignty is shared, centralism concentrates sovereignty within one governmental structure. *Centralism* is based on a federal parliament. In this parliamentary structure, the federal parliament has a general power to make laws for the peace, order, and good government within the respective country.

Centralism can also be referred to the concentration of power to formulate policy within an organization at one level. From a political perspective, the term *centralism* is used to denote centrism. Centrism is the political positioning between conservatism and liberalism (Mueller, 2001).

Branches of Government

Governmental power and authority at the national level is separated among the three governmental branches—executive, judicial, and legislative. Executive power is vested in the president of the United States, judicial power is vested in the U.S. Supreme Court, and legislative power is vested in the U.S. Congress. Governmental power and authority at the state level maintains a similar governmental structure that separates delegated state powers within the state among three governmental branches.

Executive

The executive branch executes the law through policy enforcement. The executive branch also proposes law to the legislature, issues and enforces regulations, and approves or vetoes proposed legislation. The major components of the executive branch are the Executive Office of the President (EOP), presidential cabinet, and cabinet departments. These areas are presented in Chapter 3.

Legislative

Congress has three powers that provide the foundation for its influence in the policy process: the power to make all laws, the power to tax, and the power to spend. The legislative branch is composed of two chambers—the Senate and the House of Representatives. Legislative members are frequently referred to as congressional officers or members of Congress. The Senate has 100 seats, representing two members from each state. Senators are elected for 6-year terms. The House of Representatives currently has 435 seats in which representation is based on the respective state's population size. This allocation is reviewed every

10 years based on results of the national decennial census. Representatives are elected for 2-year terms. Each congressional officer is assigned to one or more committees in the respective chamber. Chapter 4 provides more information on the legislative branch.

Judicial

The judicial branch is the final interpreter of constitutional and federal statutory law, preserves individual rights and constitutional structure, and develops a body of case law for precedence. Chapter 5 presents information on the judicial branch of government.

Federal Budget Process

The federal budget process is a collaborative effort between the executive and legislative branches of government. The president, as the official leader of the executive branch of government, sets the national spending agenda, outlined in what is known as the presidential budget. The legislative branch of government evaluates the budget and allocates spending. The federal budget fiscal year extends from October 1 through September 30. The federal budgeting process begins each year in early February. The Senate and House of Representatives compose budget resolutions for their respective chambers. The federal budget should be passed during March through each respective chamber. Once the budget is passed, a conference committee, with representation from each chamber, convenes to propose a single budget resolution with an anticipated passage date of April 15. **Box 2-7** presents the budget process timeline.

After the budget resolution is passed, budget reconciliation legislation is composed along with appropriation bills. The reconciliation bill is legislation that reconciles the governmental revenue (primarily from taxation) with the amount of money the government proposes to spend during the respective fiscal year. In contrast, an appropriation bill is legislation that prescribes the amount of funding received by each respective program named in the federal budget.

During the budget process, each committee involved in composing the various budget bills will hear public testimony. This is an excellent opportunity to influence the amount of funding allocated to a specific program. **Box 2-8** presents some budget terminology. **Figure 2-3** outlines the budgeting process.

BOX 2-7   BUDGETING PROCESS TIMELINE

First Monday in February
Deadline for submission of president's budget.

February 15
Deadline for submission of Congressional Budget Office (CBO) report on projected spending for the forthcoming fiscal year.
CBO examines president's budget.
CBO examines economic impact of president's budget.

Six Weeks after the President's Submission
Deadlines for the congressional standing committees to submit comments regarding the president's budget to the House and Senate budget committees.

March
House and Senate budget committees develop separate budget resolutions.
House Budget Committee reports in March, and the full House votes on the budget resolution about a week later.

April 1
Deadline for Senate Budget Committee to report budget resolution.
Full Senate expected to act on its budget resolution about a week later.

April 1–15
House and Senate conference committees develop a conference report on a budget resolution.
Each respective chamber votes on the resolution from the conference committee.

April 15
Congress expected to complete action on the concurrent budget resolution, generally referred to as the budget resolution, or the budget.

April 15–May
Authorizing committees develop reconciliation legislation.
Reconciliation legislation reported to budget committees of each respective chamber.
Budget committee acts on this proposed legislation (reconciliation legislation) and sends it to the respective chamber floor.
Each respective congressional chamber acts on this reconciliation legislation.
After passage, a House and Senate conference committee develops a report for final authorizing legislation.

(continues)

BOX 2-7 BUDGETING PROCESS TIMELINE (CONTINUED)

May 15
Target date for the House to consider annual appropriations bills.

June 10
House Appropriations Committee reports out, approves, and sends to the floor the final annual appropriations bill for a vote.

June 15
Congressional target date to complete action on reconciliation legislation.

June 30
Target date for the House to complete action on annual House appropriations bills.

July 1–September 30
Senate completes action on Senate appropriations bills.
House and Senate conference committees complete action on appropriations conference reports and bring them to the floors their respective chambers.

September 30
Congressional fiscal year ends.

October 1
New fiscal year begins.

BOX 2-8 FEDERAL BUDGET TERMINOLOGY

Appropriations Bill
Prescribes the amount of money dedicated to a respective program in the federal budget

Authorization Bill
Provides a government agency the legal authority to fund and operate its programs

Balanced Budget
A federal budget in which revenues and expenses (spending) are equal in the respective year

Budget Authority
Federal government's legal authority to spend a specified amount of money for a certain purpose, in accordance with congressional laws established and approved by the president

---

BOX 2-8   FEDERAL BUDGET TERMINOLOGY (CONTINUED)

Discretionary Spending
Funding that is not set each year; each year the funding level is debated and decided during the appropriations process.

Entitlement Spending
This is mandatory spending; funding of these programs is required by law and they must be funded in full each year.

Federal Debt
This is the total of all past federal budget deficits, minus the federal government repayments on this debt.

Federal Securities
These are the financial obligations, such as Treasury Bonds, held by the federal government that require payment at a future date.

Inflation
An increase in prices

Obligations
Binding financial obligations held by the federal government

Omnibus
An omnibus bill is a budget that contains all 12 appropriation bills into one bill.

Reconciliation Bill
Legislation that balances federal revenue and expenses

Sequestration
Across-the-board spending cuts enacted by legislation limiting discretionary spending

Subsidy
Direct assistance provided by the federal government to individuals or businesses

Supplemental Appropriation
Funding provided beyond the appropriation level that was provided for in regular budget process

---

State Constitutions

Each state has its own state constitution. A state constitution is generally modeled after the U.S. Constitution. The state constitution outlines the government structure of the state and the powers and duties of each branch of government

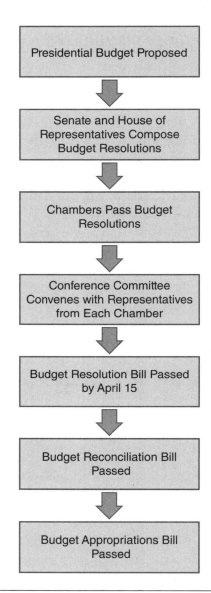

Figure 2-3   Federal Budgeting Process

within the state. Generally, the governmental powers that are not designated to the federal government in the Constitution, nor prohibited by the Constitution, are reserved for the states or the citizens. **Box 2-9** presents the typical rules of law or policy content provided for in a state constitution.

BOX 2-9   STATE CONSTITUTION CONTENT

- Purpose of constitution
- Government purpose
- Outlines citizens' rights and due process
  - Property
  - Privacy
  - Intrusion
  - Expression
  - Religion
  - Assembly and petition
  - Voting
  - Fire arms
  - Discrimination
  - Jury, trial, prosecution, access to courts
- State sovereignty
- Distribution of power among branches of government
  - Defines legislative terms of office
  - Defines legislative process
  - Provides the structure and powers of the executive agencies
  - Appointment process of officials
  - Membership of boards and commissions
  - Judicial court structure and powers
  - Judicial procedures—appeals
  - Jury structure and selection
- Defines municipalities
  - Provides home rule charters and government plans
  - Local officials
  - Incorporation procedures
  - Intergovernment cooperation
  - Election procedures
- Finance
  - Power to tax
  - Tax structure and base
  - Tax approval process

(continues)

BOX 2-9   STATE CONSTITUTION CONTENT (CONTINUED)

- ◆ Revenue-producing property
- ◆ Bonding
- Transportation
  - ◆ Transportation system
  - ◆ Funding
- Education
  - ◆ Public education system
  - ◆ Governance of education system
  - ◆ Boards and commissions
- Natural resources
  - ◆ As a revenue resource
  - ◆ Protection of resources
- Policies regarding public officials and employees
- Code of ethics
- Police power
  - ◆ Structure of state police
- Military power
- Methods to amend state constitution

City Charters

A city charter is a document that outlines a city's or municipality's governmental structure and laws. The city charter must be in alignment with the state constitution and U.S. Constitution. A city charter is also known as a municipal charter. **Box 2-10** presents the typical outline of a city charter.

BOX 2-10   COMPONENTS OF A CITY CHARTER

- Preamble or purpose
- Defining of geographical boundaries and geopolitical units
- Office of mayor
- Government structure and powers
- City council
- District commissions or geographical organizational units and governance structure and power
- Budgeting process

> **BOX 2-10   COMPONENTS OF A CITY CHARTER** (CONTINUED)
>
> - Local taxation
> - City planning
> - Defining of city property
> - Public safety offices
>   - Fire
>   - Police
>   - Medical/emergency systems
> - Parks and recreation
> - Executive agency departments—structure, power, and responsibilities
> - Historical landmark developments and designation
> - Local judicial system
> - Local election
> - Code of ethics

International Governing Bodies

The United States participates with other countries in governance structures that engage in international policymaking, for example, the World Health Organization and the United Nations.

The World Health Organization (WHO) develops policy that directs and coordinates health initiatives within the United Nations system. WHO provides global leadership in health research agenda setting, establishing national guidelines and standards that are evidence-based, proposes multiple-policy options based on the best evidence, and provides technical support in assisting with the provision, monitoring, or assessment of health. The WHO has assumed shared responsibility for ensuring equitable access to health care and to defend against transnational threats to health and safety.

The United Nations is an international policy organization with a commitment to maintaining international peace and security, assisting development of friendly nations, promoting social progress, and supporting better standards of living. The United Nations engages in a multitude of activities that include but are not limited to peacekeeping, peace building, conflict prevention, humanitarian assistance, environmental and refugee protection, disaster relief, disarmament, protection of human rights, gender equality, economic development, promoting international health standards, and expanding food production. In addition, the United Nations supports the development of democratic systems. The United Nation's activities occur through a structure of five principal organs: General Assembly, Security Council, Economic and Social Council, Secretariat, and International Court of Justice.

Summary Points

- Government is an entity, organization, or institution that provides the structure of rule within a defined country or nation.
- The three primary functions of the U.S. Constitution are to allocate power between the federal government and the states (federalism), divide power among the three branches of government (separation of power), and limit the amount of government power (protection of individual liberties).
- The U.S. Constitution is the supreme law of the land.
- Federalism separates the legal scope of authority into two governmental tiers: federal and state.
- The federalism structure sets up a hierarchy of powers.
- Total preemption exists when the federal government assumes all power over state laws.
- Partial preemption exists when a policy of the same or similar topic exists at the national and state levels.
- The three underlying principles of police power are to promote the greater public good, permit the restriction of private interest to promote public good, and permit pervasiveness of state powers.
- *Parens patriae* power provides the state with inherent power through sovereignty to safeguard citizens of the state.
- Governmental power and authority at the national level is shared among the three governmental branches—executive, judicial, and legislative
- Executive power is vested in the president of the United States.
- Judicial power is vested in the U.S. Supreme Court.
- Legislative power is vested in the U.S. Congress.
- The federal budget process is a collaborative effort between the executive and legislative branches of government.
- The federal budget fiscal year extends from October 1 through September 30.

References

Gostin, L. O., & Wiley, L. F. (2016). *Public health law: Power, duty, restraint* (3rd ed.). Oakland, CA: University of California Press.

Grad, F. (2005). *The public health law manual* (3rd ed.). Washington, DC: American Public Health.

Longest, B. (2015). *Health policymaking in the United States* (6th ed.). Washington, DC: Association of University Programs in Health Administration.

Mueller, D. (2001). Centralism, federalism, and the nature of individual preferences. *Constitutional Political Economy, 12*(2), 161–172.

Executive Branch: Federal Governmental Agencies and Appointed Bodies

The executive branch of the U.S. government exercises policymaking powers through elected officials, official executive departments, and other executive-level agencies. The most powerful office in the executive branch is the office of the president of the United States. The U.S. Constitution balances the power of the executive branch through the power bases of the legislative and judicial branches.

The Executive Branch Power Base

The executive branch of the government's powers is vested in the president of the United States. The president serves as the chief administrative or executive officer of the executive branch. As leader of the executive branch, the president serves as head of state and commander in chief of the armed forces. In the United States, the president also serves as leader of all ceremonial functions. The primary responsibilities of the president are the development of policy; implementation and enforcement of policy by Congress; and appointment of his leadership team, the cabinet, and all heads of federal agencies. Presidential powers can be executed through several policy instruments—executive order, presidential proclamation, presidential directive, presidential determination, and presidential memorandum. **Table 3-1** presents the definitions of these presidential instruments.

The Presidential Election

The American voters elect the president of the United States. In order to qualify for the presidential office a candidate must be at least 35 years of age, a natural-born citizen of the United States, and resident in the United States for 14 years prior to the election.

49

TABLE 3-1 PRESIDENTIAL POLICY INSTRUMENTS (PRESIDENTIAL POWERS)

POLICY INSTRUMENT	DEFINITION
Executive order	A directive provided to agencies and officers of the executive branch of government to manage operational activities of the respective agencies
Presidential proclamation	A general statement made on a matter of public policy that applies outside the government
Presidential directive	A form of executive order that is issued with the advice and consent of the National Security Council
Presidential determination	A statement or document released by the president's White House staff that provides a determination on a topic or issue that results in an official executive branch policy or position; may be a memorandum required by statute that must be issued before a specific action is taken
Presidential memorandum (hortatory memorandum)	A memorandum letter that is issued to manage and govern the activities, direct the practices, or guide policies of the departments and agencies within the executive branch; less prestigious action than an executive order

Electoral College

The president is elected through an electoral college system. The presidential election occurs on the first Tuesday in November of every fourth year. The population of the 50 states apportions the Electoral College. Each state provides an electoral member for each member of their congressional delegation, with the District of Columbia receiving three votes. The electors cast the votes for president on behalf of the American people. The electors meeting occurs on the first Monday after the second Wednesday in December after the presidential election.

There are currently 538 electors in the Electoral College. A majority of the 270 electoral votes is required to elect the president. The allocation of electoral votes varies by state. Some states have a "winner take all" system that pledges all electoral votes to the presidential candidate with the majority of popular votes. Electors are expected to cast their vote in alignment with the pledged votes. However, electors can vote independently, sometimes with penalties. An elector who casts an electoral vote for someone other than the candidate of the party that was pledged to vote for or does not vote for anyone is called a *faithless elector*.

After the election, the governor prepares a Certificate of Ascertainment listing all the presidential candidates and the electors. This certificate declares the winning presidential candidate in that state. The electoral votes are counted in a joint session of Congress on January 6 of the year following the presidential election. **Box 3-1** presents the presidential election cycle in the United States.

BOX 3-1   PRESIDENTIAL ELECTION CYCLE

- Spring of the year prior to election—Candidates announce intention to run for office.
- Summer of the year before election to spring of election year—Primary and caucus debates occur.
- State primaries are conducted by states, voting occurs through secret ballot.
- Caucuses are private meetings run by political parties, speeches are given on the candidates, votes are taken by caucus organizers for each candidate and delegates allocated in alignment with the vote.
  - Open primaries or caucuses—members can vote for any political party candidate.
  - Closed primaries or caucuses—members must be registered with the political party to vote for one of its candidates.
- January to June of election year—Primary elections and caucuses hold elections.
- July to September of election year—Political parties hold nominating conventions to select their presidential candidates.
- September to October—Presidential candidate debates are held.
- Tuesday after the first Monday in November—Presidential election is held.
- First Monday after the second Wednesday in December after the presidential election—Electors cast votes.
- January 6 of the year following presidential election—Congress counts electoral votes.
- January 20—Presidential inauguration day is held.

President of the United States (POTUS)

The president, as head of state, commander in chief, ceremonial leader, and head of governmental executive agencies leads the entire executive branch of government. The president is considered the most powerful person in the country, primarily because of the breadth of information possessed by the president domestically and internationally. The president is vested with information that includes but is not limited to confidential, secret, and top-secret intelligence; knowledge of foreign officials working for the U.S. intelligence community; control of the "nuclear football"; briefings on spy satellite intelligence and cyber technology intelligence; secret directives provided through special presidential policy instruments; counterterrorism reports; personal and political information on world leaders; and access to all domestic intelligence from the country's infrastructure to economics and all the information provided by the president's cabinet (Graff, 2017).

The president appoints cabinet members who are responsible through delegated authority to manage and lead the operations of their respective executive agencies. In addition to the cabinet, the Executive Office of the President (EOP) provides immediate staff support to the president.

The president is considered the chief policymaker in the United States and the most influential participant in the policymaking process. In addition to promoting national policy agendas, the president has the power to execute immediate policy in the form of an executive order or influence policy through various presidential policy instruments. Other policy powers of the president are:

- Signing legislation into law or vetoing bills
- Negotiating and signing treaties (requires congressional ratification)
- Interpreting and clarifying existing laws for executive officers
- Extending pardons and clemencies

The president is constitutionally required "from time to time" to provide a State of the Union address to Congress and the American people. The president uses this opportunity to outline the executive branch's national policy agenda and to inform Congress and the American people of the impact of current national policies.

Executive Office of the President

The Executive Office of the President (EOP) was developed in 1939 by President Franklin D. Roosevelt to facilitate the daily operations of the White House and presidential duties. The White House Chief of Staff is an advisor to the president and manages the entire EOP. The Office of the Press Secretary manages the White House Communications Office. The press secretary provides daily briefings to the media on behalf of the president to include policy issues and presidential activities. The National Security Council director advises the president on foreign policy, intelligence, and national security issues. Other councils or offices in the EOP include:

- Council of Economic Advisers
- Council on Environmental Quality
- National Security Council and Homeland Security Council
- Office of Administration
- Office of Management and Budget
- Office of National Drug Control Policy
- Office of Science and Technology Policy
- Office of the United States Trade Representative
- Office of the Vice President
- Executive Residence
- The White House

As an extension to the EOP, several offices and departments within the White House support the operations of the executive branch:

- Office of Cabinet Affairs
- Office of the Chief of Staff
- Office of Communications
- Office of Energy and Climate Change Policy
- Office of the First Lady
- Office of the Social Secretary
- Office of Health Reform
- National Security Advisor
- Office of Legislative Affairs
- Office of Management and Administration
- Oval Office Operations
- Office of Political Affairs
- Office of Presidential Personnel
- Office of Public Engagement and Intergovernmental Affairs
- Office of the Press Secretary

- Office of Scheduling and Advance
- Office of the Staff Secretary
- Office of the White House Counsel
- Office of White House Policy
- White House Military Office

The President's Cabinet

The president's cabinet serves as an advisory body to the president, and each cabinet member serves as the chief executive of his or her respective executive department. There are 15 cabinet members, generally members of the presidential succession line. The president's cabinet members are appointed by the president and confirmed by the Senate. The title of "secretary" is provided to each chief executive of a department, except the Justice Department, the head of which is the Attorney General. The 15 executive departments are:

- Department of Agriculture
- Department of Commerce
- Department of Defense
- Department of Education
- Department of Energy
- Department of Health and Human Services
- Department of Homeland Security
- Department of Housing and Urban Development
- Department of Interior
- Department of Justice
- Department of Labor
- Department of State
- Department of Transportation
- Department of Treasury
- Department of Veterans Affairs

The secretary of each department is directly responsible to the president. **Box 3-2** provides a summary of the duties of each department.

BOX 3-2   EXECUTIVE DEPARTMENT POLICY RESPONSIBILITIES

- Department of Agriculture (USDA)
    - Oversees farming, agriculture, and food production
    - Supports needs of farmers and ranchers
    - Promotes agricultural trade and production
    - Ensures food safety
    - Protects natural resources and fosters rural communities
    - Focuses on hunger in America
- Department of Commerce
    - Promotes economic development
    - Promotes technological innovation
    - Supports business community
    - Issues patents and trademarks
    - Focuses on improving environment and oceanic life
    - Formulates telecommunications and technology policy
    - Promotes U.S. exports
    - Enforces trade agreements
- Department of Defense
    - Deters war
    - Protects national security
    - Provides military forces
- Department of Education
    - Promotes academic achievement and preparation of students
    - Fosters educational excellence
    - Ensures equal access to educational opportunities
    - Administers federal financial aid programs
- Department of Energy (DOE)
    - Promotes energy security
    - Supports development of reliable, clean, and affordable energy
    - Ensures nuclear security
    - Protects the environment
- Department of Health and Human Services (DHHS)
    - Protects the health of all Americans
    - Provides essential human services

(continues)

BOX 3-2   EXECUTIVE DEPARTMENT POLICY RESPONSIBILITIES (CONTINUED)

    Prevents disease outbreaks

    Assures food and drug safety

    Provides health insurance, administers Medicare and Medicaid

    Manages National Institutes of Health, Food and Drug Administration, and Centers for Disease Control and Prevention

- Department of Homeland Security

    Prevents and disrupts terrorist attacks

    Protects American people, infrastructure, and key resources

    Responds at the time of a national incident

    Patrols borders, protects travelers and transportation infrastructure

    Enforces immigration laws

    Promotes emergency preparedness

- Department of Housing and Urban Development (HUD)

    Develops national housing policy

    Improves and develops American communities

    Promotes home ownership and rent subsidy

    Enforces fair housing laws

    Provides mortgage and loan insurance

    Administers public housing and homeless assistance programs

- Department of Interior

    Protects natural resources

    Promotes recreational opportunities

    Protects fish and wildlife

    Honors responsibilities to native populations and cultures

    Manages dams and reservoirs

    Protects national parks and protected species

- Department of Justice

    Enforces laws

    Ensures public safety against foreign and domestic threats

    Provides leadership in preventing and controlling crime

    Ensures fair and impartial justice for all Americans

- Department of Labor

    Ensures strong American workforce

    Promotes job training programs

BOX 3-2   EXECUTIVE DEPARTMENT POLICY RESPONSIBILITIES (CONTINUED)

    Promotes safe working conditions

    Sets minimum hourly wage and overtime pay

    Ensures fair and equal employment opportunities

    Protects retirement and healthcare benefits

- Department of State

    Develops and implements president's foreign policy

    Counters international crime

    Provides assistance to U.S. citizens and foreign nationals living or traveling abroad

    Promotes and maintains diplomatic relationships

- Department of Transportation

    Ensures safe and efficient transportation systems

- Department of Treasury

    Promotes economic prosperity

    Advises and enforces security of United States and international financial systems

    Produces nation's coins and currency

    Collaborates to promote global economic growth

    Predicts and prevents financial crisis

- Department of Veterans Affairs

    Administers veterans' benefit programs

    Operates veterans' medical care system

    Provides burial assistance

    Administers programs for veterans such as disability compensation, home loans, life insurance, rehabilitation

---

Executive Branch Independent Agencies

In addition to the departments in the executive branch that have representation in the president's cabinet, several independent agencies are critical to the function of the executive branch of government. These administrative agencies are divisions of the government that enforce and administer policies in the form of laws and regulations. These independent agencies and their primary functions are outlined in **Box 3-3**.

BOX 3-3   INDEPENDENT AGENCIES FUNCTIONS

- Central Intelligence Agency (CIA)
    Conducts counterintelligence
    Conducts foreign intelligence
    Maintains national security
- U.S. Commission on Civil Rights
    Investigates complaints of discrimination
- Consumer Product Safety Commission
    Reduces risk of injuries and death from consumer products
    Formulates and enforces product safety standards
- Corporation for National and Community Service
    Supports the American culture of citizenship, service, and responsibility
- Environmental Protection Agency (EPA)
    Protects human health and natural environment (air, water, and land)
- Equal Employment Opportunity Commission (EEOC)
    Promotes equal opportunity in employment
    Enforces federal civil rights laws
- Farm Credit Administration (FCA)
    Responsible for examining and regulating the Farm Credit System
- Federal Communications Commission (FCC)
    Regulates interstate and international communications by radio,
        television, wire, satellite, and cable
- Federal Deposit Insurance Corporation (FDIC)
    Insures bank deposits
- Federal Election Commission (FEC)
    Enforces Federal Election Campaign Act
- Federal Maritime Commission
    Responsible for the regulation of ocean-borne transportation in foreign
        commerce
- Federal Mediation and Conciliation Service (FMCS)
    Preserves and promotes labor management peace and cooperation
- Federal Reserve System
    Ensures stable financial system
    Regulates credit conditions and loan rates
    Regulates banks

BOX 3-3   INDEPENDENT AGENCIES FUNCTIONS (CONTINUED)

- Federal Trade Commission (FTC)

  Enforces federal antitrust and consumer protection laws

  Ensures capital system of healthy competition, free of unfair restrictions; and fair consumer policies

- General Services Administration (GSA)

  Provides government workplaces by constructing, managing, and preserving government buildings and by leasing and managing commercial real estate

  Offers private sector professional services, equipment, supplies, telecommunications, and information technology to government organizations and the military

- International Trade Commission

  Holds investigative responsibilities on matters of trade

  Investigates the effects of dumped and subsidized imports on domestic industries and conducts global safeguard investigations

  Adjudicates cases involving imports that allegedly infringe on intellectual property rights

- National Aeronautics and Space Administration (NASA)

  Develops space exploration programs, artificial satellites, and rocketry

- National Archives and Records Administration (NARA)

  Maintains National Archives

- National Endowment for the Arts (NEA)

  Supports arts community

  Funds museums, artists, and arts-related programs

- National Endowment for the Humanities

  Supports research, education, preservation, and public programs in the humanities

- Director of National Intelligence

  Integrates foreign, military and domestic intelligence in defense of the homeland and of U.S. interests abroad

- National Labor Relations Board (NLRB)

  Monitors relations between unions and employers in the private sector

  Investigates unfair labor practices by unions and employers

(continues)

BOX 3-3   INDEPENDENT AGENCIES FUNCTIONS (CONTINUED)

- National Mediation Board

    Facilitates labor-management relations within railroads and airlines systems

    Endeavors to minimize work stoppages in the airline and railroad industry

- National Science Foundation (NSF)

    Promotes science and engineering research and educational programs

- National Transportation Safety Board (NTSB)

    Investigates civil aviation, railroad, highway, and marine accidents

    Develops transportation standards

- Nuclear Regulatory Commission

    Licenses and regulates nonmilitary use of nuclear energy

- Office of Personal Management (OPM)

    Recruits and retains government workforce

- Securities and Exchange Commission (SEC)

    Administers federal securities laws

    Protects investors in securities markets

- Selective Service System (SSS)

    Provides human resources to the armed forces

- Small Business Administration (SBA)

    Provides financial and technical assistance to promote business development

- United States Postal Service

    Provides reliable, affordable, and universal mail service

---

Order of Presidential Succession

The Presidential Succession Act of 1792 outlines the order of succession to the presidency if the president should become incapacitated. This ensures continual functioning of the executive branch of government and protects the security of the American people and the country's infrastructure. The order of presidential succession is:

- Vice President
- Speaker of the House
- Senate President pro tempore
- Secretary of State

- Secretary of Treasury
- Secretary of Defense
- Attorney General (Department of Justice Secretary)
- Secretary of Interior
- Secretary of Agriculture
- Secretary of Commerce
- Secretary of Labor
- Secretary of Health and Human Services
- Secretary of Housing and Urban Development
- Secretary of Transportation
- Secretary of Energy
- Secretary of Education
- Secretary of Veterans Affairs
- Secretary of Homeland Security

The Vice President

The election of the vice president occurs along with that of the president by the Electoral College. The vice president is considered the second in command. The vice president assumes the duties and responsibilities of the president if the president is unable to perform them. This assumption of authority might be permanent or temporary, and may be the result of death, resignation, or temporary incapacitation of the president, or a vote of concern by the vice president and the majority of the president's cabinet regarding the president's ability to function. In accordance with the U.S. Constitution, the vice president received the formal Electoral College tally votes for president and vice president from the states. The vice president is required to open the Electoral College voting certificates from the states in the presence of the Senate and House of Representatives. The vice president serves as the president of the Senate. In the role of Senate president, the vice president has no vote but can cast the deciding vote on the occasion of a tie vote. The daily oversight of the Senate is normally undertaken by the majority party leader.

Czar

The president of the United States has the authority to appoint officials who are responsible for specialized areas of policymaking. These individuals generally have a title associated with that specialized area. In the United States, the term "czar" has been used to refer to these individuals. Czar is an informal title. At the time of appointment, the president determines the scope of authority and administrative responsibilities for the prospective czar. This appointment process is conducted as a measure to ensure efficient policymaking in areas of great concern or crisis.

Office of the First Lady of the United States (FLOTUS)

The spouse of the president administers the Office of the First Lady of the United States. The role and responsibilities of this office have evolved over time and change with each First Lady. The First Lady has her own personal staff to implement the activities of the Office of the First Lady. The typical functions of the First Lady and her staff are to serve as hostess for the White House, manage all social and ceremonial events of the White House, and represent her office regarding official state business. The staff of the Office of the First Lady includes but is not limited to a social secretary, chief of staff, press secretary, chief floral designer, executive chef, and other White House staff. The First Lady usually selects an area of interest in which to become involved on behalf of the American people. She might serve as a spokesperson, use her position to implement policymaking, and may engage in political activities that impact the policy agenda within this area of interest. The level of attention provided to these issues can impact public awareness, shape a policy agenda, and lead to formulation and adoption of policy.

The First Lady of the United States is considered by many as one of the most powerful positions. As First Lady, she has continual access to the president and, by nature of her relationship with the president, has his confidence. She is exposed to a plethora of political and policy information with the ability to provide advice and counsel in confidence to the president. The First Lady has more direct public exposure by nature of her position and fewer security measures. In this position, she is able to interact and provide grassroots information to the president on the public's opinion and temperament. FLOTUS is the "hidden power" of the executive branch.

White House Fellows and Interns

The White House Fellows program provides young Americans with an opportunity to engage in policymaking activities in the executive office. The White House Fellows enjoy a full-time paid position working with White House staff, cabinet secretaries, and other executive officers. During their tenure, they engage in roundtable discussions and study domestic and international policy. Their responsibilities might include chairing interagency meetings, design and implementation of federal policies, drafting speeches for their executive officer such as a cabinet secretary, and agency representation on Capitol Hill.

In contrast, the White House intern is an unpaid position. A White House intern acquires leadership skills and professional experience in preparation for a future in public service. The intern performs duties as assigned with a focus on increasing knowledge regarding the functions and policymaking of the executive branch.

Executive Offices: State and Local Governmental Level

A governor and mayor hold the chief executive offices at the state and local government level, respectively. In addition, some cities are further divided into municipalities or counties that have a similar elected official of the executive branch of government, for example, a county president. The managerial operational activities of elected officials at the state, city, or local level is analogous to those of the federal executive office. As a representative of the executive branch of government, these officials are responsible for administering laws, enforcing state constitutions or city charters, and serving as chief executive officer. **Boxes 3-4** and **3-5** outline some responsibilities and duties of these elected chief executive offices at the state and local level.

BOX 3-4   GUBERNATORIAL RESPONSIBILITIES

- Signs bills into state statutes; may use line item veto if permitted by state constitution and law
- Executes executive orders
- Administers legislative recommendations
- Monitors activities of executive departments of the state government
- Provides legislature with general and fiscal information regarding the current "state of the state"
- Creates and submits an operating budget for state legislature approval
- Collaborates with state board of pardons, serves as the last court of resort
- Appoints and removes executive officials, members of boards and commissions
  - Generally requires state senate confirmation
- Serves as commander in chief of state's military
- Convenes special legislative sessions
- Declares special elections
- Serves as official spokesperson for state

BOX 3-5 MAYORAL RESPONSIBILITIES

- Submits city budget to city council for approval
- Appoints executives of city offices
- Appoints advisory committees and commissions
- Serves as official spokesperson for city
- Signs city ordinances into laws or executes veto power
- Enacts ordinances, resolutions, and other legislative orders from city council
- Executes executive orders
- Recruits city business
- Executes official city contracts
- Manages city utility services
- Promotes city living
  - Promotes arts, cultural affairs, parks and recreation, tourism industry
- Engages in community activities
- May preside over city council meetings
- May deliver tie-breaking vote on city council
- May call city council into special meetings
- Manages health and safety services in city
  - Fire department
  - Police department
  - Health department

Local government structures follow a similar democratic process for policy formulation as that for federal and state legislatures. At the local level, a city council proposes new laws as resolutions or referrals, ordinances, or bills. These policy instruments are heard before the city council or local governing body to be considered and voted into law.

Summary Points

- The executive branch of government exercises policymaking powers through elected officials, official executive departments, and other executive-level agencies.

- President of the United States is the most powerful position in the executive branch.
- The president serves as the chief administrative or executive officer of the executive branch.
- The president, as head of state, commander in chief, ceremonial leader, and head of governmental executive agencies, leads the entire executive branch of government.
- Electoral College process elects the U.S. president, not popular vote.
- The president appoints cabinet members.
- The president is considered the chief policymaker in the United States and the most influential participant in the policymaking process.
- The vice president is considered the second in command.
- The vice president presides over the Senate.
- The president's cabinet serves as an advisory body to the president and each cabinet member serves as the chief executive of his or her respective executive department.
- The order of presidential succession is established by the Presidential Succession Act.
- The president of the United States has the authority to appoint officials who are responsible for a specialized area of policymaking, sometimes known as a czars.
- The typical functions of the First Lady and her staff are to serve as hostess of the White House, manage all social and ceremonial events of the White House, and represent her office regarding official state business.
- White House Fellows and interns engage in activities of the executive branch of government and may participate in various aspects of policymaking.

References

Auerbach, J., & Peterson, M. (2005). *The executive branch*. Oxford University Press.

Graff, G. (2017, January/February). The government secrets Trump is about to discover. *Politico Magazine*, 22–26.

Hi man, B. (2011). *The executive branch*. Mitchell Lane Publishers. Newark, Delaware.

Shambaugh, G., & Weinstein, P. (2016). *The art of policymaking: Tools, technologies and processes in the modern executive branch*. CQ Press – Sage Publications, Thousand Oaks, CA.

Legislative Branch: Role in Policy

The legislative branch of government consists of elected officials that represent the citizens of the United States. The legislative branch of government is known as the Congress of the United States, and it comprises two chambers: the House of Representatives and the Senate. It is through the legislative branch of government that representative democracy occurs.

Legislative Structure: Congress of the United States

The role of the legislative branch in policymaking is the passage of public laws for the entire country. In the Congress, the legislative work of developing laws for our country is primarily accomplished through standing committees in each chamber. There are special committees in each chamber and joint committees with bicameral membership. The two chambers are considered to have equal voice in the development of policy and legislation. In the policymaking process, bills that are passed by each chamber must be signed by the president or governor prior to becoming law. These bills are required to be signed within 10 days or they become law automatically.

House of Representatives

The House of Representatives (House) is responsible for originating all revenue bills. The House also holds the power to impeach the president and other federal officers. Every bill that originates within the House must also be passed and approved by the Senate. Reciprocally, the House must pass and approve every bill that originates in the Senate.

Senate

The U.S. Senate was created to function as a legislative body in which each state has equal representation. The Senate is considered the most powerful chamber of Congress. The Senate has the power to conduct the impeachment trial of a president. The Senate is considered the senior legislative body of the Congress. In addition to bill passage, other functions of the Senate include:

- Ratification of treaties
- Ratification of presidential or gubernatorial appointments
- Conducting impeachment trials once the House of Representatives passes a bill of impeachment
- Consenting to legal declaration of war

The vice president of the United States serves as the president of the Senate. The president of the Senate does not have a vote unless there is a tie. Senate presidency is the primary constitutional role of the vice president.

Political Parties

A democracy supports the ability of individuals and groups to affiliate with a political party. A democracy requires an informed citizenry that has the ability to openly and freely engage in debate on issues, problems, politics, and policy solutions. The U.S. Constitution supports the engagement of democratic processes that permit all voices to be heard without fear of retaliation. Political parties provide the formal structure from which democracy is practiced. Political parties are considered basic institutions through which public opinion is translated into policy (Roskin & Cord, 2016).

Political parties integrate the values and belief systems of a group of persons into governmental policy by establishing a policy platform. Political parties provide critical functions to our democracy: (1) to provide for the orderly transfer of power within the party to continually foster a specific policy agenda; (2) to offer policy alternatives consistent with the party values and beliefs; (3) to serve as a vehicle of innovation and ideas for specific causes; (4) to educate the public on policy issues; and (5) to provide for the succession planning of governmental leaders (Roskin & Cord, 2016). The most prominent political parties in the United States are the Democratic Party and the Republican Party. Political ideology consists of the beliefs held by individuals regarding the manner in which government should operate within a society. **Box 4-1** presents common political ideology terminology. Political ideology influences the manner in which individuals vote, types of policies to be prioritized, arrangement of societal elements, and policymakers' decisions regarding policy agendas and policy formulation (SparkNotes Editors, 2010).

BOX 4-1   POLITICAL IDEOLOGY TERMINOLOGY

- Absolutism—supports a single ruler who should have control over every aspect of government and people's lives; believes in divine right of kings; emphasizes a strong sense of order, clear law of nature (God), natural hierarchy or power structure among the people, wisdom of traditional values
- Anarchism—promotes a stateless society; proposes to eliminate reliance on authority; promotes no governmental structure
- Communism—classless social structure; communal ownership; authoritarian approach with violent measures
- Conservatives (considered the "right")—favor small government and low taxes; support a strong military and use of force to advance foreign policy; oppose abortion and gay rights; support gun ownership and increased Christian doctrine; promote personal responsibility, individual liberty, and traditional American values
- Environmentalism—belief in the obligation to protect natural resources from human excesses
- Fascism—nationalistic, militaristic, totalitarian political ideology with desire for absolute power; promotes racial superiority doctrines, ethnic persecution, imperialist expansion, genocide; favors masculinity, youth, and power of violence
- Feminism—belief that women are equal to men and that women should be treated equally by law
- Fundamentalism—belief that religious context is absolute and literal, not contextual in interpretation
- Liberals (considered the "left")—balance civil rights with personal freedoms; support higher taxes on the wealthy; generally reject unregulated free markets; support a strong middle class; believe government should achieve equal opportunity and equality for all
- Moderates—take a midway position between conservatives and progressives; value balanced budgets
- Nazism (National Socialism)—rejects liberalism, democracy, rule of law, human rights; stresses subordination of the individual to the state and strict obedience to the ruler; combines fascism, anticommunism, racism, and anti-Semitism
- Nihilism—related ideology to anarchism; emphasizes periodic destruction of government and society as a means of starting anew

(continues)

BOX 4-1   POLITICAL IDEOLOGY TERMINOLOGY (CONTINUED)

- Political faction—a group of individuals with a common political purpose; a political faction may be a "party within a political party"; an influential group within a group; purpose of a political faction is to advance a policy agenda, prevent adoption of alternative policies, and support individuals with similar views to positions of power within the political party
- Progressives—thought of as a forward thinkers; support increased funding for education, welfare, food stamps, infrastructure, higher taxes on the rich and corporations, criminal justice reform, aggressive environmental laws; favor unions; promote government intervention to enforce social justice and economic fairness
- Socialism—emphasizes collectivism, public ownership, central economic planning, economic equality

Reproduced from SparkNotes Editors. (2010). SparkNote on political ideologies and styles. Retrieved on January 21, 2017 from http://www.sparknotes.com /us-government-and-politics/political-science/political-ideologies-and-styles/

Democratic Party

The Democratic Party pledges a commitment to keeping our nation safe and expanding opportunity for every American. The Democratic Party's commitment is reflected in their party platform or agenda that emphasizes strong economic growth; affordable health care for all Americans; retirement security; open, honest, and accountable government; and securing our nation while protecting our civil rights and liberties. To understand the political environment and the policies formulated by each respective political party, it is critical to have a basic understanding of their party platform or agenda. The Democratic Party platform includes:

- Raise incomes and restore economic security for the middle class
  - Raising worker's wages
  - Protecting worker's fundamental rights
  - Supporting working families
  - Helping more workers share in near-record corporate profits
  - Expanding access to affordable housing and house ownership
  - Protecting and expanding Social Security
  - Ensuring a secure and dignified retirement
  - Revitalizing our nation's postal service

- Create good paying jobs
  - Building 21st century infrastructure
  - Fostering a manufacturing renaissance
  - Creating good-paying clean energy jobs
  - Pursuing our innovation agenda: science, research, education, and technology
  - Supporting America's small businesses
  - Creating jobs for America's young people
- Fight for economic fairness and against inequality
  - Reining in Wall Street and fixing our financial system
  - Promoting competition by stopping corporate concentration
  - Making the wealthy pay their fair share of taxes
  - Promoting trade that is fair and benefits American workers
- Bring Americans together and remove barriers to opportunities
  - Ending systemic racism
  - Closing the racial wealth gap
  - Reforming our criminal justice system
  - Fixing our broken immigration system
  - Guaranteeing civil rights
  - Guaranteeing women's rights
  - Guaranteeing lesbian, gay, bisexual, and transgender rights
  - Guaranteeing rights for people with disabilities
  - Respecting faith and service
  - Investing in rural America
  - Ending poverty and investing in communities left behind
  - Building strong cities and metropolitan areas
  - Promoting arts and culture
  - Honoring indigenous tribal nations
  - Fighting for the people of Puerto Rico
  - Honoring the people of the territories
- Protect voting rights, fix our campaign finance system, and restore our democracy
  - Protecting voting rights
  - Fixing our broken campaign finance system
  - Appointing judges
  - Securing statehood for Washington, DC
  - Strengthening management of federal government

- Combat climate change, build a clean energy economy, and secure environmental justice
  - Building clean energy economy
  - Securing environmental and climate justice
  - Protecting our public lands and waters
- Provide quality and affordable education
  - Making debt-free college a reality
  - Providing relief from crushing student debt
  - Supporting historically black colleges and universities and minority-serving institutions
  - Cracking down on predatory for-profit schools
  - Guaranteeing universal preschool and good schools for every child
- Ensure the health and safety of all Americans
  - Securing universal health care
  - Supporting community health centers
  - Reducing prescription drug cost
  - Enabling cutting-edge medical research
  - Combating drug and alcohol addiction
  - Treating mental health
  - Supporting those living with autism and their families
  - Securing reproductive health, rights, and justice
  - Ensuring long-term care, services, and supports
  - Protecting and promoting public health
  - Ending violence against women
  - Preventing gun violence
- Principled leadership
- Support our troops and keep faith with our veterans
  - Defense spending
  - Veterans and service members
  - Military families
  - A strong military
- Confront global threats
  - Terrorism
  - Syria
  - Afghanistan
  - Iran
  - North Korea

- Russia
- Cybersecurity and online privacy
- Nonproliferation of nuclear, chemical, and biological weapons
- Global climate leadership
- Protect our values
  - Women and girls
  - Lesbian, gay, bisexual, and transgender people
  - Young people
  - Religious minorities
  - Refugees
  - Civil society
  - Anticorruption
  - Torture
  - Closing Guantanamo Bay
  - Development assistance
  - Global health
  - HIV and AIDS
  - International labor
- A leader in the world
  - Asia-Pacific
  - Middle East
  - Europe
  - Americas
  - Africa
  - Global economy and institutions (Democratic Platform Committee, 2016).

Republican Party

The Republican Party supports the individual over the government. This party advocates reducing the size of government, streamlining bureaucracy, and returning power to the individual states. The primary Republican Party platform or agenda consists of:

- Restoring the American dream
  - Rebuilding the economy and creating jobs
  - Fair and simple taxes for growth
  - Our tax principles
  - A competitive America

- ◆ A winning trade policy
- ◆ Freeing financial markets
- ◆ Responsible home ownership and rental opportunities
- ◆ America on the move
- ◆ Building the future: Technology
- ◆ Building the future: America's electric grid
- ◆ Start-up century: Small business and entrepreneurship
- ◆ The federal reserve
- ◆ Workplace freedom for a 21st-century workforce
- ◆ A federal workforce serving the people
- ◆ Reducing federal debt
- A rebirth of constitutional government
  - ◆ We the people
  - ◆ The judiciary
  - ◆ Administrative law
  - ◆ Defending marriage against an activist judiciary
  - ◆ The First Amendment: religious liberty, constitutionally protected speech
  - ◆ The Second Amendment: our right to keep and bear arms
  - ◆ The Fourth Amendment: liberty and privacy
  - ◆ The Fifth Amendment: protecting human life, protecting private property, intellectual property rights
  - ◆ The Ninth Amendment: the people's retained rights
  - ◆ The Tenth Amendment: federalism as the foundation of personal liberty
  - ◆ Honest elections and the electoral college
  - ◆ Honest elections and the right to vote
- America's natural resources: agriculture, energy, and the environment
  - ◆ Abundant harvests
  - ◆ A new era in energy
  - ◆ Environmental progress
- Government reform
  - ◆ Making government work for the people
  - ◆ Balancing the budget
  - ◆ Preserving Medicare and Medicaid
  - ◆ Saving Social Security
  - ◆ Protecting Internet freedom
  - ◆ Immigration and the rule of law

- - Reforming the treaty system
  - Internal Revenue Service
  - Audit the pentagon
  - Improving the federal workforce
  - Advancing term limits
  - Regulation: The quiet tyranny
  - Crony capitalism and corporate welfare
  - Honoring our relationships with American Indians
  - Americans in the territories
  - The territory of Puerto Rico
  - Preserving the District of Columbia
- Great American families, education, health care, and criminal justice
  - American values
  - Marriage, family and society
  - A culture of hope
  - Education: a chance for every child
  - Academic excellence for all
  - Choice in education
  - Title IX
  - Improving higher education
  - College costs
  - Restoring patient control and preserving quality in health care
  - Protecting individual conscience in health care
  - Better care and lower costs: tort reform
  - Advancing research and development in health care
  - Putting patients first: reforming the Food and Drug Administration (FDA)
  - Advancing Americans with Disabilities
  - Ensuring safe neighborhoods: criminal justice and prison reform
  - Combatting drug abuse
- America resurgent
  - A dangerous world
  - Confronting the dangers
  - Supporting our troops: resources to do their job, standing by our heroes
  - Citizen soldiers: National Guard and reserve
  - Honoring and supporting our veterans: a sacred obligation

- America: the indispensable nation
- Challenges of a changing Middle East
- Our unequivocal support for Israel
- U.S. leadership in the Asian Pacific
- Renewing the European alliance
- Family of the Americas
- Africa: the promise and the challenge
- Sovereign American leadership in international organizations
- Defending international religious freedom
- America's generosity: international assistance that makes a difference
- Advancing human rights
- Liberty to captives: combatting human trafficking
- Facing 21st-century threats:
  - Cybersecurity in an insecure world
  - Protection against an electromagnetic pulse
  - Confronting Internet tyranny (Republican National Convention Committee, 2016).

National Independent American Party

The National Independent American Party (NIAP) desires to preserve independence out of the love for God, family, and country. The NIAP purpose is to bring America back to the original intent of the Founding Fathers. Spirituality forms the foundation of America. The primary NIAP platform or agenda consist of:

- Christian heritage
  - God
  - Christian nation
- Family
  - Traditional family
  - Morality
- Citizenship
  - Patriotism
  - Civic duty
- Unalienable rights
  - Life
  - Liberty
  - Property

- Education
  - Stewardship
  - Nongovernment schools
- Economy
  - Free enterprise
  - Taxation—substantial tax reform
  - Money and banking
- Society
  - Vigilance
  - Entitlement programs
  - Substance abuse and gambling
  - Crime
- Natural resources
  - Environment—dynamic balance between development and conservation
  - Energy
- U.S. Constitution
  - Inspired document from the Almighty God
  - Branches of government—does not support laws that delegate authority to regulatory agencies, branches of government
  - Bill of Rights—all rights are God-given and inseparable from the people
  - Constitutional Convention—discourage any attempt at a Constitutional Convention
- Government
  - Function—must be founded in faith in God, moral laws, Declaration of Independence, U.S. Constitution, Bill of Rights, and Holy Scriptures
  - Bureaucracy—abolish regional governments, unconstitutional federal agencies
  - Congressional leaders are public servants representing the citizens needs to uphold and defend the Constitution
  - States rights—all rights not delegated to the federal government belong to the states or to the people
  - Elections—right of every public citizen to seek an elected office in accordance with the Constitution
- Defense
  - War and conflicts—wars must be congressionally declared
  - Our troops—love, honor, and sustain our troops

- ◆ Readiness—favor military defense budgets, technology, supplies, storage, and manpower
- ◆ National security—oppose antiterrorist legislation that results in the loss of personal freedom and civil rights
- U.S. Sovereignty
  - ◆ Sovereign America—true sovereignty lies in the people
  - ◆ International relations—oppose attempt to regulate and govern other countries, oppose international trade agreements that diminish America's economic self-sufficiency, sovereignty, independence, or exportation of jobs
  - ◆ Global government—oppose globalization or a one-world government (National Independent American Party, 2012).

Libertarian Party

The Libertarian Party seeks a world of liberty in which all individuals are considered sovereign over their lives. The respect for individuals is considered a precondition for freedom and a prosperous world. The Libertarian Party political platform or agenda is based on the following basic principles:

- Personal liberty
  - ◆ Self-ownership—individuals own their bodies
  - ◆ Expression and communication—full freedom of expression and to oppose government censorship, regulation, or control of communication and technology
  - ◆ Privacy—individual privacy and government transparency
  - ◆ Personal relationships—sexual orientation, preference, gender, or gender identity should have no impact on the government's treatment of individuals
  - ◆ Abortion—people can hold good-faith views on both sides of this issue
  - ◆ Parental rights—right to raise their children in accordance with their own standards and beliefs
  - ◆ Crime and justice—criminal laws should be limited
  - ◆ Death penalty—oppose death penalty by the state
  - ◆ Self-defense—the only legitimate use of force is in the defense of individual rights of life, liberty, and property
- Economic liberty
  - ◆ Property and contract—freedom to obtain, retain, profit from, manage, or dispose of one's property

- Environment—protect our environment and ecosystems
- Energy and resources—government should not subsidize or control energy
- Government finance and spending—all persons should be able to keep the fruits of their labor, abolish the Internal Revenue Service
- Government employees—repeal requirement to join or pay dues to a union, prefer defined contribution plans
- Money and financial markets—favor free markets with unrestricted competition among banks and depository institutions
- Marketplace freedom—free markets with rights of individuals to form corporations, cooperatives, and other entities based on voluntary association; oppose government subsidies and bailouts
- Labor markets—employment agreements between private employers and employees are outside the scope of government
- Education—best provided by a free market, education of children is a parental responsibility
- Health care—freedom of individuals to determine their level of health insurance, health care they want, and who provides their care; believes in choice for all aspects of medical care including end-of-life decisions
- Retirement and income security—retirement planning is an individual responsibility, phase out of government-sponsored Social Security system

- Securing liberty
  - National defense—maintenance of a sufficient military, avoid entangling alliances, and abandon attempt to act as policemen for the world
  - Internal security and individual rights—country defense requires adequate intelligence but it cannot take priority over civil liberties
  - International affairs—seek peace with the world, end current U.S. government policy of foreign intervention to include military and economic aid, condemn use of force
  - Free trade and migration—support removal of government impediments to free trade, economic freedom requires unrestricted movement of humans and financial capital across national borders
  - Rights and discrimination—all people are born with certain inherent rights, condemn bigotry, government should not deny nor

abridge individual human rights based on sex, wealth, ethnicity, creed, age, national origin, personal habits, political preference, or sexual orientation

- ◆ Representative government—support representative election at federal, state, and local levels, end tax-financed subsidies to candidates or parties
- ◆ Self-determination—right of individuals to alter or abolish government if it becomes destructive individual liberty
- Omissions—silence does not imply approval (Libertarian Party, 2016).

Tea Party

The Tea Party is not a typical party but a grassroots movement comprising members from the Democratic, Republican, Libertarian, and Independent political parties. The Tea Party focuses on creating an awareness to issues that challenge the nation's security, sovereignty, or domestic tranquility. There is a strong focus on the Judeo-Christian beliefs that are fundamental to the intended values based on the founding documents written by our Founding Fathers. The members pledge to support a conservative interpretation of the U.S. Constitution and Bill of Rights. The 15 non-negotiable core beliefs are:

- Illegal aliens are in the U.S. illegally.
- Pro-domestic employment is indispensable.
- A strong military is essential.
- Special interests must be eliminated.
- Gun ownership is sacred.
- Government must be downsized.
- The nation's budget must be balanced.
- Deficit spending must end.
- Bailout and stimulus plans are illegal.
- Reducing personal income taxes is a must.
- Reducing business income taxes is mandatory.
- Political offices must be available to average citizens.
- Intrusive government must be stopped.
- English as our core language is required.
- Traditional family values are encouraged (Tea Party, 2016).

Role of Congressional Members

Members of Congress engage in the entire policymaking process. Congressional members must be well informed regarding multiple issues and be able to generate multiple policy alternatives as well as take firm policy positions. **Table 4-1**

TABLE 4-1   CONGRESSIONAL OFFICERS' ROLES AND RESPONSIBILITIES

ROLE	RESPONSIBILITIES
SENATE OFFICERS	
President	Role of vice president
	Casts a tie-breaking vote
	Makes parliamentary decisions, which may be overturned by a majority vote
President Pro Tempore	Presides in absence of president of Senate
	Most senior or highest-ranking senator
Presiding Officer	Member of the majority party
	Maintains order and decorum
	Recognizes members to speak
	Interprets the Senate's rules, precedents, and practices
Sergeant at Arms	Chief security officer
	Preserves order
Secretary	Chief legislative officer
	Elected by full Senate
	Affirms accuracy of bill text
	Supervises all printing of the bills, reports, and publications
Secretary for the Majority	Nominated by the majority leader and approved by the majority party
	Supervises phone directory, messengers, organizes meetings
	Briefs senators on votes and pending legislation
	Conducts all polls
Secretary for the Minority	Nominated by minority leader
	Responsibilities are analogous to secretary of the majority

(continues)

TABLE 4-1   CONGRESSIONAL OFFICERS' ROLES AND RESPONSIBILITIES (CONTINUED)

ROLE	RESPONSIBILITIES
OFFICERS OF THE U.S. HOUSE OF REPRESENTATIVES	
Clerk of the House	Presides at opening of Congress
	Receives credentials of members
	Notes voting tally and certifying bill passage
	Formal preparation of all legislation
	Maintains and distributes documents
Director of Nonlegislative and Financial Services	Operational and financial responsibility
	Oversees House post office and finance office
Doorkeeper of the House	Arranges for joint sessions and joint meetings of Congress
	Announces messages from president and Senate
	Announces the arrival of the president to address Congress
Speaker of the House	Presiding officer, elected by the majority party
	Appoints committee chairs, all special committees, and conference committees
	Primarily casts tie-breaking vote
COMMON SENATE AND HOUSE OFFICERS	
Committee Chairperson	Most senior member of the majority party assigned to that committee
Floor Leaders	Majority leader and the minority leader
Majority Leader	Elected by the majority party in each house to serve as the spokesperson
	Manages and schedules the legislative and executive business in the respective chamber
Minority Leader	Elected by the minority party in each chamber
Parliamentarian	Advises the Senate and House on the interpretation of parliamentary procedure
Ranking Member	Member of the party who has the most seniority
Whip	Legislator chosen to assist the leaders of the majority and minority parties to secure votes

presents the roles and responsibilities of congressional members. The manner in which a congressional member approaches policymaking is dependent upon that member's decision-making ability. Congressional members who support the basic tenet of *bounded rationality* perceive that policymaking processes and the respective political actions are intentionally rational in nature and follow a linear procedural process. *Substantive rationality* assumes complete rationality in which the congressional member has complete information prior to making a decision, weighing the pros and cons of each policy alternative solution. *Procedural rationality* uses mental shortcuts to process incoming policy information and engage in decision-making processes (Smith & Larimer, 2016).

Regardless of which cognitive processes are employed to generate policies, most policymakers are not fully rational. This lack of rationality results from congressional members having to engage in policymaking activities without complete information, and having limited policy and political perspective to completely weigh all pros and cons of each policy alternative solution prior to decision making. Congressional members are assisted in the policymaking process by legislative staff. **Box 4-2** presents the typical responsibilities of legislative staff positions. In addition, **Figure 4-1** outlines a typical organizational chart for a congressional office.

BOX 4-2   LEGISLATIVE STAFF POSITIONS

Administrative Assistant (AA) or Chief of Staff (COS)

- Manages the office operations
- Responsible for hiring
- Chief assistant to the congressional or legislative member

Legislative Assistant (LA)

- Analyzes legislation and the implications of the legislative policy change
- Provides policy briefings
- Works with other congressional or legislative assistants with the respective member's office and from other members' offices

Legislative Director (LD) or Senior Legislative Assistant or Legislative Coordinator

- Manages and coordinates the work of all legislative assistants

Press Secretary or Communications Director

- Handles media relations
- May write member's speeches

(continues)

BOX 4-2 LEGISLATIVE STAFF POSITIONS (CONTINUED)

- Maintains contact with constituents through newsletters or other mediums of correspondence
- May maintain media coverage in home state, district, or local area

Appointment Secretary or Scheduler

- Schedules member's activities
- Exerts some control over member's calendar and access to member

Personal Assistant, Secretary, or Executive Secretary

- Provides clerical duties for member
- May assist with personal tasks

Caseworker or Constituent Services Representative

- Handles individual constituent needs and concerns
- Maintains communication between individual constituents and the member and member's other staff regarding constituent's needs and concerns

Legislative Correspondent

- Answers correspondence

Office Manager

- Handles the operational functions of the office without the political involvement of the administrative assistant
- Handles staff and scheduling of office workers, volunteers

Systems Administrator, Technology Administrator

- Maintains the office technology, networks, etc.

District Director, District Coordinator, or District Legislative Coordinator

- For congressional members, this individual manages legislative activities and office at home

Receptionist or Staff Assistant

- Greets visitors
- Answers phone
- May assist with managing member's email

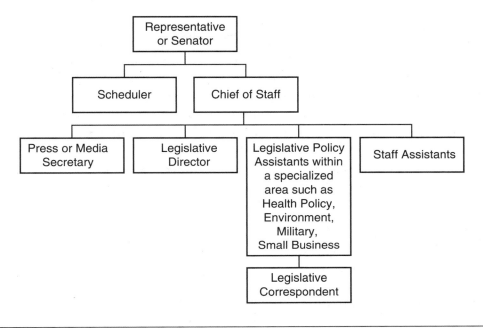

Figure 4-1   Sample Organizational Chart of Congressional Office Staff

Congressional Election Process

Every 2 years states hold congressional elections. During these elections, voters elect all members of the House and one-third of the Senate. Voting rights, other than those rights provided by the U.S. Constitution, are prescribed by state laws and electoral procedures. Replacements for congressional members who are unable to complete their term of office may be appointed by the governor or the governor may call a special election, depending on the state electoral laws and procedures. **Table 4-2** presents the minimum qualifications for congressional office. **Box 4-3** presents common terminology of the U.S. electoral process.

TABLE 4-2   CONGRESSIONAL CANDIDATE ELIGIBILITY CRITERIA

MINIMUM ELIGIBILITY CRITERIA	HOUSE OF REPRESENTATIVES	SENATE
Age	25 years	30 years
Length of citizenship	7 years	9 years
State residency	Required	Required

BOX 4-3 CONGRESSIONAL ELECTION TERMS

- Midterm elections—elections held between presidential elections or in the middle of a president's term
- Primary election—election that occurs by members of and only between candidates within the specific political party
- General election—election that occurs by all voters and among all candidates
- Special election—election to replace a member of Congress that occurs between regular elections

---

Formation of Law

The formation of law is rooted in the legislative process. Laws are generated through a process that is initiated with the composing of a bill. A bill can be composed by anyone but can only be introduced in a legislative body as a bill by an elected official such as a state legislator or congressional official. Legislators introduce bills for multiple purposes. For example, the intent when introducing legislation may not be the adoption of the bill in the form of a law, at a specific time. Legislators file bills as a medium in which to declare a position on an issue, to appease constituents or special interest groups, for publicity, or to demonstrate productivity as a member of Congress.

Once a bill is composed, it is sent to the clerk of the respective legislative chamber. The bill at this point is placed in a hopper. Often, legislation is introduced simultaneously in both chambers. However, a senator can postpone the introduction of a bill by a colleague by 1 day by voicing an objection. Every bill introduced in Congress has a lifetime of 2 years. The bill must be passed into law within 2 years or it dies by default. **Figure 4-2** outlines the formation process by which a bill becomes a law.

Legislative Committees

Legislative committees form the framework of the policymaking process. **Table 4-3** presents legislative committee responsibilities. As each chamber of the legislature has rules and procedures for handling proposed bills, so does each legislative committee. Bills are referred to the respective committee for action. *Standing committees* have permanent jurisdiction over specific types of bills. Some standing legislative committees have the authority to both authorize and allocate proposed laws. This concentrates a significant amount of power and influence over an issue within a specific committee. In contrast to a standing

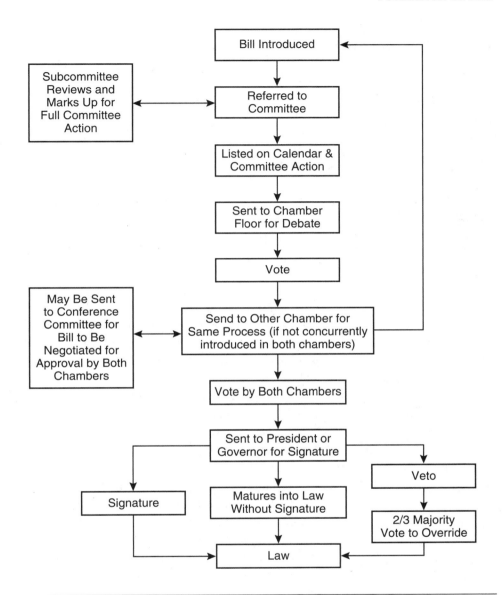

Figure 4-2   Legislative Process: How a Bill Becomes Law

committee, the legislative leadership can appoint a *select committee* to manage a proposed problem or bill. A *joint legislative committee* is a committee that has representation from both the Senate and the House of Representatives. A *conference committee* is a type of joint committee that is typically assigned to work out differences in two respectively similar bills.

TABLE 4-3   LEGISLATIVE COMMITTEE RESPONSIBILITIES

COMMITTEE	RESPONSIBILITIES
SENATE COMMITTEES	
Appropriations	Appropriates funds and implements new spending under the authority of the Congressional Budget Act
Budget	Responsible for the federal budget, concurrent budget Resolutions and Congressional Budget Office
Commerce, Science, and Transportation	Responsible for interstate commerce and transportation; Coast Guard; coastal zone management; communications; highway safety; inland waterways; marine fisheries; merchant marine and navigation; nonmilitary aeronautical and space sciences; oceans, weather, and atmospheric activities; interoceanic canals; regulation of consumer products and services; science, engineering, and technology research, development, and policy; sports; standards and measurement
Finance Committee	Responsible for health programs under the Social Security Act and health programs financed by a specific tax or trust fund; Medicaid; Medicare
Governmental Affairs	Responsible for budget and accounting measures; census and statistics; federal civil service; congressional organization; intergovernmental relations; District of Columbia; organization and reorganization of executive branch; postal service; efficiency, economy, and effectiveness of government; the U.S. archives
Health, Education, Labor, and Pension	Measures relating to education, labor, health and public welfare; aging; biomedical research and development; Occupational Safety and Health, including the welfare of minors; private pensions plans; public health

TABLE 4-3   LEGISLATIVE COMMITTEE RESPONSIBILITIES (CONTINUED)

COMMITTEE	RESPONSIBILITIES
Judiciary	Responsible for civil liberties; constitutional amendments; parental rights; family privacy
Special Committee on Aging	Issues that affect older Americans, including Medicare, prescription drugs, long-term care, and Social Security

HOUSE COMMITTEES

Appropriations	Responsible for appropriation of the revenue for the support of the government; transfers of unexpected balances; new spending authority under the Congressional Budget Act
House Energy and Commerce	Responsible for biomedical research and development; consumer affairs and consumer protection; food and drugs; health and health facilities; interstate energy committee
Committee on Government Reform	Responsible for budget and accounting measures, generally; the overall economy, efficiency, and management of government operations and activities, including federal procurement; public information and records; relationship of the federal government to the states and municipalities
Judiciary	Responsible for civil liberties; constitutional amendments; subversive activities affecting the internal security of the United States
Transportation and Infrastructure	Responsible for federal management in emergencies and natural disasters; flood control and improvement of rivers and harbors; oil and other pollution of navigable waters, including inland, coastal, and ocean waters; marine affairs (including coastal zone management) as they relate to oil and other pollution of navigable waters; roads and the safety thereof; transportation and transportation safety

(continues)

TABLE 4-3   LEGISLATIVE COMMITTEE RESPONSIBILITIES (CONTINUED)

COMMITTEE	RESPONSIBILITIES
Ways and Means Committee	Responsible for customs, collection districts, and ports of entry and delivery; reciprocal trade agreements; revenue measures; revenue measures relating to the insular possessions; bonded debt of the United States; the deposit of public moneys; transportation of dutiable goods; tax-exempt foundations and charitable trusts; national Social Security

The leadership structure of a legislative committee consists of a committee chairperson and committee members. The chair of the committee is a member of the majority party. The chairperson is responsible for setting the agenda, conducting meetings, and managing the fiscal resources of the respective committee.

Legislative committees engage in a variety of critical activities. These activities are vital to the formation of policy. In addition, each of these activities serves as a point in the policymaking process at which constituents can influence the outcome of the proposed legislation. Typical activities in which committees engage include:

- Hearings—provide an opportunity for testimony; can be public or closed
- Legislation markup—the process of editing, changing, or rewriting aspects of the proposed legislation or bill in public meetings (in accordance with the "sunshine rules"), with national security or related issues being the only exceptions
- Reports—outline the legislative intent of the bill, history of the bill, purpose and scope, changes proposed, fiscal impact, and sometimes summarize the dissenting opinions in relation to the proposed legislation

The legislative committee bears considerable responsibility for ensuring that proposed legislation reaches final passage into law. Potential committee actions are:

- Approve with or without amendments
- Rewrite or revise the bill

- Report the bill out to the full chamber favorably or unfavorably
- Take no action on the bill and let it die

Legislative Floor Action

Once the committee presents a bill, it can be placed on the calendar. The legislative body can take votes on a proposed bill by voice, division, or recorded voting. In *voice voting*, members state their answer in support or opposition as either yea or nay. A *division vote* requires a head or hand count on the proposed legislation. A *recorded vote* records each legislator's name and position on the respective proposed legislation.

Executive Action

The executive leader (president, governor, or mayor) has the authority to sign, veto, or return legislation to the legislature with a detailed objection. If the executive leader does not take action within 10 days, the bill becomes law. If the legislature adjourns before the 10-day period expires, the unsigned bill does not become law by default. It is considered to be defeated by a *pocket veto*. If the executive leader vetoes a bill, it requires a two-thirds vote of Congress to overturn the veto.

Senate Confirmation

The U.S. Constitution requires that the Senate confirm the appointment of high government officials who are nominated by the president. The Senate confirmation process consists of three steps:

- Presidential nomination—The president submits in writing the name of a nominee. The nomination is read on the Senate floor and provided a number.
- Confirmation hearings—The Senate parliamentarian refers the nomination to the respective committee for review and confirmation hearings.
- Senate vote—The Senate reviews the committee's recommendation on the floor in a closed executive session. Nominations are open to unlimited debate. The Senate may confirm, reject, or take no action. Confirmation requires a simple majority vote. Once the Senate has acted, the secretary of the Senate communicates the decision, in writing, to the president. If the Senate is in recess for greater than 30 days or is in adjournment, the nomination must be returned to the president. During this time, the president can exercise a temporary appointment that ends at the conclusion of the Senate's next session unless the Senate confirms the appointment during the session.

Types of Law (Legal Policy)

There are four main types of law in the United States: constitutional; legislative; judicial or common; and administrative. Laws are established at the local, state, and federal levels. Law developed at the lower levels should not conflict with high-level law and should be consistent with higher law. This is in accordance with hierarchical supremacy of a system of federalism. It is acceptable for laws developed at the lower level to be more specific than higher-level laws providing they are consistent with national law. Law is considered a type of policy, typically referred to as legal policy. There are several types of legal policy that originate from our federalist structure. These types are constitutional law, legislative law, and judicial or case law.

Constitutional law is the supreme law of the land. Constitutional law is derived from federal and state constitutions. The U.S. Constitution establishes the general government of the nation and grants powers to the federal and state governments. The Constitution is the highest law that exists, and no other law can overrule it. The state constitution is the highest law at the state level, but can be invalidated by the federal constitution (Gostin & Wiley 2016).

Legislative law is developed through the legislative processes at the national or state level. Passage of laws by Congress or a state legislature results in legislative law or policy. These laws or policies are frequently known as *state statutes*. Local governing bodies such as city councils promulgate laws known as ordinances (Aiken, 2004).

Judicial law, or *common law*, is also known as *case law*. Judicial law or policy is developed through decisions rendered in the judicial court system. Judicial law is founded on the principles of justice, reason, and common sense. Every decision made in a courtroom by a judge contributes to the development of judicial law. Judicial law can be either civil or criminal. Civil law protects individuals and enforces the rights, duties, and other legal relations that exist between private citizens. Criminal law consists of concerns that threaten society such as criminal or unlawful behavior toward another individual (Aiken, 2004).

Executive agencies of the government promulgate regulations, as described in Chapter 3. Regulations are considered *administrative laws* or policies. Laws that are generated from regulatory agencies are known as regulations. In addition to developing regulations, executive agencies have police power to enforce these regulations.

Summary Points

- The legislative branch of government is known as the Congress of the United States.
- The Congress is composed of two chambers—the House of Representatives and the Senate.

- The House of Representatives is responsible for originating all revenue bills.
- House of Representatives also holds the power to impeach the president and other federal officers.
- Every bill that originates within the House must also be passed and approved by the Senate and vice versa.
- The Senate is considered the most powerful chamber or house of Congress.
- The vice president of the United States serves as the president of the Senate.
- A democracy requires an informed citizenry that has the ability to openly and freely engage in a debate on issues, problems, politics, and policy solutions.
- The most prominent political parties in the United States are the Democratic Party and the Republican Party.
- The Democratic Party pledges a commitment to keeping our nation safe and expanding opportunity for every American.
- The Republican Party supports the individual over the government, reducing the size of government, streamlining bureaucracy, and returning power to the individual states.
- Legislative committees form the framework of the policymaking process.
- Bills are referred to their respective committee for action.
- Standing committees have permanent jurisdiction over specific types of bills.
- A joint legislative committee is a committee that has representation from both the Senate and the House.
- A conference committee is a type of joint committee that is typically assigned to work out differences in two respectively similar bills.
- If the executive leader does not take action within 10 days, a bill becomes law.
- If the legislature adjourns before the 10-day period expires, the unsigned bill does not become law by default.
- Congressional eligibility consists of age, state residency, and citizenship requirements
- The U.S. Constitution requires that the Senate confirm the appointment of high government officials who are nominated by the president.
- There are four main types of law in the United States: constitutional, legislative, judicial or common, and administrative.

- Constitutional law is the supreme law of the land.
- Legislative law is developed through the legislative processes at the national or state level.
- Judicial or common law, also known as case law, is developed through decisions rendered in the judicial court system.

References

Aiken, T. (2004). *Legal, ethical, and political issues in nursing* (2nd ed.). Philadelphia, PA: F. A. Davis.

Democratic Platform Committee. (2016). *The 2016 democratic party platform.* Retrieved from https://www.demconvention.com/wp-content/uploads/2016/07/Democratic-PartyPlatform-7.21.16-no-lines.pdf

Gostin, L. O., & Wiley, L. F. (2016). *Public health law: Power, duty, restraint* (3rd ed.). Oakland, CA: University of California Press.

Libertarian Party. (2016). *2016 Libertarian party platform.* Retrieved from https://www.lp.org/platform/

National Independent American Party. (2012). *Platform of the National Independent Amercan Party.* Retrieved from http://www.independentamericanparty.org/about-the-iap/platform/

Republican National Convention Committee. (2016). *2016 republican platform.* Retrieved from https://www.gop.com/the-2016-republican-party-platform/

Roskin, M., & Cord, R. (2016). *Political science: An introduction* (13th ed.). London, England: Pearson.

Smith, K. B., & Larimer, C. W. (Eds.). (2016). *The public policy theory primer* (3rd ed.). Boulder, CO: Westview Press.

SparkNotes Editors. (2010). *SparkNote on political ideologies and styles.* Retrieved on January 21, 2017 from http://www.sparknotes.com/us-government-and-politics/political-science/political-ideologies-and-styles/

Tea Party, Inc. (2016). *About us.* Retrieved from http://www.teaparty.org/about-us/

Judicial Branch: The Court System

The judicial branch is primarily responsible for the interpretation of legislation and policy and the development of case law. Case law is considered legal policy. The courts, through the litigation process, are a means to enforce legislative and regulatory requirements and hold others accountable to the law. In addition, the litigation process uses the courts to enforce rights and responsibilities in accordance with legal policy.

Structure of Judicial Branch

The judicial branch is structured into two divisions in accordance with our federalist perspective. The two judicial branch divisions are federal courts and state courts. Each division also has lower courts (**Figure 5-1**). The federal courts have jurisdiction over the U.S. Constitution and federal laws and regulations. Similarly, state courts have jurisdiction over the state constitution and state laws and regulations. The supreme courts at the federal and state level are interconnected regarding appeals. An appeal of a state Supreme Court decision may be filed with the U.S. Supreme Court. A Supreme Court decision is considered the highest legal decision and results in national policy for all citizens in our country.

Supreme Court of the United States (SCOTUS)

The U.S. Constitution vests the judicial power of the United States in one Supreme Court. It is considered the highest tribunal in the nation for all cases and controversies that arise under the Constitution or laws of the United States. This Court serves as the final interpreter and arbiter of the law. The Supreme Court is considered the guardian and interpreter of the U.S. Constitution. This Court

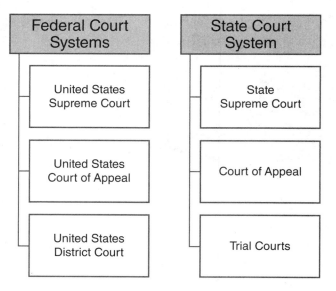

Note: Cases are generally initiated in the lowest court system and appeal upward to the highest court, such as the U.S. Supreme Court or state supreme court.

Figure 5-1   U.S. Court System

renders final decisions on specific cases; it does not provide advisory opinions, but gives legal opinions in the form of final court decisions.

The term of the Supreme Court begins on the first Monday in October and lasts until the first Monday in October of the following year. Court sessions continue from October to late June or early July. The term is divided into what is known as "sittings." During the sittings, the Justices hear cases and deliver opinions with intervening recesses, when they consider the business of the Court. Sittings and recesses alternate at about 2-week intervals. During a Supreme Court hearing, each side is provided 30 minutes of argument. There is no jury or witnesses in the hearing.

The process for appointing a Supreme Court Justice involves the president and Congress. **Box 5-1** outlines the process for the appointment of a Supreme Court Justice. The president may nominate anyone to the Supreme Court; the Constitution does not set any qualifications for service as a Justice. Justices hold office during what is called "good behavior," which is understood to mean to serve for the remainder of their lives. Justices may resign or retire. A Justice can be removed through a congressional impeachment process (Rosdeitcher, 2009).

BOX 5-1   SUPREME COURT JUSTICE APPOINTMENT PROCESS

- White House staff prepares profiles of potential candidates and conducts initial vetting (such as a review of published rulings, articles, speeches, personal and professional values and beliefs).
- President nominates a candidate after review of vetted information.
- Senate Judiciary Committee vets the candidate's credentials and backgrounds (personal life, financial background, and past legal opinions/decisions).
- Senate holds confirmation hearing.
- Committee votes.
- Committee vote on candidate is sent to full Senate.
- Senate debates candidate on Senate floor.
- Nomination confirmed through Senate vote of simple majority.

Federal Court System

The authority to create and abolish federal courts is established through the U.S. Constitution. The only court that cannot be abolished is the Supreme Court. Generally, federal courts have jurisdiction over civil and criminal actions dealing with federal laws. The federal court is presided over by a federal judge appointee. The federal judge generally retains this appointment until death, retirement, or resignation. Federal judges are expected to execute their duties with ethical behavior in upholding the law. Failure to do so may result in impeachment for improper or criminal conduct. The federal court system is administered by a chief judge or justice. The Clerk of Court maintains the court's records and finances. In addition, the Clerk of Court also provides support services, sends communications in the form of official notices and summons, and manages court reports and interpreters.

State Court System

The state court system interprets and enforces state laws under the auspices of the state government structure. State governments share power with a federal government. In accordance with the Tenth Amendment to the U.S. Constitution, all governmental powers not granted to the federal court system by the Constitution are reserved for the states and counties. **Figure 5-2** presents a typical state court system structure and function.

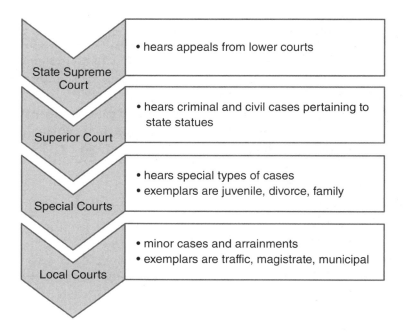

Figure 5-2   State Court System Structure and Function

Special Court Systems

The U.S. Congress has the authority to establish special legislative courts whose judges are appointed by the president and approved by the Senate for a life-long term. These special legislative courts are established through the legislative process. The two special courts that currently exist are the U.S. Court of International Trade and the U.S. Court of Federal Claims. In addition, the U.S. Attorneys or state attorneys general can exercise a unique system with which to bring forth a trial, known as a grand jury. In a grand jury, a jury convenes with government attorneys, court reporters, interpreters as needed, and witnesses to determine if there is sufficient evidence to indict an individual or "probable cause" that a suspect has committed a criminal act.

The U.S. Court of International Trade has authority over cases involving international trade and customs. The U.S. Court of Federal Claims has authority over claims for monetary damages alleged against the U.S. government, disputes over federal contracts, or the unlawful seizure of private property by the government. A grand jury may be convened for cases involving charges of a federal or state level crime.

Jurisdiction

Jurisdiction represents the scope of authority for a case. There are several types of jurisdiction: geographic, subject matter, or personal. *Geographic jurisdiction* typically represents the geographic or political locality boundaries that are encompassed within the respective court's scope of authority. *Subject matter jurisdiction* concerns the specific area of law in which the respective court has a defined scope of authority. Lastly, *personal jurisdiction* is the extent to which a court has authority over an individual or business entity. For the purpose of disposing enforcement of legal policy on corporations, a corporation is treated as an individual in the federal and state judicial systems.

Litigation Process

The litigation process consists of three stages—the pre-litigation stage; litigation stage, which extends from the period of discovery to the point at which the case is heard before the court; and the post-litigation stage that attends to rendering the court's judgment and formulating the findings into future policy as case law.

Pre-litigation Stage

The pre-litigation stage begins when an individual, usually a plaintiff, first meets with an attorney. The initial meeting with an attorney consists of an intake process that includes the following: (1) collection of personal data; (2) discussion of the complaints and allegations; (3) completion of necessary release forms allowing the attorney to represent the plaintiff; and (4) collection of supportive evidence in relation to the allegations.

Litigation Stage

The litigation stage is initiated when the first legal document is filed in the proper court jurisdiction. During this initial process, the case is assigned a docket number. The initial filing of documents for a legal case occurs in the court clerk's office. Typical initial documents that are filed might include a summons, a complaint, an answer, interrogatives, requests for documents, subpoenas, and various motions. **Table 5-1** presents legal policy terminology used in the litigation process. An important aspect of the litigation stage is the discovery process.

The discovery process seeks to identify the facts of the case, collect evidence, and gather other information supporting the case. It is during the discovery process that the attorney may file subpoenas, request documents, compose interrogatives, require physical or mental examinations, introduce admissions of fact, secure testimony and opinions of experts, and conduct depositions. The conducting of a deposition with the plaintiff, defendant,

TABLE 5-1   TERMINOLOGY USED IN LITIGATION PROCESS

Adjudicate	To make a decision, settle, or decree
Affidavit	A written declarative statement provided under oath
Allegation	A legal assertion that must be proved or supported with evidence
Alleged	Something that is claimed or asserted; charged
Amicus brief	An unsolicited legal opinion provided by an *amicus curiae*, or "friend of the court," who is not party to a case. The court must grant permission for this information to be filed. This strategy is often used by advocacy groups as a tool to advance certain opinions before the court.
Answer	A reply by the defendant or the defendant's attorney that states the manner in which the defendant intends to respond to the allegation
Appeal	A request to another court to reverse the previous court's decision based on an error
Arbitration	A binding process in which both sides agree to permit an external nonbiased arbitrator to render a decision on the disagreement or conflict
Breach	Failure to act in accordance with a duty
Class action	A case in which a large number of plaintiffs pursue litigation under the same case and case number
Complaint	A legal document that sets forth the basic facts and reasons for the legal action
Continuance	Postponement of the proceedings in a hearing, trial, or other judicial proceeding
Cross-examination	Questioning of a witness by the opposing side
Defendant	Person, company, or institution against whom a claim or charge is filed
Depose	To have a deposition rendered
Deposition	A testimony of a witness taken based on interrogatories not in open court
Direct cause	Act or event directly resulting in the injury

TABLE 5-1   TERMINOLOGY USED IN LITIGATION PROCESS (CONTINUED)

Discovery	Part of the pre-trial phase of litigation; the process by which evidence from the plaintiff and defendant is identified through securing documents and testimony such as a deposition
Expungement	A process by which a record, or portion of a record, is officially erased or removed from public record
Guardian *ad litem*	A lawyer appointed to defend or prosecute a case on behalf of a party who is incapacitated by age or other condition
Indictment	A formal accusation by a prosecutor set forth in a criminal case
Injunction	A court order prohibiting a person or agency from doing something
Interrogatives	A set of written questions that must be answered
Judgment	A final decision and order of the court
Jurisdiction	The boundaries that determine the scope of judicial authority
Malpractice	Deviation from accepted professional standards, by omission or negligence, that causes harm
Mediation	A nonbinding process in which a mediator attempts to assist two opposing sides to reach a decision or settlement that is amenable to both parties
Motion	A request made to the judge by a litigant. Legal documents filed by attorneys to facilitate the litigation process that request the court leader to make a decision on the case
Motion for judgment	A plea filed by a plaintiff that sets forth the plaintiff's claim and request for a judgment in the plaintiff's favor
Motion for summary	A request that the court provide an immediate ruling judgment on behalf of the requesting party
Motion *in limine*	Motion "at the threshold"; a motion made before the start of the trial that certain evidence may or may not be presented during the litigation process

(continues)

TABLE 5-1   TERMINOLOGY USED IN LITIGATION PROCESS (CONTINUED)

Motion to dismiss	A request that the court decide the case or render a decision; that there is no solution that could be rendered by the court
Negligence	Failing to do something that should have been done, or doing something that should not have been done
Nolo contendere	Means "I will not contest it"
Petition	A formal request to a court to take a specific action on a matter
Plaintiff	A person, company, or institution who files a suit in the court
Plea	Statement by a defendant regarding guilt or innocence
Pleadings	Formal allegations by the parties of their respective claims, testimony, or request
Precedent	A previous decision or proceeding provided by another case or court decision
Probable cause	Reasonable grounds for the existence of facts that warrant investigation
Product liability	A product that is the cause of the injury that leads to litigation
Proximate cause	Causation in which an event that occurred prior to or immediately prior to an injury is associated with the injury
Request for document production	A written request in which one side requests the other side to produce documents that pertain to the case
Restitution	The act of making good, whole, or equivalent for any loss, damage, or injury
Sealed	A document or file closed from review
Statute of limitations	The period in which the potential for litigation remains an option
Subpoena	A legal document that commands someone to appear, testify, or produce a document
Subpoena *duces tecum*	A legal order for a person to appear at a deposition or trial and produce "tangible evidence" in the case

TABLE 5-1   TERMINOLOGY USED IN LITIGATION PROCESS (CONTINUED)

Summons	A legal document sent to the defendant that informs that individual that a legal proceeding has been initiated
Tort	A wrongful act in which another is injured, property is damaged, or reputation is harmed. Torts can be intentional or unintentional.
Tortfeasor	Person who commits a tort
Trial *de novo*	A new trial or retrial in which the whole case is retried
Venue	Location or site of the court trial
Verdict	The formal decision or finding regarding guilt or innocence

Data from Garner, B. (2014). *Black's law dictionary* (10th ed.). St. Paul, MN: Thomson West; Rudolph, E. G. (2009). *How to be a professional legal nurse consultant.* Memphis, TN: Jurex Center for Legal Nurse Consulting.

and experts is a critical element of the discovery process. A deposition is a formally structured interview process in which legal counsels from both sides are present with an individual providing the testimony under oath. A court reporter records the deposition verbatim. The deposition serves as evidence and can be entered in the court system during the litigation process (**Box 5-2** and **Box 5-3**). The deposition is a source of evidence; therefore, it is critical that any individual who is deposed carefully read and correct the transcripts of the deposition. The deposition provides further leads for the continued investigation and discovery of evidentiary facts (Garner, 2014; Gostin & Wiley, 2016; Rudolph, 2009).

Another integral component of the discovery process is the conducting of legal research. Legal research produces valuable evidence to be utilized during the court litigation process. The purpose of legal research is to identify relevant case law that can provide guidance for legal strategy, assess the merits of the case, and identify judicial precedent in similar cases. During the legal research process, the attorney or a designee conducts a comprehensive assessment of professional or scientific literature and reviews relevant case law that serves as legal policy (Aiken, 2004; Rudolph, 2009). **Box 5-4** outlines a legal research process to identify relevant legal cases.

BOX 5-2   DEPOSITION PURPOSE

A deposition during the litigation stage will enable the legal team to:

- Discover information regarding the facts of the case
- Evaluate the case's strengths and weaknesses
- Evaluate the knowledge of the witnesses
- Identify and develop a legal strategy
- Determine the relevance of documents to the case
- Discover the facts and circumstances of the allegation–complaint
- Preserve the testimony of a witness for a future date
- Determine the potential extent of injury
- Determine the credibility of potential witness
- Explore the extent of expert witness expertise
- Create evidence for trial

BOX 5-3   DEPOSITION GUIDELINES

The following are guidelines for an individual being deposed:

- Present a copy of your curriculum vitae (CV).
- Review all documents and pertinent information.
- Conduct a review of relevant literature and evidence in relation to your expert opinion.
- Review any personal documentation regarding the incident.
- Review the format of the deposition with legal counsel prior to the deposition.
- Provide an honest testimony.
- Speak slowly, with clear pronunciation.
- Maintain eye contact.
- Answer only the question; do not elaborate on any questions or provide additional information not requested. Provide concise answers.
- Ask for clarification at any point if you do not understand the question.
- Always pause before answering a question to provide legal counsel with an opportunity to object.
- If asked the same question twice, answer in the same manner or request the recorder to read your previous answer.

BOX 5-3   DEPOSITION GUIDELINES (CONTINUED)

- Avoid answering in an absolute manner, such as "I always . . ." or "I have never. . . ."
- Follow the lead of your legal counsel in answering questions.
- Do not provide speculations; only answer factual questions.
- If you do not know the answer, state "I do not know."
- If you do not recall or remember the events, state "I do not remember."
- Do not argue with legal counsel.
- Thoroughly review the transcript of your testimony and correct errors.

BOX 5-4   LEGAL RESEARCH PROCESS

- Define the legal issue—DISPUTE is an acronym used to prepare for and frame the boundaries of the legal research:
  - Did you identify all the relevant parties in the case?
  - Is the location of the event important?
  - Some important items or objects important to the case are identified.
  - Place the events in chronological order.
  - Understand the events that gave rise to the issue involved in the case.
  - Take into consideration the potential opposing counsel's arguments.
  - Evaluate the legal remedy or relief sought in the case.
- From the defined legal issue—identify search terms.
- Conduct a broad search on the open web (Lexis web, Google scholar, case law).
- Use primary and secondary sources.
- Search secondary authorities—law reviews, treatises, practice guidelines, and news reports.
- Search primary authorities—case law, statutes, regulations, and regulatory annotations.
- Perform final validation using a comprehensive database. Shepard's database provides a comprehensive search on a topic with expert analysis.
- Synthesize and analyze findings.
- Write legal research brief.

The final aspect of the litigation stage is the court trial in the judicial system. The trial is the hearing of the case in the presence of a judge. In some instances, the judge may hold pre-trial hearings to shorten the trial period. During pre-trial, the judge may render rulings on issues such as the qualification of witnesses, credibility of experts, admissibility of evidence, and response to motions filed. The trial consists of several phases such as jury selection, opening statements, presentation of evidence by the plaintiff's and defendant's legal counsel, closing arguments, judge's instructions to the jury, jury deliberations and findings of case, and verdict. In some cases, the court case is tried only in the presence of a judge.

Post-litigation Stage

The jury or judge renders a final decision in each court case. This decision is known as the verdict. The decision or verdict rendered in response to a specific case formulates legal policy in the form of case law.

Types of Policy Formulated

Policy is formulated through the judicial system by the establishment of legal precedents and case law. This process is referred to as judicial policymaking. In judicial policymaking, the judge and court, acting as a collective entity, engage in an active role of policy implementation through the interpretive process. Case law in a system of jurisprudence is based on existing legal policy and judicial precedents. Case law is policy that is formulated through the judgment or verdict rendered in the judicial court system. Case law is also referred to as common law or judge-made law. Case law can define both civil and criminal policy within the respective jurisdiction of the judicial system.

A precedent is a policy that is established through an earlier judicial decision. *Stare decisis* ("let the decision stand") is the principle that establishes the basis for judicial precedence. This encourages adherence to previous case findings with substantially comparable facts and situations. Therefore, the development of case law serves as a precedent or policy by which future cases will be interpreted within the judicial system.

Nurses' Role in Judicial System

The effect of litigation within the judicial system is the establishment, affirmation, or clarification of rights at the local, state, or national level. Nurses can use their knowledge within the judicial system to serve as a legal nurse consultant or expert witness.

Legal Nurse Consultant

A legal nurse consultant is a professional who integrates nursing knowledge with knowledge of the legal system and process. The legal nurse consultant is as a member of the legal team. Legal nurse consultants are valuable resources who assist attorneys and judges in formulating legal policy. The duties of a legal nurse consultant include reviewing and evaluating medical-nursing legal cases, educating attorneys and clients regarding medical-nursing issues, reviewing and interpreting medical records, serving as an expert witness, testifying in a deposition or court, assessing the extent of damages, and conducting legal research (Rudolph, 2009). In addition, the legal nurse consultant can present a chronological summary of a case with an analysis of the case's merits in the form of an executive summary for the attorney or judge. This task expedites the rendering of a legal opinion or strategy.

Other healthcare professionals can integrate their discipline-specific knowledge with the legal system and processes to serve as legal consultants. The legal nurse consultant model can be used to form a legal specialization within other healthcare professional disciplines. Nurses or other healthcare professionals can engage in the legal system as consulting experts or testifying experts. Both of these roles assist the attorney in determining the merits of the case and providing consultation regarding the legal case. However, there are differences in the role requirements. The consulting expert can provide consultation regarding his or her respective discipline and other areas involving the case. The consulting expert's information is not discoverable in the legal case unless it is used by an expert witness. In contrast, the expert witness provides testimony only in the witness's scope of practice and the information is considered discoverable in a legal case. The role of the expert witness is further explained below.

Expert Witness

Nurses and other healthcare professionals serve as expert witnesses to provide information relevant to the case. An expert witness is an individual who has an identified area of expertise based on education, skills, credentials, qualifications, and experience (Aiken, 2004). Nurses who serve as expert witnesses generally provide testimony regarding the expected nursing standard of care within a healthcare environment. To be accepted as an expert witness, the nurse's or other healthcare professional's credibility in terms of education, experience, and credentials must be demonstrated by the team's attorney. The judge, on behalf of the judicial system, may then qualify the nurse or other healthcare professional as an expert witness in the court system. **Box 5-5** presents the responsibilities of an expert witness.

BOX 5-5   EXPERT WITNESS RESPONSIBILITIES

- Present expert evidence that is independent and uninfluenced or biased
- State the facts or assumptions upon which the opinion is based—provide references and citations as appropriate
- Provide opinion only within the expert's area of expertise and identify questions or content that is outside that area of expertise
- Ensure that an opinion rendered on incomplete information or data is known as a provisional opinion
- Must inform the court if there is a change in opinion resulting from a change in data/evidence/information or after reviewing other litigation material
- Provide copies as evidence of information used to formulate an opinion
- Must cooperate with other parties in the dispute
- Never assume the role of advocate while in the role of expert witness
- Should not omit material facts that may detract from the concluded opinion

---

Summary Points

- The judicial system is structured into two divisions—federal and state courts.
- The federal courts have jurisdiction over the U.S. Constitution and federal laws and regulations.
- State courts have jurisdiction over the state constitution and state laws and regulations.
- An appeal of a state Supreme Court decision may be filed with the U.S. Supreme Court.
- A Supreme Court decision is considered the highest legal decision.
- The only court that cannot be abolished is the Supreme Court.
- The president nominates a Supreme Court Justice and the nominee is confirmed by the U.S. Senate.
- Justices are appointed for life but can be removed by congressional impeachment.
- Federal courts have jurisdiction over civil and criminal actions dealing with federal laws.
- The federal court is presided over by a federal judge appointee.

- A federal judge generally retains appointment until death, retirement, or resignation.
- All governmental powers not granted to the federal court system by the Constitution are reserved for the states and counties.
- In a grand jury, a jury convenes with government attorneys, court reporters, interpreters as needed, and witnesses to determine if there is sufficient evidence to indict an individual or "probable cause" that a suspect has committed a criminal act.
- Jurisdiction represents the scope of authority for a case.
- Geographic jurisdiction represents the geographic or political locality boundaries that are encompassed within the respective court's scope of authority.
- Subject matter jurisdiction concerns the specific area of law in which the respective court has a defined scope of authority.
- Personal jurisdiction is the extent to which a court has authority over an individual or business entity.
- The litigation process occurs in three stages: pre-litigation, litigation, and post-litigation.
- The judicial system produces policy in the form of legal precedents and case law.
- A precedent is a policy established through an earlier judicial decision.
- Case law is policy formulated through the judgment or verdict rendered in the judicial court.
- A legal nurse consultant is a professional who integrates nursing knowledge with knowledge of the legal system and process.
- An expert witness is an individual who has an identified area of expertise based on that witness's education, skills, credentials, qualifications, and experience.

References

Aiken, T. (2004). *Legal, ethical and political issues in nursing* (2nd ed.). Philadelphia, PA: F. A. Davis.

Garner, B. (2014). *Black's law dictionary* (10th ed.). St. Paul, MN: Thomson West.

Gostin, L. O., & Wiley, L. F. (2016). *Public health law: Power, duty, restraint* (3rd ed.). Oakland, CA: University of California Press.

Rosdeitcher, S. (2009). *Supreme court adjudication and the qualifications of supreme court nominees—* Brennan Center for Justice at New York University School of Law. Accessed on March 11, 2017 at http://www.brennancenter.org/sites/default/files/legacy/Rosdeitcher-%20Supreme%20Ct%20Adjudication.pdf

Rudolph, E. G. (2009). *How to be a professional legal nurse consultant.* Memphis, TN: Jurex Center for Legal Nurse Consulting.

Healthcare Systems

The U.S. healthcare system is a complicated and complex governmental and nongovernmental system of care provided to individuals, families, groups, and communities. Healthcare policymakers influence the healthcare system through policy formulation, policy revisions, policy analysis, and policy evaluation. Healthcare policy influences the financial aspects of healthcare delivery systems, and the financial allocation of funds for health care influence the development and implementation of healthcare policies. Healthcare policy is directly and indirectly linked to the funding of health care. Civic competence requires a knowledge base in the structure and financing of healthcare systems. This chapter provides a broad and simplistic overview of limited aspects of the healthcare delivery system to provide a foundation from which to approach and understand healthcare policymaking in the United States.

Overview of United States Healthcare System

The U.S. healthcare system has been described as the best but most expensive healthcare system in the world. The healthcare system has been frequently described as a complex entity of fragmented, uncoordinated, and inefficient care delivery systems. Healthcare policymakers have focused on these negative healthcare system descriptors as opportunities to transform the U.S. healthcare system. An overview of the healthcare system is provided through an explanation of the organization and financing of healthcare services.

The healthcare system consists of isolated care and integrated systems of care delivered through independent providers, group providers, ambulatory healthcare services, home-based healthcare and hospice services, inpatient hospital and hospice services, emergency medical services, and nongovernmental community-based organizations that deliver a variety of healthcare services. The healthcare system has also been criticized as the best healthcare system that is a nonsystem.

TABLE 6-1   FIVE PILLARS OF THE HEALTHCARE SYSTEM

PILLAR	DESCRIPTION
Access	Ability of individuals and families to obtain the needed healthcare services
Quality	The degree to which healthcare services are provided to individuals and populations based on current best evidence that increases the attainment of the desired health outcomes
Cost	Health-related expenditures required to deliver healthcare services to individuals and populations
Equity	Attainment of the highest level of health for all persons based on their needs
Population health	The attainment of health outcomes of a group of individuals

The resultant structure of the healthcare system is derived from the influence of external forces on policy that has shaped the healthcare delivery system. These external forces that have and do influence policy include historical events, financing, political climate, socioeconomic structures, socialization, and provider and consumer preferences. Healthcare system structures focus on achieving five goals—access, quality care, cost containment, equity, and population health. There has been a paradigm shift from illness care to health promotion and disease prevention that has influenced healthcare policy and the structure of the healthcare system to achieve these five goals. **Table 6-1** describes the five pillar goals of the healthcare system. Managed care systems are a combined funding and structure of healthcare services as a means to achieve these five goals.

Managed care is a broad term that describes payment mechanisms and the organizational structure or system of healthcare services. Managed care consists of health maintenance organizations (HMOs), preferred provider organizations (PPOs), point-of-service (POS) organizations, exclusive provider organizations (EPOs), physician hospital organizations (PHOs), and integrated delivery systems (IDSs). **Table 6-2** describes the features of these managed care systems.

Models of Healthcare

Models of healthcare provide the foundation of the healthcare paradigm that structures the healthcare system. There are several basic goals of healthcare

TABLE 6-2   MANAGED CARE SYSTEMS

SYSTEM	DESCRIPTION
Health maintenance organization (HMO)	• Provides services on a prepaid basis • Members pay a fixed monthly fee for the provision of healthcare services • Members must receive care from healthcare providers within the HMO network • Members select a primary care provider (PCP)
Preferred provider organization (PPO)	• A group of healthcare providers and/or hospitals that provides medical services only to a specific group • PPO providers deliver services at a discounted rate to members
Point-of-service (POS) organization	• Combines characteristics of HMO and PPO • Like an HMO, no deductible is paid with a minimal copayment when receiving care from an in-network provider • Like a PPO, members select a PCP from within the network
Exclusive provider organization (EPO)	• Network of providers or groups of providers who entered into an agreement with an insurer to provide coverage to subscribers and members • Healthcare services are provided only if members receive care rendered by providers and hospitals within the network plan
Physician hospital organization (PHO)	• A legal organization that bonds hospitals and healthcare providers • The legal organization is usually jointly owned by physicians and a hospital • Typically is a for-profit, partnership, or limited liability corporation
Integrated delivery system (IDS)	• A network of healthcare institutions organized under a parent holding company/business entity • An organized, coordinated, and collaborative network that links various healthcare providers and settings to provide a coordinated, vertical continuum of care

models: sustain a healthy population; assess, diagnose, and manage health alterations at the individual, group, community, and population level; and protect individuals, families, organizations, and institutions from financial devastation during the provision of healthcare services.

Four Basic Models

The four basic models of healthcare systems are the Beveridge, Bismarck, national health insurance, and out-of-pocket models. Healthcare systems in countries throughout the world can be categorized into one of these four basic healthcare models or an integration of two or more of these models.

Beveridge Model

The Beveridge model is named after William Beveridge, who was a British National Health System social reformer. In the Beveridge model of health care, health care is financed by the national government through a taxation system. In this system of health care, the majority of hospitals are owned by the national government. In this system of care, healthcare providers are employees of the national government. Private healthcare providers also receive their payment for healthcare services from the national government.

Bismarck Model

The Bismarck model is named for the Prussian Chancellor Otto von Bismarck. In the 19th century, Chancellor Bismarck invented the welfare state during the unification of Germany. The Bismarck model uses healthcare insurance that is jointly financed by both employers and employees through a payroll deduction process. These insurance plans are designed to cover everyone without the ability to make a profit from the delivery of healthcare services.

National Health Insurance Model

The national health insurance model is composed of elements from both the Beveridge and Bismarck models. The healthcare providers are employed primarily through the private sector. Payments for healthcare services are provided through a government-coordinated insurance program that every citizen is required to pay into. This model of health care drives down healthcare cost because there is a single payer source with a large segment of the healthcare market to negotiate healthcare service pricing.

Out-of-Pocket Model

The out-of-pocket model is a common model of health care in developed, industrialized countries. In the out-of-pocket model, the recipients of the healthcare services are responsible for paying for the delivery of healthcare services from their own finances.

Healthcare Funding

The U.S. healthcare system has multiple models of healthcare funding. Healthcare funding or financing is the allocation and mobilization of funds to healthcare providers and patient population groups to provide healthcare services. The process of allocating healthcare funding, generating revenue, and managing healthcare expenditures through government and nongovernment programs requires the development and implementation of programmatic and fiscal policies that influence and impact the ultimate policies of the healthcare system. The largest funder of healthcare services in the United States is the federal government; therefore, the federal government generates a considerable amount of policy that influences healthcare service delivery. **Table 6-3** outlines the government insurance programs, Medicare and Medicaid. The federal government emerged as a significant payer of healthcare services in the 1960s. In 1965, Congress passed legislation establishing the Medicare and Medicaid programs as Title XVIII and Title XIX, respectively, of the Social Security Act. This was a major healthcare policy reform at that time. Medicare is a program of services designed to meet the healthcare needs of the elderly, severely disabled, and persons with renal disease. Medicaid is a federal and state program designed to fund health care for low-income households and disabled persons.

The three essential payment mechanisms for healthcare services are government insurance programs, private insurance programs, and personal out-of-pocket payment. **Table 6-4** provides a brief summary of the healthcare financing structures.

Not all of the healthcare services provided in the United States are funded to achieve a result of revenue generation. The provision of care without the generation of actualized revenue is considered uncompensated care. Uncompensated care includes both charity care and bad debt. Charity care is provided to the patient with no charges generated and no payment expected. An institution may engage in charity care due to policy mandates or mission fulfillment. Bad debt is care provided when payment was expected but not received.

Healthcare Reform

The U.S. Census Bureau statistics report that nearly 50 million Americans were without health insurance in 2010. The World Health Organization (WHO) reported that the United States spent more money on health care (1) per capita and (2) as a percentage of gross domestic product (GDP) than any other industrialized country in the world (Rak & Coffin, 2013). The WHO ranked the U.S. healthcare system as having the highest cost and as 37th in overall performance and 72nd in overall level of health among its 191 member nations (Rak & Coffin, 2013).

TABLE 6-3   SERVICES PROVIDED BY GOVERNMENT INSURANCE PROGRAMS

GOVERNMENT INSURANCE PROGRAM	SERVICES
PROGRAM	
Medicare (federal program)	
Part A—Hospital Insurance	• Inpatient hospital care • Skilled nursing facility care • Some home health care • Hospice care • Hospital coverage includes semiprivate accommodations, meals, operating and recovery room fees, laboratory procedures, x-rays, medications, nursing care, therapy services • Critical access hospital care
Part B—Supplemental Medical Insurance (SMI)	• Voluntary insurance • Physician and outpatient services • Physical and occupational therapy services • Some home health care
Prescription drug coverage	• Pay a monthly premium for this coverage • Designed to lower prescription drug cost
Medicaid (federal and state matching program)	• Federal law requires coverage of low-income families, qualified pregnant women and children, and individuals receiving Supplemental Security Income (SSI) • Financial eligibility is determined by modified adjusted gross income (MAGI) • Nonfinancial eligibility requirements must also be met
Children's Health Insurance Program (CHIP)	• Provides comprehensive benefits to children • An expansion of Medicaid program • Includes early and periodic screening, diagnostic, and treatment (EPSDT) services • Vaccinations are a required coverage for CHIP states

TABLE 6-4   HEALTHCARE FINANCE STRUCTURES

TYPE OF FINANCIAL STRUCTURE	STRUCTURE AND PAYMENT SOURCE
Fee-for-service (FFS)	• Payment is provided by funder for each service rendered • No incentives for preventive care, prevention of hospitalization, or reduction of diagnostic test
Accountable care organization (ACO)	• Consist of a group of providers across different organizational settings such as hospitals, clinics, ambulatory care facilities • Focus on prevention and care coordination • Joint shared responsibility for quality, cost, and care to a patient population • Cost increase with an uncoordinated system of care • For costs higher than expected benchmark, there may be penalties to the ACO • When ACO is under the cost target and meets or exceeds benchmark, members share the cost savings as revenue
Bundled payment system or episode of care	• Cost for the provision of all the healthcare services for a patient for a specific episode of care is bundled together in one payment • Focuses on prevention of complications
Pay-for-coordination	• Payment is provided beyond the fee-for-service model to pay for the coordination of care between primary care providers and specialists
Pay-for-performance (P4P)	• A value-based reimbursement • Payment is provided based on the accomplishment of specific metrics of quality and efficiency
Capitation (partial or full)	• Payment is based on a per member per month (PMPM) system based on the patient's age, race, sex, lifestyle, medical history, and benefit design • Payment rates are based on expected healthcare usage

(continues)

TABLE 6-4   HEALTHCARE FINANCE STRUCTURES (CONTINUED)

Self-pay	• Patient pays the burden of all healthcare services received
Private insurance	• Private contract issued by an insurer to assist in the payment for a set of prescribed predetermined benefits
Philanthropic funds	• Funds may be restricted or nonrestricted • Funds support payment for healthcare services as directed by the donors' intent
Investment income	• Healthcare institutions may indirectly fund health care through investment income, trust, endowments

These health and financial statistics were a catalyst for President Barack Obama to initiate a transformative change in U.S. healthcare policy.

Affordable Care Act Overview

President Barack Obama, on March 23, 2010, signed the Patient Protection and Affordable Care Act (Affordable Care Act, or ACA) into law. This law enacted the single largest expansion in health insurance since the creation of the federal Medicaid and Medicare programs in 1965 (Humphreys & Frank, 2014). The law proposed to address the fundamental healthcare system problems characterized by high healthcare costs and poor accessibility to health insurance and quality health services (Shaw, Asomugha, Conway, & Rein, 2014).

The ACA goal was to improve accessibility and quality for more Americans by making health insurance more affordable through the implementation of a comprehensive program of healthcare delivery reforms that provided consumer protections, regulations, taxes, subsidies, and the introduction of health insurance exchanges (Vincent & Reed, 2014). The ACA is projected, by 2019, to provide 25 million more Americans with affordable health insurance (Shaw et al., 2014).

ACA provides the availability of health insurance by expanding Medicaid to cover America's poorest nonelderly adults (those with annual incomes below 138% of the federal poverty level (FPL); providing economic subsidies to nonelderly adults with annual incomes of 100-400% of FPL and who lack access to employer coverage so they can purchase insurance on the new health insurance exchange marketplace; and requiring all nonelderly adults with higher income levels to obtain health insurance coverage or pay a fine for noncompliance (Price & Eibner, 2013).

Social Determinants of Health as Policy Framework

Determinants of health are factors that are considered to influence an individual's health. Determinants of health can be fixed or modifiable factors. Fixed factors are unchangeable such as age, race, and genetic profile. Modifiable factors are changeable such as lifestyle choices, social networks, environment, and education (**Figure 6-1**).

The nationally accepted framework for determinants of health is the social determinants of health (SDH). The WHO defines social determinants of health as "the conditions in which people are born, grow, live, work and age, including the health system. These circumstances are shaped by the distribution of money, power, and resources at the global, national, and local levels (WHO, 2013, para 1). It is important to note that the Healthy People 2020 initiative expanded the WHO definition of social determinants of health to include policies, programs, and institutions and other aspects of the social structure, including the government and private sectors, as well as community factors as components of the SDH (Mahony & Jones, 2013; U.S. Department of Health and Human Services, 2010; WHO, 2013).

The SDH framework can be used to formulate, modify, analyze, and evaluate health policy. Each element of the SDH framework should be considered in

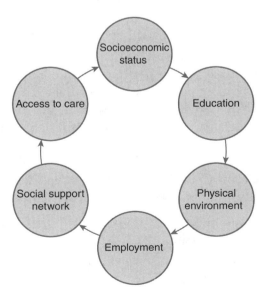

Figure 6-1   Social Determinants of Health Framework

the formulation, modification, analysis, and evaluation of health policy. These elements of the SDH model have been determined to impact the health of individuals and populations. Key elements of the SDH model for consideration in the policymaking process include:

- Poverty—lack of the ability to access basic resources;
- Economic inequality—gap between the wealthy and poor in society;
- Social status—position of rank within a society or considered standing within the community frequently based on income, education, and social affiliation;
- Stress—social and psychological conditions that provoke anxiety, insecurity, low self-esteem, social isolation, and personal lack of control;
- Education—knowledge level;
- Social exclusion—denial of an opportunity to fully participate as a societal member;
- Employment—access to income generation and control over work life;
- Social support—access to emotional resources; and
- Food security—ability to access, acquire, and consume sufficient quantity and quality of safe food (Mahony & Jones, 2013).

Interrelationship of Healthcare Systems and Policy

Healthcare systems and policy are interrelated. Policy formulation, modification, evaluation, and research inform the structure of the healthcare system. Healthcare systems generate policy at both the micro-, meso-, and macro-system levels. The micro-system in health care is an individual or small group of people or a small system that works in a coordinated and integrated manner to provide care to a subpopulation of patients. A micro-system evolves over time to consist of integrated clinical and business goals and objectives, linked processes, shared information, and integrated procedures to produce quality outcomes. Micro-systems are considered the building blocks of an organization. A micro-system of a healthcare system is considered to consist of five Ps—purpose, patients, professionals, processes, and patterns:

- Purpose—aim and mission;
- Patients—recipient of care;
- Professionals—healthcare providers delivering healthcare services;
- Processes—system of interrelated mechanisms of achieving an outcome; and
- Patterns—system's way of doing the "work" of health care.

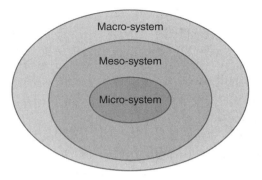

Figure 6-2   Micro-, Meso- and Macro-Systems of Healthcare

A meso-system in health is between the micro- and macro-systems. The meso-system supports the micro-system of an organization. The macro-system is the larger contextual system that is composed of the meso-system and micro-systems to deliver healthcare services. **Figure 6-2** illustrates the relationships of these systems.

Summary Points

- The U.S. healthcare system is a complicated and complex governmental and nongovernmental system of care.
- Civic competence requires a knowledge base in the structure and financing of healthcare systems.
- The healthcare system consists of isolated care and integrated systems of care delivered through independent providers, group providers, ambulatory healthcare services, home-based healthcare and hospice services, inpatient hospital and hospice services, emergency medical services, and nongovernmental community-based organizations that deliver a variety of healthcare services.
- Healthcare system structures focus on achieving five goals—access, quality care, cost containment, equity, and population health.
- Managed care consists of health maintenance organizations (HMOs), preferred provider organizations (PPOs), point-of-service (POS) organizations, exclusive provider organizations (EPOs), physician hospital organizations (PHOs), and integrated delivery systems (IDSs).
- Models of health care provide the foundation of the healthcare paradigm that structures the healthcare system.

- There are several basic goals of healthcare models: sustain a healthy population; assess, diagnose, and manage health alterations at the individual, group, community, and population level; and protect individuals, families, organizations, and institutions from financial devastation during the provision of healthcare services.
- The basic models of health care are the Beveridge, Bismarck, national health insurance, and out-of-pocket models.
- In the Beveridge model of health care, health care is financed by the national government through a taxation system.
- Bismarck model uses healthcare insurance that is jointly financed by both employers and employees through a payroll deduction process.
- In the national health insurance model, payment for healthcare services is provided through a government-coordinated insurance program that every citizen is required to pay into.
- In the out-of-pocket model, recipients of the healthcare services are responsible for paying for the delivery of healthcare services from their own finances.
- Healthcare funding or financing is the allocation and mobilization of funds to healthcare providers and patient population groups to provide healthcare services.
- The largest funder of healthcare services in the United States is the federal government.
- The three essential payment mechanisms for healthcare services are government insurance programs, private insurance programs, and personal out-of-pocket payment.
- The provision of care without the generation of actualized revenue is considered uncompensated care.
- Uncompensated care includes both charity care and bad debt.
- The ACA goal was to improve accessibility and quality of health care for more Americans by making health insurance more affordable through the implementation of a comprehensive program of healthcare delivery reforms that provided consumer protections, regulations, taxes, subsidies, and the introduction of health insurance exchanges.
- Social determinants of health framework can be used to formulate, modify, analyze, and evaluate health policy.

References

Humphreys, K., & Frank, R. G. (2014). The Affordable Care Act will revolutionize care for substance use disorders in the United States. *Addiction*, *109*(12), 1957–1958.

Mahony, D., & Jones, E. (2013). Social determinants of health in nursing education, research, and health policy. *Nursing Science Quarterly, 26*(3), 280–284.

Price, C., & Eibner, C. (2013). For states that opt out of Medicaid expansion: 3.6 million fewer insured and $8.4 billion less in federal payments. *Health Affairs, 32*(6), 1030–1036.

Rak, S., & Coffin, J. (2013). Affordable Care Act. *The Journal of Medical Practice Management: MPM, 28*(5), 317–319.

Shaw, F. E., Asomugha, C. N., Conway, P. H., & Rein, A. S. (2014). The Patient Protection and Affordable Care Act: Opportunities for prevention and public health. *The Lancet, 384*(9937), 75–82.

U.S. Department of Health and Human Services. (2010). *Healthy people 2020: An opportunity to address social determinants of health in the US.* Retrieved from http://www.healthypeople.gov/2020/about/advisory/SocialDeterminantsHealth.pdf

Vincent, D., & Reed, P. G. (2014). Affordable care act: Overview and implications for advancing nursing. *Nursing Science Quarterly, 27*(3), 254–259.

World Health Organization. (2013). *Social determinants of health.* Retrieved on June 17, 2017 from http://www.who.int/social_determinants/en/

Global, International, and Planetary Health Policy

A shared vision proposed by the Centers for Disease Control and Prevention (CDC) is to have a world where people have healthier, safer, and longer lives. To achieve such a vision, there must be policy and political awareness of the interconnection between domestic and international affairs that impact individual-, community-, and population-level health. At a time when people are connected to each other so readily and can travel across borders with general ease, the awareness of and impact of international and global health on domestic health and national security issues are essential to protect and promote population-level health. The CDC's global health mission is to protect and improve health globally through science, policy, partnership, and evidence-based public health action (CDC, 2012). This mission of the CDC is built upon the realization of the connection between domestic, international, and global health to protect the U.S. population. By the CDC that form a foundation of its global health strategy are:

- Health impact—improve the health and well-being of people around the world;
- Health security—improve capabilities to prepare for and respond to infections and other emerging health threats;
- Health capacity—build a country with strong public health capacity;
- Organizational capacity—maximize the potential of and utilization of CDC global programs and initiatives (CDC, 2012).

International and Global Health Defined

The terms *international health* and *global health* are frequently used interchangeably to mean the same thing. These terms are interrelated but have common definitional elements with some distinct differences. Both terms,

Figure 7-1   Public, International, and Global Health Relationships.

international health and *global health*, are considered to be associated with public health. Therefore, both international and global health policies impact public health policy. Public health is generally considered or viewed as focusing on the health of a population of a specific country or community. Because of the strong association between international, global, and public health, public health is considered to be international or global health for the public good (Beaglehole & Bonita, 2010).

International health focuses on health issues and policy between two nations or countries. A focus of international health has been on infectious diseases, maternal and child health, and health of low-income populations. Therefore, some consider international health and policy to focus on the interrelationships between two or more nations. In contrast, global health encompasses a broader perspective (Beaglehole & Bonita, 2010).

Global health focuses on health issues and policy from a perspective that includes all nations and environmental influences on health. Global health deals with worldwide population issues that impact health across all sectors of the world and is not limited to only the health sector (Beaglehole & Bonita, 2010). **Figure 7-1** presents the interrelationship of public, international, and global health.

Planetary Health Defined

To safeguard the health of the human population, the health of the planet needs to be maintained. Planetary health is the health of human civilizations and the natural systems on which humans depend (Whitmee et al., 2015). Planetary health focuses on the alterations in climate, water, land, and ecosystems that are impacting the health of our planet, which has implications for human health.

It is considered an interdisciplinary and transdisciplinary approach to addressing the environmental changes that have an impact on the planet and human health while also addressing political, economic, and social systems.

The Rockefeller Foundation–Lancet Commission on Planetary Health Report indicates that the changes in the structure and function of the earth's natural systems pose a growing threat to human health. This report presents data that the human population is healthier than ever with a longer mean global life expectancy, decreased poverty in the world, and decreased child mortality rate (under 5 years of age). However, this has occurred along with risks posed to our planet that include increases in carbon dioxide emissions, ocean acidification, energy use, tropical forest loss, water use, and fertilizer use (Whitmee et al., 2015). Recommendations to act on planetary health include awareness of planetary health issues, reducing food waste, health diets with low environmental impact, better governance, more efficient water usage, ending deforestation, family planning, city planning, and strengthening health systems globally. Planetary health as a global health concept includes developing health system resilience. Global health system resilience is the capacity to prepare for, respond to, maintain, and reorganize core health system functions during times of normalcy and crisis. Key components of a resilient health system are information, financing, service delivery, human resources, medicines and technology, and governance. Policies that impact international, global, and planetary health in a comprehensive manner can positively impact healthcare systems and the health of individuals.

Global Health Policy

Global health policy is the formulation, implementation, and evaluation of various types of policy that impact individuals, communities, states, nations, and the world as an entire entity. Every policy does not have a potential direct global policy impact; however, every policy, even domestic policy, has a potential indirect global policy impact. Global health policy transcends national, international, and transnational policy. Global policy focuses on policymaking as a process that flows among networks of activity and interaction between international and transcontinental groups. There are six main foci that are considered interconnections in global health policy:

- Globally relevant risks and collective action problems—all countries are linked and interdependent;
- International policy coordination—national policy should consider the impact on other countries' national policy and coordinate policies for maximum global effectiveness;

- Normative beliefs of global governance impact policymaking such as free markets, democracy, and hierarchies;
- Change from national-level to "bloc"-level policymaking—policymaking in a regionalist manner such as with the European Union and United States;
- Transition from single-polar to multipolar governance—governance, not just policymaking, occurring at a regional level; and
- Innovations in global governance—innovations to address unique emerging risks (Held, Dunleavy, & Nag, 2010).

Some global health policy trends that need to be addressed include rising noncommunicable diseases, aging populations, global urbanization, inequity, and climate change.

Global Health Organizations

Global health organizations can be governmental or nongovernmental organizations that focus on international and global health. In addition to formal global health organizations, some associations and organizational societies have global health as a priority focus area. Several prominent global health organizations are presented below.

World Health Organization

The World Health Organization (WHO) is the directing and authorizing authority within the United Nations focusing on global health. The decision-making body of WHO is the World Health Assembly. An executive board is composed of 34 members elected for 3-year terms. An annual board meeting is held in January. The WHO is headed by the Director-General.

The WHO policymaking process consists of submitting a resolution or motion by a WHO Assembly member. A preliminary impact analysis is conducted by the WHO Director-General. Then, the policy proposal is submitted to the respective WHO committee for examination. Once the proposal passes through the WHO committee, it is considered for adoption by a vote in the World Health Assembly.

The WHO provides leadership on critical health matters, shapes a research agenda, establishes norms and standards, articulates ethical evidence-based policy options, provides technical support to members, and monitors health situations and assesses health trends. The work of the WHO is carried out in the following areas:

- Health systems—promotes universal health coverage, integrated person-centered healthcare services, strong health information systems, and evidence-based policymaking
- Noncommunicable diseases—generally chronic health issues, including violence and injuries
- Promoting health through life span—promotion of health and well-being throughout an individual's life span
- Communicable diseases—prevention and treatment of diseases originating from person to person and animal/vector to human transmission
- Preparedness, surveillance, and response—provides leadership in the coordination of health responses to disasters, crisis situations; conducts risk assessments; provides technical guidance, supplies, and financial assistance; monitors health situation during a disaster or crisis
- Corporate services—consists of legal advice and counsel, supports communications and disseminates information, supplies health experts, and provides building services

North Atlantic Treaty Organization

The North Atlantic Treaty Organization (NATO) consists of 28 member countries. NATO provides an opportunity for member countries to come together to consult and make decisions on security issues. It is considered both a political and military alliance that promotes democratic values and encourages consultation and cooperation on security issues with the desire for a peaceful resolution.

United Nations

The United Nations (UN) is an international organization with 193 member states. The UN has the power to take action on a variety of international health-related issues such as peace and security, climate change, sustainable development, human rights, disarmament, terrorism, humanitarian and health emergencies, gender equality, governance, and food production. At the UN meetings, a forum is provided for member states to express their views in the General Assembly, the Security Council, Economic and Social Council, and other committees as a mechanism for international governments to find areas of agreement and to resolve problems and conflict. The UN also has the power to uphold international laws among member states.

World Trade Organization

The World Trade Organization (WTO) is an international organization that promotes open trade for the benefit of all. The WTO provides a forum for negotiating agreements aimed at reducing barriers to international trade and ensuring a level playing field for trade negotiations among all countries, regardless of wealth. WTO contributes to the economic growth and development of countries. A country's economic growth and development impact human health. WTO provides legal counsel and settles disputes among members. Specific activities of WTO are:

- Negotiating the reduction or elimination of trade obstacles such as tariffs;
- Administering and monitoring the application of WTO rules for trade and intellectual property;
- Monitoring and reviewing trade policies;
- Settling disputes among members;
- Building capacity (knowledge, skills, abilities, and assets) for developing countries' government officials;
- Assisting countries to become members of WTO;
- Conducting and disseminating economic research and trade data; and
- Explaining the purpose and functions of WTO to the public.

Pan American Health Organization

The Pan American Health Organization (PAHO) is a specialized international health agency for the Americas. PAHO works with countries in the region to improve and protect the people's health. Specifically, PAHO works to fight communicable and noncommunicable diseases, strengthen health systems, and respond to emergencies and disasters. PAHO is committed to ensuring that all people have the access to health care they need, whenever it is needed.

American Red Cross

The American Red Cross's mission is to prevent and alleviate human suffering at the time of emergencies by mobilizing volunteers and donors. The American Red Cross works in areas of disaster relief, blood donation, training and certification programs, military families, and international services. The international services provide disaster relief, vaccination against measles, disaster preparedness, reconnecting families separated by war or other disaster, and educating individuals about international humanitarian law.

World Neighbors

World Neighbors is an international development organization working to eliminate hunger, poverty, and disease in the poorest and most isolated villages in Asia, Africa, and Latin America. World Neighbors focus areas are hunger, poverty, disease, and environment.

Global Policy Issues

Health issues at the individual, community, and country level impact the global policy agenda. In addition to health issues, there are nonhealth policy issues that have the potential to directly or indirectly impact the health of a population. This is supported by the social determinants of health framework presented in Chapter 6. **Box 7-1** presents a list of global policy issues. It is critical to consider that policy is interrelated—domestic policy influences international and global policy, and international and global policy influences domestic policy.

Global Politics

Global politics occurs through several mechanisms. Each country has elected or appointed government officials who serve as representatives for their country

---

BOX 7-1   GLOBAL POLICY ISSUES

- African population explosion: fastest growing in the world
- UN's continued support for political elections
- Nuclear weapons
- Women's wage equality
- Access to clear water
- Hunger and malnutrition
- Human immunodeficiency virus (HIV)/acquired immune deficiency syndrome (AIDS)
- Children's access to education and health care
- Climate change
- Immigration and refugee displacement
- Genocide
- Landmines and explosives
- Human rights
- Polio
- Aging society
- Atomic energy
- Decolonization
- Democracy
- Access to food

on matters of international and global policy. In addition, elected leaders of countries engage in global leadership directly. Global health organizations also provide a forum or venue in which multiple country representatives can dialogue and propose global policy.

Secretary of State

The secretary of state is appointed by the president with the consent of the Senate. The secretary of state serves as the president's chief foreign affairs advisor. The secretary of state also advises the president on negotiating foreign affairs; advises the president on the appointment of ambassadors, ministers, consuls, and other diplomats; advises on the recall and dismissal of foreign diplomats; participates in international conferences, organizations, and agencies; negotiates, interprets, and terminates treaties and international agreements; supervises U.S. immigration laws abroad; provides information to Americans on the political, economic, social, cultural, and humanitarian conditions in foreign countries; promotes beneficial economic discourse between the United States and other countries; administers the Department of State and issues passports; and supervises the Foreign Service of the United States.

Ambassadors

An ambassador is a credentialed diplomat sent to a country to serve as the official representative of the home country. An ambassador is considered the highest-ranking diplomat within a state. The host country permits the foreign ambassador to have a secure territory known as an embassy. Ambassadors, along with their staff and physical property and vehicles, are generally afforded diplomatic immunity in the host country. The role of an ambassador is to form and maintain international relations in the areas of peace, war, trade, economics, culture, environment, and human rights; collect and report information that affects national interest; provide advice and council to the home country; represent the views of the home country; host international delegations; and influence the foreign government in relation to the home country's policy agendas. An ambassador may also represent the home government at state dinners.

Diplomats

Diplomat is a broad term used to describe an official representing a country abroad. The secretary of state and ambassadors are considered U.S. diplomats. Other individuals may be appointed as a diplomat to represent the interest and policies of their country. During this special appointment period, these individuals may be afforded diplomatic immunity and privilege to conduct the business of their country.

BOX 7-2   TYPES OF GLOBAL POLICY INSTRUMENTS

- Treaties
- Economic sanctions—to regulate commerce
- Referendums
- Resolutions
- Immigration restrictions and bans
- Taxation
- Declaration of war
- Foreign aid
- Trading of foreign intelligence

Global Policymaking Process

The global policymaking process is dependent upon two factors—the policy-maker and type of policy. Global policymakers can be elected officials, such as the president, secretary of state, and congressional leaders. In addition, global health organizations can enact policies that have a global impact. Domestic policy can have international and global implications. Global policies can consist of various types of policies and policy instruments written into a policy. **Box 7-2** presents a listing of some of the types of global policies and instruments.

Summary Points

- The CDC's global health mission is to protect and improve health globally through science, policy, partnership, and evidence-based public health action.
- The terms *international health* and *global health* are frequently used interchangeably to mean the same thing.
- Both terms, *international health* and *global health*, are considered to be associated with public health.
- Public health is generally considered or viewed as focusing on the health of a population of a specific country or community.
- International health focuses on health issues and policy between two nations or countries.
- Global health focuses on health issues and policy from a perspective that includes all nations and environmental influences on health.

- Global health deals with worldwide population issues that impact health across all sectors of the world and is not limited to only the health sector.
- Planetary health is the health of human civilizations and the natural systems on which humans depend.
- Planetary health focuses on the alterations in climate, water, land, and ecosystems that are impacting the health of our planet, which has implications for human health.
- The Rockefeller Foundation–Lancet Commission on Planetary Health Report indicates that the changes in the structure and function of the earth's natural systems pose a growing threat to human health.
- Key components of a resilient health system are information, financing, service delivery, human resources, medicines and technology, and governance.
- Global health policy is the formulation, implementation, and evaluation of various types of policy that impact individuals, communities, states, nations, and the world as an entire entity.
- Global health organizations can be governmental or nongovernmental organizations that focus on international and global health.
- The World Health Organization (WHO) is the directing and authorizing authority within the United Nations focusing on global health.
- North Atlantic Treaty Organization (NATO) is considered both a political and military alliance that promotes democratic values and encourages consultation and cooperation on security issues with the desire for a peaceful resolution.
- United Nations has the power to take action on a variety of international health-related issues such as peace and security, climate change, sustainable development, human rights, disarmament, terrorism, humanitarian and health emergencies, gender equality, governance, and food production.
- World Trade Organization (WTO) is an international organization that promotes open trade for the benefit of all.
- Pan American Health Organization (PAHO) is a specialized international health agency for the Americas.
- American Red Cross's mission is to prevent and alleviate human suffering at the time of emergencies by mobilizing volunteers and donors.
- World Neighbors is an international development organization working to eliminate hunger, poverty, and disease in the poorest and most isolated villages in Asia, Africa, and Latin America.

- The secretary of state serves as the president's chief foreign affairs advisor.
- An ambassador is a credentialed diplomat sent to a country to serve as the official representative of the home country.
- An ambassador is considered the highest-ranking diplomat within a state.
- *Diplomat* is a broad term used to describe an official representing a country abroad.
- Domestic policy can have international and global implications.

References

Centers for Disease Control and Prevention. (2012). *CDC global health strategy: 2012–2015*. Atlanta, GA: CDC. Retrieved from https://www.cdc.gov/globalhealth/strategy/index.htm

Beaglehole, R., & Bonita, R. (2010). What is global health? *Global Health Action, 3,* 514.

Held, D., Dunleavy, P., & Nag, E.-M. (2010). Editorial statement. *Global Policy. 1,* 1–3.

Whitmee, S., Haines, A., Beyrer, C., Boltz, F., Capon, A., Souza Dias, B., . . . & Yach, D. (2015). Safeguarding human health in the Anthropocene epoch: Report of the Rockefeller Foundation–Lancet Commission on planetary health. *Lancet, 386,* 1973–2028.

Public Health Policy

Public health law is a form of legal policy. As a form of legal policy, public health law is considered a population-based, community-level intervention that protects and maintains the public's health and safety. As a legal policy, failure to comply with the policy results in some type of punitive or disciplinary action. Public health law integrates concepts from law, medicine, health care, and public health (Gostin & Wiley, 2016).

Public Health Law Defined

Definitions of public health law abound. The word "law" is frequently used to refer to the legal system, legal processes, the legal profession, and legal knowledge and learning. Public health law is defined within the context of public health policy, since public health law is considered public policy. Longest (2015) defines public health law as laws related to health, which can be enacted at any level of government. Gostin and Wiley (2016) define public health law as the legal powers and duties of the state that assure conditions of health for the people and limit the use of state powers to constrain autonomy, privacy, liberty, proprietary, or other legal protected rights.

Gostin and Wiley's definition lists five essential characteristics of public health law: (1) the government is responsible for public health activities, (2) a population-based focus is assumed, (3) public health addresses relationships between the state and the population, (4) population-based services are delivered grounded in science, and (5) public health officers have the power to coerce individuals and businesses into actions that protect the health of the population (Gostin & Wiley, 2016).

Foundation and Scope of Public Health Law

The scope of public health law is based on the hierarchy of legal power derived from federal constitutions, state constitutions, city charters, administrative regulations, and judicial decisions. Public health law originates from five basic legal sources of authority—constitutions, international agreements, legislation, regulations, and case law. Public health law follows the policy concept of supremacy. The U.S. Constitution is the supreme law of the nation and reflects national values in relation to public health. At this level, public health laws are generated as a direct extension of the Constitution either through executive, legislative, or judicial actions. For example, federal regulation by the Occupational Safety and Health Administration promulgates rules and regulations to safeguard worker safety and health based on federal legislation implemented through an executive agency.

The next level in the hierarchy occurs at the state level with the development of statutes. Similarly, these state statutes designed to protect the health of the general population may be formulated and developed in either the executive, legislative, or judicial branch of government.

Judicial decisions can generate public health policy. Judicial decisions are precedent-setting policy or case law that generally interprets the intent of other policies developed through the executive or legislative branch. The courts also have the power to hold a statute or executive act null and void if it violates any law generated at a higher level in the federalist system, such as the state charter or the U.S. Constitution. This is known as judicial review (Garner, 2014; Gostin & Wiley, 2016). **Figure 8-1** presents eight steps in the hierarchy of legal authorization in the United States.

- U.S. Constitution
- Treaties and federal statutes
- Federal regulations
- State constitutions
- State statutes
- State regulations
- Local authority
- Common law

Higher

Lower

Figure 8-1   Eight Steps in the Hierarchy of Legal Authorization in the United States

Constitutional Law

Constitutional law originates from the U.S. Constitution. Constitutional law outlines the limitations of power of and the organizational structure for the U.S. government. Constitutional law provides individuals with fundamental rights and freedoms through its articles and amendments.

Public Health Laws

Public health laws focus on the health of the general population or public. Some public health laws are considered germane to the general health and welfare of the citizens of this country. The following public health legal policies are presented: individual rights, compulsory examination, quarantine and isolation, licensure and registration, inspection and searches, embargo and seizures, and nuisances.

Individual Rights: Due Process

An individual's rights are protected through the Bill of Rights in the U.S. Constitution and bills of rights developed at state levels. The Bill of Rights in the Constitution consists of the first 10 amendments and a portion of the Fourteenth Amendment. The Fourteenth Amendment provides individuals with dual citizenship in the nation and their state of residence, entitling them to the rights outlined at both the national and state level (Grad, 2005). The Fifth and Fourteenth Amendments prohibit the government from depriving individuals of life, liberty, or property without due process of law (Gostin & Wiley, 2016).

The due process clause provides two separate obligations: a substantive element and a procedural element. The substantive element requires the government to provide significant reasons and justifications for invading an individual's personal freedoms or removing that person's property rights. The procedural element requires the government to provide an individual with notice and to ensure a fair process in the removal of freedoms or property. The fair process consists of a notice, a hearing, and access to an impartial decision maker (Gostin & Wiley, 2016). **Table 8-1** presents public health legal policy that protects the individual.

Compulsory Examination

Compulsory examinations are considered mandatory medical examinations. These require careful consideration and justification. The right to refuse treatment is embedded in ethical principles. Public health laws or policy may override the common law and authorize mandatory examination and treatment.

TABLE 8-1   PUBLIC HEALTH POLICY: PROTECTION OF INDIVIDUAL

PUBLIC HEALTH POLICY CONCEPT	PURPOSE, FUNCTION, OR POLICY INTENT
1st Amendment	Freedom of religion, speech, press, and right of assembly (advertising cannot be misleading)
4th Amendment	Freedom from unreasonable search and seizure
5th Amendment	Protection against self-incrimination and double jeopardy (double prosecution or trial for the same offense, or two separate offenses that arise from one set of facts)
6th Amendment	Right to a speedy, public trial with an impartial jury, right to confront witnesses, right to counsel
8th Amendment	Freedom from cruel and unusual punishment
14th Amendment	Provides dual citizenship in the United States and state of residence
Right of privacy	Parts of our lives are not the government's business; freedom to seek or refuse treatment
Separation of religion and state	No law may interfere with religious beliefs (protection is limited if there is public concern); limits government's financial assistance to religious institutions or activities
Search and seizure	Permits search for evidence and seizure of evidence with an executed warrant; evidence gained with an illegal search or seizure is inadmissible in criminal proceedings
Violations of public health laws	Punishable as misdemeanors; can be tried separately under state and federal law if violation is both a state and federal crime (double jeopardy permitted)
Writ of *habeas corpus*	Judicial order; commands the jailer or other person detaining a prisoner to physically bring the prisoner before the court so that lawfulness of the detention can be determined

States support the public health provision for compulsory examination and treatment based on three interests: health preservation, harm prevention, and preservation of effective therapies (Gostin & Wiley, 2016). Public health officers have statutory authority for compulsory examination if there is sufficient belief that a communicable disease exists; a compulsory examination cannot be based on mere suspicion (Grad, 2005). Compulsory examination can be mandated as a requirement for licensure, which is considered a privilege, such as testing for sexually transmitted diseases prior to the issuance of a marriage license. In the presence of an epidemic, public health officials can require compulsory examinations, without concern for due process (Grad, 2005). In these situations, there must be concern for the greater good of the public that outweighs an individual's risk and freedoms. **Table 8-2** presents public health legal policy that may restrict individual freedom to preserve the public's health.

TABLE 8-2   PUBLIC HEALTH POLICY: RESTRICTIONS OF INDIVIDUAL OR GOODS

PUBLIC HEALTH POLICY CONCEPT	PURPOSE, FUNCTION, OR POLICY INTENT
Compulsory examination	Required examinations such as in cases of communicable diseases or periodic screenings, or threatened epidemic; does not violate individual liberty or privacy if there is sufficient justification
Isolation and quarantine	Can quarantine individuals for some communicable diseases; complete restriction of the person and possibly household contacts; misdemeanor to break quarantine or to destroy the quarantine sign; can impose on the basis of reasonable belief; some states require actual order of confinement in the form of a warrant issued by a magistrate; public health official not liable if measures taken in good faith

(continues)

TABLE 8-2   PUBLIC HEALTH POLICY: RESTRICTIONS OF INDIVIDUAL OR GOODS (CONTINUED)

PUBLIC HEALTH POLICY CONCEPT	PURPOSE, FUNCTION, OR POLICY INTENT
Emergency commitment	To allow the state to provide emergency assistance (mental illness) to an individual; must be based on recent specific act, threat, or behavior or omission; examination must occur within a specified time period; supported by a written physician statement; generally valid for 48 to 72 hours
Committed individuals	Right to prompt and adequate humane treatment; right to reasonable safety, use of least restrictive measures; need a preponderance of evidence indicating there is no longer a danger present before release
Embargo	An order prohibiting the removal or use of items by affixing a tag or marking on the goods warning that it must not be removed; purpose is to prevent the dissemination of dangerous goods; owner has right to due process
Condemnation	Typically used with an embargo or seizure; an order for the destruction, denaturing, sale, or re-exportation of goods or return to owner carried out by court proceedings; cost of destruction is the responsibility of the owner

Quarantine and Isolation

Quarantine policy originates principally from local and state powers. The states' power to quarantine is preempted by federal law pursuant to the federal government's power over commerce. The First International Quarantine Rules were adopted in 1852. The current promulgation of international quarantine laws originates from the World Health Organization (Gostin & Wiley, 2016).

Quarantine orders must be based on reasonable belief, not merely suspicion. The enforcement of a quarantine policy consists of complete restriction of a person or persons to a specific location (Grad, 2005). This is generally enacted as a measure to prevent the transmission of communicable infectious diseases. In contrast, isolation is the separation of individuals with a communicable infectious illness from the general public during the period of communicability (Gostin & Wiley, 2016). In an isolation order, persons may come into contact with an infectious person provided the appropriate protection and isolation guidelines are adhered to as a means to prevent promulgation and transmission of infection.

Licensing and Registration

A licensure is a privilege extended to an individual or institution for a specific purpose. Licensure power originates at the local or state government level. Licensure process is initiated through the passage of legislation that prohibits certain acts without the possession of a license to engage in the specified activities (Grad, 2005). Licensure power permits an executive agency of the government to promulgate rules and regulations governing certain prohibited acts. The acceptance of a license by an individual or institution implies consent to submit to the conditions of the regulatory agency. A license is formal permission by an executive agency through the delegated authority to engage in specific acts not allowed to those without the license (Gostin & Wiley, 2016). **Table 8-3** presents public health legal policy for institutions, businesses, or environments that preserves the public's health.

TABLE 8-3   PUBLIC HEALTH POLICY: INSTITUTIONS, BUSINESSES, OR ENVIRONMENT

PUBLIC HEALTH POLICY CONCEPT	PURPOSE, FUNCTION, OR POLICY INTENT
Licensure	Permission to operate within the defined rules and regulations of the license; a condition of accepting the license is consent to continuing control of the regulatory agency; licensure does ensure due process rights
Searches and inspections	Search implies looking for particular conditions (also known as those that constitute a violation of the law; administrative searches); inspection is a visitation or survey to determine whether or not conditions deleterious to the health and welfare of the public exist; must be a supporting statute for the search or inspection

(continues)

TABLE 8-3   PUBLIC HEALTH POLICY: INSTITUTIONS, BUSINESSES, OR ENVIRONMENT (CONTINUED)

PUBLIC HEALTH POLICY CONCEPT	PURPOSE, FUNCTION, OR POLICY INTENT
Exclusionary rule	Evidence seized during an administrative inspection usually cannot be used in criminal proceedings
"Plain view" doctrine	Evidence of criminal activity inadvertently discovered in the course of a legitimate public health inspection or other administrative search can be admissible if in plain view during the search or inspection activity
Public nuisance	An offense against the public; characterized by an interference with the public right to pursue normal conduct of life without threat to health, comfort, or repose; defined by statutes or ordinances
Private nuisance	Interference with the use or enjoyment of private property; subject to damages by tort law; injunctions to stop interference
Violations order	An administrative order from a public health official or agency informing property owner of the existence of a lawful violation
Orders to abate	Order to stop the activity or condition creating a violation
Order to cease and desist	Order to end the prohibited condition
Compulsory disclosure	Must be permitted by law; power to require reports and inspect books, records, or premises

The licensure process establishes a system of continued monitoring and supervision for the purpose of protecting the public's health, safety, and welfare (Gostin & Wiley, 2016; Grad, 2005). Licensure provides an individual with property rights and ensures the right to procedural due process before the person or institution license is suspended or revoked. Licenses can be denied, suspended, or revoked; however, these disciplinary actions require a clear notice to the affected party, a hearing, a right to counsel, a right to secure evidence by subpoena, and the right to confrontational cross-examination of an accuser (Grad, 2005). When there is imminent public danger or concern for the health, welfare, and safety of the public, an authorized administrator will assess the situation to determine the potential dangers and may invoke a summary suspension of the license as an immediate public protective measure with formal due process to occur at a later time. Licensure cannot be suspended or revoked without proper due process unless there is a determination of immediate public health danger.

Registration is a process of identification of and record keeping on certain individuals. Registration is simply a listing, while licensure specifies requirements that must be satisfied prior to being licensed (Grad, 2005). A registry is a listing without any preestablished conditions.

Search and Inspection

A *search* occurs when an official is looking for conditions that violate laws or for instruments that may have been used in criminal activity. An *inspection* is a visitation or survey to determine if conditions that are deleterious to the public's health exist. Inspection does not include the aim of uncovering criminal evidence. Inspections are generally conducted on a routine basis and involve an evaluation for compliance with public laws or policies. The Fourteenth Amendment provides protection from unreasonable searches (Grad, 2005).

Administrative search warrants are generally required to inspect residential and private commercial facilities (Gostin & Wiley, 2016). However, a public health official can conduct a search if there is a legislative statute that provides the authority for such activity. An inspection or search without a warrant can be conducted under three conditions: (1) when legally valid consent justifies an administrative search; (2) in an emergency to avert any immediate threats to the public's health or safety; and (3) under the "open fields" doctrine by which a public health office may search a public place. Pervasively regulated businesses, such as the food industry and health care, forfeit some rights of privacy and are subject to routine searches. Inspections are permitted without a warrant for a licensed business with a substantial public health significance. The acceptance of some licenses by businesses waives their right to privacy and permits public health officials to conduct routine searches. Public health officials can secure a search warrant by merely demonstrating specific evidence of an existing violation in health or safety regulations, or for a valid reason that is in the public health's interest (Gostin & Wiley, 2016). Most states require a search warrant issued by a judge (Grad, 2005). Evidence secured during an administrative inspection cannot be used in criminal investigations unless the evidence was in plain view during the inspection. The "plain view" doctrine allows criminal evidence to be used if the evidence was in plain view of the public health inspector during the search (Grad, 2005).

Embargo and Seizure

Articles or items are *embargoed* by tagging or marking the article with a statement such as "this article is in violation of the law" (Grad, 2005). An embargo prohibits further use or removal of the identified articles. An embargo is placed when the articles are considered to pose a public health threat, as in the case of dangerous dissemination of contaminated or potentially infected goods. An embargo is a public health preventive measure. In contrast to embargo, *seizure* takes possession of goods that belong to another (Grad, 2005).

Nuisances

A *private nuisance* is the unreasonable interference with the use or enjoyment of private property (Gostin & Wiley, 2016; Grad, 2005). Private nuisances are subject to tort law, and injunctions can be issued to stop the interference. A *public nuisance* is unreasonable interference with the community's use and enjoyment of a public place; or interference with the right to pursue the normal conduct of life without a threat to health, comfort, or repose (Gostin & Wiley, 2016; Grad, 2005). Public nuisance is typically defined by local ordinances or statutes. Public nuisances are subject to legal action by injunction or criminal prosecution.

The cessation of a public nuisance is fundamental to maintenance of a healthy environment. The following policy strategies can be implemented in order to stop the public nuisance:

Summary abatement order. This order directs action to remove the offending condition prior to a hearing or court authorization. A summary abatement order is justified if there is significant and imminent risk or threat to the public's health.

Violations order. This is an administrative order from a state or federal health officer or agency that informs the property owner of a legal violation.

Order to abate. An order to abate requires the cessation of an activity or condition within a time period detailed in the order. The time period typically provides the individual with a "reasonable amount of time" to stop the activity.

Order to cease and desist. This is an order to end a prohibited condition.

Injunction. This is a court order that directs a person to perform a specific activity or refrain from engaging in a specific activity (Grad, 2005).

Personal Health Law and Policy

Personal health law is the scope of law that deals with individual persons and family health. Personal health law includes personal health insurance policies and laws governing personal injury. In addition, personal health law includes laws that provide legal guidance with regard to an individual's access to healthcare services. Laws that pertain to the impact that other individuals or the environmental may have on an individual's health are also considered a type of personal health law.

Environmental Health Law

Environmental health law is the scope of law that provides legal guidance concerning human impact on the environment and natural resources, and also the impact of the environment on humans. Environmental health law includes legal guidance regarding the use and disposal of toxic substances. In addition, environmental health laws provide guidance regarding our personal living space, such as radon exposure levels within our homes.

Occupational Health Law

Occupational health law is the scope of law that provides legal guidance regarding an individual's work environment. The Occupational Safety and Health Administration (OSHA) is the executive agency that primarily develops occupational regulations to protect the employee within the work environment. The Occupational Safety and Health Act provides the legal authority for OSHA to develop regulations governing the workplace.

Statutory Law

Statutory law is based on formal statutes. Statutes are written laws enacted by the federal, state, or local legislative bodies. Federal statutes are published and codified in the US Code. Congress and state legislatures enact acts and statutes. In contrast, at the local level, counties or parishes enact ordinances. These enactments govern human behavior, provide access to programs, and restrict certain activities that negatively impact individuals and groups. All statutes or ordinances must be consistent with the respective state's constitution and the U.S. Constitution.

Administrative Law

In the executive branch of government, executive-level agencies and organizations act within the scope of administrative law to enact their missions. Administrative laws exist at both the federal and state level to govern the practice of executive agencies. Administrative procedure acts at both the federal and state levels outline the legal procedures of administrative law. Administrative law provides basic procedural safeguards for federal and state regulatory systems and defines the scope of judicial authority over the federal or state agencies.

Administrative laws outline the process of developing regulations within the respective executive agencies. The rules and regulations developed by executive agencies are subject to challenge. These challenges are typically based on procedural rather than substantive grounds. The judicial system has deferential preference to the respective executive agencies' expertise and are unlike to interfere with the substantive decision rendered by the executive agency. However, procedural challenges are heard especially if there is concern with interference with an individual's basic constitutional rights. The judicial system can also be engaged in the legal process within the scope of administrative law if an executive agency has been requested to act and it did not act. The judicial system could be requested to render a judicial review and decision.

The executive agency acting within the scope of administrative law must maintain consistency with constitutional law and relevant statutes and judicial precedence. Judicial review of an executive agency would take into consideration the following:

- Extent to which the executive agency stayed within constitutional and statutory authority
- Proper interpretation of applicable laws and statutory language
- Proceedings were conducted in a fair manner, ensuring the individual's right to due process
- Rendered decisions are not arbitrary, capricious, or unreasonable
- Rendered decisions are based on substantial evidence

Tort Law

A tort is a wrongful act that creates harm. A simple characterization of a tort is a civil wrong committed by one person against another person. The idea behind tort law is that the harm or injury that occurs as a result of a wrongful act can be compensated and that antisocial behavior is discouraged. Tort law does not include breach of contract cases. Intentional torts are intentional or willful acts that violate another person's rights or property, resulting in some type of harm. The primary factor of relevance in an intentional tort is the individual's intent in the action. Intent implies that the person acted for the purpose of causing or inflicting injury. The motive or purpose of the act has a critical role in determining the amount of liability resulting from the act. The purpose of tort law is to provide a remedy for the wrongs committed to the person or property. **Table 8-4** provides a differentiation between tort law and criminal law cases (Garner, 2014). There are several types of intentional torts, including assault and battery, false imprisonment, intentional infliction of emotional stress, and land trespass (Garner, 2014).

Assault is the threat or attempt to inflict effective physical contact onto another person. Battery is the invasion of another person's privacy by unpermitted touch. False imprisonment is the unlawful and intentional confinement

TABLE 8-4   DIFFERENTIATION OF TORT AND CRIMINAL LAW

TORT LAW	CRIMINAL LAW
Parties	
Filed by plaintiff or victim of wrongful act	Filed on behalf of the people of a state or the United States.
Burden of proof	
Civil burden of proof is more than 50% certainty	Beyond a reasonable doubt (probability of certainty of guilt beyond reasonable doubt is about 97%)
Expected outcomes	
Generally monetary compensation Focus is on making an individual whole	Focuses on punishing the offender
Options to achieve outcomes	
Settlement, trial, dismissal, or arbitration	Trial, plea bargain, or dismissal of case
Requirement to testify	
Tort case can force a person to testify, Fifth Amendment will only protect from testimony if the witness could be subject to criminal prosecution	Fifth Amendment prevents a person from being compelled to testify against himself
Impact of laws	
Derived from common or judge-made laws	Prosecutions filed if there is a statute or law that criminalizes the conduct

of another person within fixed boundaries in which the person is harmed by this confinement. Intentional infliction of emotional stress is the invasion of another person's peace of mind. Land trespassing is the unlawful interference with another person's possession of land by intruding on the property, failing to leave the property, or placing something on the property (Garner, 2014).

In an intentional tort, the individual committing the tortuous act had requisite knowledge and the will to commit the wrongful act. In contrast, a nonintentional tort occurs when negligent conduct results in harm to another person. Negligence is failing to act when an individual should have acted to prevent harm to another person (Garner, 2014). Negligence is based on the provision of prudent care. Therefore, negligence consists of doing something that another prudent healthcare professional would not do or failing to do something that another prudent healthcare professional would have done under the same or similar circumstances.

A third type of tort is quasi-intentional tort. A quasi-intentional tort results from the spoken word and includes defamation, invasion of privacy, and breach of confidentiality. Defamation is the oral or written communication to a third party about a person that is false with the intent to injure that person's reputation. Slander is defamation using oral communication, and libel is defamation using written communication. Invasion of privacy violates another person's right to be alone without the unreasonable interference of his or her personal life. Breach of confidentiality is providing an individual's private information to other parties without that individual's expressed consent (Garner, 2014).

Summary Points

- Public health law is a form of policy.
- Public health law is considered a population-based, community-level intervention that protects and maintains the public's health and safety.
- Law is frequently used to refer to the legal system, legal processes, the legal profession, and legal knowledge and learning. Public health law is defined within the context of public health policy, since public health law is considered public policy.
- Public health law can be defined as the legal powers and duties of the state that assure conditions of health for the people and limit the use of state powers to constrain autonomy, privacy, liberty, proprietary, or other legal protected rights of individuals.
- The U.S. Constitution is the supreme law of the nation and reflects national values in relation to public health.

- Constitutional law outlines the limitations of power of and the organizational structure for the U.S. government.
- The Bill of Rights in the Constitution consists of the first 10 amendments and a portion of the Fourteenth Amendment.
- The Fourteenth Amendment provides individuals with dual citizenship in the nation and their state of residence, entitling them to the rights outlined at the national and state levels.
- The Fifth and Fourteenth Amendments prohibit the government from depriving individuals of life, liberty, or property without due process of law.
- The due process clause provides two separate obligations: a substantive and a procedural element.
- Compulsory examinations mandate a medical examination.
- States support the public health provision for compulsory examination and treatment based on three interests: health preservation, harm prevention, and preservation of effective therapies.
- Quarantine and isolation are enacted to prevent the transmission of communicable diseases.
- A license is a privilege extended to an individual or institution to engage in specific activities that are legally protected.
- Registration is a process of identification of, and record keeping on, certain individuals. It is a listing or roster.
- A *search* occurs when an official is looking for conditions that violate laws or for instruments that may have been used in criminal activity.
- An *inspection* is a visitation or survey to determine if conditions that are deleterious to the public's health exist.
- Search warrants are usually issued by a judge.
- Embargo and seizure prohibit the use or removal of materials as a measure to protect the public's health.
- Nuisances interfere with another's property or right to enjoyment.
- Environmental health law is designed to protect and preserve environmental resources.
- Occupational health law governs the workplace environment.
- Statutory law is based on formal statutes, which are written laws enacted by federal, state, or local legislative bodies.
- Administrative law governs the activities of executive-level agencies.
- Tort law governs wrongful acts that create harm to another.
- Assault and battery are torts.
- Torts can be intentional or unintentional.

References

Garner, B. (2014). *Black's law dictionary* (10th ed.). St. Paul, MN: Thomson West.

Gostin, L. O., & Wiley, L. F. (2016). *Public health law: Power, duty, restraint* (3rd ed.). Oakland: CA: University of California Press.

Grad, F. P. (2005). *The public health law manual* (3rd ed.). Washington, DC: American Public Health Association.

Longest, B. (2015). *Health policymaking in the United States* (6th ed.). New York, NY: Health Administration Press.

Policy Formulation and Implementation

CHAPTER

9

Policy formulation and implementation are stages of the policymaking process that occurs within a context of political activity to ensure that a policy issue arrives on the policy action agenda. Policy formulation and implementation stages continue to be impacted by political activities throughout the entire policymaking process. The policy formulation and implementation stages of policymaking continue to be a transformative period during which policy continues to be influenced and defined by societal needs and political agendas. The context in which policy formulation occurs impacts the eventual policy that is formulated and implemented into practice.

Policy formulation and advancement require a clear and concise problem statement and consensus among constituents and stakeholders. Constituents and stakeholders generate significant influence on the context of policy development. To be effective in policy formulation, the policymaker should be able to:

- Promote a consistent message;
- Communicate a common shared perspective and solution;
- Promote a desired vision and policy endpoint;
- Remain visible;
- Promote appealing and innovative solutions;
- Substantiate policy recommendations with evidence, research, and science; and
- Tailor policy communication to the audience using brief, high-impact communication medium and channels (Ridenour & Trautman, 2009).

Policy Development Context

Policy development is contextually dependent. The context in which policy development occurs includes the various policy agendas, political spheres, and interdependent discourse among various individuals and interest groups that represent scientific, social, and governmental interests. Constituents engaged in the policy development and formulation process negotiate with policymakers regarding the authorization and allocation of scarce resources while balancing the public's need against multiple other competing interests.

The various factors that influence the policy development context consists of public and societal needs, special-interest group desires, political agendas, social and economic pressures, personal desires, and governmental influence. The context for policy development influences the political process, political maneuvers, and strategies implemented; frames the policy issue; and impacts the resultant intent of the policy formulated. An aspect that influences the policy development context is the public's perspective.

Public Policy Perspective: Pluralist and Elitist

The public's perspective regarding the policy can influence the context in which the policy is developed. The public's perspective changes as societal needs and desires change. Two primary public perspectives that influence policy development are pluralistic and elitist. The pluralist perspective embraces the idea of multiple special interests affecting the development of policy as a means of ensuring equal representation in the policymaking process. Pluralists support the view that competing special interest groups should engage in the policy development process. From the pluralist perspective, the various competing special interest groups are viewed as counterbalancing forces in the policy development process as a means to ensure that the ultimate policy developed presents the best interest of the public. Group theory provides a supporting theoretical foundation for the pluralist perspective. Truman (1993) summarizes the essential tenets of group theory politics as follows: (1) special-interest groups are essential linkages between the people and the government; (2) interest groups compete with each other in the political process to create a counterbalance of special interest; (3) no special-interest group is dominant; and (4) special-interest group competition is fair (Longest, 2015; Truman, 1993).

In contrast to the pluralist perspective, the elitist values the input of a select few individuals in the policy development process. The elitist considers special-interest groups to be ineffective and powerless (Longest, 2015). For the elitist, the majority of the policy power structure lies in the hands of a few who are influential through their financial wealth. In addition, the elitist entity may be a small group of individuals who are most influential owing to their personal or professional positioning among networks of policymakers or through their affiliations. These groups of individuals are frequently referred to as the "power elite." The power elite have a financial basis from which to directly or indirectly influence framing of policy issues and impact policy development. The central tenets of the power elitist theoretical basis are as follows: (1) real power rests with a small proportion of the general population; (2) members of the power elite have similar values and interests; (3) incremental policy change is preferred over radical transformative change; and (4) the elitists ensure that policy does not erode their power bases (Dye, 2017; Porche, 2003). The elitist perspective has been characterized as primarily concerned with self-interest.

Policy Formulation

Policy formulation occurs within a context of high political diplomacy and negotiation. The policy formulation process is a dynamic and continuous process that occurs within a larger political arena. The manner in which policy is formulated is referred to as the policy formulation approach. These approaches are described below:

Policy Formulation Approaches

There are two general approaches to policy formulation: rational and incremental (Mason, Gardner, Outlaw, & O'Grady, 2016). The type of policy approach informs and shapes the policy development process. In addition, the policy formulation approach impacts the sequence of activities that occur during the political process of policymaking.

The *rational* approach reflects "real-world" goals. In the rational approach, policymakers define the problem; identify and rank social values aligned with the policy goals; examine policy alternative solutions in relation to both the positive and negative consequences of each alternative; conduct a cost and benefit analysis; compare and contrast options; and finally, select the policy that achieves the resolution that most closely aligns with social values and meets the most needs (Mason et al., 2016).

In the *incremental* approach, policymakers initiate small policy changes in an evolutionary manner over time. Most policymaking is incremental. The incremental approach begins with the current *status quo* and alters the current policy through a series of incremental changes in relation to the expressed desire. The incremental approach permits greater involvement and permeation over time of various political systems within the political arena. Both approaches to policy formulation are dependent on the policy agenda, political environment, and policy issue.

In contrast to these two approaches, another possible approach to policy formulation is transformational. A *transformational* approach to policy formulation is comprehensive in nature. Transformational policy formulation proposes widespread policy change to entire programs or systems at once. Even though the proposed changes in the form of policy occur at one point in time, the implementation of various aspects of the transformational policy change may occur over a longer period.

The policymaking approach is dependent upon the context of policy formulation and the type of policy developed. The policy developer must be cognizant of the policymaking process and approval authority for the respective type of policy. An essential component of deciding on the policy formulation approach is the policy approval process. For example, the policy generation process of an executive governmental agency is dependent upon administrative law procedures that outline the promulgation process for the development of rules and regulations; whereas an organization's policy formulation may be dependent upon a governance structure of organizational committees, membership or stakeholder input, and final board approval.

Policymakers in the Governmental Branches

The governance power structure in the United States is balanced through the development of three branches of government: the executive, legislative, and judicial. Through this governmental structure, the main policymakers are executives or bureaucrats, legislators, and judiciary officials such as judges.

The policymakers in the executive branch primarily consist of presidents, governors, mayors, and city council officials. These executive branch officials prepare proposed legislation that may require legislative action. Frequently, the policymakers at the executive level can initiate immediate policy through the issuance of an executive order. In addition, these executive officials are responsible for the development of rules and regulations that "operationalize" the implementation of policy that was legislatively authorized. The executive agency officials, or bureaucrats, also collect, analyze, and transmit information that can influence the development of future policy (Longest, 2015).

Legislators are responsible to their voting public or constituency. Legislators are responsible for considering the pros and cons of each policy issue based on the public or their constituency's best interest. Legislators serve as the primary drafters of policy at the federal and state levels (Longest, 2015).

Judicial officials establish policy through the interpretation of laws, interpretation of federal and state constitutions, interpretation of rules and regulations of executive agencies, and the establishment of judicial procedures (Longest, 2015). In their role as interpreters, the judicial branch representatives also declare laws as constitutional or unconstitutional, which sets future precedent for policy development and formulation. Judicial officials interpret the intent and meaning of policy, which accordingly impacts the manner in which policy may be implemented (Longest, 2015).

Drafting Policy Proposals

Policy proposal ideas can originate from multiple sources. The executive branch of government is expected to initiate policy proposals that Congress can approve (Dye, 2017). In addition, "executive communication" from the executive branch influences or initiates policies that may be drafted by others outside the executive branch. Members of the legislative branch also initiate policy proposals. In addition, citizens, organizations, and special interest groups can petition the government, through the First Amendment, to formulate policy. The proposed policy generated by these groups can be in the form of ideas, solutions, or drafted policy that may be introduced into the process by an elected official (Longest, 2015).

Legislative staff members are an influential group that directly and indirectly affects the drafting of policy proposals. Once a problem is on the policy agenda, elected officials frequently delegate proposal drafting to a member of their legislative staff team. In addition, legislative staff members are the gatekeepers that control access and the flow of information to elected officials. Therefore, legislative staff members indirectly control policy by controlling access to an elected official (Weissert & Weissert, 2000). Staff members frequently provide long-term consistency in an elected governmental office. Legislators and executive officers are elected and change office or may be subjected to term limits. Legislative staffers provide the historical and institutional memory helpful to newly elected officials. Frequently, legislative staff members orient the new legislator to current and critical policy issues, thus further shaping the elected official's policy agenda. As expected, this relationship between elected officials and the legislative staff is dependent upon trust. Other indirect influence on policy proposals by legislative staff occurs through the execution of their normal duties such as research, scheduling, communicating with constituents, and writing draft policy proposals (Dye, 2017).

The drafting of policy proposals is the result of a team effort. Any member of the legislature or executive branch can draft a bill; however, only an elected official of the legislative branch of government can introduce a bill. Once a legislator agrees to officially sponsor a bill, that legislator is responsible for the language of the bill. **Box 9-1** provides some recommended best practices for drafting legislation (Peters, 2012).

BOX 9-1   BEST PRACTICES FOR DRAFTING LEGISLATION

1. Legislative intent is clearly expressed.
2. Proposed legislation does not conflict with existing legislation.
3. Legislation is constitutionally permitted.
4. Legislation is organized.
   a. Internally—definitions section, applicable provision listed first, exceptions presented, similar ideas grouped together, penalties listed last
   b. Externally—provide number or reference to permit tracking of legislation
5. Use words appropriate to their definitions; use words in a consistent manner throughout legislation content.
6. Use repetitive statements to communicate a consistent message—describe actions and concepts the same way throughout the legislation.
7. Write succinctly—eliminate language that does not contribute to the legislation's meaning or intent.
8. Use captions that describe the legislation's subject.
9. Use headings to outline different sections of legislation.
10. Provide transition language in legislation (Peters, 2012).

Legislative Oversight of Policy

Bills introduced into the legislative process are numbered sequentially by date of introduction and referred to the appropriate standing committee. Each legislative committee has a specific scope of legislative authority. Bills that have broad focus may be referred to more than one standing committee for consideration and action. This type of legislative oversight occurs during policy formulation. Legislative oversight also occurs after a bill is signed into law.

Once a bill becomes law, the authorizing body frequently employs the evaluation process to determine the effectiveness of the law. This evaluation data is reported to the legislative oversight committee. The legislative oversight committee is responsible for monitoring the implementation and effectiveness of the policy as detailed in the law.

The most powerful source of legislative oversight occurs through the continual appropriation of funds for each respective law. The Legislative Reorganization

Act of 1946 mandates oversight of laws by the legislative branch of government (Longest, 2015). This oversight is expected to achieve the following:

- Ensure adherence to the intent of the law
- Improve efficiency, effectiveness, and economy of governmental operations
- Assess the ability of the executive agency to manage and achieve the implementation of the law
- Ensure the implementation of policy in the public's best interest (Longest, 2015)

Nurses and Other Healthcare Professionals as Policymakers

Nurses and other healthcare professionals' discipline-specific knowledge and experience within the healthcare system provides them with a unique knowledge and experiential base from which to influence the development of policy. Nurses and other healthcare professionals can assume many roles in the policymaking process. The nurse or other healthcare professional as a scientist or researcher generates or validates the scientific basis that provides essential foundational evidence to support or refute various elements of the proposed policy. They can serve as members or organizers of special interest groups that focus on specific policy issues. These professionals can work with lobbyists or as lobbyists. Lobbying is the process used to influence policymakers through the political process. Nurses and other healthcare professionals have served as electioneers. Electioneering is the process of using personal and professional networks to assist a political candidate to secure an elected office. Nurses and other healthcare professionals are cautioned to ensure that their engagement in electioneering is conducted as private citizens and not as representatives of their employer unless there is clear expressed permission. As electioneers, nurses and other healthcare professionals serve as community mobilizers. They also engage directly with the legislative branch as advocates.

Nurses and other healthcare providers can participate as legislative advocates. Legislative advocacy is a process of collaborating with policymakers or policymaking bodies to gather support or influence the policy development process. The legislative advocacy process consists of (1) marshaling allies, (2) coordinating organizational advocacy structure to promote communication and decision making among the marshaled allies, (3) developing or partnering with coalitions, (4) collecting evidence and data regarding the policy issue, (5) defining and piloting the policy message, (6) revising the message and developing a communication or social media network, (7) cultivating relationships with the media to promote communication, and (8) diffusing the message into the public and political structures that have the ability to influence the policy (Porche, 2003). Advocacy will be further explored in Chapter 15.

Nurses and other healthcare professionals provide expert testimony regarding policy issues. Nurses and other healthcare providers have many personal and professional experiences that reinforce relevance to the policy issue. These providers can also serve as experts and provide expert opinion testimony that substantiates a position supported by scientific evidence and professional experience. In addition, nurses and healthcare professionals are members of the public. Therefore, they can provide personal testimony that adds a personal dimension to policy issues that impact the public and healthcare systems. Personal testimony provides a first-hand account of the impact of policy on the individual.

Interprofessional Policymaking

Nurses and other healthcare professionals can exert considerable power as an interprofessional policymaking team. **Box 9-2** presents critical definitions to interprofessional policymaking (IPEC, 2016, 2011). Interprofessional policymaking teams remove the discipline-specific silos to formulate policy with a focused intent that meets multiple disciplinary needs at one time while representing a unified perspective to the final policymaking authority. Interprofessional policymaking requires nurses and other healthcare professionals to deliberately work together during the entire policy formulation and political process. Multiple disciplines engaged in policymaking together require consultation and collaboration as interprofessional competencies during both the policy formulation and political processes. Interprofessional policymaking

---

BOX 9-2   INTERPROFESSIONAL DEFINITIONS

Interprofessional education—two or more professions that learn about, from, and with each other to promote collaboration and to mutually improve health outcomes

Interprofessional collaborative practice—two or more professionals from different disciplines who work together to deliver the highest-quality patient care

Interprofessional teamwork—different professions working cooperatively, in a coordinated manner to collaborate to achieve a common mutual goal

has the potential to generate substantive health systems focused policy that improves population level health.

Consultation

Consultation is the process of seeking advice, opinion, or guidance of another healthcare professional. The consultant serves in multiple roles—advocate, expert, educator, and collaborator. There are two types of policy consultation— expert or process consultation; therefore, consultation involves one professional discipline providing the other with information or advice on processes. The consultation process of providing information is known as expert, knowledge, or information consultation. Process consultation focuses on advising the consultee on the policymaking process to also include political processes. Process consultation focuses on advising on the "how to" of resolving problems through policy formulation. **Box 9-3** presents stages of the consultation process.

Collaboration

Collaboration is a process in which two or more healthcare professionals work together, with each professional contributing from his or her respective area of expertise. Collaboration is a recursive process that requires multiple professionals to work together as colleagues respecting each other's scope of practice and boundaries to achieve a mutual policy goal. In contrast to consultation, in collaboration, both professional parties bring to the table their respective knowledgebase within a context of shared power to deliberately work together to develop a shared vision with a shared policy purpose and intent. Collaboration is considered a joint venture with shared power and authority. **Box 9-4** presents attributes of policy collaboration.

BOX 9-3   CONSULTATION STAGES

- Entry—request for assistance, contract negotiation, delineation of role and responsibilities, problem exploration, problem identification
- Engagement—information gathering, problem clarification, mutual goal setting
- Resolution—solution searching, policy selection, developing political strategies
- Evaluation—assessing the policy consultation process
- Termination—ending the consultation process

BOX 9-4   POLICY COLLABORATION ATTRIBUTES

- Shared power and authority
- Joint venture
- Cooperative endeavor
- Shared decision making
- Interprofessional team approach
- Shared responsibility
- Nonhierarchical relationships

Policy Models

Policy models provide a framework that specifies the processes through which policy evolves, develops, and emerges as a solution to a policy issue or problem. There are multiple models that provide frameworks that can be utilized to understand the policymaking process, intervene in the policymaking process, analyze policy, evaluate policy, and develop other strategies to politically influence future policy models.

Kingdon's Policy Stream Model

The Kingdon policy stream model describes the policy development process as occurring through three streams: problem, policy, and political. These three streams might be envisioned as free-floating, waiting for a "window of opportunity" to open for policy development. The window of opportunity is an alignment of the three streams into an environment that is considered prime for policy development.

The problem stream is the problem that is identified within the policy agenda. The problem stream poses a challenge for policymakers to focus on the problem and to provide a policy solution. The policy stream consists of the potential policy alternatives that can be developed and implemented to resolve the problem. The goals and ideas of the policy also constitute the policy stream. In addition, policymakers such as legislative staff, researchers, congressional members, and special-interest groups are a part of the policy stream. In the policy stream, Kingdon envisions policies as free-floating, in search of a problem or person who is ready to assume the policy development challenge to link that policy with a problem. The political stream characterizes the persons involved in politics and the political environment that influence the policy agenda. When at least two of the three streams align, the context is primed, and the window of opportunity is considered open for policy development. Kingdon's policy stream model is also used to analyze policy. The stream's framework provides the primary three elements—problem, policy options, and politics—from which to analyze policy development and implementation (Kingdon, 2011).

Ambiguity and Multiple Streams Model

Ambiguity and multiple streams model uses Kingdon's three streams—problems, policies, and politics—to explain how policy is formulated under conditions of ambiguity. Ambiguity is considered a state in which there are many ways of thinking about an issue, problem, or policy solution. Ambiguity is operationalized contextually. This policy model expands from the three streams to have five structural elements—problems, policies, politics, policy window, and policy entrepreneurs. Policy stream consists of the various issues or problems that policymakers desire to be addressed. Policies are the "primeval soup" of potential policy solutions. Politics consists of three elements—the national mood, pressure-group campaigns, and administrative or legislative turnover. Policy window emerges when the three streams are joined together at critical moments when policy solutions can be pursued or implemented. Policy entrepreneurs are individuals, groups, or corporations who attempt to align the three streams to create a policy agenda, formulate policy, or implement policy (Sabatier & Weible, 2014).

The ambiguity and multiple streams model uses attention, search, and selection as elements to produce policy results. Policymakers' attention must be focused on the policy agenda. Attention can be supported by opportunity, formal position in an organization, institutional structure, and symbols that are both emotive and cognitive. The element of search is the seeking of solutions and the availability to search for resources to impact the policymaking process. The search process is influenced by the structure of policy networks. Policy networks work to generate ideas for the "primeval soup." Selection is the manipulating of strategies and skills of policy entrepreneurs to align the streams of problems, policies, and politics into one package that frames an issue and primes constituents and stakeholders to support one preferred policy solution within a context of ambiguity. This policy model provides a lens to address the policy using policy entrepreneurs to create a clearly framed issue among the context of ambiguity (Sabatier & Weible, 2014).

Stage-Sequential Model

The stage-sequential systems model identifies sequential stages for the policy development process. The stage-sequential model consists of four stages: policy agenda setting, policy formulation, program implementation, and policy evaluation (Mason et al., 2016).

The first stage is policy agenda setting. The identification and distinction of an issue versus a problem determines its placement within the policy agenda. This identification of a problem that needs a resolving policy initiates the policy agenda-setting stage. The identified problem is framed into a policy concern. The policy agenda-setting stage attempts to place the issue or problem on the policy agenda for action. Placement on the policy agenda can assume one of three levels of consideration: discussion, action, or decision. The discussion agenda merely places the issue or problem within the policymaker's scope of attention. The action agenda signifies that the problem is moving through to the policy formulation phase. The decision agenda denotes the last phase of stage one. The decision agenda legitimizes the problem that will be confronted by policymakers during the legislative or regulatory process (Mason et al., 2016).

Policy formulation represents the second sequential stage. Policy formulation consists of collecting information on the issue or problem, analyzing the information, disseminating the information to various constituencies, and drafting legislation. All interested stakeholders and constituency groups should be engaged in the provision of valuable information to inform the policy formulation process.

Stage three focuses on program implementation. In the program implementation stage, the executive agency or body charged with, or authorized to, develop the program or implement the policy must begin to draft guidelines, rules, or regulations to operationalize the policy. Proposed drafts of the guidelines, rules, or regulations are generally published in a public medium to provide the general public with an opportunity for comment. Typical publications are the Federal Register, State Register, or an official publication of the appropriate regulatory agency.

Program evaluation constitutes the last sequential stage. The program evaluation stage attempts to answer the question, "Did the policy effectively achieve what it was formulated to achieve?" The program evaluation stage determines the extent to which a program has accomplished the intended goals and objectives as designed by the policymakers. The ultimate question to be answered during this stage is "Did the policy resolve the problem?" In addition to evaluating the outcome of the policy, the process of implementing the policy is also evaluated and reported to the responsible authorizing body (Mason et al., 2016; Porche, 2003).

Richmond-Kotelchuck Model

The Richmond-Kotelchuck model was developed to support prevention policies in the public health arena. The model identifies three essential elements for prevention: knowledge base, political will, and social strategy. All three of these elements are considered essential for prevention policy development to occur (Atwood, Colditz, & Kawachi, 1997).

The knowledge base in this model represents the scientific and administrative evidence used to make informed policy decisions (Richmond & Kotelchuck, 1991). This knowledge base is the area of concentration for research and analysis by public health professionals. This in-depth involvement is critical to the development of a scientific base with which to influence public health prevention policy.

Political will is society's desire and commitment to develop and fiscally support new programs, and provide or modify the existing support to established programs in alignment with the knowledge base and social strategies. Political will is dependent on a group's ability to influence policymakers such as politicians, legislators, stakeholders, and special-interest groups. The scientific knowledge base influences political will and vice versa (Richmond & Kotelchuck, 1991).

Social strategy is the use of the scientific knowledge base and the political will environment to develop public health prevention policy. The social strategy capitalizes on existing social networks and relationships to initiate and improve desired programs (Atwood et al., 1997).

Local Public Health Policy Model

An example of a local public health policy model, described by Upshaw and Okun (2002), was used to influence livestock operations that impacted the public's health. This model consists of five major processes that facilitate the formulation of public health policy: preparing to act; clarifying the role and approach; involving the community; communicating the rule and rationale; and adopting, implementing, and evaluating the rule.

Advocacy Coalition Framework

The advocacy coalition framework uses a coalition as the policy force for policy formulation. A coalition is formed by like-minded individuals with shared values and beliefs who join forces to produce a coordinated effort over time to generate policy. Policy change occurs through coalition changes in three different ways—external perturbation upsets the status quo or balance between existing advocacy coalitions and ignites a desire for a policy formulation, a new advocacy coalition gains power with voice to influence policy formulation, or an existing advocacy coalition changes its beliefs and resulting policy solutions. A communication strategy used by advocacy coalitions to promote policy interest is the professional forum. Through these professional forums, advocacy coalition members use evidence and research to support their policy solutions (Ritter & Bammer, 2010; Sabatier & Weible, 2014).

Narrative Policy Framework

The narrative policy framework provides a narrative structure and content to guide and influence policymaking. A narrative is a story with a temporal sequence of events that has an unfolding plot that culminates in a moral to the story (Jones & McBeth, 2010; Sabatier & Weible, 2014). Narratives are considered powerful in shaping beliefs and actions. This framework proposes to tell a story or narrative to guide thinking and decision making regarding policy solutions. Policy narratives should contain minimal qualities. **Box 9-5** presents the minimal narrative qualities. The narrative policy framework uses information, communication strategies, media, and a story to influence policymaking. Narratives can be used to shape and measure policy beliefs and a coalition's strength and stability. Advocacy groups engage in policy narratives as a means to influence the public's opinion and policymaker's preferences. Policy narratives impact policy formulation at the micro-, meso-, and macro-levels. At the micro-level, policy narratives impact an individual's opinion. The meso-level explores the impact of narratives on subsystems. Macro-level influences policy at the institutional or organizational level (Jones & McBeth, 2010; Sabatier & Weible, 2014). The narrative policy framework can also be used to analyze policy.

Policy Feedback Model

The policy feedback model addresses a wide spectrum of political dynamics using four major streams of inquiry, each composed of several tributaries. Policies shape the four major streams, which in turn further shape public policy (**Figure 9-1**) in a feedback loop. The meaning of citizenship is the reciprocal relationship between government and ordinary people (an individual's legal status as a citizen or member of society). Policies have an effect on the form of governance through their impact on the government's capacity and the political knowledge and ability of public officials to influence policy and transform policymaking processes. Policies influence the power of special-interest groups, associations, and other organizations with a policy agenda. Political agendas

---

BOX 9-5   MINIMAL NARRATIVE QUALITIES

- Setting or context of the policy
- Plot—a description of the relationships among the various aspects of the policy
- Characters—policy actors, interest groups, constituents, stakeholders
- Moral of the story—the potential policy solutions

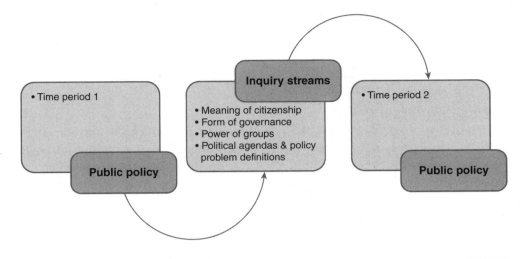

Figure 9-1   Policy Feedback Inquiry Streams

and the manner in which policy problems are framed and defined are impacted by public policy. These four streams of inquiry are influenced by public policy and influence future public policy. For example, in the meaning of citizenship stream, public policy shapes the goods, services, rules, and regulations that individuals either gain, lose, or must comply with which in turn impact the level of the individual's civic engagement to influence policy (Sabatier & Weible, 2014).

Institutional Analysis and Development Framework

The institutional analysis and development (IAD) framework consists of understanding the logic, design, and performance of institutional arrangements in a variety of settings. The first step in applying the IAD framework is to have a shared problem that individuals are working to resolve. This step of identifying the conceptual unit of the problem is referred to as the "action arena." An action arena is a social space where individuals interact, exchange goods and services, solve problems, compete, and dominate one another. The action arena is the focal unit of analysis for the IAD framework. Within the action arena are the action situation and actors. The action situation comprises a set of participants, specific positions filled by the participants, allowable actions and their linkage to outcomes, potential outcomes linked to individual sequences of action, information available to participants, and the costs and benefits assigned to actions and outcomes. Actors are the individuals or groups influencing the action arena. This framework proposes several rules that impact the participants assigned to positions, actions assigned to positions, information linked to potential outcomes, control over potential outcomes, and the net cost and benefits assigned to potential outcomes. The rules that impact the exogenous elements of an action situation are boundary, position, choice, information, aggregation, scope, and payoff (Sabatier & Weible, 2014).

Social Ecological Systems Framework

The social ecological systems (SES) framework further elaborates the IAD framework. In the SES framework, four main types of components impact the primary elements of SES. These four components are governance systems, actors/users, resource systems, and resource units. These four components are involved in interactions that lead to specific outcomes that impact related ecosystems. The SES framework proposes that governance systems, actors/users, resource systems, and resource units interact via action situations as described in the IAD framework to produce outcomes of common interest (Sabatier & Weible, 2014).

Analysis of Determinants of Policy Impact Model

The analysis of determinants of policy impact (ADEPT) model attempts to explain and influence policy development and impact policy implementation with four determinants: goals, obligations, resources, and opportunities. Goals represent what the constituents or stakeholders "want or desire" in the policy. Obligations are the professional duties of policymakers and politicians in the policymaking process. Resources are both the fiscal and human capital and ability to propose policy. Opportunities are the organizational, political, and public opportunities that emerge from changes in public awareness and engagement in the policy to provide the opportunity for policy readiness. The ADEPT model proposes that these four determinants influence the intention to act on policy. The alignment of goals, obligations, resources, and opportunities lead to policy impact in the form of policy output and policy outcomes (Rütten, Gelius, & Abu-Omar, 2011).

Centers for Disease Control and Prevention Policy Process Model

The Centers for Disease Control and Prevention (CDC) embraces the fact that policy is an effective strategy to improve the health of populations. The CDC proposes a policy process that has two overarching domains: (1) stakeholder engagement and education and (2) evaluation. In this model, there are five process domains: problem identification, policy analysis, strategy and policy development, policy enactment, and policy implementation. **Figure 9-2** is a depiction of the CDC policy process model (CDC, 2012).

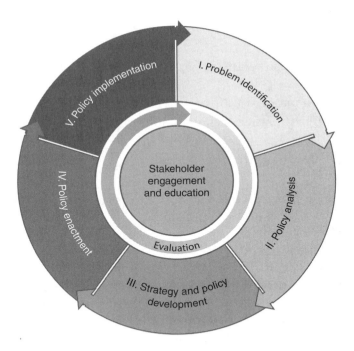

Figure 9-2   CDC Policy Process Model

Reproduced from Centers for Disease Control and Prevention. (2012). *Overview of CDC's policy process*. Atlanta, GA: Centers for Disease Control and Prevention, US Department of Health and Human Services.

The overarching domain of stakeholder engagement and education occurs throughout the five process domains. Stakeholder engagement and education ensures that key stakeholders are identified and connected with decision makers. The CDC suggests that key stakeholders are those affected by the proposed policy and the general public. Essential activities in the stakeholder engagement and education domain are:

- Identify key stakeholders such as supporters, opponents, community members, decision makers, policymakers;
- Assess key stakeholders' knowledge, attitudes, and needs;
- Implement a communication plan and strategies to deliver relevant and timely messages and materials; and
- Connect with stakeholders by soliciting input, guidance, suggestions, and feedback on proposed policy.

Evaluation is the second overarching domain that impacts all five process domains. Evaluation occurs as a formal assessment during each step of the policy process focusing on policy impact and outcomes. The essential activities in the evaluation domain are:

- Develop an evaluation plan that measures needs, purpose, and user impact;
- Conduct evaluation during each process step; and
- Disseminate evaluation results to policymakers and stakeholders.

The process domains provide a framework to guide the policy formulation process. The problem identification domain focuses on clarifying and framing the policy issue and the effect of the issue on population health. Policy analysis domain focuses on identifying policy options that address the policy issue. In the policy analysis domain, the various policy options are evaluated for their effectiveness, efficiency in implementation, and feasibility. The strategy and policy development domain activities emphasize strategy development to promote policy adoption and operationalization of the policy. Policy enactment domain works with the authoritative body to follow internal and external procedures to approve, adopt, or enact the policy. Policy implementation domain is the translation of the policy into action, monitoring the policy adoption, and ensuring full implementation of the policy into practice. **Table 9-1** provides a list of essential activities for each of these five domains (CDC, 2012).

Executive Policymaking: Executive Orders and Memorandums

An executive order is a legally binding directive issued by the chief officer of the executive branch of government at the national, state, or local level. Executive orders are a type of legal policy and can be issued by a president, governor, or mayor. Executive orders generally deal with domestic issues. Executive orders do not require congressional or legislative approval to take effect; the officer who issues the order determines the effective date. To ensure a balance of power, as required by our Constitution, Congress or most state legislative bodies can overturn an executive order with a two-thirds majority vote. An executive memorandum is an executive action taken to clarify, manage, or direct the action of departments or agencies within the executive branch. A memorandum generally directs a department or agency to take some action or to do something. Executives can also issue an executive proclamation. An executive proclamation does not have the power of law but provides a public statement to make known the executive's position on a policy issue, problem, or matter. An executive proclamation can be symbolic and ceremonial in intent, such as making a declaration to honor an individual or recognize a specific group.

TABLE 9-1   CDC PROCESS DOMAIN'S ESSENTIAL ACTIVITIES

DOMAIN	ESSENTIAL ACTIVITIES
Problem identification	• Collect and summarize relevant epidemiological data about problem/issue (morbidity and mortality statistics, social determinants of health in relation to problem/issue) • Define characteristics of problem/issue—scope, severity, trends, fiscal impact • Determine gaps in data as a means of collecting relevant data • Frame the problem/issue in terms of population health
Policy analysis	• Conduct a literature search or review of evidence-based practice to identify policy options • Describe the relationship of the policy options on the impact of the epidemiology and characteristics of the problem/issue • Determine fiscal impact of policy options • Identify feasibility of policy adoption from an operational and political perspective • Assess each policy option and prioritize policy options for adoption
Strategy and policy development	• Identify the authoritative body, structure, or process for policy approval • Identify the operational needs for policy implementation • Develop a strategy to secure approval from stakeholders and policymakers • Draft the policy
Policy enactment	• Enact the policy approval process
Policy implementation	• Translate the policy into practice • Promulgate rules, regulations, or other guidelines needed for implementation of the policy • Implement all parameters of the policy • Coordinate resources and build stakeholder and community capacity for policy implementation • Use process evaluation methods to assess success of policy implementation • Develop and implement a postimplementation policy sustainability plan

Modified from Centers for Disease Control and Prevention. (2012). *Overview of CDC's policy process.* Atlanta, GA: Centers for Disease Control and Prevention, US Department of Health and Human Services.

Incremental Policy Formulation

Incremental policy formulation or policymaking describes a slow evolution of policy. Incremental policy formulation may occur when there is not enough political support to ensure that a transformational policy change will be approved by policymakers. Incremental policymaking can use existing policies as a foundation from which to expand the original intent of a policy. The long-term goal, a desired new policy, is hoped to be achieved over time, and often employs utilization of the media to frame policy, and prime policymakers and constituents. This process represents small successive changes to an existing policy so that over time, the entire intent of the policy has been transformed.

Incremental policymaking is considered a conservative policymaking approach. The incremental approach to policymaking allows policymakers to avoid political struggles that require extensive justification for new policy. However, incremental policymaking has been considered a disjointed approach to policymaking that yields confusing and contradictory policies. Adhering to a comprehensive strategic plan will prevent disjointed policymaking when using this incremental approach. An incremental policymaking plan should include:

- A comprehensive policymaking goal that describes the desired policy intent
- An agenda-setting plan that describes what policies will be developed and a timeline for placement on the action policy agenda
- Identified policy modifications with a timeline for policymaking
- Development of a long-term political strategy for each policy modification that will occur over time
- Development of policy evaluation plans to provide data that support each successive policy modification

Policy Instruments

Policy instruments are the tools used by policymakers to achieve a desired policy intent or outcome. A policy is sometimes considered a collection of policy instruments. Policy instruments are written into policy to achieve a desired outcome. Policy instruments can take the form of mandates and inducements. Mandates are policies that oblige individuals or organizations to take or not take certain actions. Inducements are the provision or transfer of funds for the provision of goods, services, or behaviors. Policy instruments are critical to the design of policy and are impacted by the politics of policymaking. These instruments are

---

BOX 9-6   LIST OF POLICY INSTRUMENTS

- Taxation
- Fares
- Financial incentives
- Punitive or disciplinary action
- Subsidies
- Quotas
- Allocation of goods and services
- Distribution of goods and services
- Physical restrictions
- Licensing
- Price control
- Economic disincentives

---

considered the substance or content that forms the policy. Policy instruments are also critical to the implementation of policy (**Box 9-6**).

Transformative Policy Formulation

Transformative policy formulation is considered a rapid-cycle type of policy formulation. In transformative policy formulation, the policy seeks to implement a policy of remarkable change from the current policy state. Three properties of transformative policy formulation are selective specific focus, process orientation, and engagement of multiple policy instruments to secure rapid change. Policymakers who propose transformative policy formulation are innovative and entrepreneurial with a tolerance for risks. Transformative policy formulation stimulates policymakers to go above and beyond incremental policy expectations to transition rapidly to the desired policy state.

Policy Implementation Process

A critical element for effective policy implementation is the ability to develop systems in which there are clear and strong linkages between the constituent's goals, governmental goals, proposed policy, and planned activities or programs. Policy implementation refers to connecting the intention of the policy to the outcomes or results achieved from the policy (Smith & Larimer, 2016). Buse,

Mays, and Walt (2012) propose the following necessary conditions for effective policy implementation:

- Clear and logically established objectives that are consistent with a common goal
- Sufficient evidence to support a relationship between the proposed policy and the expected outcome
- Implementation process that facilitates compliance by implementers (incentives and sanctions)
- Committed administrative and legislative support for implementation
- Assurance that required resources are available
- Clear communication
- Support from the public, interest groups, and all branches of government
- Stable socioeconomic conditions Buse, Mays, and Walt (2012).

Similarly, from a statutory perspective, seven elements have been identified as critical to policy implementation: clear goals; adequate causal theory linking the policy alternatives to the problem causes; adequate resources; hierarchical integration of executive agencies responsible for policy implementation; decision rules to guide the executive agencies implementation processes; commitment from the executive agency to implement policy in alignment with its intent; and formal participation by constituents who support the policy objectives and who are impacted by the policy objectives (Smith & Larimer, 2016).

Once a bill is legislatively passed, the governmental executive officer must sign the proposed bill, thus making it a law. With the signing of a bill into law, the policymaking process moves from policy formulation to the policy implementation. This transition of the newly signed bill into law moves responsibility from the legislative branch to the executive branch (oversight evaluation responsibility may reside with a legislative standing committee). Policy implementation is a function of the executive branch of government.

The respective executive departments and agencies have oversight responsibility for the implementation of laws (Longest, 2015). Policy implementation consists of two cyclical processes: rule making and operation. Rule making and operation are two processes that are dictated by administrative law.

Policy Implementation Planning

Policy implementation planning should begin to be considered during the policy formulation process. The implementation planning may be written into the policy by delineating the respective responsible agency, group, committee, or person for implementation. **Table 9-2** presents a policy implementation matrix to plan and monitor the process of implementing a policy. Policy implementation

TABLE 9-2 POLICY IMPLEMENTATION MATRIX						
POLICY	ACTIONS	RESPONSIBLE PARTY	TIMEFRAME	BUDGET	BUDGET SOURCE	STATUS

planning consists of multiple interrelated stages. The stages of policy implementation are outlined below:

- Define the scope of work—the policy instruments or components that need to be implemented.
- Identify the project activities for each policy instrument or component of the policy.
- Identify specific tasks to achieve each activity.
- Schedule tasks.
- Detail cost of each activity and task.
- Secure funding for activities and tasks.
- Identify other resources needed for implementation.
- Identify stakeholders' and constituents' roles in implementation.
- Engage stakeholders' and constituents' involvement in implementation.
- Monitor performance and manage risk of policy implementation (McLaughlin & McLaughlin, 2015).

Four critical components of the policy implementation planning are leading teams, managing change, communication plan, and postmortem analysis.

Team Leadership

Teams are groups of individuals who come together for a mutual purpose to achieve a common goal. Leadership is necessary through each cycle of team formation. Team formation leadership ensures that the group of individuals remain focused on implementation of the policy. The stages of team formation requiring leadership are forming, storming, norming, and performing. Forming is the establishment of a policy implementation team and linking the policy intent and goals to each individual member's personal goals. This alignment facilitates continued engagement. Storming occurs when team tensions rise. Storming is an expected phase of team formation in which power struggles emerge, blaming occurs, fault for errors are assigned, and distrust may emerge. Norming is the stage when the team members establish expected team norms, behaviors, and operations. Performing stage is the point in which the team begins to achieve the implementation of the activities and tasks necessary for policy implementation. In addition to leading teams during policy implementation, the leader is continually managing change.

Managing Change

Change involves individuals. Some individuals may be self-motivated to change, but others may need to be influenced to change. The implementation of a new policy or modification of an existing policy creates the need to manage the change process. Lewin's three-stage model of change proposes that driving and restraining forces influence change and the development of an equilibrium state (**Figure 9-3**). Driving forces are the forces that push in the direction of the desired policy change. Restraining forces are the forces that hinder the change or move in the opposite direction of the desired policy change. Equilibrium is the state in which driving and restraining forces are equally balanced and the policy change does not occur.

Policy makers can use the three stages of change to influence policy implementation. The first stage is unfreezing. Unfreezing is the process of assisting individuals and groups to let go of old behaviors and accepted practices. The second stage is movement or change. This stage consists of instituting the policy instruments and intent to generate a change in thought, feeling, and behaviors consistent with the policy expectations. In the last stage, refreezing, the policy change becomes considered the new "norm" or "status quo."

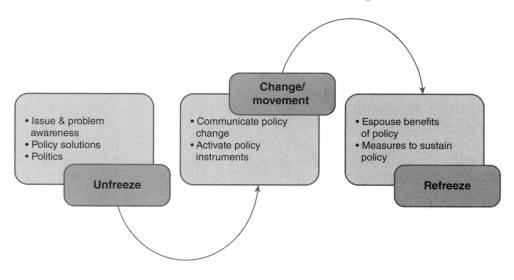

Figure 9-3   Lewin's Stages of Change: Policy Implementation

Communication Plan

In policy implementation, the communication plan details the manner in which the policy change is communicated to constituents and stakeholders. **Box 9-7** outlines the components of a policy communication plan. Policy communication is best if it addresses a specific audience about a specific policy. Four criteria are used to evaluate an effective policy communication message: it should be clear, correct, concise, and credible. Certain principles should be considered when developing a policy communication plan: it should be transparent, fact based, consistent in message, timely, demonstrate equal treatment for various audiences, and show respect for diverse opinions.

Postmortem Analysis

In policy implementation, a postmortem analysis provides the foundation for future policy development and formulation. A postmortem analysis is a critical

---

BOX 9-7   COMPONENTS OF A POLICY COMMUNICATION PLAN

- Determine communication medium
- Determine communication channels
- Define a key message and repeat the key message
- Identify policy author or spokesperson
- Explain the approval process and confirm authority for policy approval
- Describe supporting or sponsoring agencies, organizations, special-interest groups
- Communicate a need for policy—discuss political, economic, social, technological, environmental, and legal factors associated with the policy
- Describe the purpose of the policy
- Describe the expected impact or outcomes from the policy
- Describe the intended audience for the policy
- Identify constituents and stakeholders
- State the date of implementation (when it takes effect) or timeline of implementation
- Describe the impact on other policies
- Discuss related and other supporting policies, documents, and reports
- Provide contact information for further inquires

BOX 9-8   POLICY IMPLEMENTATION POSTMORTEM TEMPLATE

- Key accomplishments
  - What went right?
  - What worked well?
  - What was useful? `
- Key problem areas
  - What went wrong?
  - What processes did not work well?
  - What was the outcome of the problem areas?
  - Were there technical challenges
- Processes and schedule
  - What processes worked?
  - What factors impacted the implementation process?
  - What alterations occurred in schedule?
  - What impacted the schedule?
- Risks assessment
  - What risks emerged?
  - How were risks managed or mitigated?
- Communication
  - Effectiveness of medium?
  - Effectiveness of communication channel?
- Team assessment
  - Each team member evaluates the others
- Lessons learned

---

review of the team's performance during the policy implementation process. The postmortem analysis is not about assigning blame but is used for identifying areas for future improvement. **Box 9-8** provides a postmortem template for policy implementation.

Promulgation of Rules and Regulations

Rule making is the establishment of formal rules and regulations necessary to fully operationalize the legislative intent of the law (Longest, 2015). Rule making is also known as the policy legitimization process. Policy legitimization is considered one of the final steps in the policymaking process. Policy legitimization

---

BOX 9-9   SUMMARY OF RULE-MAKING STEPS

- Advanced notice of proposed rule making
- Notice of proposed rule making
- Notice of public hearing
- Notice of final rule
- Agency implementation and enforcement

---

occurs as a result of the open process of policymaking that permits the public to provide feedback on proposed rules and regulations through the promulgation of rules and regulation process (Dye, 2017).

The executive department or agency responsible for implementing the law must determine the intent and develop rules and regulations consistent with the legislative intent. The promulgation process requires the publication of the proposed rules and regulations for a specified period of time in the public domain to permit an opportunity for public input and comment. **Box 9-9** provides a summary of the rule-making process. The process for promulgating rules and regulations consists of:

- Publishing a "notice of proposed rule making" in the State Register or Federal Register, generally a draft of the proposed rules and regulations.
- A public comment period that permits reaction and discussion of the proposed rules and regulations. Frequently, the executive department or agency may permit interested parties to submit a request for a public hearing on the proposed rules and regulations.
- Proposed rules and regulations are revised based on public comment and or hearings.
- Publishing of the wording of the final rule in the State Register or Federal Register.
- Implementation of published rules (Longest, 2015).

Operation

After the rules and regulations have been promulgated, operationalization of the rules and regulations begins the operation process. Operation is the actual activity that occurs in carrying out the proposed law, such as conducting inspections, imposing fines, issuing permits, or starting new programs (Longest, 2015).

Diffusion of Innovation

Diffusion of innovation provides a theoretical framework in which to understand the dissemination and adoption of policy. According to Rogers (2003), an innovation can be anything that is perceived as new by an individual or group. An innovation can be an idea, practice, or resource (physical, human, or fiscal) that requires the acceptance and adoption by another individual or group. Therefore, an innovation can be a policy, or the implementation of a new program resulting from a policy. Diffusion represents the process by which an innovation is communicated through channels over time among members of a social system. This theoretical framework provides a means to understand this diffusion process and to impact the rate of diffusion.

Four main elements affect diffusion of innovations: innovation, communication channels, time, and the social system or contextual environment. Each of these elements has an essential part in the rate of diffusion or dissemination of a policy within a population. The characteristics of an innovation that impact the rate of diffusion or dissemination, and ultimately adoption, are dependent upon the innovation's relative advantage, compatibility, complexity, trialability, and observability. They are briefly described below:

- Relative advantage—degree to which an innovation is considered better than what it will supersede
- Compatibility—degree that an innovation is considered consistent with existing values, past experiences, norms, and existing policies
- Complexity—degree to which an innovation is considered easy to understand and use
- Trialability—degree to which an innovation can be trialed or piloted with the option of returning to prior state before innovation adoption
- Observability—degree to which innovation produces visible results

Communication is the process by which individuals create and transmit information from one individual to another to promote mutual understanding. The communication channel is the means by which this message is transmitted. Time impacts the diffusion process through the innovation-decision process: innovativeness and rate of adoption. This innovative-decision process is a cognitive process by which an individual or group assimilates the knowledge regarding the innovation to formulate an attitude toward the innovation and render a decision to adopt, reject, implement, or merely confirm a decision. This innovation-decision process involves five steps: knowledge, persuasion, decision, implementation, and confirmation. The innovativeness is the readiness with which an individual or group is likely to adopt innovation as characterized by five adopter categories. These adopter categories are:

- Innovators—first individuals to adopt an innovation; may serve as a gatekeepers
- Early adopters—next level of individuals to adopt an innovation; rely on opinion leaders to influence their adoption of innovation; not much ahead of the average individual in adopting an innovation; respected by peers for discrete use of new ideas
- Early majority—adoption of innovation takes longer than innovators and early adopters; act with peer base; most common adopter category; deliberate for some time before adopting an innovation; will not be the first or last to adopt an innovation
- Late majority—respond to increasing network and peer pressure to adopt an innovation; approach innovations with skepticism and cautiousness; adopt an innovation after most members of the social system have adopted
- Laggards—last persons to adopt an innovation; prefer the past as their point of reference; resistant to change; suspicious of innovation and change agents; must be certain an innovation will not fail before it is adopted

The rate of adoption is the relative speed with which an innovation is adopted among members of an entire social system. The social system is considered a system of interrelated members or units that can be composed of individuals, groups, or organizations and institutions.

Policy Modification

Policy is never perfect. As societal demands and policy agenda changes, there may be a need for modification of existing policy. In addition, mistakes of omission and commission inevitably occur during the policymaking process. Policies are modified as a means to limit any negative impact of existing policy while continuing to meet the legislative intent and the public's need. Other reasons for policy modification include resource constraints, change in goals, interest group, stakeholders, or constituents with political influence. Policy modification may be the result of policy analysis, policy evaluation, or policy research processes that identify a need for change or alteration in the existing policy. Policy modification engages several stages of the policymaking process such as agenda setting, legislation development, and promulgation of rules and regulations, depending on the extent and type of policy modification needed.

The modification can result in an alteration to the original law, an amendment to the existing law, or modification in the rules and regulations that implement the law within the respective executive department or agency.

Policy Modification versus Policy Change

Policy modification and *policy change* are terms frequently used interchangeably. Policy modification and policy change are two distinct types of policymaking activities. Policy modification alters an existing policy by either deleting aspects of the policy, modifying aspects of the policy, or extending the original policy. Policy modification is frequently used with incremental policymaking. In contrast, policy change alters the entire focus and intent of the original policy. Typically, the original policy is superseded by a new policy.

Policy Development: Expanding the Scope of Nursing Practice

At the state level, boards of nursing engage in the development, formulation, and regulation of the nursing scope of practice in accordance with the statutory authority. As societal need dictates, boards of nursing engage in a process of policy development to meet these societal needs within the respective state's legal statutory policy governing the scope of nursing practice. Frequently, this requires the development and formulation of policy in the form of statutes or rules and regulations that expand the existing scope of nursing practice. In addition, boards of nursing can formulate proclamations, resolutions, position papers, declaratory statements, or advisory opinions as policies.

The policy development process for boards of nursing to explore expansion of the nursing practice scope consists of the following:

- Examining the existence of statutory authority that permits the expansion of the nursing scope of practice
- Exploring the history of practice for nurses who will engage in the expanded scope
- Analyzing the requisite educational, training, and experiential requirements for the expanded scope of practice
- Critiquing and synthesizing literature (with a focus on empirical research) that supports the expanded scope of nursing practice
- Determining the presence of or need for regulations that support this expanded scope of nursing practice
- Documenting the verifiable need for nurses to engage in the expanded scope of nursing practice

- Analyzing the evidence that supports the expanded scope of practice in relation to the impact of societal need, public health, and public safety

Each health professional discipline has a different regulatory process; however, other health professional boards also use similar policies for scope of practice issues. Professional regulatory boards establish the guidelines and standards to govern the methods of expanding the respective disciplines scope of practice. The method of expanding scope of practice for nursing described above is similar to that for other health professional disciplines. The policy development process presented above should be used as a general framework to guide expanding scope of practice. Nurses and other healthcare professionals should refer to their respective state regulatory board to define the specific process for scope of practice expansion within the respective state.

Policy Termination

Policy termination is an aspect of the policy process that is not frequently discussed, but should be provided the same emphasis as policy formulation and implementation. Policies that are inaccurately terminated can result in the development of other policy issues and problems. Frequently, policy termination results in the elimination of programs, fiscal retrenchments, and the redirection or expansion of existing policies and/or programs. Policy termination could even result in the closure of departments, organizations, or agencies. Occasionally at the institutional or organizational level, policy termination may result simply in the deletion of an existing outdated policy no longer necessary or the rescinding of a policy with an update replacement policy. Suspension of a policy is temporary termination of a policy, typically for a defined period of time.

Policy termination can be complete or incremental. Complete policy termination ends the cumulative policy at one specific point in time. Complete policy termination can be used as a political strategy to catch opponents "off guard" and reduce the resistance to policy termination. However, there could be considerable negative political fallout from such a precipitous maneuver if it is done abruptly and without notification. In contrast, incremental policy termination results from a progressive and consistent elimination of certain aspects of an existing policy. Incremental policy termination is frequently associated with programmatic phasing out. The slow reduction of programmatic or organizational budgets is a means of incrementally terminating an existing policy or program. This is sometimes referred to as "decrementalism" (Stewart, Hedge, & Lester, 2007). **Box 9-10** provides some policy termination recommendations.

BOX 9-10   POLICY TERMINATION RECOMMENDATIONS

- Information leaks regarding policy termination should be minimized until a comprehensive plan and justification are prepared and ready for dissemination.
- Once a plan is developed, make use of the media to prime and frame the policy termination.
- Enlarging the policy constituency builds a support base for the policy termination beyond the original policymakers and supporters.
- The policy analysis and policy evaluation should include a harm analysis from the perspectives of the policy beneficiaries, supporters, and opponents.
- Maximize on societal and ideological changes to formulate a new perspective regarding the policy.
- Consider an external agent as the policy terminator.
- Do not encroach on power prerogatives.
- Provide positive incentives for terminating the policy.
- Use political strategies to adopt another policy as a replacement to the terminated policy.
- Consider terminating only nonessential portions of a policy.

Summary Points

- Policy development is contextually dependent.
- The context in which policy development occurs includes the various policy agendas, political spheres, and interdependent discourse among various individuals and interest groups that represent scientific, social, and governmental interests.
- The context for policy development influences the political process, political maneuvers, and strategies implemented; frames the policy issue; and impacts the resultant intent of the policy formulated.
- The pluralist perspective embraces the idea of multiple special interests affecting the development of policy as a means of ensuring equal representation in the policymaking process.
- The elitist values the input of a select few individuals in the policy development process.
- Policy formulation occurs within a context of high political diplomacy and negotiation.

- In the rational approach, policymakers define the problem; identify and rank social values aligned with the policy goals; examine policy alternative solutions in relation to both the positive and negative consequences of each alternative; conduct a cost and benefit analysis; compare and contrast options; and finally, select the policy that achieves the resolution that most closely aligns with social values and meets the most needs.
- In the incremental approach, policymakers initiate small policy changes in an evolutionary manner over time.
- Legislators are responsible to their voting public or constituency.
- Judicial officials establish policy through the interpretation of laws, interpretation of federal and state constitutions, interpretation of rules and regulations of executive agencies, and the establishment of judicial procedures.
- An executive branch prepares proposed legislation for action by Congress or similar legislative body depending on the level of government.
- Citizens, organizations, and special-interest groups can petition the government, through the First Amendment, to formulate policy.
- Legislative staff members are the gatekeepers who control access and the flow of information to elected officials.
- Legislative staff members orient the new legislator to current and critical policy issues, thus further shaping the elected official's policy agenda.
- Bills introduced into the legislative process are numbered sequentially by date of introduction and referred to the appropriate standing committee.
- Each legislative committee has a specific scope of legislative authority.
- The legislative oversight committee is responsible for monitoring the implementation and effectiveness of the policy as detailed in the law.
- The nurse scientist or researcher generates or validates the scientific basis that provides essential foundational evidence to support or refute various elements of the proposed policy.
- Interprofessional policymaking removes discipline-specific silos to formulate policy.
- Consultation is the process of seeking advice, opinion, or guidance of another healthcare professional.
- Collaboration is a process by which two or more healthcare professionals work together, with each professional contributing from a respective area of expertise.

- Policy models provide a framework that specifies the processes through which policy evolves, develops, and emerges as a solution to a policy issue or problem.
- The Kingdon policy stream model describes the policy development process as occurring through three streams: problem, policy, and political.
- Ambiguity and multiple streams model combines Kingdon's three streams with the context of policy ambiguity.
- The stage-sequential model consists of four stages: policy agenda setting, policy formulation, program implementation, and policy evaluation.
- The Richmond-Kotelchuck model of policy identifies three essential elements for prevention: knowledge base, political will, and social strategy.
- The five major processes of the local public health policy model are preparing to act; clarifying the role and approach; involving the community; communicating the rule and rationale; and adopting, implementing, and evaluating the rule.
- Advocacy coalition framework uses a coalition as the policy force for policy formulation.
- Narrative policy framework provides a narrative structure and content to guide and influence policymaking.
- Policy feedback model addresses a wide spectrum of political dynamics using four major streams of inquiry, each composed of several tributaries.
- Institutional analysis and development (IAD) framework consists of understanding the logic, design, and performance of institutional arrangements in a variety of settings.
- The first step in applying the IAD framework is to have a shared problem that individuals are working to resolve.
- In the SES framework, four main types of components impact the primary elements of SES—governance systems, actors/users, resource systems, and resource units.
- Analysis of determinants of policy impact (ADEPT) model attempts to explain and influence policy development and impact policy implementation with four determinants—goals, obligations, resources, and opportunities.
- CDC proposes a policy process that has two overarching domains: stakeholder engagement and education and evaluation.
- The five CDC process domains are problem identification, policy analysis, strategy and policy development, policy enactment, and policy implementation.

- An executive order is a legally binding directive issued by the chief officer of the executive branch of government at the national, state, or local level. Executive orders are a type of legal policy.
- Incremental policymaking can use existing policies as a foundation from which to expand the original intent of a policy.
- Adhering to a comprehensive strategic plan will prevent disjointed policymaking when using this incremental approach.
- Policy implementation refers to connecting the intention of the policy to the outcomes or results achieved from the policy.
- Policy instruments are the tools used by policymakers to achieve a desired policy intent or outcome.
- Transformative policy formulation is considered a rapid-cycle type of policy formulation.
- Rule making is the establishment of formal rules and regulations necessary to fully operationalize the legislative intent of the law.
- Operation is the actual activity that occurs in carrying out the proposed law, such as conducting inspections, imposing fines, issuing permits, or starting new programs.
- Policy implementation refers to connecting the intention of the policy to the outcomes or results achieved from the policy.
- An innovation can be an idea, practice, or resource (physical, human, or fiscal) that requires the acceptance and adoption by another individual or group.
- Diffusion represents the process by which an innovation is communicated through channels over time among members of a social system.
- Four main elements affect diffusion of innovations: innovation, communication channels, time, and the social system or contextual environment.
- The characteristics of an innovation that impact the rate of diffusion or dissemination, and ultimately adoption, are dependent upon the innovation's relative advantage, compatibility, complexity, trialability, and observability.
- The innovativeness is the readiness with which an individual or group is likely to adopt innovation.
- Policies are modified as a means to limit any negative impact of existing policy while continuing to meet the legislative intent and the public's need.
- Policy modification and policy change are two distinct types of policymaking activities.
- Policy change alters the entire focus and intent of the original policy.

- A postmortem analysis is a critical review of the team's performance during the policy implementation process.
- Policy termination can be complete or incremental.

References

Atwood, K., Colditz, G., & Kawachi, I. (1997). From public health science to prevention policy: Placing science in its social and political contexts. *American Journal of Public Health, 87*(10), 1603–1605.

Buse, K., Mays, N., & Walt, G. (2012). *Making health policy* (2nd ed.). Berkshire, UK: Open University Press.

Centers for Disease Control and Prevention (CDC). (2012). *Overview of CDC's policy process.* Atlanta, GA: Centers for Disease Control and Prevention, U.S. Department of Health and Human Services.

Dye, T. (2017). *Understanding public policy* (15th ed.). Boston, MA: Pearson.

Interprofessional Education Collaborative. (2016). *Core competencies for interprofessional collaborative practice: 2016 update.* Washington, DC: Interprofessional Education Collaborative.

Interprofessional Education Collaborative Expert Panel. (2011). *Core competencies for interprofessional collaborative practice: Report of an expert panel.* Washington, DC: Interprofessional Education Collaborative.

Jones, M., & McBeth, M. (2010). A narrative policy framework: Clear enough to be wrong? *Policy Studies Journal, 38*(2), 329–353.

Kingdon, J. (2011). *Agendas, alternatives, and public policies* (2nd ed.). Boston, MA: Longman.

Longest, B. (2015). *Health policymaking in the United States* (6th ed.). New York, NY: Health Administration Press.

Mason, D. J., Gardner, D. B., Outlaw, F. H., & O'Grady, E. (Eds.). (2016). *Policy & politics in nursing and health care* (7th ed.). St. Louis, MO: Elsevier.

McLaughlin, C., & McLaughlin, C. (2015). *Health policy analysis: An interdisciplinary approach* (2nd ed.). Burlington, MA: Jones & Bartlett Learning.

Peters, A. (2012). Ten best practices for drafting legislation. *Journal of Nursing Regulation, 3*(1), 49–51.

Porche, D. (2003). *Public & community health nursing: A population-based approach.* Thousand Oaks, CA: Sage.

Richmond, J., & Kotelchuck, M. (1991). Coordination and development of strategies and policy for public health promotion in the United States. In W. Holland & R. Detels (Eds.), *Oxford textbook of public health,* (pp. 441–445). Oxford, England: Oxford Medical.

Ridenour, N., & Trautman, D. (2009). A primer for nurses on advancing health reform policy. *Journal of Professional Nursing, 25*(6), 358–362.

Ritter, A., & Bammer, G. (2010). Models of policy-making and their relevance for drug research. *Drug and Alcohol Review, 29*(4), 352–357.

Rogers, E. M. (2003). *Diffusion of innovations* (5th ed.). New York, NY: Free Press.

Rütten, A., Gelius, P., & Abu-Omar, K. (2011). Policy development and implementation in health promotion—From theory to practice: The ADEPT model. *Health Promotion International, 26*(3), 322–329.

Sabatier P., & Weible, C. (2014). *Theories of the policy process* (3rd ed.). Boulder, CO: Westview Press.

Smith, K. B., & Larimer, C. W. (Eds.). (2016). *The public policy theory primer* (3rd ed.). Boulder, CO: Westview Press.

Stewart, J., Hedge, D., & Lester, J. (2007). *Public policy: An evolutionary approach* (3rd ed.). Boston, MA: Wadsworth-Cengage Learning.

Truman, D. (1993). *The governmental process.* Berkeley, CA: University of California Institute of Governmental Studies.

Upshaw, V., & Okun, M. (2002). A model approach for developing effective local public health policies: A North Carolina county responds to large-scale hog production. *Journal of Public Health Management Practice, 8*(5), 44–54.

Weissert, C., & Weissert, G. (2000). State legislative staff influence in health policy making. *Journal of Health Politics, Policy and Law, 25*(6), 1121–1148.

Policy Analysis

Policies that have been formulated and implemented must be continually analyzed for currency with the political climate, social issues, and best evidence. Policy analysis provides valuable data that can assist with policy modifications. Policy formulation and modification is not the end of the policymaking process. Policies should be continually analyzed during all phases of the policymaking process, including agenda setting, policy formulation, policy drafting, rule making, policy implementation, and policy modification. Policy analysis is a strategy used to identify current policy issues and to assist in constructing policy formulation and modification strategies. Policy analysis also provides a perspective into the world of politics (Dye, 2017; Longest, 2015).

Policy analysis critically appraises the context in which an agenda, issue, or policy exists. Policy analysis is initiated with an interpretive analysis of the policy and a review of the historical evolutionary context of the policy. This policy analysis process may generate information regarding congruence between the present policy, and past and present political and social contexts. If there is significant incongruity in the policy analysis results, the analysis may initiate an in-depth policy evaluation; or the analysis alone could lead to policy modification recommendations. The product of policy analysis is a clear description of the problem, identification of policy solutions or alternatives, courses of action with expected outcomes, and a contextual understanding of the policy problem and comprehensive understanding of the policy.

Policy analysis can be conducted on three levels. Hudson and Lowe (2008) propose that macro-, meso- or micro-level policy analysis can be utilized. Macro-level analysis encompasses the broad parameters that influence policy such as global economics and globalization. Meso-level analysis focuses on the policymaking process through implementation and the individuals and groups that develop the policy. Therefore, the meso-level focuses on policymaking and policy implementation. Micro-level policy analysis focuses on the engagement between consumers or constituents and policymaking agencies or individuals and their personalities. The micro-level of policy analysis focuses on an individual's engagement, beliefs, and values that impact the policymaking process. In addition, the policy analysis model chosen will depend upon the intent of the analysis. Examples of different approaches are examination of the specifics of the policy process (agenda setting, policy development, etc.); analysis of a substantive policy area (environmental health, smoking cessation, etc.); a prescriptive focus to determine what policy should be; or an empirical approach to existing policy. Therefore, prior to engaging in policy analysis, the analyst should define the level at which the policy will be analyzed and the overall purpose and intent of conducting the policy analysis. The policy analysis process should clearly indicate if policy analysis is at the macro-, meso-, or micro-level. In addition, policy recommendations generated from the policy analysis should also indicate the level (macro-, meso-, or micro-) at which these recommendations are targeted.

Policy Analysis Models

There are two primary foci of policy analysis—analysis *of* policy or analysis *for* policy. Analysis *of* policy is a retrospective process that explores the determination of policy and what constituted the policy. Analysis of policy examines how policy evolved onto the policy agenda, the process of formulation of the policy, and rationale for the context of the policy. In contrast, analysis *for* policy is prospective issue or problem analysis that explores what may result if a respective policy is formulated and implemented (Buse, Mays, & Walt, 2012).

Policy analysis is dependent upon access to data sources. Data sources used in policy analysis are outlined in **Box 10-1**. An accurate policy analysis is dependent upon the use of valid and reliable documents. **Box 10-2** presents some questions to pose and consider when using documents as a data source in policy analysis.

Process Model

The process model identifies the stages of policymaking and then analyzes the determinants associated with each of the respective stages. In the process model, the policy analyst uses any policymaking model as the framework with which to conduct policy analysis (Lester & Stewart, 2007). **Figure 10-1** presents a conceptual policy analysis framework. The framework proposes the broad conceptual areas of content, process, actors, and context.

BOX 10-1   POLICY ANALYSIS DATA SOURCES

- Policy documents
  Legislation
  Journals
  Academic books
  Position papers
  Copies of public testimony
  Annual organizational reports
  Reports from think tanks, interest groups, consultants, governmental
    and nongovernmental agencies
- Interviews
- Focus groups
- Policy evaluation reports

BOX 10-2   DOCUMENT ANALYSIS

- Who authored the document? What are the author's political
  affiliations?
- Who published the document? What are their vested interests?
- What prompted the writing of the document?
- Does the document contain primary or secondary data sources? Is
  the document, in its entirety, a primary or secondary data source, or
  combined?
- What is the authenticity of the documents?
- How did the document frame the issue or problem?
- Is the document clear and logical?
- Can the document's contents be corroborated with other sources of
  data?
- Are there contradictory or competing interpretations of the document?

Substantive Model

The substantive model analyzes the policy from the perspective of the policy
issue. This analysis is usually conducted by policy content experts in the focus
area. Policy analysts who engage in policy analysis using a substantive approach

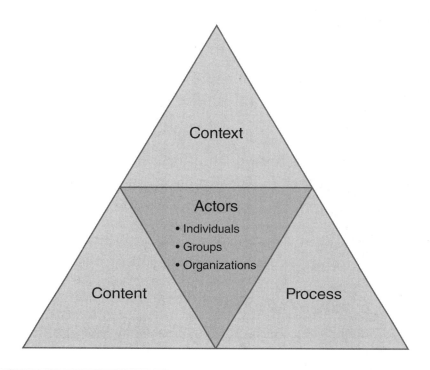

Figure 10-1   Policy Analysis Framework

must be familiar not only with the content but also with the political bodies and strategies used in policymaking in the focus area. This policy analysis model's focus area of emphasis is on the substantive content of the policy in relation to the root causes of the policy issue or problem. This model focuses less on the process and political aspects of the policy.

Eightfold Path

An eightfold path describes an iterative problem-solving process used to clarify the policy problem and determine policy solutions (Bardach & Patashnik, 2016). The eight iterative steps in this model are:

- Defining the problem
- Assembling the evidence
- Constructing policy alternatives
- Selecting the criteria

- Projecting the outcomes
- Confronting the trade-offs
- Deciding
- Telling the story (Bardach & Patashnik, 2016)

Defining the problem is the first critical step. The problem should be defined in quantifiable terms. These quantifiable terms permit the determination of the magnitude of a problem. In addition, the defining terms provide a baseline from which to evaluate the policy effect later. The defining of the problem permits the root causes of the problem to be determined. This differentiates the causes of the problem from the antecedent's associated factors, or consequences.

Assembling the evidence consists of collecting the data. Evidence assembly consists of reviewing the literature, conducting surveys to collect primary data, and synthesizing best practices. In the course of this process, people as a source of evidence will lead to other people, people will lead to pertinent documents, pertinent documents will lead to people, and documents will lead to other documents. Thus, evidence assembly is a tool that can provide cumulative evidence.

Constructing policy alternatives generates multiple policy options to resolve the problem or issue. It is from the policy alternatives generated that the final policy option is selected based on an evaluation of the appropriateness of the policy alternative to the problem.

Criteria selection determines the value system that will be used to evaluate the acceptability of a policy alternative. Typical selection criteria used are efficiency in terms of cost-benefit analysis; justice (equality, equity, and fairness); freedom (free from government control, equality before law, free speech, religious freedom, privacy); legality; political acceptability; robustness and improvability; and linguistic clarity.

Outcome projection attempts to hypothesize the outcomes that will occur in relation to adoption and implementation of the policy alternative. Outcome projection also assists in identifying unanticipated consequences that may occur.

Confronting the trade-offs is the decision process to determine the acceptable trade-off in positive and negative terms that will be permitted with the adoption of various policy options. The trade-off confrontation can be used to eliminate policy alternatives that do not meet the selection criteria and lead to more positive benefits.

Deciding and telling the story are the last two steps in the process. A final selection must be made from among the multiple policy alternatives. Telling the story consists of redefining the problem, reconceptualizing the policy alternatives, reconsidering the criteria, reassessing the outcomes, and reevaluating the trade-offs from the perspective that the selected policy alternative is the best. The storytelling must consider the audience, communication medium, and narrative story that connects the policy decision to the audience (Bardach & Patashnik, 2016).

Logical-Positivist Model

The logical-positivist model, also known as the behavioral or scientific approach, uses a deductive reasoning approach to policy analysis. The logical-positivist model begins with a theory or theoretical framework that guides the policy analysis inquiry process. The analyst then generates a model, and hypothesis testing examines the propositional relationships of the theoretical model. Data are collected and analyzed using either comparative or correlative measures, and findings are reported. This process is very similar to the research or scientific method process (Lester & Stewart, 2007).

Participatory Policy Analysis

Participatory policy analysis (PPA) is a model that maximizes the democratic process. PPA uses a model that seeks input from participants to ensure that the ideals of a deliberative democracy are included in the generation of policy alternatives. This policy analysis model directly engages the constituents into the policymaking and analysis processes (Smith & Larimer, 2016).

Forecasting Model

The forecasting model of policy analysis focuses on an assessment of health technology. This model involves policy analysis with the perspective of technology adoption. Forecasting requires that the policy analyst accept the context of the analysis while avoiding the biases within the context. This model consists of forecasting cost and efficacy of technology innovation. If the policy involves technology and technology innovation, the forecasting model may be used alone or in combination with other policy analysis models. There are six levels of technological forecasting involved in the policy analysis. These levels must each be analyzed in the forecasting model:

- The specific intervention;
- Alternative interventions that achieve the same purpose, cost, and efficacy;

- Technical accomplishments and requirements;
- Social and economic effects possible with the technical accomplishments;
- Social and economic effects predicted to result from the technical accomplishments; and
- Secondary and indirect effects of the predicted technical accomplishments (McLaughlin & McLaughlin, 2015).

The recommended methods of forecasting are:

- Gathering expert opinion;
- Time series analysis of data over time;
- Sampling potential users and conducting surveys;
- Correlation and causal modeling to predict outcomes; and
- Simulation and system modeling to evaluate the interaction of multiple variables. (Gilfillan, 1952; McLaughlin & McLaughlin, 2015)

Political Feasibility

The political feasibility model analyzes the right fit between the policy ideas and the values and interest of the stakeholders or constituents. This model focuses more on the political adoptability of the policy than the policy content. Political feasibility model measures the policy actor's ability, in a specific period of time, to influence activities to impact the adoption and implementation of policy. The actor's level of influence is known as political leverage. Four sets of variables frame the thinking of political feasibility:

- Main actors—most politically influential persons and what they intend (for example, at the federal level, the main actors are congressional members, president, or other equivalent executive; nongovernmental main actors are interest groups, media, scientists, and other experts)
- Other inputs such as political climate, state of the economy, public opinion, and technological capabilities (this includes election cycle, constituent relations, campaign and fundraising activities and supporters, political party and interest group agendas, economy, political trading of favors and support, legislative body adjournment activities and timing, personal issues of legislators, and unexpected events)

- Interplay of main actors and other inputs; and
- Threshold for adoption (McLaughlin & McLaughlin, 2015; Dror, 1969).

The political feasibility mode emphasizes the importance of the authorizing environments to policy adoption. The authorizing environment refers to the main actors from whom authorization must be received in order to survive a political environment and succeed. The methods used to analyze the political feasibility uses a force field analysis, which consists of assessing the driving forces (for) and the restraining forces (against) of the issue and the policy.

The most politically feasible solutions often involve the "client politics," in which there is strong advocate support from the clients of the policy. Stakeholder analysis is an essential assessment parameter of the political feasibility model (McLaughlin & McLaughlin, 2015) and is critical to policy analysis.

Economic Viability

Policy formulation frequently involves the allocation and appropriation of scarce resources. The economic viability model analyzes policy from the economic and financial perspective. The process to conduct an economic viability analysis includes:

- Define the issue;
- Agree on the intervention and its effectiveness;
- Agree on mechanism of implementation;
- Select the analytical approach—what impact will the proposed policy have on supply and demand for services? (approaches to consider—cost-effectiveness analysis, return on investment, internal rate of return)
  - Agree on the resources required
    - Determine the relevant costs
  - Agree on the outcome produced
    - Determine the value of the outcomes produced
- Calculate discount and inflation adjustments for future cost and benefits;
- Determine and plan for important uncertainties;
- Compute the ratios;
- Identify the financing models;
- Consider distributional effects; and
- Compare with competing alternatives (McLaughlin & McLaughlin, 2015).

Value Analysis

The value analysis model focuses on taking into account the values important to the policy. These values may or may not be considered during political processes but should be assessed as a component of a robust policy analysis. Values to be considered are:

- Equitable access;
- Efficiency and value;
- Privacy and confidentiality;
- Informed consent;
- Personal responsibility;
- Quality, variability, and malpractice reform;
- Professional ethics;
- Consumer sovereignty;
- Social welfare;
- Rationing; and
- Process equity (McLaughlin & McLaughlin, 2015).

Five "E" Model

The five "E" model proposes a simple policy analysis based on five essential variables:

- Effectiveness;
- Efficiency;
- Ethical considerations;
- Evaluation of alternative policy options; and
- Establishment of positive recommendations for change and what is feasible to be established (Kirst-Ashman, 2016).

Policy Analysis Process

The policy analysis process includes both intuitive and empiric components. The policy analysis process may involve one or more of the policy frameworks discussed above within the policy analysis plan. Smith and Larimer (2016) describe the policy analysis process as an inquiry process that uses multiple methods of information gathering to produce policy-relevant information. The policy analysis process proposed by Smith and Larimer includes:

- Defining the problem
- Identifying the alternative policy course of actions

- Linking potential policies to outcomes
- Estimating the outcomes from each policy alternative
- Comparing the greatest impact and outcomes that will be generated among the various policy alternatives
- Selecting the most preferred policy alternative with the greatest potential impact and outcomes

A simple method for executing this process might be:

- Write down each potential policy decision or policy solution.
- Divide the paper in half under each potential policy decision or solution. Write the pros and cons for each policy decision or solution with the pros on one side and the cons on the other.
- Add a third column along with the pros and cons. In the third column, assign weights to each of the pros and cons, reflecting the level of importance or desirability.
- Balance the pros and cons—strike out each pro and each con that cancel each other.
- Analyze the pros and cons to determine which side has the most weight.
- Use the final weights of the pros and cons of each policy solution to inform the decision-making process (Smith & Larimer, 2016).

The following framework has been described by Hewison (2007) as a foundation for a nurse manager's analysis of policy. The framework below was proposed for nursing but can be used to guide other healthcare professionals. The framework is:

- Identify the level of policy analysis: macro-, meso-, or micro-level;
- Use a nursing meta-paradigm to frame policy analysis that focuses on
  - Person (humanistic perspective)
  - Health
  - Environment
  - Nursing or other health professional discipline
- Examine the policy environment
  - Understanding of policy environment
  - Response to organization's policy environment
  - Manner in which organization's policy environment is shaped
- Develop an understanding of the manner in which the policy is developed

- Examine original sources of information generated during the policy development process to include parliamentary or legislative speeches, debates, committee minutes, official reports, government reports and documents, statistics, etc. Each policy document should be analyzed to:
  - Develop a summary description of the main policy aims or objectives
  - Establish the status of the policy document in comparison to other relevant documents
  - Link policy document to other previous and associated policy documents
  - Identify central policy themes or tenets
  - Identify the area of practice impacted (can use nursing or the respective discipline's meta-paradigm) (Hewison, 2007).

Problem or Issue Analysis

An initial step in policy analysis is to analyze the problem or issue framing the need for policy development and formulation. Problem or issue analysis is a systematic process used to describe and explain the interrelationships of multiple antecedents or background variables affecting a societal concern (Porche, 2003).

A critical step in problem or issue analysis is distinguishing whether the area of concern is a real *problem* or merely an *issue* of concern. The ability to differentiate among problem situations, policy problems, and policy issues is critical to determining the most appropriate policy solutions. Problem or issue differentiation is dependent on stakeholders, constituencies, and policymakers' perceptions of the area of concern. A policy failure can be the result of inaccurately stating or characterizing the problem or issue. In addition, areas of policy concern that are *issues* can eventually evolve into what is considered a policy *problem*. The first step in discerning if the area of concern is a problem or issue is to explore the area's placement within the policy agenda framework.

Issue Analysis Process

The differentiation of a problem and issue requires an analysis of the respective area of concern. This analysis is a 12-step process. During the analysis, debate and inquiry into the issue are encouraged, thus engendering insightfulness, inquisitiveness, and refusal to accept simple answers for complex queries

(Porche, 2003). The following steps outline a process for the analysis of an area of concern and differentiation of the area as a problem or issue:

Identification of the area of concern. Identification of the area of concern clarifies the underlying and related concerns. Causes, potential effects, and interested parties are identified. The manner in which the area of concern may receive attention on the policy agenda is analyzed.

Background. The context of the concern is analyzed through an assessment of social, economic, ethical, political, and legal factors that are forcing the area of concern to rise to the level of the policy agenda.

Stakeholders and constituents. All direct and indirect stakeholders and constituents are identified.

Position analysis. Stakeholders' and governmental officials' (in the executive, legislative, and judicial branches of government as necessary) positions on the area of concern are analyzed.

Political analysis. The political climate is analyzed.

Statement of concern. A narrative statement is written delineating the boundaries of the concern. The concern statement may be altered throughout this analysis process.

Interaction analysis. The interrelationships of this area of concern with other issues or problems on the policy agenda are analyzed.

Policy identification. Potential policy options and alternatives are analyzed.

Outcome identification. Desired outcomes are identified.

Policy recommendation. The optimal policy solution for the area of concern is recommended.

Impact assessment. The depth and breadth of the area of concern is analyzed in terms of the magnitude of this impact, the possible attachment of the concern to other policy issues and problems, political context of the concern, and the potential for a finding of *issue* versus *problem*. A *problem* will have the greatest magnitude of potential impact, a network of attachment to other issues and problems, highly charged political attention, constituency and stakeholder readiness for action, and placement on the policy agenda for action.

Determination. Determination is the final labeling and framing of the area of concern as an issue or problem. It is contextual and changes as the policy agenda and political climate changes.

The final determination of whether the public health area of concern is an issue or problem is largely decided by interested parties and policymakers within the context of the area of concern. The magnitude of the concern frequently differentiates issue from problem. An area of concern considered a problem that needs policy intervention is frequently subjected to a detailed problem analysis. This process further structures the problem to facilitate policy development and formulation. There is some redundancy in the process of conducting an analysis of issues and problems, but this only leads to further clarification of the area of concern (Porche, 2003).

Problem Analysis Process

Problem identification consists of the following four steps: problem sensing, problem search, problem definition, and problem specification. Problem sensing is the recognition and felt existence of a problem. The problem sensing step analyzes the problem situation. The problem search step discovers the multiple representations of the problem, multiple stakeholders involved, and multiple worldviews of the problem. Problem definition formally characterizes the problem as a substantive problem. In the problem definition step, the problem is characterized in basic and general terms, and a conceptual framework of the problem is presented. The last step, problem specification, formalizes the problem through agenda setting, identifying constituents' needs, conducting public opinion polls, and assessing the opposition's position and strength in relation to the problem.

Several methods are used to structure or define a problem including the following:

Boundary analysis. Identify the boundaries of the problem by posing the questions: What are the various facets of the problem? Who are the interested stakeholders and constituents? What are the multiple views regarding the problem?

Concept analysis. Analyze the multiple concepts presented and discussed in the problem.

Hierarchy analysis. Analyze the potential causes as possible, plausible, or actionable.

Synectics. Analyze the similarities and differences of the problems.

Brainstorming. Use this technique to generate goals, ideas, and policy strategies.

Multiple perspectives analysis. Generate multiple explanations of the problem and potential policy strategies.

Assumption analysis. Identify and synthesize multiple assumptions underlying problem and policy solutions.

Argumentation mapping. Assess the accuracy of each assumption.

Problem structuring is critical to policy development and formulation. Problem structuring identifies the problem from the eye of the beholder, discovers and analyzes hidden assumptions about the problem, diagnoses possible causes, maps policy solutions, synthesizes conflicting views, and assists in designing new policy outcomes. The critical nature of problem structuring ensures that the correct problem is identified and that it is correctly characterized and solved through the development and formulation of the correct policy. The policy solution must match the problem.

Policy Analysis Methods

Policy analysis methods are the processes used to collect information and data for the purpose of analyzing policy and political variables influencing policy. Policy analysis methods include both qualitative and quantitative methods. Qualitative methods include but are not limited to case studies, interviews, and focus groups. Quantitative methods include but are not limited to surveys, questionnaires, and secondary data analysis.

Bill or Law Analysis

A bill is proposed legislation that is being considered by a legislative body and executive officer (president, governor, mayor, etc.) who has authority to approve the bill. A law is legislation that has been approved or passed by a legislative body and approved or signed by an executive officer. During policy analysis, it may be necessary to analyze bills or laws related to the policy issue or problem that are currently in effect, in the approval process, being formulated, or being considered for formulation. **Box 10-3** presents basic components of a bill or law. Bill or law analysis is a systematic process to critically appraise the components of the bill or law. This analysis can identify areas of strength, weaknesses, limitations, and opportunities for modification or change of existing law. A bill or law analysis is written in a narrative summative format. **Box 10-4** presents the components of a bill or law analysis process and the format for a narrative summative report on a bill or law. An analysis of a bill is not a one-time process. Bills must continually be analyzed during the approval process. The analysis should be succinct, concise, objective, and analytical. Attention should be given to the words *shall* and *may*. Each has a specific meaning: *shall* means an action is statutorily required; *may* means an action is considered optional.

- Conduct comprehensive bill or law search to identify legislation on the policy issue or problem area—includes legislation at the national,

---

BOX 10-3   COMPONENTS OF BILL OR LAW

- Legislative body and session number
- Bill status
  - Floor amendment—changes made to a bill when it is debated on the floor of the full House or Senate
  - Engrossed—bill has been passed by the chamber in which it was filed, all amendments are incorporated
  - Enrolled—bill has passed both chambers of the legislature in identical form and is prepared for approval signatures
  - Title
- Bill or law number
- Statement of intent—how the legislation intends to solve a problem
- Body of the bill
- Rulemaking authority—what is the approval process or who has authority to approve?
- Author's name—name of individual who composed legislation
- Sponsor's name—name of individual introducing the legislation
- Articles—an article is one subject area
- Legislative history—chronologically states the actions taken on the bill or law
- Fiscal impact statement—cost associated with implementing the bill or law
- Signature lines
- Effective date

---

  state, or local level and in surrounding geographical areas or by other organizations, associations, or institutions

- Analyze if the title is representative of the policy intent and bill or law
- Identify and critically summarize position papers, resolutions, policy briefs, and other documents that are source documents or that summarize the proposed bill or law
- Identify and describe the policy issue or problem area intended to be impacted
- Summarize existing legislation on the policy issue or problem

---

BOX 10-4   BILL OR LAW ANALYSIS PROCESS AND REPORT FORMAT

- Identify the policy instruments for the implementation of the policy intent
- Trace the bill or law's history and amendments; identify what changes were made by whom and what approvals were secured and by whom
- Conduct a cost to benefit analysis on the bill or law's fiscal impact
- Identify opponents and supporters of the bill
- What executive agency is responsible for implementation?
- What executive agency or body is responsible for policy evaluation?
- Read edited content—content added is generally underlined; content deleted from an existing law is generally enclosed in brackets and marked through with a line; content that is added to replace existing language is placed immediately before the old content and underlined, with old content in parentheses and striked through

---

A Summative Policy Analysis Process

Policy analysis is conducted on developed policy for a variety of reasons. Policy analysis facilitates a clearer understanding of the policy's intentions, expected outcomes, and interrelationships with other policies. Policy analysis is also conducted by regulatory agencies as a measure of rule making to implement required programs and to initiate policy modifications.

Policy analysis is a systematic process using methods that critically appraise the extent to which the policy is a viable and implementable solution to a problem and whether the policy will be acceptable to affected stakeholders and constituents given the current social fabric of society (Taub, 2002). There is a lack of consensus on the processes with which to structure the public health policy analysis process. The author recommends the following process as one possible method of conducting policy analysis (Porche, 2003):

> *Critical policy review.* The policy needs to be read repeatedly until there is clear understanding of the policy's intent and the various directives buried in the policy. The essential components of the policy should be outlined and correlated to current and past issues or problems. The policy should be reviewed for inconsistencies or gaps. The critical policy review should include an analysis of any components of the policy that appear to be unrelated amendments to the policy. The boundaries

of the policy should be defined during this process. The policy boundaries inform the policy search process and parameters of the policy search.

Policy search. Conduct a comprehensive policy search that focuses on the problem. Policies that are affected by, or related to, the public health policy should also be analyzed. The related impact of one policy on another, or contradictions in two related policies should be assessed. Each of the related policies should undergo policy analysis.

Historical analysis. The time period in which the policy was developed should be reviewed in relation to social, economic, political, and environmental factors that influenced the policy. The values, beliefs, and political affiliations of the policymakers who drafted the policy at that time should be reviewed. Refer to Appendices A and B to determine the political context present during the respective time period at the national level.

Authorization analysis. Analyze the authorization legislation for the respective policy. Determine the scope of the authorization and the executive agency responsible for the implementation of the policy.

Budgetary analysis. Analyze the appropriation of funds to support the policy. Determine which components of the policy had the largest appropriation of resources. This provides some idea of legislative priorities in regard to the policy.

Public health issue and problem analysis. The issues surrounding the policy should be analyzed. The analysis should also address the problems identified in the policy as it currently exists.

Stakeholder and constituency identification. Actual or potential stakeholders, constituents, and special-interest groups should be identified. The political positions of these groups regarding the problem and policy under review should be analyzed.

SWOT analysis. Identify the strengths, weaknesses, opportunities, and threats (SWOT) to the potential policy. The SWOT analysis should focus on the current analysis of the problem and the viability and adequacy of the existing policy to solve the problem.

PESTEL analysis. A PESTEL (political, economic, social, technological, environmental, legal) analysis is used for macro-environmental factors that may affect the organization. **Figure 10-2** outlines the elements of a PESTEL analysis.

Gap analysis. The provisions of the current policy in relation to the current needs should be appraised. Any gaps between the current policy

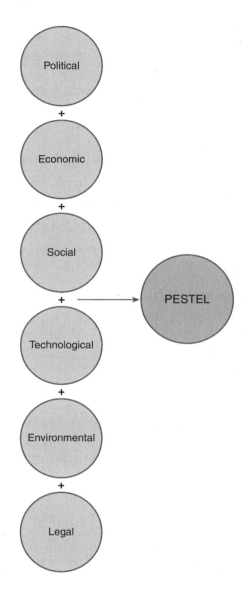

Figure 10-2   PESTEL (Political, Economic, Social, Technological, Environmental, Legal) Elements

and the needs to address the current issue or problem should be identified as potential areas for policy development, formulation, or modification.

Executive summation. A concluding brief summation of each of these steps should be developed and presented to policymakers. The final component of the executive summation should include recommendations for policy development, formulation, or modification. The final recommendations should include suggestions for authorization and allocation legislation. In addition, recommendations for the assignment of the implementation to the respective executive agency and the responsible legislative committee for the policy evaluation should be included.

Prioritization. Recommendations provided in the executive summation should be prioritized for policy development, formulation, modification, and implementation.

Summary Points

- Policy analysis provides valuable data that can assist with policy modifications.
- Policy formulation and modification is not the end of the policymaking process.
- Policy analysis is a strategy used to identify current policy issues and to assist in constructing policy formulation and modification strategies.
- The product of policy analysis is a clear description of the problem, identification of policy solutions or alternatives, courses of action with expected outcomes, and a contextual understanding of the policy problem and comprehensive understanding of the policy.
- Macro-, meso-, or micro-level policy analysis can be utilized.
- Analysis *of* policy is a retrospective process that explores the determination of policy and what constituted the policy.
- Analysis *for* policy is prospective and explores what may result if a respective policy is formulated and implemented.
- The substantive model analyzes the policy from the perspective of the policy issue.
- Eightfold path describes an iterative problem-solving process used to clarify the policy problem and determine policy solutions.

- The forecasting model of policy analysis focuses on an assessment of health technology.
- The political feasibility model analyzes the right fit between the policy ideas and the values and interest of the stakeholders or constituents.
- The economic viability model analyzes policy from the economic and financial perspectives.
- The value analysis model focuses on taking into account the values important to the policy.
- Five "E" model assesses effectiveness, efficiency, ethical considerations, evaluation of policy options, and establishment of positive change.
- Logical-positivist model uses a deductive reasoning approach to policy analysis.
- Participatory policy analysis (PPA) uses a model that seeks input from participants to ensure that the ideals of a deliberative democracy are included in the generation of policy alternatives.
- The policy analysis process is an inquiry process that uses multiple methods of information gathering to produce policy-relevant information.
- Problem or issue analysis is a systematic process used to describe and explain the interrelationships of multiple antecedents or background variables affecting a societal concern.
- A critical step in problem or issue analysis is distinguishing whether the area of concern is a real *problem* or merely an *issue* of concern.
- The final determination of whether the public health area of concern is an *issue* or *problem* is largely decided by interested parties and policy-makers within the context of the area of concern.
- Problem identification consists of the following four steps: problem sensing, problem search, problem definition, and problem specification.
- Problem structuring identifies the problem from the eye of the beholder, discovers and analyzes hidden assumptions about the problem, diagnoses possible causes, maps policy solutions, synthesizes conflicting views, and assists in designing new policy outcomes.
- Policy analysis is a systematic process using methods that critically appraise the extent to which the policy is a viable and implementable solution to a problem and whether the policy will be acceptable to affected stakeholders and constituents given the current social fabric of society.

References

Bardach, E., & Patashnik, E. M. (2016). *A practical guide for policy analysis: The eightfold path to more effective problem solving* (5th ed.). Thousand Oaks, CA: CQ Press.

Buse, K., Mays, N., & Walt, G. (2012). *Making health policy* (2nd ed.). Berkshire, UK: Open University Press.

Dye, T. (2017). *Understanding public policy* (15th ed.). Boston, MA: Pearson.

Hewison, A. (2007). Policy analysis: A framework for nurse managers. *Journal of Nursing Management*, *15*(7), 693–699.

Hudson, J., & Lowe, S. (2008). *Understanding the policy process: Analysing welfare policy and practice* (3rd ed.). Bristol, UK: The Policy Press, University of Bristol.

Kirst-Ashman, K. (2016). *Introduction to social work & social welfare: Critical thinking perspectives*. Empowerment series. Independence, KY: Cengage Learning.

Lester, J., & Stewart, J. (2007). *Public policy: An evolutionary approach* (3rd ed.). Stamford, CT: Wadsworth/Thomson Learning.

Longest, B. (2015). *Health policymaking in the United States* (6th ed.). New York, NY: Health Administration Press.

McLaughlin, C., & McLaughlin, C. (2015). *Health policy analysis: An interdisciplinary approach* (2nd ed.). Burlington, MA: Jones & Bartlett Learning.

Porche, D. (2003). *Public & community health nursing practice: A population-based approach*. Thousand Oaks, CA: Sage Publications.

Smith, K. B., & Larimer, C. W. (Eds.). (2016). *The public policy theory primer* (3rd ed.). Boulder, CO: Westview Press.

Taub, L. (2002). A policy analysis of access to health care inclusive of cost, quality, and scope of services. *Policy, Politics and Nursing Practice*, *3*(2), 167–176.

Policy Research and Evaluation

R esearch is the planned, systematic collection and analysis of data that answer relevant questions within the existing state of science. Research results in generalizable knowledge. The research community consists of researchers—scientists, scholars, practitioners, academicians, students of various disciplines, and constituents. The research community has the ability to influence policymakers through several processes. The general processes in which a researcher can influence policymakers are documentation and dissemination of research findings, policy analysis, and prescription for the use of research findings through the communication of research implications.

Research is a tool that can be used to influence policy and policymakers. Research data can be used to influence the perceived impact of an issue and provide baseline data from which to evaluate policy impact and outcomes. Both quantitative and qualitative data can provide critical information to influence policymaking. Hanney, Gonzalez-Block, Buxton, and Kogan (2003) assert that research-informed policies are a secondary research output that can later be utilized as data for systematic review to inform future policy.

Policy Research

Policy research can be used to analyze a problem or as a means to further define the boundaries and context of an identified problem. Policy research is a tool to generate, gather, and disseminate information that informs the actions of policymakers. Weiss and Bucavalas (1980) propose four characteristics that define what is considered useful research by policymakers. These four characteristics are research quality, conformity to expectations, action orientation, and challenge to the status quo. Therefore, policymakers are seeking not just to find solutions in policy research but also to challenge the current political and policy paradigm. Six recommendations to increase policymakers' use of policy research are:

- Understand information needs.
- Understand the policymaking process.
- Target research findings to specific audiences and provide action-oriented policy recommendations from the research findings.
- Communicate research findings in understandable terms.
- Connect research findings to existing knowledge or expectations.
- Provide the context of the research findings and promote public debate of the findings.

Policy research consists of study that relates to or promotes the public interest and produces generalizable knowledge to the larger population. Policy research is a broad term used to describe the comprehensive and systematic intellectual approach to the examination of problems.

Researchers and policymakers are sometimes considered to travel in parallel universes. There needs to be increased communication between researchers and policymakers. A critical challenge for the researcher is translating scientific evidence into an appropriate, substantial, and effective public policy (Brownson, Royer, Ewing, & McBride, 2006). Brownson and coworkers (2006) identify eight major challenges for both the scientific and policymaking community:

- Clash of cultures;
- Timing of policy decisions and time required to complete research study, time from research results to publication;
- Ambiguous findings—policymakers may desire precise data and estimates;
- Balance of advocacy and objectivity in the research process;
- Personal demands;
- Information overload from multiple studies and literature;
- Lack of relevant data; and
- Language of policymaking and science.

In addition, to the suggestions provided above to promote the use of research for policymaking, Brownson and coworkers (2006) propose the following recommendations to close the gap between researchers and policymakers:

- Publish findings early in abbreviated form—short research briefs, press releases, write editorials on findings;
- Provide testimony on findings;
- Educate legislative staffers on research findings;

- Develop and utilize policy surveillance systems to identify policy issues that can be linked to research findings; and
- Cultivate political champions for your research.

Policy Research Process

The research process is a decision-making process based on the scientific process. The scientific process consists of posing a question, conducting background research on the subject area (reviewing literature), developing a hypothesis, testing the hypothesis, analyzing the data, drawing conclusions from the findings, and communicating the results. Fain (2013) proposes that the research process consists of five phases: selecting and defining the problem, selecting a research design, methods, data analysis, and research utilization. **Figure 11-1** outlines a summary of the phases of the research process.

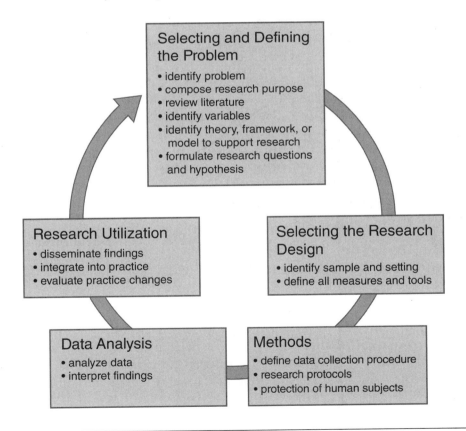

Figure 11-1   The Research Process

The policy research process integrates the research and policymaking processes (Wakefield, 2001). Policy research can be utilized to identify policy solutions or to generate knowledge in relation to information gaps regarding policy issues. Policy research involves quantitative, qualitative, and mixed-method research designs. The research design selected is determined by the policy research question posed and the knowledge gap. Some policy research may be evaluative-type research of a program implemented from a policy, or action-type research focusing on the behaviors of politics, policymakers, and individuals implementing the policy. The following process is suggested to facilitate the policy research process:

- Define the policy issue and the policy through a comprehensive review of the related relevant issues. The first step of a policy research project may be the conducting of an analysis of the existing or proposed policies.
- Conduct a review of scientific literature and statistical data.
- Develop research questions, study purpose, and hypotheses as appropriate. Some research variables to consider in policy research are information regarding policy environment, policy action agenda, political actions and behaviors of policymakers and constituents and constituent groups, public opinion, and communication patterns.
- Select the research design.
- Select the research methods.
- Select data analysis methods.
- Propose study findings and results.
- Identify limitations of the study.
- Identify further recommendations to include practice implications, policy solutions, and future area of policy research. The research recommendations should be written to provide direction to policymakers regarding policy solutions or strategies to resolve the policy issue based on study findings.
- Disseminate findings through scholarly publications, oral presentations, and distribution to appropriate policymakers, legislative bodies, and executive agencies; produce reports that can be posted in the public domain; inform media of findings; prepare testimonies on findings.

The different processes for political decision making and research further create a gap between researchers communicating with policymakers and

TABLE 11-1   COMPARISON OF SCIENTIFIC AND POLITICAL DECISION-MAKING PROCESSES

SCIENTIFIC DECISION-MAKING PROCESS	POLITICAL DECISION-MAKING PROCESS
• Identify problem	• Identify problem
• Develop hypothesis	• Make a political judgment on the issue
• Organize study	• Build political support
• Conduct study	• Propose new policy initiative
• Analyze data	• Assess constituents and stakeholder support
• Publish results	• Assign resources

policymakers using research. **Table 11-1** outlines the two parallel processes of decision making in science and political processes (Brownson et al., 2006).

Research Designs and Methods

A research design is the overall blueprint or plan that outlines the process by which the research will be conducted. Research methods are the specific techniques the researcher uses to collect data. The research design and methods selected are determined by the supporting research and evidence, research questions, resources, and human subject protection factors. The research design can be qualitative, quantitative, or mixed-method.

Qualitative research is embodied by observations and analysis captured in words, statements, and narratives. Qualitative designs or approaches are described in **Box 11-1**. Various methods are used to collect qualitative data (**Box 11-2**). Qualitative data analysis involves the analysis of words and behaviors. **Box 11-3** presents a review of qualitative data analysis techniques. Qualitative research designs can be used in policy research for analyzing elected official speeches, examining campaign speeches, and conducting interviews with elected officials, other policymakers, and constituents and stakeholders.

Quantitative research collects numerical data from a sample with the intent of generalizing to a larger population. **Box 11-4** presents a summary of

---

BOX 11-1   QUALITATIVE DESIGNS/APPROACHES

- Phenomenology—describe the lived experience
- Ethnography—describe cultural characteristics
- Grounded theory—theory development
- Historical—describe or examine past events as a means to understand current events
- Biographical—in-depth study of one individual
- Case study—an in-depth analysis of one person, family, group, community, or institution

---

BOX 11-2   QUALITATIVE METHODS

- Interview
  - Individual
  - Focus group
- Observation
  - Direct
  - Indirect
- Document analysis
- Recorded review
  - Narratives or stories
  - Archives
  - Logs
- Audio or videotape
- Field notes
- Journaling

BOX 11-3   QUALITATIVE DATA ANALYSIS TECHNIQUES

- Classification and ranking of data
- Thematic analysis
- Constant comparative analysis
- Narrative analysis
- Conceptual approach
  - Concept formation, development, reduction, modification, and integration
- Content analysis of written data

BOX 11-4   QUANTITATIVE RESEARCH DESIGNS

- Experimental—test hypotheses
  - ◆ Three essential elements—control group, randomization, and intervention
- Quasi-experimental—lacks a randomization of true experimental design
- Descriptive—observes, describes, or documents what exists
- Correlational—investigates the relationships between and among variables
- Survey—uses interviews or questionnaires to generate data
- Evaluation—determines if the policy achieved the expected goals, objectives, or outcomes

---

quantitative research designs. Quantitative research analysis involves mathematical and statistical data analysis using descriptive and inferential statistics. Quantitative policy research can include opinion surveys, satisfaction ratings, and campaign polling data.

Mixed-methods research integrates quantitative and qualitative research designs to answer a research question. There are six mixed-method design strategies (**Box 11-5**).

Other components of a research design are sampling, setting, instrumentation or measurement, data collection, data analysis, and human subject protection. Sampling is the process of selecting an individual from a population's sampling frame. There are various types of sampling techniques (**Box 11-6**). Setting is the place in which the research study occurs. Instrumentation involves the measurement or operationalization of linking study variables to numerical data. Two critical requirements of measurement are reliability and validity. Reliability is the extent to which the instrument produces stable and consistent results over time. Validity is the extent to which an instrument measures the concepts it is expected to measure. Data collection draws from either primary sources or existing sources. Primary data are collected by the researcher for the purpose of the research study. Existing data, also known as secondary data, have already been collected or are obtained through sources that already exist. Human subject protection focuses on assuring ethical practices in accordance with the ethical principles of respect for persons, beneficence, and justice.

BOX 11-5   MIXED-METHOD DESIGN STRATEGIES

- Sequential explanatory
  - Explain or interpret findings of a quantitative study
  - Collect and analyze quantitative data after the collection and analysis of qualitative data
- Sequential exploratory
  - Explore a phenomenon
  - Collect and analyze qualitative data after quantitative data collection and analysis
- Sequential transformative
  - Collect either quantitative or qualitative data first, then integrate both quantitative and qualitative data
- Concurrent triangulation
  - Use two or more methods to confirm, cross-validate, or corroborate findings
  - Collect data concurrently
- Concurrent nested
  - Use one primary approach, either qualitative or quantitative, with the other approach embedded into the primary approach
- Concurrent transformative
  - Use theoretical perspective to guide all methodologies

BOX 11-6   SAMPLING TECHNIQUES

- Random—each subject has equal and independent chance of selection
- Systematic (nth technique)—every nth subject or record is selected
- Stratified—subjects are divided into strata based on a specific characteristic, then they are sampled from each stratum
- Convenience or opportunity—sample subjects who are readily available are selected
- Purposive—subjects are selected based on a special characteristic, experience, or knowledge of the group sampled
- Quota—data is gathered from subjects possessing identified characteristic and in the same quota

Regardless of the policy research question, design, or method, policy research is expected to be significant; relevant; aligned with policy issues, problems, and potential solutions; timely; and unbiased. Policy influences research and research influences policy in an iterative manner. The research should be considering the possible policy solutions aligned with the research results and the policymaker should identify areas of research to generate generalizable knowledge for the larger population.

Policy Research Extramural Funding

Extramural funding occurs from an external agency or source. Numerous funding opportunities exist for policy research. Chapter 17 describes the various policy institutes, their policy agendas, and funding opportunities. In addition to policy institutes, executive agencies are a source of funding for policy research.

Research Utilization

Research utilization is a systematic process by which research data and knowledge formulated from research findings are integrated into practice (Fain, 2013). The practice arena includes but is not limited to the clinical practice environment. The practice arena includes the practice of developing and formulating policy, which is known as the practice of policymaking. The utilization of research is dependent upon the last stage of the research process, research dissemination. **Table 11-2** summarizes several research utilization models.

Research Utilization Models

Research utilization models provide a framework from which to incorporate the use of research findings into the policymaking process. Some framework models for research utilization are the classic/purist/knowledge-driven model, problem-solving/engineering/policy-driven model, interactive/social interaction model, enlightenment/percolation/limestone model, political model, and tactical model. The classic/purist/knowledge-driven model uses a linear sequence of policymaking activities. In this model, research generates knowledge that then drives policymaking decisions. The problem-solving/engineering/policy-driven model also uses a linear sequence. It begins with problem identification by the

TABLE 11-2   NURSING RESEARCH UTILIZATION MODELS

The following are some select nursing research utilization models. The process of each respective model is briefly summarized:

MODEL	PROCESS
Western Interstate Commission for Higher Education	• Problem identification • Research retrieval • Research review • Development of research-based care
Conduct and Utilization of Research in Nursing	• Problem identification • Assessment of knowledge base • Design of practice change • Clinical trial • Adoption or rejection of change • Diffusion of innovation into practice • Institutional change
The Nursing Child Assessment Satellite Training Project	• Recruitment • Translation of research findings • Dissemination of findings • Evaluation

constituent who requests the researcher to explore viable policy solutions. The researcher then explores various policy solutions and recommends the most appropriate policy solution based on research findings. The interactive/social interaction model closely resembles action research. This model proposes interactions between the researchers and users of the data to frame the research questions, and to process and use the research data based on the researcher's and user's needs. The enlightenment/percolation/limestone model proposes the use of research based on the gradual "sedimentation" of insight, theories, concepts, and perspectives. In the political model, politics influences all aspects of the research process from problem identification to research dissemination and implementation. Lastly, the tactical model uses research under the duress of pressure to act on an issue. In the tactical model, policymakers act by commissioning a study on the issue of concern. This is sometimes considered a political maneuver prior to engaging in the policymaking process.

Hanney and colleagues (2003) propose a model that places policymaking within the research utilization process. The model is described to exist within the context of the reservoir of knowledge and the political and professional environments of the wider society. The stages of the model are briefly described below:

- Stage 0—This stage initiates the research needs assessment. Stage 0 interfaces with Stage 1 with project specification, selection, and commissioning.
- Stage I—This stage consists of the research inputs: prior knowledge gained forms the needs assessment data and previous research findings.
- Stage II—Stage II consists of the research process.
- Stage III—This stage consists of the primary outputs from the research (data) that directly impacts the contextual knowledge reservoir that exists. This stage interfaces with stage IV through the dissemination of the findings.
- Stage IV—This stage represents policymakers using the research data to inform policy and serves as a secondary output of the research.
- Stage V—This stage focuses on the application of research findings or utilization of research data in practice.
- Stage VI—This stage represents the cumulative final outcomes from the research that results from the implementation of the findings into practice and the resultant evaluation data, and the evaluation data from the implemented policy that resulted from the original research data findings (Hanney, Gonzalez-Block, Buxton, & Kogan, 2003).

Several nursing scientists have proposed models of research utilization that can be used in the policymaking process. These nursing research utilization models can be used by other healthcare professional disciplines engaged in the translation of science into clinical practice. Regardless of the research utilization model implemented, the basic process of research utilization consists of:

- Problem identification, clarification, and refinement;
- Assembling the research literature;
- Critiquing the research findings;
- Synthesizing the research findings;
- Assessing the applicability of the synthesized findings;

- Implementing the research-based innovation; and
- Evaluating the innovation (Fain, 2013).

Legal Research Process

The legal research process provides the foundation for a lawsuit and provides valuable information that can inform policymaking. Through the legal research process, legal policy is identified. Legal nurse consultants, paralegal professionals, and attorneys perform legal research as a means to identify case law. In addition, legal research provides information regarding the assessment of liability, value of a case, and approach to evaluate opposing counsel's trial strategy.

The legal research process includes searching for relevant case law. Each case reviewed during the legal research process contains information regarding the case name, case citation (decision date, docket number, and court name), brief case summary, headnotes or subject notes, attorney names, judge names, and the text of the case opinion. In the process of searching for case law, it is critical that the legal research process explore if the case law remains viable. The research process should explore whether the existing case law has been overturned, remanded, or cited by more recent case law. The legal research process consists of exploring relevant statutes at the local, state, and federal level that may be relevant to the issue being investigated (Garner, 2014).

The Internet as a Research Tool

The Internet serves as an excellent source of information without geographical boundaries. The Internet provides access to interlinked data without any hierarchical structure, but users will find valuable factual information mixed with misinformation. The utilization of the Internet as a research tool requires that the user discern quality information from misinformation. **Box 11-7** provides a list of criteria that can be used to evaluate Internet sites.

Policy Evaluation

Policy evaluation measures the overall effectiveness and extent to which a policy has achieved its objectives (Dye, 2017). Policy evaluation is a systematic, empirical assessment of the effects developed from the policies (Nachmias, 1979; Porche, 2003). This evaluative process focuses on measuring the impact of a policy and the implementation of that policy as intended by the policymakers. Policy evaluation poses the questions "What have we done?" and "What was the impact and/or outcome?"

BOX 11-7 INTERNET SOURCE EVALUATION CRITERIA

- Website
  - ◆ Title of website is consistent with URL address.
  - ◆ The website domain is consistent with information presented (edu for education, com for company, gov for government, org for an organization, mil for military, and net for network of computer).
  - ◆ Website has stable and active URLs for all links.
- Authorship
  - ◆ The author is cited.
  - ◆ The author's academic credentials, certifications and licenses, and organizational affiliations are noted.
  - ◆ The author's contact information is provided.
  - ◆ Author's curriculum vitae or resume is published.
  - ◆ Author is known in the field.
  - ◆ Author is referenced by another known author or respected professional in the field.
  - ◆ Biographical information is included.
- Analog to peer review
  - ◆ Links to webpage by professor or other recognized professional are seen.
  - ◆ Webpage is included in college course readings.
  - ◆ Another professional organization or society has links to webpage.
  - ◆ Content is referenced by others in the field.
- Timeliness
  - ◆ A copyright date is present.
  - ◆ Revision dates are posted.
- Content
  - ◆ There is evidence of peer review.
  - ◆ Content presents facts or opinions.
  - ◆ Content has appropriate depth and breadth.
  - ◆ Information is consistent with other sources.
  - ◆ Evidence of conflict of interest or bias is not present.
  - ◆ Document presents balanced perspective on the issue.

(continues)

The effect of policy should be measured based on the intent of the policy and impact on the policy's target population. Dye (2017) suggests that evaluation of the policy should focus on its effects on real-world conditions. Real-world effects that should be measured in the evaluation process are (1) impact on the target problem, (2) impact on the targeted group, (3) impact on nontargeted groups (spillover effects), (4) impact on future and immediate conditions of the problem, (5) direct cost in terms of resources devoted, (6) indirect costs, and (7) net analysis of benefits to costs.

Sabatier and Weible (2014) propose that policy evaluation criteria should consist of economic efficiency, equity through fiscal equivalence, redistribution equity, accountability, morality conformance, and adaptability. Economic efficiency is determined by the net benefits associated with the policy allocation or reallocation of resources. Fiscal equivalence is determined by equality between a constituent's contributions to an effort and their benefits derived from the result. Redistribution equity occurs when resources are redistributed to poorer constituents. Accountability represents a sense of responsibility to the constituents whose resources are used and whom the policy should impact. Morality conformance ensures that policies comply with the value system, beliefs, and ethical norms. Lastly, adaptability is the extent to which the policy can be applied to other populations and situations.

The evaluative responsibility for policy may be articulated in the policy. Several strategies are used to evaluate the effectiveness of policy. Dye (2017) identified the most common strategies for conducting a policy evaluation: (1) congressional or oversight committee hearings, (2) annual program reports to Congress or an oversight committee, (3) on-site visits, (4) tracking of program benchmarks, (5) comparison of program to some professional standard, and (6) ongoing evaluation of constituent complaints. In addition, the General Accounting Office (GAO) is an arm of Congress established in 1921 that maintains the authority to audit federally funded programs' operations and finances. The GAO submits its findings to Congress and other oversight committees as appropriate, as an evaluative measure of programs developed and implemented as a result of public health policy (Dye, 2017; Longest, 2015).

Public accountability requires a comprehensive evaluation of the impact of policies in terms of the intent and expected outcomes of the policy. Porche (2003) suggests the following process as a procedure to evaluate policies:

- Conduct a public health policy analysis.
- Identify the goals and objectives of the policy.
- Identify public health data to measure the effectiveness of the public health policy.
- Identify the articulated timelines in the public health policy.
- Collect data on the chronological implementation of the policy.
- Collect public health data indexes that measure the impact of the policy on the public's health.
- Determine the extent to which the public health policy objectives have been met.
- Identify intervening variables or circumstances that may have a negative impact on the maximum effectiveness of the public health policy.
- Provide recommendations to improve the impact of the public health policy.
- Disseminate findings to policymakers, stakeholders, and special-interest groups (Porche, 2003).

Policy Evaluation Models and Process

Policy evaluation provides data that documents the influence of policies on policy issues and problems. In addition, policy evaluation provides data on program outcomes that resulted from the development and implementation of policies that authorized and allocated funds for programs. Decision-making processes and implementation strategies regarding current and future allocation of scarce resources use evaluation data. Three reasons to evaluate programs that are developed as a result of policies, are to provide elected officials and policymakers with evaluation data to demonstrate program accomplishments and provide that the legislative mandates or administrative policy requirements have been met; guide program decision making; and determine the level of improvements in health outcomes that are directly or indirectly linked to the program (Green & Kreuter, 2004).

Monitoring

Monitoring should be included as an essential element in the evaluation plan as it provides continual feedback about the policy. Monitoring is an ongoing measurement, providing information about the policy accomplishments and progress toward the preestablished policy goals, objectives, and outcomes. Program monitoring is defined by Rossi, Lipsey, and Freeman (2004) as a systematic documentation of critical components of program performance that are indicative of whether the program is functioning as the program was planned and intended or by some comparable standard or benchmark. Program monitoring can include such variables as service utilization, program organization, and outcomes. Therefore, this definition regarding program monitoring can serve as the basis for a policy monitoring definition. The following policy monitoring definition is provided to guide policy monitoring activities. Policy monitoring is a systematic process of collecting data related to policy issues or policy that provides a concurrent analysis of the policy issue or policy in relation to the expected goals, objectives, or outcomes of the policy issue or policy (Porche, 2003).

Structure, Process, and Outcome

The structure, process, and outcome model of evaluation was proposed by Donabedian (1996), who provided this evaluation framework based on his management perspective. Structure evaluation assesses the environment in which policy is developed and implemented, and includes measures such as organizational structure, resources and resource allocation, policy adherence, legal requirements, and management and staff qualifications. Process evaluation measures the extent to which the policy is implemented as planned. Outcome evaluation determines the extent to which the policy has achieved the expected goals and outcomes.

Formative versus Summative

Formative and summative evaluations differ based on the evaluation time period. Formative evaluation occurs at designated periods of time during the implementation of the policy. Formative evaluation data provide the foundation for the summative evaluation. In a program structure that has objectives that lead to the accomplishment of program goals, the objectives' evaluation at designated time periods may correlate with the formative evaluation process. Formative evaluation is sometimes referred to as the ongoing periodic evaluation. In this same program structure, the summative evaluation occurs at the conclusion of a designated period of time in which specific goals should have been achieved. Summative evaluation data are used in the decision-making process to determine if the program goal and outcome were achieved. Summative evaluation is associated with the policy's long-term expectations (Porche, 2003).

Impact versus Outcomes

Impact evaluation measures the immediate results achieved from the intended policy. In contrast, outcome evaluation measures results that are achieved in relation to resolving the root cause or associated factors. For example, the impact may be the number of persons who receive a service resulting from the new program developed through the authorization policy. However, the outcome would be the extent to which the problem is resolved resulting from the new program. An exemplar for a policy to reduce the rate of human immunodeficiency virus (HIV) infection in a specific population would consist of the impact evaluation analyzing the results of the number of persons educated or number of condoms distributed, depending on the program design. In contrast, the outcome evaluation would be an analysis of the reduction in the incidence of HIV infection in the specific population for which the program was developed.

Process versus Outcome

Process evaluation analyzes the extent to which the policy is implemented in the manner planned. In contrast, outcome evaluation analyzes the extent to which the policy solution has affected the problem. The outcome evaluation seeks to measure what a policy has actually achieved. In policy outcome evaluation, it is necessary to link outcomes directly to the various aspects of the policy. These associated or causal relationships strengthen the need for the evaluation data collected. Additionally, in policy outcome evaluation, there should be a discernment between the gross and net policy outcomes. The gross policy outcome consists of all the changes in the outcome variables observed when evaluating the policy. A formula for gross policy outcome measures is:

$$\text{Gross outcome} = \text{Effects of policy} + \text{Effects of extraneous variables to policy} + \text{Design effects}.$$

The net policy outcome consists of the changes in the outcome variables that can be reasonably attributed to the implementation of the policy with a clear associated or causal relationship. Net policy outcome measures are more difficult to ascertain.

Efficiency Analysis

Efficiency analysis involves an evaluation of the cost benefit and cost effectiveness of policies. Efficiency analysis provides critical data to policymakers regarding the allocation of scarce resources among the various policy initiatives. In a cost-benefit analysis, the policy outcomes are expressed in monetary terms as described previously. In a cost-effectiveness analysis, the policy outcomes are expressed in substantive terms. For example, a smoking cessation policy that focused on reducing the negative health impacts of smoking would have a cost-benefit analysis that examined the dollar savings from reduced medical care cost for smoking-related illnesses compared to the policy implementation cost. In comparison, a cost-effectiveness analysis of the same policy would estimate the dollars that have been expended to convert a smoker to a nonsmoker.

Utilization-Focused Evaluation

Utilization-focused evaluation's basic premise focuses on utility and actual use. The primary focus of utilization-focused evaluation is the intended use of the data to inform policy and policy issues for policymakers and constituents. The guiding principles of utilization-focused evaluation are systematic inquiry, competence, integrity and honesty, respect for people, and responsibility for the general and public welfare. Utilization-focused evaluation proposes a collaborative approach to policy evaluation based on several premises. Utilization-focused evaluation does not prescribe a specific model or process but actually proposes a framework or philosophical approach to policy evaluation. Some of the utilization-focused premises are:

- Intended use of data by policymakers and constituents is the driving force.
- The use of evaluation data is considered with the initial design of the evaluation plan.
- Personal factors, interest, and commitments impact use of data.
- Stakeholder analysis is critical.
- Useful evaluations are designed and adapted to certain situations.
- Stakeholders or users are engaged in the evaluation planning process.
- Evaluators should be active, reactive, and adaptive during the evaluation process (Fetterman, Kaftarian, & Wandersman, 2014; Porche, 2003).

Logic Evaluation Model

Logic models are utilized to link program inputs (resources) and activities to program outcomes. Logic models are a tool used to: (1) identify short-term, intermediate, and long-term program outcomes; (2) link program outcomes to each of the program activities; (3) select indicators; and (4) explain to decision makers the time necessary to achieve the respective long-term program outcomes.

The components of a logic model are inputs, activities, outputs, and outcomes (short-term, intermediate, and long-term). Inputs are the resources that are placed into a program such as staff, partnering organizations, equipment, materials, and direct and in-kind funding. Activities are the events that occur to implement the program. Outputs are the direct products of the program activities. The outcomes are the intended effects of the program. Short-term outcomes are the immediate effects of the program. Some typical short-term outcomes are knowledge, attitudes, and skills. Intermediate outcomes include changes in behavior, normative change, and policy changes. Long-term outcomes are typically achieved after years of program implementation. Long-term outcomes are typically measured in changes in morbidity and mortality data. **Table 11-3** and **Figure 11-2** present a logic model template and a sample logic model.

A logic evaluation model can be constructed with five steps. The five steps to constructing a logic evaluation model are:

- Step 1—Collect relevant background information regarding the policy or program.
- Step 2—Describe the policy problem and the contents of the policy or program.
- Step 3—Define the elements of the logic model—inputs, activities, outputs, short-term outcomes, intermediate outcomes, and long-term outcomes.
- Step 4—Draw the logic model in a figure.
- Step 5—Verify the logic model.

TABLE 11-3   LOGIC EVALUATION MODEL TEMPLATE

INPUTS	ACTIVITIES	OUTPUTS	SHORT-TERM OUTCOMES	INTERMEDIATE OUTCOMES	LONG-TERM OUTCOMES
Example Health education staff	Smoking cessation counseling	Smoker counseled on cessation options	Increased knowledge	Quit attempts Reduced tobacco use	Smoking cessation

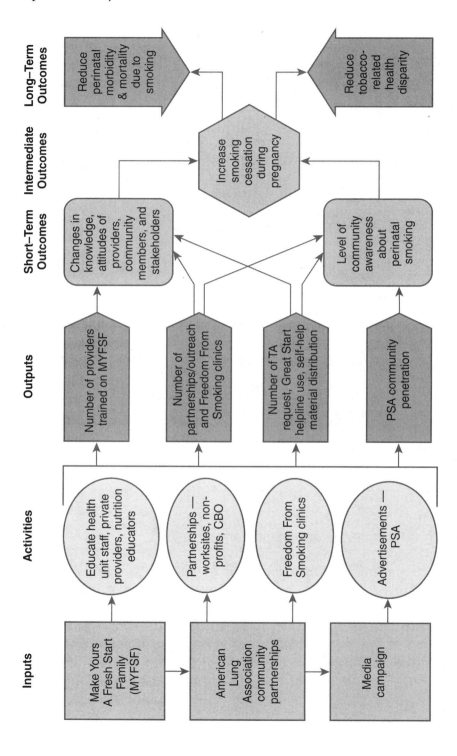

Figure 11-2 Perinatal Smoking Cessation Program Logic Evaluation Model

Research and Evaluation Informing Policy Formulation and Modification

Evaluation models and processes provide the guidance to ensure that the evaluation is correctly designed to generate the data and findings required to develop or modify existing policy. A sound policy evaluation must originate with a clear evaluation purpose and specific aims or objectives that guide the evaluation process. The evaluation questions, purpose and aims direct the appropriate evaluation model and process to be implemented. Patton (2008) provides four criteria for evaluation models:

- Utilization—Evaluation provides valuable information to stakeholders.
- Feasibility—Evaluation is realistic, prudent, diplomatic, and frugal.
- Propriety—Evaluation is conducted in a legal and ethical manner with regard to the welfare of those involved and impacted.
- Accuracy—Evaluation process yields adequate and precise information.

Each evaluation model will utilize an evaluation research design. The research designs presented earlier in this chapter can be used to conduct policy evaluation research. The evaluation design selected will depend on the evaluation question, purpose, aims, and evaluation model.

Multiple models and processes have been presented for the policy evaluation process. The following policy evaluation process is proposed as a means to use evaluative data to inform the policy modification process. This proposed policy evaluation process is based on Porche's (2003) previous recommendations regarding an evaluation process for program evaluation and concepts presented in this chapter. The proposed policy evaluation process is:

- Engage policy and policy issue stakeholders, constituents, and policymakers.
- Define the purpose and objectives/aims of the policy evaluation.
- Describe the policy issue or problem.
- Describe existing policy, related or associated policies, previous policies, and policy alternatives.
- Design the evaluation plan.
- Collect evaluation data.
- Analyze evaluation data.
- Compose findings.
- Draw conclusions.
- Identify recommendations for practice, education, future research, and policy initiatives.
- Disseminate findings.

BOX 11-8 GUIDELINES FOR LINKING PUBLICATIONS TO POLICY

- Explicitly link manuscript topic and title to policy.
- Frame the research findings or theoretical information within the current policy context.
- Background section of manuscript should reference and cite relevant policy.
- Manuscript should address populations of interest to policymakers.
- Language of manuscript should be understandable to policymakers.
- Manuscript should include policy-relevant content in the literature review and discussion sections.
- Manuscript should have information that can be used in multiple phases of the policymaking process.
- Manuscript content should be useful to political action committees, advocates, and special-interest groups.
- Explicit policy terms should be used as keywords.
- Use current policy agenda terminology in manuscript and keywords.
- Manuscript should propose implications for policy in the conclusion.

Policy Evaluation Dissemination

Dissemination should serve as the last phase of both the research and policy evaluation process. **Box 11-8** provides guidelines that promote the linking of the scholarly literature with policy.

Summary Points

- Research is the planned, systematic collection and analysis of data that answer relevant questions within the existing state of science.
- The research community consists of researchers—scientists, scholars, practitioners, academicians, students of various disciplines, and constituents.
- Research is a tool that can be used to influence policy and policymakers.
- Policy research can be used to analyze a problem or as a means to further define the boundaries and context of an identified problem.

- Policy research is a tool to generate, gather, and disseminate information that informs the actions of policymakers.
- The scientific process consists of posing a question, conducting background research on the subject area (reviewing literature), developing a hypothesis, testing the hypothesis, analyzing the data, drawing conclusions from the findings, and communicating the results.
- Policy research involves quantitative, qualitative, and mixed-method research designs.
- Research utilization is a systematic process by which research data and knowledge formulated from research findings are integrated into practice.
- Research utilization focuses on integrating research findings into practice based on the findings from formal, systematic research investigations.
- The legal research process provides the foundation for a lawsuit and provides valuable information that can inform policymaking.
- The research process should explore whether the existing case law has been overturned, remanded, or cited by more recent case law.
- The legal research process consists of exploring for relevant statutes at the local, state, and federal level that may be relevant to the issue being investigated.
- Policy evaluation measures the overall effectiveness and extent to which a policy has achieved its objectives.
- Policy evaluation poses the questions "What have we done?" and "What was the impact and/or outcome?"
- Policy evaluation provides data on program outcomes that resulted from the development and implementation of policies that authorized and allocated funds for programs.
- Monitoring is an ongoing measurement, providing information about the policy accomplishments and progress toward the preestablished policy goals, objectives, and outcomes.
- Policy monitoring is a systematic process of collecting data related to policy issues or policy that provides a concurrent analysis of the policy issue or policy in relation to the expected goals, objectives, or outcomes of the policy issue or policy.
- Structure evaluation assesses the environment in which policy is developed and implemented; process evaluation measures the extent to

which the policy is implemented as planned; and outcome evaluation determines the extent to which the policy has achieved the expected goals and outcomes.

- Formative evaluation occurs at designated periods of time during the implementation of the policy.

- Summative evaluation occurs at the conclusion of a designated period of time in which specific goals should have been achieved.

- Impact evaluation measures the immediate results achieved from the intended policy.

- Outcome evaluation measures results that are achieved in relation to resolving the root cause or associated factors.

- Process evaluation analyzes the extent to which the policy is implemented in the manner planned.

- Efficiency analysis involves an evaluation of the cost benefit and cost effectiveness of policies.

- The guiding principles of utilization-focused evaluation are systematic inquiry, competence, integrity and honesty, respect for people, and responsibility for the general and public welfare.

- Logic models are utilized to link program inputs (resources) and activities to program outcomes.

- The components of a logic model are inputs, activities, outputs, and outcomes (short-term, intermediate, and long-term).

References

Brownson, R., Royer, C., Ewing, R., & McBride, T. (2006). Researchers and policymakers: Travelers in parallel universes. *American Journal of Preventive Medicine, 30*(2), 164–172.

Donabedian, A. (1996). Evaluating the quality of medical care. *Milbank Quarterly, 44*, 166–204.

Dye, T. (2017). *Understanding public policy* (15th ed.). Boston, MA: Pearson.

Fain, J. A. (2013). *Reading, understanding, and applying nursing research* (4th ed.). Philadelphia, PA: F. A. Davis Company.

Fetterman, D., Kaftarian, S., & Wandersman, A. (2014). *Empowerment evaluation* (2nd ed.). Thousand Oaks, CA: Sage.

Garner, B. (2014). *Black's law dictionary* (10th ed.). St. Paul, MN: Thomson West.

Green, L., & Kreuter, M. (2004). *Health promotion planning: An educational and ecological approach* (4th ed.). London, UK: Mayfield.

Hanney, S., Gonzalez-Block, M., Buxton, M., & Kogan, M. (2003). The utilization of health research in policy-making: Concepts, examples and methods of assessment. *Health Research Policy and Systems, 1*(2), 1–28.

Longest, B. (2015). *Health policymaking in the United States* (6th ed.). New York, NY: Health Administration Press.

Nachmias, D. (1979). *Public policy evaluation*. New York, NY: St. Martin's.

Patton, M. Q. (2008). *Utilization-focused evaluation* (4th ed.). Thousand Oaks, CA: Sage Publications.

Porche, D. (2003). *Public and community health nursing: A population-based approach*. Thousand Oaks, CA: Sage.

Rossi, P. H., Lipsey, M. W., Freeman, H. E. (2004). *Evaluation: A systematic approach* (7th ed.). Thousand Oaks, CA: Sage Publications.

Sabatier, P. A., & Weible, C. M. (Eds.). (2014). *Theories of the policy process* (3rd ed.). Boulder, CO: Westview Press.

Wakefield, M. (2001). Linking health policy to nursing and health care scholarship: Points to consider. *Nursing Outlook, 49*(4), 204–205.

Weiss, C., & Bucavalas, M. (1980). *Social science research and decision-making.* New York, NY: Columbia University Press.

Evidence Informing Policymaking

Health policy formulation and modification based on evidence and data strengthens the support for policy decisions. Developing data-driven capabilities to support policymaking depends on identifying the constituents and/or stakeholders while answering four questions: (1) What are the policy problems? (2) What data are available to support policy decisions? (3) What do the data indicate about the current state of the problem/situation? and (4) What policy options are supported by data? (AHRQ, 2004). Using data to support policy decision is dependent upon constituent or stakeholder perspectives, political feasibility, timing, funding, and available data. Evidence-based, quality improvement, and population data can inform the policymaking process.

Evidence-Based Practice Frameworks

Evidence-based medicine or nursing practice expands the concept of research utilization. Research utilization focuses on integrating research findings into practice based on the findings from formal, systematic research investigations. In contrast, evidence-based medicine or nursing practice integrates research findings but also integrates information from best practices, clinical expertise, patient values, and other sources of information (Melnyk & Fineout-Overholt, 2015). Research utilization is considered a narrower term than evidence-based practice. Evidence-based practice assists with closing the publication gap. The publication gap exists when researchers or experts have information and data to inform practice but have not disseminated the findings yet into literature retrievable by the public. Evidence-based practice uses hierarchies of evidence to evaluate the effectiveness of interventions and to determine the strength of evidence. The evidence hierarchies inform the appropriateness or readiness of the respective information for integration into practice. **Boxes 12-1** and **12-2** outline types of evidence and some evidence-based practice hierarchies,

---

BOX 12-1   TYPES OF EVIDENCE

- Research-based data
- Opinion-based
- Expert panels
- Patient views
- Professional expertise and experience
- Quality improvement
- Infection control
- Financial data
- Process and outcome evaluation data
- Population and demographics (population science) data
- Morbidity and mortality statistics

BOX 12-2   EVIDENCE HIERARCHIES

American Association of Critical-Care Nurses

A. Meta-analysis of multiple controlled studies or meta synthesis of qualitative studies
B. Randomized or Nonrandomized well-designed controlled studies
C. Qualitative, descriptive, or correlational studies, integrative or systematic reviews, randomized trials
D. Peer reviewed standards
E. Expert opinion or multiple case reports
F. Manufacturer recommendations (Armola et al., 2009)

Stetler Evidence Hierarchy

I. Systematic, statistical review of multiple controlled studies (e.g., meta-analysis)
II. Systematic interpretive, table-based integrative review of multiple studies primarily of quantitative research
III. Experimental studies
IV. Quasi-experimental studies

BOX 12-2   EVIDENCE HIERARCHIES (CONTINUED)

V. Systematic, interpretive, tabular integrative review of multiple studies primarily of *qualitative* research

VI. Nonexperimental studies, such as correlational, descriptive research, as well as qualitative research

VII. Systematically obtained, verifiable evaluation data from the literature

VIII. Consensus opinion of respected authorities, e.g., a nationally known guideline group (With permission from Cheryl B. Stetler; Stetler, 2001, 2002)

Joanna Briggs Institute (JBI) Evidence Levels for Effectiveness

1 – Experimental designs

    1.a – Systematic review of randomized controlled trials (RCTs)

    1.b – Systematic review of RCTs and other study designs

    1.c – RCT

2 – Quasi-experimental designs

    2.a – Systematic review of quasi-experimental studies

    2.b – Systematic review of quasi-experimental and other lower study designs

    2.c – Quasi-experimental prospectively controlled study

    2.d – Pre-test – post-test or historic/retrospective control group study

3 – Observational-Analytical designs

    3.a – Systematic review of comparable cohort studies

    3.b – Systematic review of comparable cohort or other lower study designs

    3.c – Cohort study with control group

    3.d – Case-controlled study

    3.e – Observational study without a control group

4 – Observational-Descriptive designs

    4.a – Systematic review of descriptive studies

    4.b – Cross-sectional study

    4.c – Case series

    4.d – Case study

5 – Expert Opinion and Bench Research

    5.a – Systematic review of expert opinion

    5.b – Expert consensus

    5.c – Bench research/single expert opinion (With permission from Joanna Briggs Institute; Joanna Briggs Institute, 2013)

respectively (Stetler et al., 1998). Spector (2010) outlines the following steps for evidence-based healthcare regulation policy as a means to inform policymaking:

- Question formulation—Convert the information needed regarding regulatory practice into an answerable question.
- Identify and collect evidence—Review the literature and collect other information and data relative to the proposed question.
- Appraise the evidence—Critically appraise all evidence and note the level of evidence using an evidence hierarchy.
- Process data—Extract data; synthesize findings from multiple data and information sources; and integrate findings into a recommendation.
- Disseminate findings—Report to a larger audience or constituency.
- Evaluate effectiveness and efficiency—Evaluate this evidence-based regulatory practice process from the stage of question formulation to disseminating findings.

Several frameworks or models exist to provide a process for evidence-based practice that can be used to determine the best policy solution based on the best evidence. **Box 12-3** summarizes several key evidence-based practice models (DiCenso, Guyatt, & Ciliska, 2005; Hughes, 2008; Melnyk & Fineout-Overholt, 2005; Stetler, 1994; Stetler et al., 1998). Evidence-based practice models can be utilized to determine the best evidence to inform policy decisions and as a means to evaluate the impact and outcome of policy recommendations. **Box 12-4** presents criteria for the evaluation of evidence-based practice models (Gawlinski & Rutledge, 2008).

Evidence-based practice for policy generation results in a final outcome policy formulation or policy change. The Joanna Briggs Institute (JBI) suggests that an evidence-based practice recommendation include specific components. FAME represents the JBI-suggested components—feasibility, appropriateness, meaningfulness, and effectiveness in recommendations based on evidence synthesis.

Quality Improvement

Quality improvement is another evidence source of data to provide input for policy development and modification. Quality improvement continually strives to move from a state of "good" to "great" while embracing change. The focus of quality improvement is achieving quality. The structure, process, and outcome

BOX 12-3   EVIDENCE-BASED PRACTICE FRAMEWORKS—MODELS

ACE Star Model
- Knowledge discovery
- Evidence synthesis
- Translation into practice recommendations
- Implementation into practice
- Evaluation

Iowa Model
- Population-or knowledge-focused trigger
- Topic prioritized for organization relevance
- Assemble teams
- Assemble relevant research and literature
- Critique and synthesize research and literature for use in practice
- If there is insufficient data, conduct research study
- If there is sufficient data to implement practice change, pilot change and evaluate
- Used data from pilot evaluation or research study to institute change
- Evaluate outcomes
- Disseminate findings

Stetler Model
- Preparation
  - Identify, sort, and select relevant research evidence
  - Consider all influential factors
  - Affirm priorities
  - Define purpose of investigation
- Validation
  - Critique and synthesize information gathered in preparation phase
- Comparative evaluation—decision making
  - Evaluate synthesized data according to fit of setting, feasibility, substantive evidence, current practice
  - Decide to use, not use, or consider use

(continues)

BOX 12-3   EVIDENCE-BASED PRACTICE FRAMEWORKS—MODELS (CONTINUED)

- Translation—application
  - Decide to use now in practice
  - Consider use but conduct an evaluation of an implementation pilot
- Evaluation
  - Evaluate routine practice outcomes

Joanna Briggs Institute (JBI) Model of Evidence-Based Health Care
- Evidence generation
  - Discourse
  - Experience
  - Research
- Evidence synthesis
  - Theory
  - Methodology
  - Systematic review
- Evidence (knowledge) transfer
  - Systems
  - Information
  - Education
- Evidence utilization
  - Embed system organizational change
  - Practice change
  - Evaluation of impact on system/process outcome

BOX 12-4   EVIDENCE-BASED PRACTICE MODEL EVALUATION CRITERIA

- Organization of the model is clear and concise.
- Concepts of the model are clear and concise.
- Diagrammatic representation of the model allows quick assimilation of the concepts and relationships among the concepts.
- Diagrammatic representation of the model permits quick assimilation of the organization of the steps of evidence-based change.
- Model is comprehensive.
- Model is easy to use in policy.
- Model can be applied to typical policy issue.

evaluation approach is one approach suggested by Donabedian (1996) to improve quality. Deming (1982) identified 14 points of quality:

- Constancy—Create constancy of quality improvement purpose.
- Philosophy—Adopt a quality improvement philosophical perspective.
- Statistical data—Engage in data-based decision making.
- Price—Price cannot be the central focus when focusing on quality.
- Problem solving—Focus on problem identification and continually work to alleviate the problem or improve the problem level.
- Personnel training—Training is imperative to ensure quality.
- Supervision—Delegate appropriately with quality control measures in place.
- Fear—Decrease fear inherent with making improvements.
- Barriers—Eliminate system barriers.
- Methods—Goals and methods are aligned.
- Quotas—Eliminate quotas.
- Pride—Create a culture of pride.
- Education—Education is the basis for knowledge.
- Management—Top-level and upper-echelon support is critical to successful quality improvement efforts (Porche, 2003).

Quality improvement is one aspect of total quality management. Total quality management, as proposed by Deming (1982), consists of several basic principles: customer focus, a continuous quality improvement obsession, continual improvement systems, unity of purpose, teamwork, employee involvement in the entire process, education and training regarding quality and quality improvement, a scientific approach, and a long-term commitment to quality (Porche, 2003). In addition, total quality management is based on the trilogy of quality proposed by Joseph Juran: quality planning, quality control, and quality improvement as interrelated processes (Defeo, 2016). Quality planning consists of identifying customers, identifying customer needs, product development to address needs, establishing quality goals, developing processes to achieve quality goals, and improving process capability to achieve quality goals. Quality control consists of selecting the aspects of the policy, service delivery, or product development to control through a continual analysis of measuring specific quality indicators. Quality improvement consists of establishing the need for improvement, identifying projects for improvement, organizing the quality improvement project, conducting causal analysis for quality defects, identifying causes, implementing corrective action, evaluating corrective action plans, and providing controls to ensure integration of correction actions for continual improvement in the policy quality.

The Institute for Healthcare Improvement (IHI) suggests six aims for qual-
improvement policies in health care: safe, effective, patient-centered, timely,
ıcient, and equitable care. They also add three goals: improving the patient
experience, reducing cost, and improving population health.

Model for Improvement: PDCA/PDSA Quality Improvement

PDCA/PDSA is a common quality improvement model. PDCA stands for plan,
do, check, and act, and PDSA stands for plan, do, study, and act. PDCA/PDSA
is a systematic process that uses learning and knowledge generated during the
improvement implementation process to continually improve the product,
service, or process. This is a process-oriented simple model that can be used
to plan, do policy implementation, study impact of policy implementation,
and act on the data from the PDCA/PDSA cycle to further modify the policy.
Figure 12-1 presents the PDCA/PDSA model. The PDCA/PDSA cycle consists
of the following processes:

- Identify customers and policy stakeholders.
- Implement PDCA cycle
  - Plan—Plan the improved service.
  - Do—Implement quality improvements.
  - Check/Study—Determine results and evaluate quality
    improvements.
  - Act—Integrate improvements into systems to maintain quality.
- Analyze—Measure long-term quality outcomes resulting from im-
  provements (Porche, 2003).

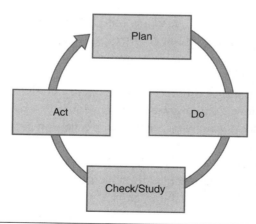

Figure 12-1   PDCA/PDSA Model

Define, Measure, Analyze, Improve, Control (DMAIC)

Define, measure, analyze, improve, and control (DMAIC) is a data-driven quality improvement strategy to improve processes. Improvements based on DMAIC can lead to the formulation or modification in process-related healthcare policies. **Figure 12-2** presents the phases of DMAIC. The five phases of DMAIC are:

- Define—define the problem, improvement activity, opportunity for improvement, goals, or constituent/stakeholder needs;
- Measure—measure process performance;
- Analyze—analyze processes to determine root causes of variation, error, or poor performance;
- Improve—implement policy that focus on improving processes by eliminating, preventing, or managing the problem's root causes; and
- Control—ensure policy addresses strategies for continued improvements and future process performance.

Define, Measure, Analyze, Design, Verify (DMADV)

Define, measure, analyze, design, and verify (DMADV) is a process methodology used sometimes when the focus of improvement is on new processes, not a change. This is presented in **Figure 12-3**. DMADV's application to policy would focus on defining constituent and stakeholder needs, measuring constituent and stakeholder needs, finding policy process options to meet these needs, designing a policy that meets these needs, and verifying that the policy process achieves the expected process metrics.

Failure Mode and Effect Analysis (FMEA)

Failure mode and effect analysis can be used to generate causative data to support developing policy resolutions. The goal of FMEA is to prevent errors

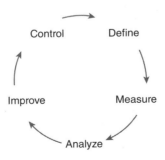

Figure 12-2   DMAIC Model

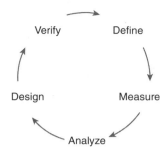

Figure 12-3   DMADV (Define, Measure, Analyze, Design, and Verify) Model

by attempting to identify the manner in which processes fail. The five steps of FEMA are:

- Define the problem/topic.
- Assemble a team.
- Develop a process map for the problem with each step and substep numbered consecutively.
- Conduct a hazard analysis—identify the cause of failure modes, score each mode using a standard hazard matrix, use a decision tree to define points of action.
- Develop desired policy actions and desired policy outcomes (Hughes, 2008).

Benchmarking

Benchmarking is a term used throughout the quality improvement process. Benchmarking is the measuring and comparing of results to best performers. Policy benchmarking would consist of measuring and comparing the results of a new policy formulated or modified to a policy known to generate the expected outcomes in an effective, efficient, and cost-effective manner. The two types of benchmarking are internal and external. Internal benchmarking is used to identify and compare policy outcomes within an organization. External or competitive benchmarking compares the policy outcomes to those of other successful organizations.

Population Outcomes

An ultimate goal of policymaking is the improvement in population outcomes. The achievement of policy outcomes focuses on four broad goals—(1) improving the overall population health based on morbidity and mortality statistics (2) improving the health-related quality of life, (3) eliminating the disparities within the population, and (4) improving the state of the social determinants of health. Policymakers should focus on the achievement of these four broad population-based policy outcomes. Population-based policymaking targets improving the health outcomes of groups of individuals with an aim to improve the health of an entire human population.

Evidence-Based Practice Informing Policy Formulation and Modification

Data have the ability to drive policy decision making. However, data need to be critically appraised prior to implementation. Data considered to be "groundbreaking" or new have the potential to move policymakers toward action. Due diligence is necessary to appraise data from research, evaluation, evidence-based practice, and quality improvement initiatives. STAR is an easy-to-remember acronym that outlines steps to ensure this appraisal occurs prior to policy formulation and modification. STAR represents:

- Stop—review the issue or problem;
- Think—critically appraise the data;
- Act—formulate policy options and evaluate alignment of data to policy solutions/options; and
- Review—review each policy option and data before selecting best policy option with the supporting data.

Another acronym, SBAR, can also assist with using data to formulate policy. SBAR stands for:

- Situation—the policy issue or problem and the data that support the policy issue or problem;
- Background—historical analysis of issue or problem;
- Assessment—data that supports policy solutions; and
- Recommendation—alignment of policy issue or problem with the data supported/driven solutions.

Dissemination

A distinguishing factor between evidence-based practice and quality improvement as compared to research is the ability to generalize findings. Evidence-based practice and quality improvement results are limited in generalizability as compared to the findings of research. Regardless of the generalizability, findings generated from quality improvement projects and evidence-based practice or synthesis projects should be disseminated to expand the potential impact of the findings. The dissemination of these findings facilitates the building of a knowledge base in an area of inquiry. Methods of dissemination consist of, but are not limited to:

- Published manuscripts or reports
- Conference podium presentations
- Conference poster presentations
- Institution-based presentations, newsletters, poster displays
- Policy briefs on findings
- Position statements on findings
- Press release about findings

Summary Points

- Health policy formulation and modification based on evidence and data strengthen the support for policy decisions.
- Using data to support policy decision is dependent upon constituent or stakeholder perspectives, political feasibility, timing, funding, and available data.
- Evidence-based medicine or nursing practice expands the concept of research utilization.
- Research utilization focuses on integrating research findings into practice based on the findings from formal, systematic research investigations.
- Evidence-based practice uses hierarchies of evidence to evaluate the effectiveness of interventions and to determine the strength of evidence.
- The basic principles of total quality management are customer focus, a continuous quality improvement obsession, continual improvement systems, unity of purpose, teamwork, employee involvement in the entire process, education and training regarding quality and quality improvement, a scientific approach, and a long-term commitment to quality.
- Institute for Healthcare Improvement six aims are safe, effective, patient-centered, timely, efficient, and equitable care with three goals of improving the patient experience, reducing cost, and improving population health.
- PDCA stands for plan, do, check, and act.

- Define, measure, analyze, improve, and control (DMAIC) is a data-driven quality improvement strategy to improves processes.
- Define, measure, analyze, design, and verify (DMADV) is a process methodology used sometimes when the focus of improvement is on new processes, not a change.
- Failure mode and effect analysis can be used to generate causative data to support developing policy resolutions.
- The goal of FMEA is to prevent errors by attempting to identify the manner in which processes fail.
- Policy benchmarking consists of measuring and comparing the results of a new policy formulated or modified to a policy known to generate the expected outcomes in an effective, efficient, and cost-effective manner.

References

Agency for Healthcare Research and Quality (AHRQ). (2004). *Monitoring the health care safety net.* Washington, DC: Agency for Healthcare Research and Quality.

Armola, R. R., Bourgault, A. M., Halm, M. A., Board, R. M., Bucher, L., Harrington, L., . . . Medina, J. (2009). Upgrading the American Association of Critical-Care Nurses' Evidence-Leveling Hierarchy. *American Journal of Critical Care, 18*(5), 405-409.

DiCenso, A., Guyatt, R., & Ciliska, D. (2005). *Evidenced-based nursing: A guide to clinical practice.* St. Louis, MO: Elsevier Mosby.

Deming, E. (1982). *Quality, productivity, and competitive position.* Cambridge, MA: Massachusetts Institute of Technology.

Defeo, J. (2016). *Juran's quality handbook: The complete guide to performance excellence* (7th ed.). New York, NY: McGraw-Hill.

Donabedian, A. (1996). Evaluating the quality of medical care. *Milbank Quarterly, 44,* 166–204.

Gawlinski, A., & Rutledge, D. (2008). Selecting a model for evidence-based practice changes. *AACN Advanced Critical Care, 19*(3), 291–300.

Hughes, R. (2008). *Patient safety and quality: An evidence-based handbook for nurses* (Vol. 3). Washington, DC: Agency for Healthcare Research & Quality.

Joanna Briggs Institute Levels of Evidence and Grades of Recommendation Working Party. (2013). *New JBI Levels of Evidence.* Retrieved from https://joannabriggs.org/assets/docs/approach/JBI-Levels-of-evidence_2014.pdf

Melnyk, B. M., & Fineout-Overholt E. (2015). *Evidence-based practice in nursing & healthcare: A guide to best practice* (3rd ed.). Philadelphia, PA: Wolters Kluwer Health.

Porche, D. (2003). *Public and community health nursing: A population-based approach.* Thousand Oaks, CA: Sage.

Spector, N. (2010). Evidence-based nursing regulation: A challenge for regulators. *Journal of Nursing Regulation, 1*(1), 30–36.

Stetler, C., Brunnell, M., Giuliano, K., Morsi, D., Prince, L., & Newell-Stokes, V. (1998). Evidence-based practice and the role of nursing leadership. *Journal of Nursing Administration, 28*(7/8), 45–53.

Stetler, C. (1994). Refinement of the Stetler/Marram model for application of research findings into practice. *Nursing Outlook, 42,* 15–25.

Stetler, C. (2001). Updating the Stetler Model of research utilization to facilitate evidence-based practice. *Nursing Outlook, 49*(6), 272–297.

Stetler, C. (2002). *Evidence-based practice and the use of research: A synopsis of basic concepts & strategies to improve care.* Washington, DC: NOVA Foundation.

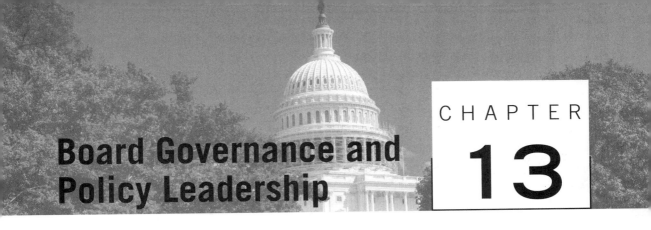

Board Governance and Policy Leadership

Nurses and other healthcare professionals are active members of professional organizations, associations, and for-profit and nonprofit organizations that generate policy through board membership. Board governance and policymaking as a board member constitute an essential leadership competency for nurses and healthcare professionals. Leadership requirements for board governance is dependent upon the understanding of board structure and functions along with knowledge regarding governance at the local, state, national, or international level across various government and nongovernment sectors of health care.

Governance Defined

Governing and governance are two terms that are often confused. Governing is a verb that describes the act of governance. Governance is a noun that means the process or the power of the government, administration, institutional, or association representatives to govern. Governing or governance does not mean taking complete control, rendering all decisions, or managing the day-to-day operations of an organization or system. Governing and governance are considered to include a broad set of leadership decisions and processes that reflect the social expectations, broad accountability for ethical conduct, management of conflicts of interest, assurance of financial integrity, creation and influence of strategic direction and expected outcomes, and the setting of policy (Berkowtiz, 2016).

Boards Defined

A board is a group of persons formed and organized under the authority of a formal governance document afforded the power and privileges to exercise certain authorities, provide oversight or control of certain matters, or discharge functions in a fiduciary manner. Board type is differentiated based on three

TABLE 13-1   DESCRIPTIONS OF BOARD TYPES

BOARD TYPE	CHARACTERISTICS
Not for profit	• Broad-based term that encompasses all organizations known as charities, nonprofits, nongovernmental organizations (NGOs), private voluntary organizations (PVOs), civil society groups • Tax exempt • Must demonstrate community benefit • Serves stakeholders
For profit	• Corporate board • Benefits shareholders • Pursues a profit • Transparency required

characteristics—purpose (mission), ownership, and level of authority or control. **Table 13-1** compare the types of boards.

Board Structure

Board structure provides the framework from which to govern an organization or institution. A healthy board structure builds a relationship with the chief executive officer (CEO) based on accountability, not individual tasks. In a healthy relationship, the board is concerned with total organizational performance and holds the CEO accountable. The CEO is accountable to the full board, not individual members. A healthy board must empower the CEO to fulfill the organization's mission and strategic initiatives and ensure the CEO has the necessary resources to achieve the mission. The CEO must also empower the board members to function as board members.

The board structure is the framework from which the board implements its duties. The overarching accountability of the board is to the shareholders or stakeholders. A board of directors serves as the formal leadership of the organization in accordance with the articles of incorporation and/or bylaws. The board of directors employs an executive director or CEO to provide organizational leadership and management to fulfill the mission. The board of directors operates through several policy documents such as bylaws or governance document, board operations manual, policies and procedures, and other various board governance instruments. The actual work of the board occurs through an organizational committee structure. Typical board committees are executive, audit, nominations and selections, financial, fundraising, and board development. Board ad hoc committees can consist of audit, capital campaign, special events, and research.

The board of directors and executive committee are led by the board president or board chairperson. The primary role of the board president or board chairperson is to provide the overall leadership for the board. The board president or board chairperson functions as the link between the board and CEO. In addition, the board president or board chairperson is responsible for the board agenda; coordinates committees; engages in the selection, orientation, and induction of new directors; provides counsel to other directors; serves as board spokesperson; and represents the board with key shareholders and stakeholders.

Board Responsibilities and Duties

Board functions and organizational management functions are distinct. It is important that the board and CEO duties are clear and distinct, with areas of mutual or shared authority and responsibility clearly delineated. The basic roles and duties of nonprofit boards are to:

- Determine the mission and purpose;
- Select and employ the CEO;
- Support the CEO;
- Assess CEO performance;
- Ensure organizational planning;
- Ensure the provision of adequate resources;
- Manage resources effectively;
- Determine, monitor, and improve programs and services;
- Enhance board's public image and community standing;
- Ensure legal and ethical integrity and maintain accountability;
- Recruit and orient new board members; and
- Assess board member actions and contributions.

The board's legal responsibility and liabilities are grounded in three fiduciary duties. The fiduciary duties are duty of care, duty of loyalty, and duty of obedience. These fiduciary duties are outlined in **Table 13-2**. A fiduciary is a person who holds something in trust for another. In this situation, a fiduciary is a board member who holds the organization in trust for the stakeholders or shareholders.

Other necessary board responsibilities and duties are:

- Understand financial data
  - Approve budget
  - Read and understand financial reports

TABLE 13-2 FIDUCIARY DUTIES

Type of Duties	Description of Duties
Duty to care	• Exercise reasonable care in acting on behalf of and in the interest of the organization • Exercise care in a manner of other prudent persons in similar situations • Make reasonable inquires—challenge assumptions • Exercise reasonable effort to become familiar with relevant and essential information • Use good judgment and make informed decisions • Willing to voice a dissenting opinion or vote
Duty of loyalty	• Undivided loyalty—safeguard the organization's business interest • Act in best interest of the organization • Avoidance of conflicts of interest—actual, potential, apparent, or perceived • Preserve confidentiality of the board and organization
Duty of obedience	• Obey and follow articles of incorporation, bylaws, policies, procedures, and applicable laws • Remain guardian of the mission

- ◆ Monitor budget
- ◆ File IRS Form 990
- Ensure financial stability
  - ◆ Determine revenue sources
  - ◆ Monitor expenditures
- Manage risk
  - ◆ Assess risk exposure
  - ◆ Maintain appropriate insurance to include directors' and officers' insurance
  - ◆ Ensure adequate policies and procedures are in effect.

- Define board member expectations
  - Time commitment
  - Financial commitment of board members
- Develop a strategic planning process
- Manage meetings productively
  - Establish committee structure
  - Plan meeting agenda
  - Maintain communication flow among board members and board staff
- Succession planning for board members and CEO

Successful boards have a clear delineation of board and CEO activities. Table 13-3 compares duties/activities of the board and CEO.

In contrast to the board, the management of the organization is responsible for the execution of strategic initiatives and policies and implementation of organizational operations. An effective board culture promotes robust engagement, mutual trust, and willingness to act between board members and organizational staff, and a commitment to high ethical and business standards and practices.

TABLE 13-3 COMPARISON OF DUTIES OF THE BOARD AND CEO

BOARD MEMBER DUTIES	CEO DUTIES
Oversee financial performance	Manage operations of the organization
Oversee and promote improvements in quality, safety, and service	Lead the organization and manage executive team
Improve board effectiveness and performance	Execute board policies and decisions
Fulfill fiduciary responsibility	Provide board with information and recommendations for informed decision making
Provide vision and strategic directions	Serve as organizational spokesperson
Coach CEO	Direct community involvement
Evaluate CEO performance	Model and require ethical conduct
Develop board policies and procedures	Draw board attention to key issues and matters
Provide board member orientation	

Board Competency

Membership on boards contribute to the nurse and other healthcare professional's competency base. Board membership contributes to the nurse or other healthcare provider's personal and professional abilities to shape policy, create culture change, and promote the profession's reputation and confirm the healthcare professional's legitimate position of authority within the healthcare system. An essential element of board membership is competency in an area of subject-matter relevance.

The American Hospital Association (AHA) has outlined core competencies for members of hospital and healthcare system boards. **Box 13-1** outlines the

---

BOX 13-1   AHA CORE HOSPITAL AND HEALTHCARE SYSTEM BOARD MEMBER COMPETENCY

Knowledge and skills

- Business and finance
- Healthcare delivery systems
- Human resource management

Personal competencies

- Accountability
- Achievement orientation
- Change leadership
- Collaboration
- Community orientation
- Complexity management
- Information seeking
- Innovative thinking
- Organizational awareness
- Professionalism
- Relationship building
- Strategic orientation
- Talent development and management
- Team leadership

Reproduced from American Hospital Association's (AHA) Center for Healthcare Governance and Health Research & Education Trust. (2009). *Competency-based governance: A foundation for board and organizational effectiveness.* © Used with permission of American Hospital Association.

AHA core competencies (AHA, 2009). The AHA proposes two sets of competencies necessary to link board effectiveness and organizational performance.

Curran (2015) proposes a set of competencies for nurses to serve on boards. Curran proposes the following experience and behaviors serve as board competencies for nurses:

- Holistic view of the impact of board decisions on others;
- Compatibility to work across disciplines;
- Accountability to stakeholders or shareholders;
- Ethical morals and integrity that generate trust;
- Experience with organizational operational issues;
- Risk management knowledge;
- Ability to proactively anticipate and make decisions;
- Verbal and written communication skills;
- Action oriented;
- Focus on outcome-based decision making; and
- Desire to be a servant leader (Curran, 2015).

Board Appointment

Governing boards have appointment processes that may be formal or informal in nature. To secure a board appointment, it is critical that the nurse or other healthcare professional is familiar with the board appointment process and political processes and actions necessary to secure an appointment. Gillis (2016) proposes four preliminary questions to consider before seeking an appointment to a board:

- What area of service is of interest?
- What area of service am I able to contribute relevant expertise, personally or professionally?
- What is my level of resource commitment in terms of time, talent, and treasure?
- What are my distinguishing characteristics as compared to other candidates seeking appointment? (Gillis, 2016)

After you confirm your commitment to pursue appointment to a board, the following are actions needed to secure a board appointment:

- Prepare a biography of about 250 to 500 words
- Ensure that your résumé or curriculum vitae highlights your previous board experience or relevant experience for board membership
- Conduct an initial exploration of the board

- Mission, vision, values
    - Legal responsibilities
    - Board member roles and responsibilities/duties
    - Current board member composition
    - Strategic initiatives
    - Financial position
- Outline the required process activities to secure an appointment
- Make your interest known to members of the nominating committee or board
    - Build your network of contacts
    - Attend meetings
    - Connect with members
- Seek support from persons influential to the board
- Submit the required application and complete the required appointment process

Board Governance Document: Bylaws

Boards have a governance document typically referred to as bylaws. The organization's bylaws are the supreme governance document of the organization. Organizational bylaws must comply with all applicable laws. Organizational policies and procedures must conform to and not contradict the organizational bylaws. Basic elements of the board governance or bylaws provide the basis for the board's authority and sometimes the authority for the organization to exist as a legal entity. **Box 13-2** provides basic elements of a governance document.

BOX 13-2   GOVERNANCE DOCUMENT ELEMENTS (BYLAWS)

Offices and domicile
- Principal office
- Registered office or legal office
- Other offices

Meetings
- Place
- Number of meetings
- Special meetings
- Notice of meetings

BOX 13-2   GOVERNANCE DOCUMENT ELEMENTS (BYLAWS) (CONTINUED)

- Voting privileges
- Quorum
- Proxy voting
- Voting rights
- Voting method
- Presiding officer
- Election inspection and officers

Membership
- Types of membership categories
- Voting rights

Board, directors, or officers
- Types of positions
- Role, responsibilities, and duties of officers
- Number of members
- Qualifications
- Term of office
- Nomination and election process
- Removal from office
- Vacancies
- Number of meetings
- Notice of meetings
- Proxy voting
- Voting method
- Quorum

Committees
- Types of committees
- Membership
- Duties and authority
- Removal
- Vacancies

Indemnification clause
Method of bylaw revision or amendment procedures
Procedures or guidelines for the conducting of meetings

Board Assessment

Board assessment is a key to a successfully functioning board. Board assessment consists of assessing the board as an entity and reviewing the functions. Three fundamental areas of assessment are vision, mission, and core values; appropriate board membership; and effective board processes. Areas of assessment include individual board member profiles (**Box 13-3**), effectiveness of meetings (**Box 13-4**), board operations, individual board member contributions, and overall board assessment (**Box 13-5**).

BOX 13-3   BOARD MEMBER PROFILE ASSESSMENT

- Years of service to board
- Gender
- Age
- Race/ethnicity
- Profession
- Area of expertise
- Constituency
- Available time
- Board contributions

BOX 13-4   BOARD MEETING EFFECTIVENESS ASSESSMENT

- Agenda clear and distributed in advance
- Reports and supporting agenda documents distributed in advance
- Board members prepared for meeting
- Reports provided sufficient information for board members to make informed decisions
- Board did not engage in operational issues or micro-management
- Diversity of opinions encouraged
- Chair effectively guided meeting
- Members participated appropriately and respectfully
- Action items identified and recorded with a responsible party indicated for each action
- All board members present
- Meeting began and ended on time
- Meeting environment was conducive for the work of the board

---

BOX 13-5   BOARD ASSESSMENT

The board assessment evaluates the board's area of responsibilities. These areas can be rated as satisfactory or needs improvement. The areas for assessment are:

- Mission
- Strategic planning, thinking, and initiatives
- Program evaluation and improvement
- Fiscal management
- Risk management
- CEO relationship
- Board-staff relationships
- Public relations and advocacy
- Board selection and orientation
- Boar organization and processes
- Fundraising

Board Policymaking Process

The board governance document provides the framework for policy decision making. Bylaws should be carefully written to invest decision-making authority in accordance with the organization's preferences. Bylaws provide the scope of authority and decision-making capacity of the organization or institution's officers, committees, and members. Policymaking processes should clearly delineate the scope of authority and process for securing approvals through the formal committee structure and governing board.

Summary Points

- Board governance and policymaking as a board member constitute an essential leadership competency for nurses and healthcare professionals.
- Governing and governance are considered a broad set of leadership decisions and processes that reflect the social expectations, broad accountability for ethical conduct, management of conflicts of interest, assurance of financial integrity, creation and influence of strategic direction and expected outcomes, and the setting of policy.
- A board is a group of persons formed and organized under the authority of a formal governance document afforded the power and privileges to exercise certain authorities, provide oversight or control of certain matters, or discharge functions in a fiduciary manner.

- Board type is differentiated on three characteristics—purpose (mission), ownership, and level of authority or control.
- Board structure provides the framework from which to govern an organization or institution.
- A healthy board structure builds a relationship with the chief executive officer (CEO) based on accountability, not individual tasks.
- The board of directors operates through several policy documents such as bylaws or governance document, board operations manual, policies and procedures, and other various board governance instruments.
- The board's legal responsibility and liabilities are grounded in three fiduciary duties—duty of care, duty of loyalty, and duty of obedience.
- An effective board culture promotes robust engagement, mutual trust, and willingness to act between board members and organizational staff, and a commitment to high ethical and business standards and practices.
- An essential element of board membership is competency in an area of subject-matter relevance.
- American Hospital Association (AHA) has outlined core competencies for members of hospital and healthcare system boards.
- Boards have a governance document typically referred to as bylaws.
- Basic elements of the board governance or bylaws provide the basis for the board's authority and sometimes the authority for the organization to exist as a legal entity.
- Board assessment is a key to a successfully functioning board.
- Three fundamental areas of assessment are vision, mission, and core values; appropriate board membership; and effective board processes.

References

American Hospital Association's (AHA) Center for Healthcare Governance and Health Research & Education Trust. (2009). *Competency-based governance. A foundation for board and organizational effectiveness.* Chicago, IL: Center for Healthcare Governance.

Berkowtiz, B. (2016). President's message: Governance: An essential core competency. *Nursing Outlook*, 64, 290–291.

Curran, C. (2015). *Nurses on boards.* Indianapolis, IN: Sigma Theta Tau International.

Gillis, C. (2016). *The process of getting appointed to a Board.* Washington, DC: American Academy of Nursing, Institute for Nursing Leadership.

Institutional and Organizational/Association Policy

Healthcare institutions and other professional and community organizations and associations set policy agendas and engage in policymaking processes. Nurses and other healthcare professionals are active members of these formal institutions and organizations and associations as active policymakers. The multiple roles that nurses and other healthcare professionals fulfill increase the capacity and relevant contributions to the policymaking process. This chapter will differentiate institutions from organizations and associations for the purpose of discussion policymaking in this book. An institution is considered a legal entity approved to operate within a state that has a specific purpose and organizational structure, such as a healthcare institution. An organization or association will be referred to as a nongovernmental community-based organization or professional organization or association that has been formed to achieve a specific mission with a specific membership base or community constituency.

Defining Institutional Policy

Institutional policy is policy developed through the formal hierarchical authority structure outlined through applicable state laws and institutional governance documents. Legal formal entities that are organized into an institution should have articles of incorporation or a governance document or bylaws that delineate the hierarchical authoritative structure to form policy. It is from this governance structure that the authority to generate and implement policy originates.

An institutional member has delegated authority from the articles of incorporation or the governance document or bylaws to formulate policy or to implement his or her duties responsibly through legitimate power. If an institutional member does not have the delegated authority to act on behalf of the organization through the articles of incorporation or the governance document or bylaws, the source of legitimate power should be clearly delineated in the position or job description; otherwise, it could be challenged that the member's actions are without the appropriate authority.

The boundaries of institutional policies are limited in scope to the respective institution and its members. Institutional policies are expected to be in accordance with applicable federal, state, and local laws or legal policies. Many institutions differentiate between the terms *policy, procedures, guidelines,* and *protocols,* to be discussed below. The supreme governance document of the organization should implicate who, what position, or what representative body/board/committee in the organization is the final interpreter of institutional policy if there are areas of question, conflict, or needed clarification with the meaning, intent, or interpretation of any institutional policy.

As stated before, healthcare institutional policies must comply with the applicable local, state, and federal laws. In addition, healthcare institutions may have accreditation or national recognition programs such as The Joint Commission or American Nurses Credentialing Center's Magnet Hospital designation. These recognition programs require policies that document compliance with or achievement of those national standards.

Defining Organizational/Association Policy

A professional organization or association is sometimes also referred to as a professional body or professional society. A professional organization or association is a voluntary membership nonprofit organization or association with a profession, discipline, or specific common interest mission. Professional associations are critical to the healthcare policymaking process. These associations typically represent a large number of members from a specific profession or discipline. These associations generate national standards and competencies that are considered a form of national policy. These associations formulate national policies that generate the formulation and implementation of policies and procedures at lower association or institutional levels.

In addition to the policy-generating function of professional associations, these associations participate in the influencing of other policies through their lobbying efforts. Professional associations as nonprofit organizations are not restricted in the same manner by ethical codes or laws governing lobbying.

Types of Institutional and Organizational/Association Policy

Institutions and professional organizations or associations generate various types of policy. As stated above, institutional policy's scope of authority is generally restricted to the respective institution. However, professional organization or association policy, depending upon the organizational structure, may generate policy with a scope of authority within and external to the organization. **Table 14-1** summarizes some of the types of institutional and organizational policies developed.

Institutional and professional organizations may have a policy on policy, which is a policy that outlines the defining characteristics of a policy and the

TABLE 14-1   TYPES OF INSTITUTIONAL AND ORGANIZATIONAL/ ASSOCIATION POLICIES

TERM	DEFINITION
Policy	A statement that is a guiding principle to establish direction for an issue or statement that establishes the purpose or intent of something
Procedure	A series of prescribed steps to be followed in a consistent manner to achieve a specific expected outcome
Clinical guideline	Provides a general framework of evidence-based standards that permit flexible provider judgment based on patient needs, situation, or environmental context
Clinical protocol	Provides a specific agreed-upon procedure that is expected to be followed in the manner designated or outlined
Standard	The expected level of quality or attainment; a widely agreed upon or established level to which something is compared
Competency	The expected level of skill or performance related to a specific area of knowledge, skills, and abilities
Resolution	A resolution is a formal motion, position, or solution proposed by an executive or governing body or organization (refer to Chapter 15)
Position statement	A statement designed to educate, generate support on an issue, and formalize a position or agenda in relation to a policy issue (refer to Chapter 15)
Policy briefs	A quick explanation of the policy issue or problem and the proposed policy, along with policy and political assessments (refer to Chapter 15)

process for securing policy modifications and approvals. Some recommended areas of content for a policy on policy are:

- Purpose of policy
- Definitions and defining characteristics of the types of policy formulated and implemented such as guidelines, protocols, etc.
- Policy format, structure, and required content
  - Policy scope of authority
  - Rationale for policy
  - Related policies and supremacy policies
  - Content of policy
  - Implementation date
  - Approval signatures
  - Approval and revision dates
- Policy review and revision procedure and timelines, sunset policy provision

Organizational Politics

Politics influences the entire policymaking process (refer to Chapter 15). Organizational politics is described as a variety of activities that use influencing tactics to promote a personal, professional, or organizational interest (Jarrett, 2017). Individuals within an organization who have the power or ability to influence organization policy have considerable impact on organizational outcomes. Jarrett describes four metaphoric domains that outline the political terrain of organizational politics. Each of these four domains should be assessed and strategically mobilized or controlled as a means to influence organizational policy. These four metaphoric domains are:

- The weeds—personal influence and informal networks that rule the influence of policy;
- The rocks—individual interactions and formal legitimate sources of authority and power that are derived from title, role, and/or access to resources;
- The high ground—combines formal authority with organizational systems and uses established rules, structures, policy guidelines, and procedures as the basis of political activities to control and influence policy; and
- The woods—implicit norms, hidden assumptions, and unspoken routines that influence policy. (Jarrett, 2017)

Diagnosis of Organizational Politics

Institutional and organization/association members should be politically savvy to organizational politics as a strategy to influence policy. This is achieved through the ability to diagnose organizational politics and political structures. The following assessment framework can guide the diagnosing and understanding of organizational politics:

- Political landscape—consists of the formal, informal, and alternative hierarchies
  - Formal hierarchy—outlined by the organizational chart reporting structure
    - First indication of the political makeup and structure of an organization
  - Informal hierarchy—informal networks developed through teamwork and personal and professional relationships
    - Sometimes serve as the organizational informal gatekeepers to political power by reputation
  - Alternative hierarchy—somewhat a combination of formal and informal hierarchy—typically a person who is a "dotted line" report on the organizational chart (Krackhardt, 1990).
- Political players—each member in the organization has a role in politics—the organizational political players can be categorized as
  - The chief administrator (boss)
  - Assistant administrator (second on command)
  - "Yes" person—always agrees with administrator
  - Curmudgeon—focuses on the negative of everything
  - Vortex—person who generates drama to attract others to their position
  - Empire builder—power grabber
  - Peacemaker—strives to achieve balance and harmony
  - Brain—content expert or data-driven person
  - Rubber chicken—person who's opinion cannot be defined, focuses on the "what if," speaks a lot but contributes little substantive content
  - Parrot—repeats others' thoughts and words, uses others' ideas and opinions (Bolander, 2011)
- Cultural rules of the organization
  - Strict chain of command
  - Messenger attack

- ◆ Favoritism over performance
- ◆ Paranoid culture
- ◆ Kingpins—all decisions must be vetted by a specific set of persons
- ◆ Data drive—data rules decisions
- ◆ Decision by committee—process-oriented rules with emphasis on representation and having voice
- ◆ Emotional or gut reaction—lack of data but follows intuition
- ◆ Analysis paralysis—focuses on analysis with little definitive decision making

Mastering organizational politics is an ongoing skill that needs continual development and refinement but is critical to individual and organizational success. Some recommendations for successfully mastering organizational politics are:

- Leverage emotional intelligence;
- Data driven;
- Foster and develop personal and professional alliances and networks;
- Understanding the paradigm that frames the thinking behind the issue or problem as much as you understand the root causes of the issue or problem;
- Practice veracity;
- Focus on "what is best for the institution or organization/association";
- Promote the identification of common ground and mutual goals;
- Agree to disagree respectfully in a nonpersonal manner;
- Know when to make peace;
- Know implicit and explicit agendas of institutional and organizational/association members;
- Acknowledge your knowledge deficits; and
- Tailor your political approach to the current issue/problem, situational context, organizational culture and climate, and current political dynamics (Bolander, 2011)

Institutional Policymaking Process

Institutions have both formal and informal guidelines that support the development of institutional policies. Institutional policy formulation guidelines generally include the following:

- Identification and clarification of the issue;
- Identification of the problem;

- Determine if a policy is needed to resolve the problem;
- Consult with the appropriate administrator regarding the problem and decision to pursue a policy;
- Determine the type of institutional policy needed;
- Engage the appropriate authoritative body to generate the policy or engage the appropriate group in the policy process;
- Assign the policy drafting and formulation team;
- Analyze related policies and policies that will be directly and indirectly impacted;
- Analyze supremacy policies that the new policy must be aligned to;
- Draft institutional policy;
- Ensure that administrator with administrative oversight over the problem area remains informed and reviews and advises on policy drafts;
- Secure legal counsel review, if appropriate;
- Distribute draft policy to appropriate approval bodies for review and consideration;
- Secure policy approval through the appropriate policymaking processes of the institution;
- Distribute the policy once approved to ensure appropriate dissemination of the policy; and
- Conduct informational or education sessions on the policy using the institution's communication plan.

Organizational/Association Policy Process

As described above, the process for policy development in an organization or association should be outlined and followed based on either the policy on policy or by the governance document or bylaws. Organizational/association leaders will be held accountable by their stakeholders based on the agreed-upon process for policy formulation, adoption, and implementation as outlined in the policy on policy or governance documents.

Policy and Procedure Manual

Policy and procedure manuals are typically a book of documents that represent the institution or organization/association approved policy documents. There should be a clear connection between the institution or organization/association's policy and procedures and the respective organizational structure and mission. **Figure 14-1** describes the relationship of the documents in

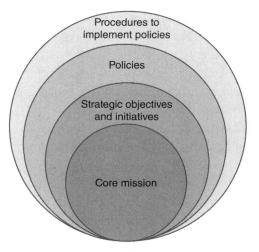

Figure 14-1   Policy and Procedure Manual Organizational Structure Relationships

the policy and procedure manual. Nurses and other healthcare providers are cautioned about purchasing predeveloped or written policy and procedure manuals. Purchased manuals must be evaluated for mission congruence; adherence to organizational structure, culture, and processes; and currency of best evidence.

Summary Points

- Healthcare institutions and other professional and community organizations and associations set policy agendas and engage in policymaking processes.
- An institution is considered a legal entity approved to operate within a state that has a specific purpose and organizational structure, such as a healthcare institution.
- An organization or association is referred to as a nongovernmental community-based organization or professional organization or association that has been formed to achieve a specific mission with a specific membership base or community constituency.
- Institutional policy is policy developed through the formal hierarchical authority structure outlined through applicable state laws and institutional governance documents.

- An institutional member has delegated authority from the articles of incorporation or the governance document or bylaws to formulate policy or to implement duties responsibly through legitimate power.
- Institutional policies boundaries are limited in scope to the respective institution and its members.
- A professional organization or association is sometimes also referred to as a professional body or professional society.
- A professional organization or association is a voluntary membership nonprofit organization or association with a profession, discipline, or specific common interest mission.
- A policy on policy outlines the defining characteristics of a policy and the process for securing policy modifications and approvals.
- Organizational politics is described as a variety of activities that use influencing tactics to promote a personal, professional, or organizational interest.
- Mastering organizational politics is an ongoing skill that needs continual development and refinement but is critical to individual and organizational success.

References

Bolander, J. (2011). *How to deal with organizational politics. The Daily MBA: Tips, tools and techniques to be a better entrepreneur.* Retrieved on June 22, 2017, from http://thedailymba.com/2011/02/28/how-to-deal-with-organizational-politics/

Jarrett, M. (2017). The 4 types of organizational politics. *Harvard Business Review*. Retrieved on June 23, 2017, from https://hbr.org/2017/04/the-4-types-of-organizational-politics

Krackhardt, D. (1990). Assessing the political landscape: structure, cognition, and power in organizations. *Administrative Science Quarterly, 35*(2), 342–369.

Politics: Theory and Practice

Politics is an integral aspect of the policymaking process. The majority of the population engages in political activities on a daily basis. However, politics is discussed and referred to as something that is negative and should not occur. This is much to the contrary. Political activity is a means to influence policymaking. What is not considered a positive aspect of influencing policymaking are illegal or unethical activities that may occur during political activities. This chapter provides a foundation to guide a professional's activities to influence the policymaking process.

Politics Defined

Politics is frequently associated with a negative connotation or belief system that encompasses something that is wrong. Politics also creates negative feelings and emotional responses such as anger, disgust, or indignation. In reality, politics and political maneuvers are a form of engagement universal to most interpersonal interactions. Politics is defined as the process of influencing someone or something to ensure the allocation of resources as desired. Politics and the political process use multiple forms of power. Politics is based on a power dynamic (Leavitt, 2009).

Constituents and Stakeholders

Constituents and stakeholders have the potential to impact policymaking as key politicians. To ensure that effective policy formulation or modification meets the needs of interested groups, constituents, and stakeholders it is beneficial to identify and cultivate these individuals and groups. The terms *constituents* and *stakeholders* are frequently used interchangeably; however, both are critical to the policymaking process even though their meanings and influential ability may be different, depending on the policy and the contextual situation. A constituent refers to an individual, group, institution, or association that is a member of a specific geographical area or political district that has the ability to elect an official who represents and votes on their respective behalf for policy. A stakeholder is an individual, group, or institution that is likely to affect or be affected by a proposed policy, someone with a general interest. Stakeholders can be further defined as primary or secondary stakeholders. Primary stakeholder is individual, group, or institution that may be directly impacted by the policy. A secondary stakeholder is an individual, group, or institution that may be indirectly impacted by the policy. Constituents and stakeholders' level of support of or opposition to a proposed policy formulation or modification should be assessed.

Constituent or stakeholder analysis is the political process of constituent or stakeholder management that involves evaluating the position of the constituent or stakeholder in relation to the proposed policy or policy modification based on specific criteria. The overall constituent or stakeholder analysis process consists of the following:

- Identify constituents and stakeholders;
- Identify the criteria by which to analyze the constituents or stakeholders;
- Prioritize the constituents or stakeholders; and
- Develop a plan of action to influence constituents and stakeholders to support or oppose the policy based on criteria analyzed.

There are several tools based on different criteria by which to analyze constituents and stakeholders. The analysis criteria can be based on power and interest (**Figure 15-1**), influence and interest (**Figure 15-2**), and influence and support (**Figure 15-3**). For each of these tools, the identified stakeholders should be placed in the appropriate quadrant. This provides a visual representation of the position of each group in relation to their support or opposition to the policy. This type of constituent or stakeholder analysis provides a process to account for and incorporate the needs of those who have an interest in the policy. The positional placement of constituents or stakeholders in relation to the policy using these tools assists with the identification of strategies to influence the constituent or stakeholders' support in alignment with the proposed policymaker's intent. For example, the Registered Nurses' Association of Ontario's (RNAO) stakeholder analysis tool (see Figure 15-3) proposes the following strategies in relation to the criteria of influence and support:

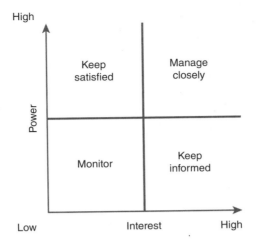

Figure 15-1   Constituent and Stakeholder Analysis: Power and Interest Analysis

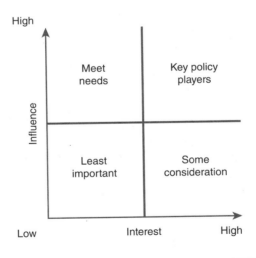

Figure 15-2   Constituent and Stakeholder Analysis: Influence and Interest

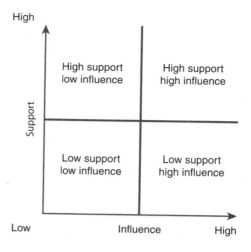

Figure 15-3   Constituent and Stakeholder Analysis: Influence and Support

1. High support and high influence—collaborate, involve, support and nurture, encourage feedback, prepare for change management, and empower;
2. High support and low influence—collaborate, encourage feedback, empower, encourage participation, prepare for change, involve at some level;
3. Low support and high influence—consensus building, relationship building, recognize needs, involve at some level, monitor, don't provoke into action; and
4. Low support and low influence—consensus building, relationship building, recognize needs; monitor, involve at some level (Registered Nurses' Association of Ontario, 2012).

Ten Tenets of Politics

Political affairs involve the competing interests of individuals, groups, and sometimes societies or countries. The following 10 tenets are provided to guide an individual's understanding of political environments as a means of promoting political power and political savvy. The 10 tenets of politics are:

- Every vote counts.
- It all starts and ends at home; constituency is important.

- Know thy friends and enemies, keep both close enough to know their political agenda.
- The majority rules; always count your votes ahead of time.
- Build political capital, develop networks of influence.
- Politics involves economics; donate funds or generate funds.
- Exercise your power, negotiate for your agenda.
- Reputations are built over time, but destroyed in an instant.
- Politics is a personal sport; the best defense is a good offense.
- Exercise the three Ps—politeness, persistence, and persuasiveness.

Political Savvy and Astuteness

Political savvy and astuteness are competencies that increase an individual's ability to influence others. Political savvy is the knowledge, skill, intuitiveness, and perception regarding the politics of a given situation. Political savvy provides an individual with the ability to garner a clear perception of the political reality of a situation within a specific situational context, and recognize the impact of multiple alternative courses of action. Political savvy can be learned and developed with experience. **Box 15-1** presents strategies for cultivating legislative relationships. Political astuteness refers to an understanding of different political agendas and power bases among various individuals, organizations, and institutions and

---

BOX 15-1   CULTIVATING LEGISLATIVE RELATIONSHIPS

- Provide the legislator and staff with substantive information in a simple and comprehensive manner. Legislators like statistics and data.
- Be concise in your discussions.
- Be specific in your request.
- Provide public testimony if requested and as necessary.
- Consider compromise but know your limits of negotiation.
- Take notes during your meeting with the legislator or staff and follow up with requested information or a note of thanks.
- Personal contact is preferred.
- Establish your constituency.
- Attend fundraisings.

the dynamic between them in relation to the proposed policy solution. Some recommended strategies to increase political savvy and astuteness are:

- Learn the policymaking process and political strategies.
- Identify key individuals and constituents.
- Use networks to gain information and communicate.
- Participate in various levels of political engagement such as grassroots efforts, political action committees, or special-interest groups.
- Increase your breadth of knowledge regarding current events by reading various newspapers of differing political opinions, books, and other publications.
- Listen to local, state, and national news programs.
- Serve on policy committees.
- Examine the local, national, or organizational culture and climate in relation to politics and the proposed policy.
- Understand the underlying social, political, and historical factors shaping local and national political realities.
- Gain experience in a legislative or judicial office.
- Secure an appointed position as a board member.

Political Power

Political power encapsulates the total means, influences, pressures, and scope of authority used to achieve outcomes desired by the power holder. Political power is the ability to exert control over the behavior of another. Political power can be exerted with decision making and without decision making. Not making a political decision can be just as powerful as making a political decision. Political power can be considered potential or kinetic power. Potential power exists when an individual has the ability to influence another individual. This power may be present but is in a dormant state. Kinetic power occurs when an individual uses his power source to actually influence the behavior of another individual. Box 15-2 presents general political strategies.

Two philosophical paradigms—monolithic and pluralistic—influence the means by which political power is used and cultivated. The monolithic paradigm model is an authoritarian framework with a fixed power structure. In the monolithic paradigm, the authoritarian position at the top of the societal structure has the most power and exerts the most control. The monolithic paradigm embraces an elitist perspective in which the privileged minority rule. In contrast, the pluralistic paradigm embraces power from a grassroots perspective, which originates from the people. The pluralistic paradigm considers each individual, and multiple individuals forming social networks, as capable of exerting political power. The pluralist paradigm embraces open competition, freedom to organize into

---

BOX 15-2   GENERAL POLITICAL STRATEGIES

- Persistence
- Incremental policy change
- Demonstration or pilot projects
- Frame the problem or policy within the context of known concerns.
- Be aware of covert messages, bring covert agendas into open
- Mobilize human capital and social networks.
- Quid pro quo—call in your favors
- Timing is critical—move when the window of opportunity exists.
- Exhibit a united front.
- Take measured risk.
- Use offensive strategies more than defensive strategies.
- Maximize your charisma.

---

interest groups, openness to lobbying, the right to freely communicate views, and intention that no elite groups dominate (Buse, Mays, & Walt, 2012).

The various stakeholders or constituents involved in policymaking processes have various levels and sources of power. The elements of power typically include instrumentalities (equipment, materials, funds), people, or information. The typical sources or types of power used to create political power include:

- Legitimate or structural—The authority associated with a specific position or role
- Reward—The ability to provide incentives or rewards to another individual for a desired behavior
- Coercive—The ability to exert a punishment on or withhold something from another individual to achieve a desired behavior
- Referent—The ability to influence others through associations with other individuals who have political power
- Expert—The ability to influence others is a result of some specialized information or knowledge
- Human resource—The ability to influence others resulting from interpersonal relationships or social networks
- Material or resource—The influence exerted by controlling access to property, natural resources, or fiscal resources
- Charisma or personal power—The ability to influence others based on certain attractive personal characteristics (Borkowski, 2015)

Political power is cultivated over time. Individuals who desire to influence policymaking should develop a political power base. The political power base can then be used at the appropriate time to influence specific policy outcomes. Several techniques to develop a political powerbase are:

- Cultivating social networks of persons who actively participate in policymaking, who remain socially connected with individuals who engage in policymaking, or who control access to individuals engaged in policymaking
- Creating a sense of obligation so that an individual needs to return a favor
- Developing a reputation as an influential individual
- Developing a base of support
- Creating a favorable image within the public domain
- Public alignment with a problem or policy
- Creating a sense of perceived dependence among stakeholders
- Forming organized groups such as coalitions (Borkowski, 2015; Harrison & Shirom, 1999)

Iron Triangles

Members of an iron triangle are congressional members, members of the executive branch of government, and special-interest groups. These three members form what is considered an unbreakable triad that proposes policy ideas and solutions. Some refer to the policy triangle as an iron-clad issue network (Smith & Larimer, 2016). The iron triangle is a type of policy monopoly. Policy monopolies consist of structural arrangements that maintain the policymaking ability within a small group of interested individuals.

Through political affiliations, special-interest groups coalesce together for a common interest and purpose. These groups frequently exhibit diverse types of political power throughout their vast networks. The groups that have and exert their political power to significantly influence policymaking are sometimes referred to as members of the "iron triangle." These iron triangles can consist of various constituents such as private interest groups, bureaucrats, and government officials who are linked together in mutually beneficial relationships. Members of the iron triangle are powerful fixtures within the policymaking arena.

Nurses' Stages of Political Engagement

Nurses should be politically involved in policy development, formulation, modification, analysis, and evaluation. Nurses' engagement in the policy process has been shaped by educational preparation, practice experience, professional engagement, and the maturity level of the nursing profession. Cohen and colleagues (Cohen, Mason, Kovner, Pulcini, & Scholaski, 1996) identified four stages that characterize the political development of the nursing profession.

The first stage is considered to range from the 1970s to the 1980s. This stage is known as the "buy-in" stage. During this stage nurses were reactive. Their reactivity was characterized by the increase of nursing's political sensitivity. The second stage, termed the "self-interest" stage, occurred from the 1980s to the 1990s. During the self-interest stage nursing political engagement was characterized by the development of nursing's political voice. In the self-interest stage, nursing organized political action or special-interest groups such as the American Nurses Association Political Action Committee. The third stage occurred during the 1990s. This stage is known as the "political sophistication" stage. In this stage, nurses began to be recognized as policymakers and healthcare leaders who had a valuable perspective and expertise in health policy. Lastly, stage four is known as the "leadership stage." This stage is characterized by nursing leadership in establishing policy agendas (Cohen et al., 1996; Mason, Gardner, Outlaw, & O'Grady, 2016). Nursing is assuming leadership as a key interest group or stakeholder through organized political participation.

Political Participation

Political participation is one political engagement maneuver. Scholzman, Burns, and Verba (1994) define political participation as any formal or informal activity that is mainstream or unconventional and occurs as a result of individual or collective action to either directly or indirectly influence what the government does. Organized political participation is the engagement in activities of groups or associations whose political engagement is organized around specific goals and a policy agenda. Nurses' decisions to engage in political activities is influenced by resources, motivation, and engagement, described further below (Verba, Scholzman, & Brady, 1995).

Nurses and other healthcare professionals represent a unique body of individuals within the policymaking arena. Nurses and other healthcare professionals possess both clinical and nonclinical knowledge in relation to health policy. As the largest segment of the U.S. healthcare system, nurses have a great potential for influencing the policymaking process through political participation. Similarly, Vandenhouten, Malakar, Kubsch, Block, and Gallagher-Lepak (2011) define political participation as activities that have the ability to influence governmental action directly by impacting the public policy or indirectly by influencing other individuals, groups, or institutions who make the policy. Political participation also involves activities that influence the election, appointment, or actions of government officials. Civic literacy is required for nurses to effectively impact policy. Civic literacy is the political knowledge and skills needed to influence policy. Verba and associates (1995) proposed a civic volunteerism model to explain an individual's decision to participate in political processes. Verba et al. (1995) identified three factors that impact an individual's level of political participation:

1. Resources—time, money, and civic skills
2. Psychological engagement—motivation, political interest, political efficacy, political information, partisanship, and family influences
3. Recruitment networks—exposure to cues to action; civic, religious, and professional association memberships; and engagement (Verba et al., 1995)

Nurses must have the resources or wherewithal to engage in the political process. Resources identified to influence nurses' participation are free time, available money, and civic skills. The second influencing factor is the nurses' motivation to engage in political activity. Political interest, personal efficacy, and partisanship influence the nurse's motivation to engage in organized political activities. The last influencing factor is opportunity, or the network of recruitment that supports political engagement. These influencing factors consist of requests or cues to action that stimulate the nurse to become involved in an organization's political activities.

Organizational Politics

Organizational politics consist of the ability to influence another individual, group, or system within an organization. An individual, group, or systems can exert organizational politics. To effectively use organizational politics as a means of effecting policy changes, an individual must engage in the diagnosis of organizational politics.

Diagnosis of Organizational Politics

The purpose of diagnosing organizational politics is to gain an understanding of the political structure and forces that effect policymaking changes within a defined organization. The process of diagnosing organizational politics consists of three steps: stakeholder analysis, force field analysis, and identifying influencing tactics.

Stakeholder analysis consists of identifying the stakeholders with vested interest in the problem or proposed solution. The stakeholder analysis consists of examining each stakeholder's position, powerbase, and organizational role such as change agent, change strategist, implementor, policy recipient, or nonparticipating stakeholder. Each stakeholder's capacity for action in the policymaking process should be assessed along with the potential impact of that action.

The force field analysis maps the balance of forces for and against a proposed policy. The force field analysis identifies the restraining and supportive or driving political forces of change within an organization. The restraining forces strive to maintain the status quo. The supportive or driving political forces attempt to advance the political agenda toward a desired outcome.

Lastly, organizational politics diagnosis identifies the influencing tactics. The influencing tactics assess the tactical means used to influence others. The tactics could consist of, but are not limited to, framing or priming an issue, controlling access to powerful individuals, forming coalitions, and threatening the use of sanctions.

Communication: The Tool of Politics

Politics involves the ability to influence the allocation of resources. The tool used to influence individuals or groups is communication. Communication is the transfer of information from the sender to the receiver through a specific medium. In the policymaking arena, communication is not only the sending of information but is also used to receive information, educate, solicit feedback, and clarify meaning. **Box 15-3** presents some political communication strategies. **Exhibits 15-1** through **15-5** provide various samples of letters and guidelines that can be used in the political engagement of legislators.

BOX 15-3   POLITICAL COMMUNICATION STRATEGIES

- First impressions occur within the first 30 seconds.
  - Your first words should count.
  - Introduce yourself clearly.
  - Repeat the name of the person you meet.
  - Smile and face the person you meet.
- Work the room.
  - Survey the room.
  - Position yourself near a group to gain entry into their conversation.
  - Make eye contact to gain entry into a conversation.
  - Shake hands for the length of the introduction.
- Use humor cautiously.
- Speak with confidence.
- Be aware of nonverbal communication.
- Listen, do not speak over another person, and do not interrupt.
- Use positive talk only, do not complain.
- Be culturally sensitive to interpersonal space.
- Exchange business cards with a note on the back to ensure you are remembered.

EXHIBIT 15-1   CONGRESSIONAL LETTER STRUCTURE

MEMBER OF THE HOUSE OF REPRESENTATIVES

The Honorable _____ (Name)
U.S. House of Representatives
Physical Address
Washington, DC 20515
Dear Representative _____ (Name)*

[*If you are writing to the Representative in his/her capacity as a committee chair, the letter should be addressed as Chairman or Chairwoman. The Speaker of the House should be addressed as Dear Speaker _____ (Name).]

MEMBER OF THE U.S. SENATE

The Honorable _____ (Name)
U.S. Senate
Physical Address
Washington, DC 20515
Dear Senator _____ (Name)*

[*If you are writing to the Senator in his/her capacity as a committee chair, the letter should be addressed as Chairman or Chairwoman. If the Senator is a majority or minority leader, the letter can be addressed as Dear Majority Leader _____ (Name) or Dear Minority Leader _____ (Name).]

EXHIBIT 15-2   GUIDELINES FOR POLICYMAKER LETTERS (CONGRESSIONAL OR STATE LEGISLATORS)

Letters to policymakers should be to the point but persuasive. Consider the following guidelines in preparing a letter to a policymaker:

- Send the letter to the correct policymaker.
- Clearly and simply state purpose of letter.
- Focus on a single topic or issue.
- Letter should be unique and personal.
- Length of letter should be no more than two pages, preferably one page.

EXHIBIT 15-2   GUIDELINES FOR POLICYMAKER LETTERS (CONGRESSIONAL OR STATE LEGISLATORS) (CONTINUED)

- Ensure that a local perspective is presented.
- Inform the policymaker of your identity—state who you are (establish constituency), and list your credentials.
- Provide factual information.
- Cite the specific bill number, proposed bill title, or name of act.
  House bill: H.R. ____
  House resolution: H.RES. ____
  House joint resolution: H.J.RES. ____
  Senate bill: S. ____
  Senate resolution: S.RES. ____
  Senate joint resolution: S.J.RES. ____
- Always close the letter with your requested action. Your request should be specific: "I request you to support/oppose . . ." or ". . . vote for/vote against. . . ."
- Use a professional and courteous tone.
- Close the letter with a reiteration of your specific request and provide all of your contact information.
- Proofread your letter for spelling, punctuation, grammar, and factual information.

EXHIBIT 15-3   SAMPLE LETTER FORMAT A

The Honorable (First and Last Names)
Physical Address
U.S. House of Representatives
Washington, DC 20515
Dear Representative (Last Name),

I am writing to request your support/opposition to H.R. _____, _____ (Title of Bill or Act). This bill was introduced by Representative _____ on _____ (date). H.R. ____ and intends to _____ _____ (cite purpose of bill).

[Next paragraph should focus on presenting your rationale for supporting or opposing the legislation. Ensure the presentation of facts and specific case information.]

(continues)

EXHIBIT 15-3   SAMPLE LETTER FORMAT A (CONTINUED)

[Concluding paragraph should iterate your request for support for, or opposition to, the legislation (by specific number and name). Offer your assistance and provide your contact information.]

Respectfully submitted,

[Name, Credentials, Address]

EXHIBIT 15-4   SAMPLE LETTER FORMAT B

The Honorable (First and Last Names)
Physical Address
U.S. House of Representatives
Washington, DC 20515
Dear Representative (Last Name),

As a constituent directly affected by (cite policy issue such as a disease, environmental issue, etc.), I am requesting your support/opposition to H.R. ___ (number), _____ (name of bill). [Thank policymaker for past legislative support in related or similar issues that supports your current request.]

[Second paragraph can focus on providing statistical data, research information, and personal experience that provides background for your request.]

[Concluding paragraph should thank policymaker for their consideration. Cite your specific request again. Ensure that you request for authorization and allocation policy. Provide your contact information.]

Respectfully requested,

[Name, Credentials, Address]

EXHIBIT 15-5   SAMPLE LETTER FORMAT C

The Honorable (First and Last Names)
Physical Address
U.S. House of Representatives
Washington, DC 20515
Dear Representative (Last Name),

EXHIBIT 15-5   SAMPLE LETTER FORMAT C (CONTINUED)

As a voter and a constituent of _____ (cite city or county and state), I urge you to support/oppose H.R. ___ (number), _____ (bill title). I also urge you to notify your colleagues in the House leadership, _____ (list names) and in the Senate _____ (list names) to inform them that you support/ oppose ____ (cite all bill numbers and titles related to the issue).

[Second paragraph should summarize your understanding of the intent of the proposed legislation. Cite your specific data and examples to support your request. You can also list your specific points of information you would like the policymaker to consider, such as "I would appreciate your consideration of the following informational points during your deliberation on ____" (cite issue—list the points, logically, and succinctly).]

[Last paragraph should make one last profound and persuasive argument regarding the impact of this proposed legislation. Cite your request one last time.]

Sincerely,

[Name, Credentials, Address]

There is also communication with legislators and legislative staff via email communication. It is recommended that email communication should follow the sample letters and guidelines format with the content of the letter inserted directly in the email, but the official letter should be attached to the email on formal letterhead with a signature.

Role of Social Media

The evolution of social media has transformed political processes. Social media is not only a means through which to communicate in policymaking but it also influences political processes through established social networks. The role of social media in politics is to promote optimal civic engagement free from boundaries and barriers within a relatively safe environment. Social media has the ability to transform the level of civic engagement and promote popular discourse. Social media provides policy and political information that is readily available, continuously accessible, and quickly disseminated, and offers a wide reach to a diverse audience.

Political Protocol

A political protocol consists of the written and unwritten rules that prescribe the appropriate manner of engaging with political and elected officials during formal functions and ceremonies. Political protocols exist to establish the order of precedence, rank, and power. Political protocol requires the utilization of appropriate titles and forms of address and the proper etiquette for introductions and seating arrangements.

Political Theory and Philosophical Perspective Overview

Political theory provides the theoretical framework that identifies the essential concepts, assumptions, and propositions that describe, explain, and predict political action, political policies, and the exercise of political power (Roskin, Cord, Medeiros, & Jones, 2017). Political theories can be systematic, ideological, empirical, or philosophical in nature. Systematic theories focus on the study of politics. Ideological theories focus on belief systems or the thought networks of political views. Empirical theories focus on quantitative data to describe, explain, and predict political behaviors. Lastly, the political philosophy theory places the study of politics within the larger nature of the universe and society. Refer to Chapter 4, Table 4-1, for a review of political ideology terminology.

Liberalism

Liberalism proposes an optimistic view based on the rational capability of individuals. Liberals believe in the ownership of private property and use of natural resources for individual human gain. Liberals emphasize support for democratic institutions, law, acceptance and tolerance of diversity, and peaceful reform (Roskin et al., 2017).

Socialism

Socialists are also referred to as Marxists. Socialism is monistic and materialistic. Socialism proposes shared property and wealth, and equal control and distribution of resources. Socialism focuses on the ability to generate product, or what is referred to as the forces of production. The material and systems used to produce the goods are owned by the state or country (Roskin et al., 2017).

Conservatism

Conservatism believes in the need to exert control and authority in society. The conservative perspective proposes that individuals with wealth and who are powerful in society have an obligation to provide resources and protect the less fortunate individuals in society. A conservative approach believes in a fundamental value system (Roskin et al., 2017).

Political System

A system is a complex whole that is greater than the sum of its parts. A system consists of a number of interrelated and interdependent parts or subsystems.

Easton (1965) describes a political system as comprising inputs, throughputs (process), and outputs. The political inputs consist of the demands, resources, and support generated from the constituents. The demands on the system also result from the constituents' needs and desires. The inputs are placed into the system to generate policy outputs. The outputs are the public policies generated to provide goods or services that meet the constituents' expressed needs and desires. The process or throughput of the political system consists of the policymaking process and political strategies that influence and impact the decision making that results in policy formulation.

Buse et al. (2012) propose that political systems can be classified into five groups, based on the degree of openness to policy solutions and alternatives. These five groups are liberal democratic regimes, egalitarian-authoritarian, traditional-inegalitarian, populist, and authoritarian-inegalitarian. The liberal democratic regime has stable political institutions that provide multiple opportunities to engage in political activities and strategies with a wide and diverse population representation. The egalitaria-authoritarian system is similar to the elitist perspective—a few ruling elite individuals and an authoritarian autocratic bureaucracy. The traditional-inegalitarian rule through traditional monarchs provides minimal opportunity for political participation in decision making. The populist system is based on single or dominant political parties. The authoritarian-inegalitarian system is associated with military-style governments that engage in repression as a form of political influence (Buse et al., 2012).

Similar to this classification, Heineman (1996) described three types of political systems: democratic, authoritarian, and totalitarian. The democratic system primarily exists in democratic societies. This system presents a political system in which political processes are decentralized and flexible. The democratic system uses interest groups, elections, and organized political parties as a means to influence policy. Authoritarian systems are characterized with strong centralized governmental control with strict limits on political activities. Free discussion, assembly, and association are limited in authoritarian systems. In the totalitarian system, propaganda is used to control the beliefs of the people and present a totalitarian and united front. In the totalitarian system, the government subordinates beliefs and behaviors to the needs of the government.

Political Process

The American democracy ensures a political process that provides each citizen with a voice. The political processes generally involve a multiparty political system. These political parties develop policy agendas and political platforms from which candidates generate their political campaign. Each candidate conducts a campaign to secure a nomination, or, for candidates who do not need a political party nomination, the campaign is used to promote their policy agenda or platform to persuade voters to support their candidacy. Constituents have an opportunity to engage in multiple aspects of the political process such as attending rallies, town hall meetings, listening to debates, reading about political candidates, and campaigning. Political strategies used in the political process are presented in a following section. **Table 15-1** provides some foundational terms inherent in the political process.

TABLE 15-1   POLITICAL TERMS

TERM	BRIEF DEFINITION
Affidavit	A sworn statement in writing, usually under oath, or an affirmation before an authorized officer or notary.
Caucus	A meeting of a local party or organized group who engages in an open forum. Formal caucuses may engage in the selection of convention delegates to the party's national convention. In some aspects, caucuses may organize to inform members and debate policy issues.
Conservatives	Individuals who emphasize free-market economic principles, prefer state and local government power over federal power, and are considered to be right of the center politically.
Convention	A meeting at the state or national level that has delegates from a political party. Delegates cast votes to nominate individuals for political office.
Delegate	An official representative selected by members of an organization or party to represent the general membership.
Electoral base	A politician or political nominee's major constituency group that provides unprecedented support and loyalty to the candidate.
Electoral college	The electoral college is a group of popularly elected representatives who formally vote on behalf of the citizens for the president and vice president of the United States as mandated by the Constitution.

TABLE 15-1   POLITICAL TERMS (CONTINUED)

TERM	BRIEF DEFINITION
GOP	Abbreviated nickname for the Republican Party, stands for "Grand Old Party."
Independent	An individual voter who is registered to vote but has not declared an affiliation with a political party.
Liberals	Individuals who are considered ideological, favor more power at the federal level and federal intervention into economic and social issues, and considered to be left of the center of the political spectrum.
Majority	A number greater than half of the total votes cast.
Platform	A position or political agenda drafted by a candidate or political party to note their policy action agenda.
Primary (closed or open)	A closed primary is an intraparty election open to only registered voters of the respective party. An open primary permits registered voters from other parties and independent registered voters to participate in the election.
Proxy	An individual authorized to act on another individual's behalf, generally a written document.
Swing voters	Individuals who are not yet committed to a policy or politician's election, these individuals may still be persuaded to vote in a particular manner; also known as "undecideds."
Third party	A political party that exists outside the Republican or Democratic parties.

Seeking an Elected Office

The decision to pursue an elected office is a decision that expands beyond the individual to include family members and significant others. The pursuit of an elected office requires a commitment of time, money, and energy. To secure an elected office, the individual must follow the candidate nomination and qualifying process for the respective elected position, including the payment of all fees. **Box 15-4** provides a listing of strategies for seeking an elected office.

BOX 15-4   STRATEGIES FOR SEEKING AN ELECTED OFFICE

- Ensure all candidate qualifications are met.
- Review the appropriate ethics rules or laws for the position.
- Ensure compliance with any local, state, and federal laws or prepare for any violations of laws to be presented in the political challenges from the opposition.
- Make a declaration of candidacy that garners media coverage.
- Declare any conflicts of interest.
- Develop a campaign agenda and schedule that details actions and strategies with specific target audiences and timelines.
- Develop your policy agenda.
- Develop a logo, slogan, and signage.
- Complete financial disclosure statements.
- Appoint a campaign team.
- Develop a campaign organizational structure with identified lines of decision-making authority.

Seeking an Appointed Office

Political appointments have a different process than that for seeking an elected office; however, political persuasion as to who should be appointed can be influenced through political maneuvers. Appointment to an office generally has a nomination process. This nomination process is designed to ensure proper vetting of the candidate before a recommendation is made to the official who makes the final decision regarding the appointment. At the state level, there may be nomination committees, professional associations, or other formal bodies that assist the governor's office to announce the office vacancy and solicit the nominations. In addition, the nomination committee, professional association, or other formal body may also conduct candidate interviews for the candidate's vetting process. After the nomination and recommendation process is completed, political persuasion can influence the choice of individual appointed. **Box 15-5** provides some suggested strategies. After the appointment, most appointed offices need to be confirmed by an authoritative body, such as the state senate.

Voting

Voting is an American's ultimate voice in political policy and is at the core of a democratic political process. Voting is a right that is exercised in the political process of elections. Elections involve four phases: voter registration, vote

---

BOX 15-5   POLITICAL STRATEGIES TO SECURE AN APPOINTED OFFICE

- Learn about the board or office—mission, strategic initiatives, current board members and their respective areas of expertise, candidate profile desired for board membership, current board or office activities, future and impending board or office challenges, alignment of your strengths and assets with the board or office.
- Attend board or any other public office meetings—ensure your presence is known.
- Speak to current board or appointed officers.
- Complete all candidacy documents correctly and in timely fashion.
- Notify influential leaders of your intent to secure the office—elected officials, appointed officials, and professional and community leaders. Build support for your nomination.
- Request that letters of support and/or oral recommendations are made to the office of appointments.
- Ensure your application has a cover letter, résumé or curriculum vitae (provide what is requested), and letters of recommendation or contact information for references.
- Once appointed, send formal notices of your appointment with thank-you notes to all individuals, groups, or organizations that may have influenced your appointment.

---

casting, collation and tabulation of votes, and certification of the results and announcement of the official results. The integrity of these phases impacts the ultimate integrity of the political process.

As a truly democratic process, voting involves four critical properties—private, incoercible, accurate, and verifiable. Voters have the right to keep their ballots secret. Voters should not be unduly influenced in any manner. In the political process, integrity of the system requires accuracy in the final tally of the results. Lastly, verifiability ensures that voters can prove to themselves that they cast a vote as intended and the vote was counted.

Political Strategies

Political strategies are the methods and processes used to influence the desired policy goals. In addition to the general political strategies presented, specific political strategies include activities in, or use of, conflict resolution, lobbying, interest groups, advocacy, media, policy briefs, policy speeches, position papers, resolutions, and coalition building.

Advocacy

Advocacy is considered any action that is in favor of, recommends, argues for a cause, supports or defends a position, represents others, or pleads a perspective, situation, or action on behalf of others. Advocacy's greatest impact can be realized through advocacy planning.

Advocacy planning occurs after there is a determination for a need to change or propose a new policy. Advocacy planning is considered "a strategic planning process that specifies goals, an implementation strategy with key stakeholder analysis, a SWOT (strengths, weaknesses, opportunities, threats) analysis, timeline, budget, and evaluation plan" (Patterson, 2008, p. 778). Advocacy planning's impact is to inform the policy agenda, shape the policy agenda, and inform policymakers regarding a specific policy solution. Patterson considers advocacy planning essential to ensure that policy change occurs. The formula proposed by Patterson for policy change consists of:

$$\text{Analysis} + \text{Advocacy planning} + \text{Action} = \text{Policy change}$$

The most common type of advocacy in politics is lobbying as individuals, political action groups/committees, or other interest groups. In addition to lobbying, advocacy activities consist of:

- Organizing groups to build a power base;
- Educating community members;
- Conducting research and disseminating findings;
- Organizing public rallies, debates, caucuses;
- Coordinating town hall–type listening sessions;
- Coordinating mass calls to legislators; and
- Educating legislators.

Some other advocacy strategies are to:

- Remain locally focused;
- Discuss reelection of legislators when advocating;
- Develop a story line that community members care about and one that attracts the legislator's attention; and
- Promote grassroots advocacy at the lowest organizational levels in the community.

Political Action Groups

Political action groups or committees are frequently referred to as PACs. PACs are the funding arm of special organizations or interest groups. These groups exert their political influence through financial contributions to a candidate's legislation or campaign. PACs use their constituents to raise funds to build their power base through the potential to make financial contributions. In addition, PACs engage in lobbying activities.

Lobbying

Lobbying is the process of approaching legislators or policymakers to present information to influence their decision making. Lobbying uses interpersonal relationships and power as a means of influencing decisions. The process of lobbying requires the individual lobbying a legislator or policymaker to be informed on the policy issue or problem. In addition, the lobbyist must be knowledgeable regarding the legislative history of the issue, the power dynamics within the context of the issue, and the position of the respective constituents of the policy. **Box 15-6** presents lobbying tips.

Lobbying can occur through letter writing, personal visits, and email. Email provides an immediate mechanism to lobby a legislator. The following fundamental questions provide direction for lobbying interaction with a legislator or legislative staff regarding a policy:

BOX 15-6   LOBBYING TIPS

- Know the issue.
- Identify the communication medium, setting, time, and purpose of each lobbying interaction.
- Share an anecdote that illustrates the problem and policy resolution.
- Provide a fact sheet.
- Provide your business card with a special note on the back of the card.
- Provide any information promised, follow up within 1 week after the visit.
- Do not become argumentative.
- Request a statement about the position of the legislator on the issue and their voting intent.
- Conclude with a thank-you note.

- What is the proposed problem the legislation will resolve?
- What is the rationale for approaching the problem with this policy?
- Does a nonlegislative solution exist? What are the possible nonlegislative options?
- Has this policy or similar policies been proposed before? If so, what was the resolution?
- What is the fiscal impact of this policy?
- Who will sponsor the legislation?
- What special-interest groups support, oppose, or remain neutral on the proposed policy? (Buppert, 2007; Ridenour & Harris, 2010).

Interest Groups

Interest groups are groups of individuals or organizations that share political, social, or other common interests and seek to influence the policymaking process. The benefits of interest groups are material, solidarity, and purposive. The material benefits exist from the sharing of tangible resources. The solidarity benefits include the power of masses or number of individuals. The purposive benefit includes ideological or issue-oriented goals. Buse et al. (2012) propose the following functions of interest groups in our society—participation, representation, political education, motivation, mobilization, and monitoring of political behavior and policy.

There are different types of interest groups. Interest groups can be classified according to organizational structure, economic focus, benefits obtained, or goals and missions. Organizational structure designates the interest group as centralized or decentralized, or by level of focus such as local, state, or national. Economic interest groups focus on the economic interests of their constituents. Benefit interest groups seek to obtain some tangible deliverable for their constituents. Lastly, goals or mission interest groups pursue a common goal or purpose.

Lobbying is the primary activity of interest groups. Interest groups use either an inside or outside strategy for lobbying. The inside strategy is direct and focused in nature within the interest group. In comparison, the outside strategy focuses on influencing the general public external to the interest group.

Media

The media has a critical role in policy agenda setting. Media literacy is a necessary competence of nurses and other healthcare providers. Media literacy is the ability to access, analyze, evaluate, create, and act using all forms of communication. Media literacy involves the ability to apply critical thinking skills to media messages analyzing all aspects of the communication. An excellent example of media literacy is debate analysis. As a competence, media literacy empowers democracy and supports the media's power structure.

The power of the media lies in the ability of editors, producers, anchors, reporters, and columnists to present policy problems or issues to the public within the public domain (Dye, 2017). The media exerts considerable influence in agenda setting. The media controls what is considered "news" and who is "newsworthy" (Dye, 2017). Those who work in the media do not necessarily control what we think but they definitely influence what we think about.

Media influence occurs through two activities, priming and framing. Priming is the psychological process used to increase the salience of an issue through the activation of previously acquired information. Priming utilizes cognitive psychology theory. In priming, the media has the ability to plant an idea or concept within an individual's mind about a specific issue or related issue. This priming facilitates the manner in which an individual thinks about or judges future information regarding the issue. Priming sets the stage for future messages regarding a policy problem or issue (Domke, Shah, & Wackman, 1998).

Framing complements the priming process. Framing is the activity used by the media to focus our attention on specific aspects of an issue while obscuring the focus on other aspects of the issue (Prouty, 2000). Framing impacts the assimilation of information regarding a policy. The frames create the boundaries within which individuals think about the policy. Two primary forms of frames are episodic and thematic (Porche, 2003). Episodic frames focus on the current person in trouble or current point of conflict in relation to a problem or issue. In contrast, thematic frames focus on the context within which the issue is unfolding. The thematic frames place the problem, issue, or policy within a broader social, political, environmental, or economic context.

Both priming and framing influence thinking regarding policy problems and policy resolutions. Priming and framing can be utilized to secure support for a specific policy issue. Therefore, they are also considered policy interventions.

Media Analysis

Media analysis facilitates the assessment of the extent to which the information presented is biased or the manner in which the information is biased. Policymakers are advised to conduct a media analysis of several sources prior to formulating an opinion. A media analysis permits an individual to critically evaluate media messages, learn who controls the media, and determine vested interest that are projected into the information presented. A media analysis consists of examining the medium of communication; who sends the message; what message is delivered; the rhetoric used to convey the message; effectiveness of the message in influencing opinions, affecting emotions, and generating

---

BOX 15-7   EDITORIAL GUIDELINES

- Opening paragraph
  - ◆ Outline the issue or problem.
  - ◆ Challenge an opinion or agree with an opinion.
  - ◆ Opening should be dramatic but factual.
- Second paragraph
  - ◆ Present your position.
  - ◆ Clearly state your rationale.
- Third paragraph
  - ◆ Acknowledge opposing thoughts or opinions.
  - ◆ Counter each opposing thought or opinion.
- Last paragraph
  - ◆ Present a call to action or challenge.
  - ◆ Be specific in your request for action.
- Signature—name, title, affiliation (if permitted), city, state

---

attention; and accuracy of the message. In addition to the use of media serving as a political strategy, responding to the media is also considered a political strategy. A typical response to the media might be an editorial or response to an editorial. **Box 15-7** presents some recommendations for writing an editorial.

Testimony

A testimony is an oral presentation delivered before a committee, organization, or an elected official. A testimony is typically an oral presentation of a position regarding a policy or policy issue. Oral testimony may be at the request or subpoena of a congressional or state legislative committee.

Oral testimonies may have severe time limitations, especially before congressional committees. It is imperative that the individual delivering an oral testimony secure the guidelines and procedures for the testimony prior to engaging in the delivery of the testimony. In the delivery of an oral testimony, adequate preparation is essential. The testifier must analyze the committee and their respective position on the policy or policy issue, research the policy or policy issue, and prepare the testimony with factual and experiential information. The oral testimony should be written so that copies can be submitted to the committee. This creates a public record of the testimony and serves as a resource for future reference. **Boxes 15-8** and **15-9** present some guidelines for the delivery of an oral testimony (Kleinkauf, 1981).

BOX 15-8   TRIAL TESTIMONY GUIDELINES

- Review all evidence and documents prior to the trial, especially your deposition.
- Wear professional attire.
- Convey confidence, sincerity, impartiality, and control.
- Speak clearly, keeping eye contact with the person asking the question, and as appropriate to the jury or judge.
- Provide succinct and precise answers.
- Answer only the question posed.
- Control your emotions and facial expressions.
- Remain within the limits of your knowledge, expertise, and credentials.
- Explain any terms that may be unfamiliar to the judge or jury.
- Do not discuss the case in public areas.
- Do not speak with any juror.

BOX 15-9   LEGISLATIVE TESTIMONY GUIDELINES

- Introduce yourself.
- Provide credentials.
- State who you are representing; it is critical to establish your constituency.
- Open with a position statement that clearly identifies the policy or issue to which you are speaking.
- Present the body of your speech using exemplars to connect with the committee and factual data to support your position.
- If speaking to a policy issue, ensure that you present your position relative to both sides of the issue with supporting evidence and exemplars.
- If presenting before a judicial committee, ensure that you discuss legal issues.
- Compare and align your testimony with other groups or organizations.
- Conclude with a specific request or call for action—be specific in what action you are requesting.
- Conclude by offering to answer questions.

(continues)

BOX 15-9   LEGISLATIVE TESTIMONY GUIDELINES (CONTINUED)

- Avoid reading directly from a written testimony.
- Avoid shuffling papers.
- Make eye contact.
- Be aware of your voice projection and body language.
- Know the titles and positions of everyone on the committee.
- Address committee members by their official and honorary titles.
- Expect and be prepared to answer questions; do not become argumentative during the question and answer session; If you disagree, respectfully inform the person you disagree with and present your position briefly.
- Follow-up is critical—always provide any information requested, and send thank-you notes.

Policy Speeches

A policy speech intersects the principles of policymaking, politics, and public speaking. Policy speeches are conducted during political campaigns and during policy agenda setting and policymaking activities. Any individual who engages in public speaking to communicate a specific position regarding a policy can render policy speeches. **Box 15-10** presents some policy speech guidelines.

Policy Briefs

Policy briefs provide a quick explanation of the policy issue or problem and the proposed policy, along with policy and political assessments. The policy briefing provides a quick and informative snapshot of the issue and policy solution. Policy briefs can be written or oral. A written policy brief is frequently referred to as a "one pager." The typical policy briefing paper includes a summary of the issue, background information, policy alternatives, various stakeholder and constituency perspectives on each policy alternative, and recommended action. An oral policy briefing should be presented in a concise and logical manner that includes the same information described for a written policy briefing. **Box 15-11** presents the format for a policy brief (Jennings, 2002). **Box 15-12** presents guidelines that can be used to evaluate the quality of a policy brief (Britner & Alpert, 2005).

BOX 15-10   POLICY SPEECH GUIDELINES

- Introduction
  - Establish credibility.
  - Connect with the audience in opening remarks.
- Body
  - Establish a slogan or memorable tagline.
  - Describe the problem: give examples, connect with the constituents, give statistics.
  - Present solutions.
  - Illustrate the points.
  - Use expert testimonials.
  - Present advantages and disadvantages.
  - Acknowledge other positions and render them nonviable.
  - Present a call to action to your audience.
- Conclusions
  - Review the problem.
  - Restate the solutions and call to action.
  - Conclude with a memorable closer.

BOX 15-11   POLICY BRIEF GUIDELINES

- Introductory statement of issue
  - Clear statement of the issue or problem to be addressed
- Context and background of the issue
  - Most effective in bulleted format
  - Concise
  - Background of the issue
  - Key regulatory and legislative history
  - Related data—statistics, demographics, recent trends
  - Current references for all data provided
- Policy options or alternatives
  - Pros and cons of each policy option or alternative
  - Timetable for action

(continues)

BOX 15-11   POLICY BRIEF GUIDELINES (CONTINUED)

- ◆ Political perspective associated with each policy option and alternative
- ◆ Placement of each policy option within the policymakers' policy agenda, values, and previous commitments
- ◆ Political vote count for each policy option if known
- Resources
  - ◆ Full references citations

BOX 15-12   POLICY BRIEF EVALUATION CRITERIA

- Quality of content
  - ◆ Cohesive and logical argument
  - ◆ Relevant research and data used
  - ◆ Integrated review of background information
  - ◆ Statements supported with references
  - ◆ Comprehensive perspective
- Organization
  - ◆ Clear statement of the issue or problem
  - ◆ Conclusions of current state of knowledge from convergent findings
  - ◆ Clear recommendations for action
- Quality of writing
  - ◆ Written at the appropriate level for the policymaker
  - ◆ Assumes no previous knowledge regarding subject matter
  - ◆ Objective and scientific
  - ◆ Appropriate use of grammar, spelling, punctuation
  - ◆ Concisely written

Position Papers

A position paper is used to educate, generate support on an issue, and to formalize a position or agenda in relation to a policy issue. A position paper typically describes the individual's or organization's position on an issue, and a recommended solution with the supporting rationale for the position. The position paper is based on evidence with a sound argument provided. In addition, a position paper can introduce an organization's philosophical intent regarding a social or political issue.

A position paper is also known as a "white paper." The term *white paper* is used less often today to remain culturally sensitive to specific populations. The term *white paper* originated from the term *white book*, which was an official government publication. **Boxes 15-13, 15-14,** and **15-15** present position paper purpose, format, and guidelines. Some organizations use a simple PICO format for the writing of a position paper, as follows:

- Problem—What is the problem or question?
- Ideas or issues—What ideas or evidence is/are in the literature?
- Complete, complement, or compatible—How does position paper advance organization and complement existing positions, and is it compatible with existing positions?
- Outcome—What is the expected outcome of the development and dissemination of the position paper?

BOX 15-13   POSITION PAPER PURPOSE

- Frame the policy discussion on the issue or problem.
- Organize and outline the position of an individual or organization.
- Formally inform other constituents about your position on the issue or problem.
- Present recommended policy solutions.
- Provide a framework from which to develop and formulate specific policies or resolutions.
- Establish a voice and credibility on the issue or problem.

BOX 15-14   POSITION PAPER FORMAT

Organizations are encouraged to develop a consistent position paper template. In addition, organizations are encouraged to have a systematic process for the development and formulation of position papers, continual analysis and review of current and past position papers, method of archiving position papers, and process for the approval of position papers that includes a period of public or organizational comment and debate. If an organization is updating or developing a new position paper, the organization should identify previous or related position statements and clarify which position statement has supremacy or takes precedence. This can be accomplished through one statement: "This position paper supersedes the position paper titled _____, ratified on _____ (date), by _____ (name of organization)."

(continues)

BOX 15-14 POSITION PAPER FORMAT (CONTINUED)

Typical format of a position paper:

- Cite the mission of the organization, organizational identity, organizational address, and constituents represented.
- Provide supporting evidence and data, factual information.
- Organize into three sections:
  - Introduction
  - Body
  - Conclusion
- Introduction
  - Identify the issue or topic of the position paper.
  - Include a thesis statement that clearly presents the main idea of the position.
- Body
  - Provide background information on the issue with supporting evidence and data.
  - Provide one idea per paragraph regarding the issue.
  - Build your argument logically with transition of thought between the paragraphs.
  - Provide a discussion of the supporting and opposing position of the argument. Clearly articulate your position and the rationale supporting your position.
  - Reference supporting organizations, legislation, regulations.
  - Cite figures, tables.
  - Provide cases or exemplars.
  - Use primary source authoritative references, interviews, expert opinions, leader statements, indisputable dates or events.
  - Use an inductive logical reasoning approach.
- Conclusion
  - Provide declaration of resolution to the issue.
  - Suggest courses of action.
  - Reinforce ideas without repeating.
- Appendixes
- References
- Authors
- Executive summary

BOX 15-15   POSITION PAPER GUIDELINES

- Use official letterhead with organizational logo.
- Cite references.
- Provide contact information for leaders quoted.
- Paper should focus on a single issue or problem.
- Thesis statement should articulate the main premise and position.
- Both supporting and opposing arguments should be recognized.
- Provide rationale for the position.
- Length should be one to two pages.
- An organizational position paper should include:
  - Brief introduction of your organization
  - Organizational history related to the issue, problem, or topic
  - Impact of issue or problem on your organization
  - Organizational current policies with respect to the issue and supporting rationale for your policies
  - Quotes from your organizational leaders about the issue or problem
  - Statistics or empirical research that supports your organization's position
  - Actions taken by your organization related to the issue or problem
  - Past position papers or resolutions adopted and ratified by organization on the issue or problem
  - Organizational opinion or suggested resolution to the issue or problem

---

Organizations generally have an approval process determined by the organization's governance document, bylaws, or operational procedures. In addition, organizations generally have an established procedure to continually improve the quality of and update position papers to ensure continual relevance of the position paper. **Box 15-16** provides procedure recommendations for approval and revision of position papers.

A communication strategy should be planned in the form of a position paper dissemination plan. The dissemination plan promotes access to and awareness of the position. A position paper dissemination plan is also a measure to secure

---

BOX 15-16   POSITION PAPER APPROVAL PROCEDURAL RECOMMENDATIONS

- Initial recommendation for the need of a position paper. Identify the mechanisms or groups that can request the development of a position paper. Identify a required position paper proposal format to include brief explanation of issue, background, purpose, expected outcome, proposed timeline for development, resources required, and fiscal impact. Position paper should have a clearly defined purpose and expected outcome.
- Approval authority. Establish the authorizing individual, group, or representatives for final approval. Clearly outline the position paper approval process.
- Position papers should contain an expiration date or identified date for review or renewal, generally not to exceed 3 years.
- Authors draft position paper using approved format.
- Factual vetting of position paper.
- Authorized approval body should review draft.
- Public comment period. Provide discussion and debate on position paper draft by stakeholders and constituents.
- Revise position paper based on stakeholder and constituent feedback.
- Clearly define possible action on position paper:
  - Adoption
  - Modification
  - Modification and adoption
  - Reject in entirety

---

support on the policy position. **Box 15-17** presents elements of a position paper dissemination plan. **Figure 15-4** summarizes the position paper development process.

A resolution is a formal motion, position, or solution proposed by an executive or governing body or organization. A resolution consists of four parts: heading, subject, preamble, and operative clause. **Box 15-18** presents guidelines for writing each of the four parts of a resolution.

BOX 15-17   POSITION PAPER DISSEMINATION PLAN ELEMENTS

- Organizational mission statement or purpose to be communicated with or on the position paper document;
- Press release—quote from author or representative of the group, association, or organization, identify embargo time and time for press release
- Professional associations and organizations—list of professional organizations that should receive a copy
- Executive and federal agencies—executive offices and agencies that should receive a copy
- Public health or medical organizations
- Briefing events on capitol hill, state legislature, or to professional associations or organizations
- Distribution to media outlets—wide distribution to media outlets such as national public radio (NPR), associated press (AP)
- Social media—post on Twitter, Facebook
- Blog—post on a blog or start a blog on the position paper
- Publications—include in a manuscript, write an editorial or letter to the editor
- Poster presentations—present poster on position statement at conferences
- Letters—direct mail letter to legislators and congressional representatives and staffers
- Provide statements on fiscal impact of position
- Identify a contact person for further information on the position paper

---

Coalition Building

A coalition is a group of individuals or group of organizations that form together around a common area of interest (Porche, 2003). Coalitions consolidate grassroots-level power and generate grassroots advocacy. Coalitions increase the political power structure by increasing the number of individuals supporting a specific policy. The power of coalitions is the ability to convene and bring together individuals from diverse perspectives to focus on a clearly

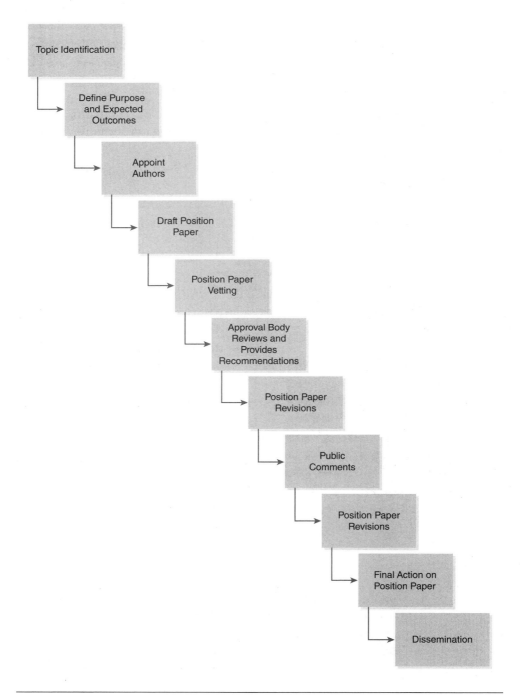

Figure 15-4   Simple Position Paper Development Process Resolutions

BOX 15-18 RESOLUTION WRITING GUIDELINES

- Format
  - Use single spacing with double spacing between clauses
  - Each line should be numbered along the left margin of the paper
  - Each clause should begin with the appropriate introductory phrase
  - Preamble clauses end with a comma and the word "and"
  - The last preamble clause should end with a period
  - Each operative clause ends with a semicolon
  - The last operative clause ends with a period
- Resolution heading
  - Provides the identification of the resolution
  - States where the resolution will be submitted
  - States the topic
  - Names the author
  - Sample heading:
    - SUBMITTED TO:
    - SUBJECT:
    - PROPOSED BY:
    - DATE:
- Preamble
  - First half of the resolution
  - Explains why the action of the operative clauses is needed
  - States any past action
  - First word of preamble clause sets the tone
  - Defines the purpose
  - Provides evidence and data to support the operative clauses
  - Initiating phrases for preamble clause:
    - Acknowledging
    - Affirming
    - Alarmed
    - Anxious
    - Appreciating
    - Approving
    - Aware
    - Bearing in mind
    - Being convinced

(continues)

BOX 15-18   RESOLUTION WRITING GUIDELINES (CONTINUED)

- Cognizant
- Concerned
- Confident
- Conscious
- Contemplating
- Convinced
- Declaring
- Deeply disturbed
- Deploring
- Desiring
- Determined
- Emphasizing
- Encouraged

- Endorsing
- Expressing
- Expecting
- Fulfilling
- Fully
- Grieved
- Guided by
- Having
- Keep in mind
- Mindful
- Observing
- Noting
- Reaffirming

- Realizing
- Recalling
- Recognizing
- Referring
- Regretting
- Reiterating
- Seeking
- Stressing
- Welcoming
- Taking into account
- Taking into consideration
- Taking note

- Operative clause
  - Tells the reader the action needed
  - First word should be a verb
  - Initiating operative phrases:
    - Accepts
    - Adopts
    - Affirms
    - Appeals
    - Appreciates
    - Approves
    - Authorizes
    - Calls upon
    - Commends
    - Concurs
    - Condemns
    - Confirms
    - Congratulates
    - Considers
    - Decides

    - Declares
    - Deplores
    - Designates
    - Directs
    - Expresses its appreciation
    - Expresses the belief
    - Expresses conviction
    - Expresses the hope
    - Expresses its regret
    - Expresses sympathy

    - Expresses thanks
    - Further invites
    - Further proclaims
    - Further reminds
    - Further recommends
    - Further requests
    - Further resolves
    - Instructs
    - Reaffirms
    - Recognizes

BOX 15-18   RESOLUTION WRITING GUIDELINES (CONTINUED)

- Recommends
- Regrets
- Reiterates
- Renews its appeal

- Repeats
- Suggests
- Supports
- Takes note of
- Transmits

- Urges
- Welcomes

---

defined purpose, in order to achieve a common goal. Coalitions ensure a broad base of ideas, opinions, and expertise. In addition, each member or organizational partner of the coalition adds a different type of resource to the coalition. The cornerstones of an effective coalition are leadership, diverse membership, and diverse resource pool. The following are some suggested steps for the formation of a coalition:

- Define needs, objectives, scope of interest, and type of influence needed from coalition members.
- Analyze the breadth of influence of the coalition members.
- Secure resources needed to establish basic infrastructure of a coalition.
- Identify potential members of the coalition. This is an iterative process—as the coalition forms, and objectives are refined, the need for a specific type of coalition member will expand the search for other coalition members.
- Develop vision and mission statements.
- Convene public meetings of the coalition.
- Utilize feedback from coalition members to refine the vision, mission, and objectives of the coalition; invite more members; and develop strategic plans that include action work plans.
- Establish the coalition's identity (name, bylaws, logo, letterhead, brand identity, etc.).
- Develop coalition materials (fact sheets, position papers, policy briefs, etc.).
- Engage in advocacy or other defined activities of the coalition.

A goal of a coalition is to advance a specific policy agenda. The primary vehicles for advancing the coalition's agenda are communication and developing a financial base. Coalitions develop extensive networks through which to publicize their perspectives. The five Rs for effective advocacy are: having the Right preparation on the issue, using the Right communicator, sending the Right message, proposing the Right request, and Repeating the advocacy or lobbying efforts as necessary to ensure success (Berkowitz & Wolff, 2000).

Political Polls

Political polls are surveys used to measure the potential of a specific candidate to win an election or to determine the level of support for a specific issue or policy. Political poll results are a means to persuade individuals to the popular public opinion; however, political polls can be framed in a manner that demonstrates partisan support in a specific direction. Political polls are conducted in most elections. Exit polls are highly influenced by election turnout by constituents. Exit polls are expected to measure actual votes (Heineman, 1996). These exit political polls shape and form public opinion and sentiment as a means to prime and frame policy.

Public Opinion

Public opinion creates a "group think" mentality that may persuade some individuals to align their beliefs and actions with the majority, particularly if it is believed that this will lead to a desired outcome. Public opinion informs and shapes policy agendas and potential policy alternatives. Public opinion is a good assessment of the national mood. Even though public opinion is a measure of the national mood, some problems with using this as a measure are that the public opinion or national mood may not reflect the public's true policy preference and that national mood is highly volatile with the ability to change without significant warning (Smith & Larimer, 2016).

Conflict Resolution

The political process results in competing problems and policy agendas. The clash of competing interests may result in conflict. Conflict may be a direct or indirect result of the political process. Conflict is an incongruence in ideas, values, or beliefs between two or more individuals or groups and can result in antagonistic actions between these factions. There are four primary types of conflict—intrapersonal, interpersonal, intergroup, and organizational. Intrapersonal conflict occurs within an individual when there

---

BOX 15-19 CONFLICT RESOLUTION COMMUNICATION STRATEGIES

- Communicate and listen
- Clarify intent
- Clarify meaning
- Summarize discussion
- Paraphrase discussion
- Evaluate congruence between written, spoken, and nonverbal

---

are conflicting values or opinions regarding the best policy alternatives. Interpersonal conflict occurs between two individuals. Intergroup conflict occurs between two or more groups. Organizational conflict can be a result of intrapersonal, interpersonal, or intergroup conflict that occurs within a defined organization. In addition to conflict resulting from incongruent ideas, values, or beliefs, conflict can be the result of disagreement regarding power and status.

Communication is the means of reducing conflict. Some communication strategies to resolve conflict are described in **Box 15-19**. Conflict resolution is the process of resolving the incongruence into a mutually acceptable solution. Other conflict resolution strategies are:

- Denial or withdrawal—Avoids the conflict with the hope that it will resolve on its own
- Suppression—Downplays the magnitude of the disagreement
- Power or dominance—Resolves conflict through the use of positional power or authority or majority rule
- Compromise—Resolves issue when both sides forfeit something of value
- Collaboration—Creates a win-win situation in which both parties focus on a mutual goal

Thomas and Kilmann (2002) propose that everyone has a preferred conflict resolution style. Thomas and Kilmann have developed a conflict instrument to measure an individual's conflict preference, known as the TKI, or Thomas-Kilmann Conflict Mode Instrument. The TKI identifies five conflict resolution modes that are used to resolve conflict:

- Avoiding—Prefer not to address the issue, may withdraw or suppress feelings and actions.

- Compromising—Identify a mutually acceptable solution that satisfies all parties involved.
- Accommodating—Neglect personal concerns to satisfy the concerns of the other party.
- Competing—Pursue own concerns at the expense of the other party.
- Collaborating—Will work with others to explore an option that satisfies both parties (Thomas & Kilmann, 2002).

Conflict Negotiation

Policy formulation and modification are wrought with conflict. Conflict negotiation skills are critical for constituents, stakeholders, policymakers, politicians, and lobbyists. Conflict negotiation is the process used to resolve conflict that consists of both sides presenting their positions while continuing to move toward an acceptable solution. Conflict negotiation is a strategy built on trust, relationship, and communication. **Box 15-20** presents conflict negotiation strategies to resolve conflicts.

BOX 15-20   CONFLICT NEGOTIATION STRATEGIES

- Assess each party's perspective of the issue
- Identify what a win-win solution would look like
- Remain focused on the problem, not feelings or beliefs
- Make no assumptions or conclusions without supporting data
- Listen without interrupting
- Remain in the present—forget the past
- Consider interest and values separately—separate personal perspectives and emotions
- Appeal to and establish overarching values for the negotiation process
- Engage in relationship-building dialogue
- Establish a common ground or cause
- Understand differences—learn as much as you can about the other party's needs, desires, interest, and values
- Avoid emotional provocation
- Use time wisely—time can be a negotiation strategy within itself

---

During conflict negotiations, sometimes an impasse is reached. An impasse is a situation in which an immediate resolution cannot be achieved. An impasse can generate feelings of frustration, anger, and disillusionment. Recommendations during an impasse consist of:

- Taking a break from negotiations for a defined period of time;
- Secure a mediator;
- Reframing the issue and potential solutions;
- Reaffirming commitment to resolution, goals, and values;
- Break the problem into manageable problem areas and resolve the components of the problem that can be resolved;
- Remain flexible but know your negotiation "bottom line of compromise";
- Validate and reaffirm areas of agreement;
- Reaffirm ground rules to the negotiation process; and
- Consider caucusing on the issue, then returning to the negotiation table.

Political Campaigns

The activity of campaigning is a political strategy that can have multiple purposes. Some of the purposes of a campaign are to create name recognition and build a political base or constituency, influence others to vote for a specific candidate, frame an issue or problem, or educate constituents regarding policies. The political campaign strategy can include working on a political campaign or running a political campaign. **Box 15-21** presents guidelines for managing a political campaign. The three cardinal principles of campaigning are know thyself, know thy voters, and know thy opponent.

BOX 15-21   CAMPAIGN GUIDELINES

- Establish an exploration committee to evaluate potential for candidacy
  - Examine the political environment
    - Analysis of constituency
    - Voter history

(continues)

BOX 15-21   CAMPAIGN GUIDELINES (CONTINUED)

- Opponent profiles
- Concurrent political races
- Media analysis
- Select a campaign manager
- Appoint a campaign committee
  - Hire staff
  - Develop campaign website
- Identify campaign strategy by writing a campaign plan
  - Develop a platform
  - Compose a brand and slogan
  - Engage in opposition research
  - Vet your opponent
  - Public opinion polls, polling, and geomapping
  - Examine campaign resources—time, money, people, and talent
  - Secure campaign funding
  - Fundraising
  - Establish communication medium
  - Identify "kitchen cabinet"
  - Establish an advisory board
  - Identify a spokesperson
  - Plan to impact voter turnout, persuade voters
  - Public appearances and speeches
  - Grassroots efforts
  - Secure endorsements and political party support
  - Publicize campaign schedule and events
  - Develop voter contact list
- Candidate development
  - Listen and lead
  - Meet opinion leaders
  - Engage in grassroots activities
  - Learn key media players
  - Learn community organizations and special-interest groups
  - Polish personal communication skills and charisma

Vetting

Vetting is a process of conducting a comprehensive background examination and evaluation of individual prior to appointing the person to a position or selecting the individual as a partner in a political campaign. Vetting can also occur before an individual is offered employment, especially for senior executive or upper echelon positions within an organization. The media engages in its own vetting process, typically within a public forum such as newspaper articles or televised news reports. The following steps are proposed as critical to ensuring a successful vetting process:

- Identify the characteristics needed for the respective position to include but not be limited to knowledge, attitude, behaviors, skills, competencies, political connections, and access to resources.
- Identify potential candidates.
- Initiate a basic demographic and personal questionnaire to learn about the person's heritage and past personal and professional experiences. If the candidate is married or partnered, conduct the same investigation of the candidate's partner.
- Administer a specialized questionnaire that focuses on the specific position for which the individual is being vetted.
- Conduct a background check that examines any illegal or criminal activity or any interactions with the legal system.
- Examine all public records on the candidate.
- If the candidate is an elected official, scrutinize all previous votes on policies.
- Evaluate each public speech and critique all published reports and scholarly articles presented by the candidate.
- Conduct a personal financial background check to include all campaign contributions, income tax filings, employment of others, and investment strategies.

Debate

A debate is a formal method of verbal argument. An argument for the purpose of a debate is a position with a justification or rationale that supports the debater's assertion on the topic or issue. Most debates center on a controversial issue. The art of debate does not always rely solely on logic and reason, and can be used to educate the public, clarify issues, develop an agenda, assert a position on a topic, and persuade the audience in the direction of a specific policy or action. Therefore, debates also rely on appeal. The winning debater is the individual who presents the best argumentative framework regarding the issue being debated. There are various types of debates.

The four typical types of debates are parliamentary, Lincoln-Douglas, cross-examination, and academic. A parliamentary debate requires no prior research on a policy issue. A parliamentary debate generally debates a resolution following accepted parliamentary procedures. Parliamentary debates rely heavily on logic, persuasiveness, and factual information. The Lincoln-Douglas debate is named after the original debate that occurred between Abraham Lincoln and Stephen A. Douglas regarding slavery. A Lincoln-Douglas debate is generally a one-on-one debate between two individuals. A Lincoln-Douglas debate generally has two individuals who engage in a verbal argumentative dialogue regarding issues centered on moral issues, policy propositions, or values. The cross-examination debate is also known as the policy debate, or the team debate. In a cross-examination debate, one team presents an affirmative position regarding a policy issue and one team presents a negative position regarding the same policy issue. An academic debate is purely for academic enhancement; it focuses on presenting information and knowledge to educate and create an awareness of the policy issue or policy. **Box 15-22** presents some general guidelines that may be used for a debate. **Box 15-23** presents a debate format.

Debates are a political strategy to inform the public and learn the opponent's beliefs, values, knowledge, and policy position. In addition, debates are symbolic in nature with contextual meaning communicated about the candidate's political ideology and policy agenda. **Box 15-24** presents the meaning of colors that are used to communicate messages in debates. Debate analysis can be used as a means of advancing the understanding of political platforms, political ideology of a candidate, and policy agenda. **Box 15-25** provides guidelines for debate analysis.

BOX 15-22   GUIDELINES FOR A DEBATE

- Debate preparation
  - Prepare background information.
  - Prepare a comprehensive bibliography and reference list to document facts.
  - Read a wide breadth of information on the topic.
  - Prepare a debate strategy to frame the argument.
  - Know your opponent's position and argument as well as know your own position.
- In a team debate, each participant should speak.
- In a debate, each team or individual typically begins with a constructive speech that presents their basic position on the issue or policy agenda.

BOX 15-22 GUIDELINES FOR A DEBATE (CONTINUED)

- Affirmative argument is typically presented first.
- Negative argument typically presents first rebuttal.
- New constructive arguments are typically not introduced in the rebuttal period, unless they answer a direct question.
- Terms used should be well understood in terms of definition and intent.
- The individual who proposes an assertion in the debate is responsible for proving the assertion.
- Evidence and logic should support each assertion.
- Facts should be accurate.
- Restatement or a quotation of an opponent's argumentative statement must be accurate.
- Plans of action presented during a debate must be clearly outlined and explained.
- Debate rules should be established that define
  - Time allotted for entire debate period
  - Time allotted for the constructive introductory statements
  - Time allotted to each speaker to present affirmative and negative statement
  - Time allotted for each rebuttal
  - Time allotted for closing statement
  - Acceptable behavior during the debate
  - Permissibility of visual aids during debate
  - Determination of whether the debate will have a rebuttal period and closing summary period or if the rebuttal period will serve as the closing summary.
- Avoid emotionally charged words.
- Exercise caution when asserting causal relationships.
- Avoid innuendo.
- Avoid rhetorical statements or the presentation of malevolent ideas.
- Do not commit *ad hominem*—attacking the presenter and not the argument.
- Do not assert your authority; argue with persuasion.
- Avoid pleading.
- Present a clear and consistent message.

BOX 15-23   DEBATE FORMATS

General Format

- Constructive opening of affirmative
- Constructive opening of negative side
- First affirmative speech
- Question and answer period
- First negative speech
- Question and answer period
- Second affirmative speech
- Second negative speech
- Third affirmative speech

Lincoln-Douglas

- First affirmative constructive statement
- Cross-examination of affirmative statements by negative side
- First negative constructive statement
- Cross-examination of negative statements by affirmative side
- First affirmative rebuttal to negative side's argument
- Negative side rebuts the affirmative side's statements
- Second affirmative rebuttal (generally the final)

Lincoln-Douglas (Team Format)

- Each team member presents an affirmative or negative statement and responds once to the other team in the cross-examination.
- First affirmative constructive statement
- Cross-examination of affirmative statements by negative team
- First negative constructive statements
- Cross-examination of negative teams by affirmative team
- Second affirmative constructive statement by another team member
- Cross-examination of affirmative statement by another negative team member
- Second negative constructive by another team member
- Cross-examination of negative statements by another affirmative team member
- First negative rebuttal

BOX 15-23   DEBATE FORMATS (CONTINUED)

- First affirmative rebuttal
- Second negative rebuttal
- Second affirmative rebuttal (concludes debate)

BOX 15-24   POLITICAL SYMBOLISM OF COLORS

Red—energy, war, danger, strength, power, determination as well as passion, desire, love, power, nobility, and attention to detail

Blue—depth, stability, trust, loyalty, wisdom, confidence, intelligence, faith, and truth

Yellow—joy, happiness, intellect, and energy

Green—growth, harmony, freshness, fertility, safety, and money

White—light, goodness, innocence, purity, virginity, safety, color of perfection, faith

Purple—combines the stability of blue and the energy of red; symbolizes royalty, power, nobility, luxury, and ambition; conveys wealth and extravagance; associated with wisdom, dignity, independence, creativity, mystery, and magic; a color of unity

Black—power, elegance, formality, death, evil, and mystery

BOX 15-25   DEBATE ANALYSIS GUIDELINES

- Fact checking—evaluate the accuracy of the information presented
- Presentation delivery—spoke confidently with conviction
- Content depth and breadth—exhibited a comprehensive understanding of the various aspects of the issue
- Reaction—what was the biggest surprise, what was learned during debate, what part of the debate changed your point of view, what changed or confirmed your point of view, what was the most interesting or contentious part of the debate and why
- Political relationship—political party affiliation of debater, alignment of debater's statements with political party platform; philosophical assumptions and basic beliefs identified of each debater
- Location—where was debate held

(continues)

BOX 15-25   DEBATE ANALYSIS GUIDELINES (CONTINUED)

- Sponsorship—who sponsored the debate, advertisements at the debate location, advertisements during the debate, advertisements after the debate
- Content analysis—word count of the debate, number of times specific words used, repetitive phrases and number of times phrases used, word choice and linguistic patterns
- Argument—identify topics of argument and each debater's position on the issue
- Moderator—who was the moderator, who sponsored the moderator, bias of moderator
- Context and environment—format of debate, position of moderator and debaters, backdrop of the debate stage, color of debate stage
- Color analysis—color of debater's clothing, accessories (tie)
- Emotional language—emotional buzzwords or phrases used by debater
- Body language—facial expressions, gestures, voice tone, appearance and performance, eye contact
- Production techniques—position of camera, use of split-screen or reaction shots, presence of music and type of music

---

Politics and Economics

Economics is the study of how individuals, groups, organizations, and societies allocate and use resources. In the policymaking process, policymakers make decisions regarding the costs and benefits of a policy solution or alternative. The two primary economic indicators in our country are the gross domestic product and the gross national product. The gross domestic product is the monetary total of all finished goods and services (public and private) produced within the nation in one year. The gross national product is the total market value of all goods and services produced in an economy during a period of time, which can be quarterly or yearly.

A frequent question for politicians regarding the policymaking process is whether to develop policy that redistributes existing resources or allocates new resources. All political and policy decisions have an economic impact if resources are necessary to implement the political or policy decision.

Politics and economics interact at two levels, microeconomic and macroeconomic. Microeconomics examines the allocation of resources at the individual decision-making level. In contrast, macroeconomics examines the allocation of resources at the aggregate national level. Whether politics and economics interact at the micro- or macroeconomic level, economic policy outcomes are generally judged according to the criteria of efficiency, equity, economic growth, and economic stability. Efficiency or allocative efficiency produces resources needed with the least possible cost. Equity refers to the fairness of the economic outcomes. Economic growth refers to an increase in the total output as the result of an economic decision. Economic stability is a state in which there are stable outputs with low inflation and maximum use of resources.

Political Analysis

Political analysis is the process of examining the political philosophy, and perspectives, structures, interactions, and networks that influence the policymaking process. The philosophical approaches that inform the political analysis process are empirical, normative, institutional, behavioral, and forces (internal and external). Empirical perspective uses observable data to analyze the political situation. The normative perspective focuses on what should be or ought to be the political activity in alignment with the espoused values. Institutional perspective analyzes the political activities in terms of the institutional culture and climate. Behavioral perspective attempts to explain, describe, and possibly predict the political behavior of individuals and groups. The forces perspective considers the internal and external forces that are exerted on an individual or group to influence their political activities (Heineman, 1996).

A political analysis examines the politics of the problem and the politics of the proposed policy. The steps of a political analysis are:

- Problem identification—This consists of determining the scope, duration, history, and sphere of impact of the problem.
- Analyzing proposed policy solutions—Each solution should be analyzed in respect to practicality, feasibility, potential outcomes, and resources needed.
- Background analysis of the problem—This analysis consists of the historical perspective of the problem, historical precedents, and past political actions with related policy problems and policy solutions.
- Identify the political structures supporting and opposing the policy solutions—This includes special-interest groups, political parties, and policy precedents generated in the executive, legislative, and judicial systems.
- Evaluate constituents—Examine who supports and opposes solutions, the presence of policy entrepreneurs, and the constituents' resource base.
- Conduct a values assessment.

- Evaluate the extent of types of resources.
- Examine the constituents' power base.

Conflicts of Interest

A conflict of interest occurs when an individual has a conflict between personal or private interest and the responsibilities associated with their position of authority. Political activity can present many potential areas of conflict of interest.

Lobbying and Government Employees

Employees of governmental agencies at the local, state, and national level may have employment-related restrictions in relation to lobbying and other types of political engagement. These requirements are typically a condition of employment. The employee does not forfeit their rights as a citizen but must be clear as to whom they represent during their advocacy and lobbying efforts. An employee may act in self-interest regarding an issue or problem to legislators but not as an agent of the employing organization. The rules and laws governing individual and organizational advocacy and lobbying activities differ. Therefore, it is vital that the respective individual is familiar with all applicable institutional, local, state, and federal laws governing individual- and organizational-level advocacy and lobbying activities.

Summary Points

- Political activity is a means to influence policymaking.
- Politics is defined as the process of influencing someone or something to ensure the allocation of resources as desired.
- Political astuteness refers to an understanding of different political agendas and power bases among various individuals, organizations, and institutions and the dynamic between them in relation to the proposed policy solution.
- Political power is the ability to exert control over the behavior of another.
- Political power can be considered potential or kinetic power.
- The monolithic paradigm model is an authoritarian framework with a fixed power structure.
- The pluralistic paradigm embraces power from a grassroots perspective, which originates from the people.
- The elements of power typically include instrumentalities (equipment, materials, funds), people, or information.

- Sources or types of political power can include: legitimate, reward, coercive, referent, expert, human resource, material, or charisma.
- Members of an iron triangle are congressional members, members of the executive branch of government, and special-interest groups.
- Nurses' engagement in the policy process has been shaped by educational preparation, practice experience, professional engagement, and the maturity level of the nursing profession.
- The purpose of diagnosing organizational politics is to gain an understanding of the political structure and forces that effect policymaking changes within a defined organization.
- Organizational politics diagnosis identifies the influencing tactics.
- A political protocol consists of the written and unwritten rules that prescribe the appropriate manner of engaging with political and elected officials during formal functions and ceremonies.
- Liberals believe in the ownership of private property and use of natural resources for individual human gain.
- Socialism proposes shared property and wealth, and equal control and distribution of resources.
- The conservative perspective proposes that individuals with wealth and who are powerful in society have an obligation to provide resources and protect the less fortunate individuals in society.
- Five political system groups are liberal democratic, egalitarian-authoritarian, traditional-inegalitarian, populist, and authoritarian-inegalitarian regimes.
- Political strategies are the methods and processes used to influence the desired policy goals.
- There are four primary types of conflict—intrapersonal, interpersonal, intergroup, and organizational.
- Lobbying is the process of approaching legislators or policymakers to present information to influence their decision making.
- Interest groups are groups of individuals or organizations that share political, social, or other common interests and that seek to influence the policymaking process.
- Seven functions of interest groups in our society are participation, representation, political education, motivation, mobilization, and monitoring of political behavior and policy making.
- The power of the media lies in the ability of editors, producers, anchors, reporters, and columnists to present policy problems or issues to the public within the public domain.

- Priming sets the stage for future messages regarding a policy problem or issue.
- Framing impacts the assimilation of information regarding a policy.
- Media analysis facilitates the assessment of the extent to which the information presented is biased or the manner in which the information is biased.
- Testimony is an oral presentation before a committee or official body providing evidence, responding to questions, or presenting a position.
- Policy briefs provide a quick explanation of the policy issue or problem and the proposed policy, along with policy and political assessment.
- Policy speeches are conducted during political campaigns and during policy agenda setting and policymaking activities.
- A position paper typically describes the individual's or organization's position on an issue and a recommended solution with the supporting rationale for the position.
- A resolution is a formal motion, position, or solution proposed by an executive or governing body or organization.
- A resolution consists of four parts: heading, subject, preamble, and operative clause.
- Coalitions consolidate grassroots-level power and generate grassroots advocacy.
- Coalitions increase the political power structure by increasing the number of individuals supporting a specific policy.
- Political polls are surveys used to measure the potential of a specific candidate to win an election or to determine the level of support for a specific issue or policy.
- Public opinion is a good assessment of the national mood.
- Vetting is a process of conducting a comprehensive background examination and evaluation of an individual prior to appointing the person to a position or selecting the individual as a partner in a political campaign.
- A debate is a formal method of verbal argument.
- Policy, politics, and economics are interrelated and inseparable.
- Economics is the study of how individuals, groups, organizations, and societies allocate and use resources.
- Political analysis is the process of examining the political philosophy and the perspectives, structures, interactions, and networks that influence the policymaking process.

References

Berkowitz, B., & Wolff, T. (2000). *The spirit of coalition.* Washington, DC: American Public Health Association.

Borkowski, N. (2015). *Organizational behavior in health care.* (3rd ed.). Sudbury, MA: Jones & Bartlett.

Britner, P., & Alpert, L. (2005). Writing *amicus curiae* and policy briefs: A pedagogical approach to teaching family law and policy. *Marriage & Family Review, 38*(2), 5–21.

Buppert, C. (2007). How to develop relationships with legislators. *Journal of Nurse Practitioners, 3*(10), 682–683.

Buse, K., Mays, N., & Walt, G. (2012). *Making health policy* (2nd ed.). Berkshire, UK: Open University Press.

Cohen, S., Mason, D., Kovner, J., Pulcini, J., & Scholaski, J. (1996). Stages of nursing's political development: Where we've been and where we ought to go. *Nursing Outlook, 44*(6), 259–266.

Domke, D., Shah, D., & Wackman, D. (1998). Media priming effects: Accessibility, association, and activation. *International Journal of Public Opinion Research, 10*(1), 51–75.

Dye, T. (2017). *Understanding public policy* (15th ed.). Boston, MA: Pearson.

Easton, D. (1965). *A systems analysis of political life.* New York, NY: Wiley.

Harrison, M., & Shirom, A. (1999). *Organizational diagnosis and assessment: Bridging theory and practice.* Thousand Oaks, CA: Sage Publications.

Heineman, R. (1996). *Political science: An introduction.* New York, NY: McGraw-Hill.

Jennings, C. (2002). The power of the policy brief. *Policy, Politics, & Nursing Practice, 3*(3), 261–263.

Kleinkauf, C. (1981). A guide to giving legislative testimony. *Social Work, 26*(4), 297–302.

Leavitt, J. (2009). Leaders in health policy: A critical role for nursing. *Nursing Outlook, 57*(2), 73–77.

Mason, D. J., Gardner, D. B., Outlaw, F. H., & O'Grady, E. (Eds.). (2016). *Policy & politics in nursing and health care* (7th ed.). St. Louis, MO: Elsevier.

Patterson, M. (2008). Nursing policy primer: Putting policy to work for your practice. *Journal of Nurse Practitioners, 4*(10), 776–779.

Porche, D. (2003). *Public and community health nursing practice: A population-based approach.* Thousand Oaks, CA: Sage Publications.

Prouty, J. (2000). *Agenda setting function of Maxwell McCombs & Donald Shaw.* Retrieved on May 4, 2017 from https://www.unc.edu/~fbaum/teaching/PLSC541_Fall06/McCombs%20and%20Shaw%20POQ%201972.pdf

Registered Nurses' Association of Ontario. (2012). *Toolkit: Implementation of best practice guidelines* (2nd ed.). Toronto, ON: Registered Nurses' Association of Ontario.

Ridenour, J., & Harris, G. (2010). Shaping public policy: The nurse regulator's role. *Journal of Nursing Regulation, 1*(1), 26–29.

Roskin, M. G., Cord, R. L., Medeiros, J. A., & Jones, W. S. (2017). *Political science: An introduction* (14th ed.). Essex, England: Pearson Education.

Scholzman, K., Burns, N., & Verba, S. (1994). Gender and the pathways to participation: The roles of resources. *Journal of Politics, 65*(4), 963–990.

Smith, K. B., & Larimer, C. W. (Eds.). (2016). *The public policy theory primer* (3rd ed.). Boulder, CO: Westview Press.

Thomas, K., & Kilmann, R. (2002). *Thomas-Kilmann conflict mode instrument.* Palo Alto, CA: CPP.

Vandenhouten, C., Malakar, C., Kubsch, S., Block, D., & Gallagher-Lepak, S. (2011). Political participation of registered nurses. *Policy, Politics, & Nursing Practice, 12*(3), 159–167.

Verba, S., Scholzman, K., & Brady, H. (1995). *Voice and equality: Civic voluntarism in American politics.* Cambridge, MA: Harvard University Press.

Policy, Law, and Politics: Ethical Perspective

CHAPTER 16

The public expects accountability in all aspects of governmental relations, including political activities and policymaking. Elected officials and their representatives and delegates are expected to avoid conflicts of interest in the policymaking process. Ethical behavior and political activity are two behaviors that can coexist and are not mutually exclusive concepts. The public expects policymakers, constituents, and policy implementers to behave in an ethical manner. In addition, expectations of accountability have been strengthened within the business community, requiring institutional and organizational policies to be formulated and implemented in an ethical manner. This chapter presents an overview of ethics to facilitate ethical policymaking and political activity.

Ethics Defined

Ethics is defined as the study of the nature and justification of principles that guide individuals to act in a moral manner that is consistent with society's customs, values, beliefs, and norms. Ethics is also described as the study of the manner in which individuals behave in a situation or as the basis for determining correct action. The field of ethics continues to evolve as societal needs change, technological advancements occur, and policies evolve (Porche, 2003).

Professional ethics "seek out the values and standards that have been developed by practitioners and leaders of a given profession over a long period of time and . . . identify those values that seem most salient and inherent" to the professional discipline (Callahan & Jennings, 2002, p. 172). Applied ethics adopts a point of view that promotes practical application in real-world ethical issues. Applied ethics focuses more on professional behavior and conduct in specific situations based on the values of a profession (Callahan & Jennings, 2002). Advocacy ethics focuses equality and social justice. These are basic theoretical frameworks that guide ethical decision making (Beauchamp & Childress, 2012). Other essential ethics terms are presented in **Table 16-1**.

TABLE 16-1   ETHICAL TERMINOLOGY

TERM	DEFINITION
Absolutism	Belief that there is one correct approach to moral life
Altruism	The regard for others
Autonomy	Principle of respect for persons and of individual self-determination
Beneficence	The principle that one should assist others; to do good
Cognitive dissonance	A discrepancy between what a person believes, knows, and values and what is perceived to be true and real.
Duty	An action or act that must occur because of a moral or legal obligation
Egoism	Behavior in which self-promotion is the sole objective
Ethical gray area	An ethical situation or problem that does not neatly fit into any one specific categorization
Ethics	Process of determining right and wrong conduct
Equality	Equal distribution
Fidelity	To keep one's promises; loyalty
Justice	Fairness
Liberty	Freedom of human action; grounded in the principle of autonomy
Morals	Qualities that are considered by society to be associated with being intrinsically good
Paternalism	A liberty-limiting principle; a practice in which a person's liberty is justifiably restricted to prevent self-harm or harm to others and to promote others' well-being
Unethical	Describes an action or conduct that violates ethical principles, accepted values, or morals
Veracity	Principle of truth telling
Vices	Negative ethical or character traits
Virtues	Positive ethical or character traits

Ethical Theories and Paradigms

Ethical theories are the frameworks that provide the context in which an individual engages in ethical decision making. Ethical theories serve as guidelines to assist with the analysis of ethical dilemmas and guide an individual in determining ethical actions. Two classical ethical theories are deontology and utilitarianism.

Deontology

Deontology is a theoretical framework based on a sense of moral obligation or duty. Deontology states that an action's moral rightness or wrongness depends on the action itself and the motivation behind the action (Beauchamp & Childress, 2012). Deontology acknowledges the moral obligation that individuals feel toward certain actions. Moral obligation refers to an individual feeling a sense of duty that requires him to act in a particular manner in response to his values, beliefs, and perspective of societal norms.

Utilitarianism

Teleology is an ethical theory that determines rightness or wrongness based solely on the expected outcomes or consequences of an action. Utilitarianism is a theoretical framework of teleology theory. The utilitarian framework proposes that the most ethical action is that which results in the greatest good for the largest number of individuals (Beauchamp & Childress, 2012). Utilitarianism does not specifically focus on the action but on the ultimate number of individuals impacted by the action.

Ethical Principles

Ethical principles evolve from an individual's guiding ethical theoretical perspective, personal paradigm regarding moral conduct, and societal expectations. Ethical theories in addition to the moral tone of society assist in the formulation of ethical principles that guide an individual's ethical behavior. In addition, ethical principles are the foundation of professional codes of ethics. Ethical principles guide an individual in the critical analysis and reasoning of an ethical dilemma. The most common principles encountered in ethics are beneficence, nonmaleficence, justice, and autonomy (Beauchamp & Childress, 2012).

Beneficence consists of norms providing the greatest benefit to an individual, group, or community. Beneficence consists of weighing the benefits of an action against the risks or costs to the individual, group, or community involved (Beauchamp & Childress, 2012).

Nonmaleficence is the ethical principle of "doing no harm." With nonmaleficence, the policymaker focuses on not causing harm to individuals, groups, or communities (Beauchamp & Childress, 2012).

Justice is the ethical principle of ensuring the fair and equitable distribution of benefits, risks, and cost. Justice is known as the ethical principle of fairness (Beauchamp & Childress, 2012).

Autonomy is the ethical principle known as "respect for persons." Autonomy provides individuals with the right to make their own autonomous decisions. This is also referred to as the right to self-determination. This principle provides individuals with the right to make free, uncoerced, and informed decisions. Autonomy is the ethical principle that provides the framework of full disclosure and informed consent (Beauchamp & Childress, 2012).

In addition to the ethical principles of beneficence, nonmaleficence, justice, and autonomy, fidelity and veracity are two other principles essential in ethical decision-making processes. Fidelity is known as promise keeping. Fidelity ensures that the policymaker delivers what was promised in the form of policy. Veracity is known as truth telling. Veracity consists of being honest in delivering information to a policymaker's constituency. Fidelity and veracity are essential for a policymaker to develop a trusting relationship with constituents.

Values Clarification

Values are beliefs that an individual or social group has regarding what is relevant and important to their belief system. Values generally have an emotional attachment. Values are continually formed throughout life as an individual develops, and as the contextual and social situation of the individual changes. Some values are permanent and some values transform as an individual grows and develops. Value formation originates within the individual's family unit and continues to evolve with socialization into different professional and societal groups. Values that typically do not change, and form the basis for other values and philosophical perspectives are considered core values. An individual's values comprise the belief system or framework that structures the manner in which an individual views the world. In other words, this value system serves as the framework that creates an individual's paradigm regarding policy and politics (Coletta, 1978).

Values form the foundation for ethical decisions. To engage in moral thoughts and actions, an individual should have a framework of values that comprise their professional and personal life. The value clarification process promotes clarity regarding an individual's personal and professional values that form the foundation for their thoughts and actions in relation to policy and politics.

The value clarification process promotes self-reflection to identify an individual's values and value system. During this process of self-reflection, the policymaker has the ability to analyze and prioritize the values that compose their value system through a process of refinement. Raths, Harmin, and Simon (1966, 1978) defined a seminal process of values clarification. The process consists of choosing, prizing, and acting. In accordance with this process, a value is that which meets more than two criteria resulting from these three processes (see **Figure 16-1**).

Choosing consists of three criteria: choosing freely, choosing from alternatives (thoughts and actions), and choosing after thoughtful consideration of the consequences of each alternative. The next process, prizing, consists of two criteria: cherishing and being happy with the choice, and willingness to affirm the choice within a public arena. Lastly, the acting process is defined by doing

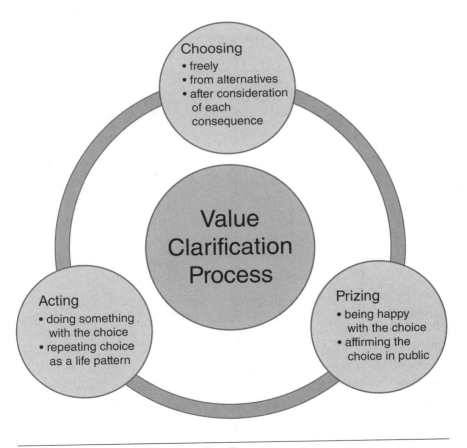

Figure 16-1   Value Clarification Process

something with the choice, and repeatedly acting in the same manner as a life pattern. Collectively, these three processes define the value clarification process that identifies an individual's values that for the basis for that person's personal and professional policymaking paradigm. This same process can be used by groups, organizations, and associations to identify and clarify their values.

The value clarification process assists each individual or organization in the identification of core values. Core values are the fundamental beliefs that an individual or organization holds as guiding principles that direct behavior and action. These core values are critical in determining policy ideology, policy agendas, selecting policy alternatives, and the manner in which an individual or organization conducts political activities. During the decision-making process and conducting of policy research, an individual or organization should continually reflect on these core values to guide decision making, behavior, and actions. **Box 16-1** provides a value clarification exercise to assist an individual with determining the values that make up that person's value system. This process of self-reflection increases an individual's personal understanding and self-awareness.

BOX 16-1   VALUES CLARIFICATION EXERCISE

The following is a list of personal and professional values. Carefully consider each value. Rate each value using the following scale:

   1 = Not at all important to me
   2 = Not very important to me
   3 = Moderately important to me
   4 = Very important to me
   5 = Essential to me

Value	Meaning	Rating (1 to 5)
Achievement	Accomplishment of a desired goal	
Aesthetics	Appreciation for beauty	
Altruism	A genuine regard and devotion to the interest of others	
Autonomy	Freedom of self-determination	
Diversity	Appreciation for differences or variation	
Emotional well-being	Freedom from anxiety; piece of mind; inner feelings of pleasure	
Excellence	Highest quality	

BOX 16-1   VALUES CLARIFICATION EXERCISE (CONTINUED)

Family	Maintain strong sense of relationship to genetic relatives or group of choice
Health	Freedom from disease or pain; general condition of well-being
Honesty	Being truthful; straightforwardness of conduct
Integrity	Quality of having high moral principles, being reliable and trustworthy
Justice	Quality of being impartial, just, and fair
Knowledge	Attainment of information or truth, power of knowing
Love	Affection or admiration for another
Loyalty	Maintaining an allegiance to a person, institution, political body, or another entity
Morality	Belief in and maintenance of ethical standards
Pleasure	An agreeable emotion of satisfaction or gratification
Power	Ability to influence others or exert control
Professionalism	Adherence to a set of values comprising statutory professional obligations, formally agreed codes of conduct, and the informal expectations aligned with the respective discipline
Recognition	Providing attention as a means to convey significance and importance
Respect	Positive feeling of esteem or admiration for another person or entity; deference toward another person or entity
Security	A feeling of safety or comfort
Skill	Ability to execute a specific technical expertise
Spirituality	Belief in or feeling of connection with a higher being
Wealth	An abundance of material possessions or resources
Wisdom	Insight, good sense, good judgment, intuitive knowledge

Ethical Influence of Culture and Religion on Policy

An individual's values are influenced by his or her culture and religious beliefs. These individual cultural and religious values can influence organizational values as organizational values are a collective set of values of the individual members. These cultural and religious values will impact an individual's ethical decision-making processes with a resulting impact on policy formulation. Similarly, an individual's political ideology and political affiliations will be grounded on the fundamental basis of that person's personal beliefs and values originating from his culture and religion. It is essential that during policy and political analysis, culture and religion of the individuals and collective group are considered to ensure a comprehensive understanding of the underlying value dynamics that may be influencing the policy and political decisions and activities. The basic elements of culture that should be considered when analyzing its impact on policy are beliefs, values, symbols (anything used to stand for something else), norms, language, roles, customs and traditions, religion, and social collectives/organization (family patterns, social classes). The basic elements of religion that should be considered when analyzing its impact on policy are beliefs and religious behavioral norms (supernatural powers), rituals and ceremonies, sacred objects, symbols, ideology, and sects (small groups within the larger religious group).

Ethical Decision-Making Process

An ethical dilemma arises when there is a conflict in the principles, duties, rights, beliefs, or values of one individual, group, population, or community with another or with societal expectations (Beauchamp & Childress, 2012). A reflective process that generates solutions or alternatives to the ethical dilemma is known as the ethical decision-making process.

Ethical decision-making processes facilitate the selection of an ethical resolution by outlining the steps that promote an understanding of the ethical dilemma and the preferred resolution. Ethical theoretical perspective and ethical principles are used in the ethical decision-making process to analyze the ethical dilemma. Several decision-making processes can be used to assist with ensuring that an individual selects the most ethical behavior within the given contextual situation. The two processes presented next are similar, but differ in the method by which the final ethical decision is rendered.

This author (Porche, 2003) proposed the following steps as a reflective process to reason through an ethical dilemma:

- Define the ethical dilemma.
- Outline the conflicting ethical issues and principles resulting from both sides of the ethical dilemma.
- Identify the constituency impacted at all policy levels and on both sides of the dilemma.
- Collect data relevant to both sides of the ethical dilemma.
- List alternative policy options to resolve the ethical dilemma.
- Describe the consequences for each policy option listed.
- Analyze each policy option in relation to the preferred ethical theoretical paradigm, and ethical principles or codes of ethics.
- Determine which policy option would be the best and most ethical resolution.
- Draft policy that represents the ethical resolution selected.
- Ensure that the policy is implemented with the ethical intent and context that provided the framework to develop the policy.
- Evaluate the implementation and consequences of the ethical resolution. Consider the impact of the ethical resolution on each constituency (Porche, 2003).

An ethical decision-making process has been proposed by the Josephson Institute of Ethics. This decision-making process consists of five principled reasoning steps:

1. Clarification
   a. Determine what must be decided.
   b. Formulate a full range of alternative decisions.
   c. Eliminate any alternative decisions that have any unethical actions.
   d. Prioritize the decisions hierarchically in relation to ethical principles.
2. Evaluate—Consider all decisions in terms of practicality, ethics, benefits, burdens, and risk to all individuals involved.
3. Decide
   a. Make the best decision based on personal conscience and appropriateness of action.
   b. Consider the following: Are you treating others as you would want to be treated? Would you be comfortable if your reasoning and decision were to be made public? Would you be comfortable if your children were observing your behavior?

4. Implement
   a. Develop a plan to implement the decisions.
   b. Maximize benefits while reducing cost and risks.
5. Modify and monitor
   a. Evaluate and adjust the plan to new information.
   b. Monitor the effects of the decisions.
   c. Revise plan of action based on new information (Josephson Institute of Ethics, 1999. ©Josephson Institute of Ethics, 1999. Reprinted with permission.).

Codes of Ethics

Codes of ethics are derived from normative ethics. Ethical codes are used to transmit moral guidelines of a professional discipline or professional group. These ethical codes represent the values inherent in a profession or professional group (Beauchamp & Childress, 2012).

Ethical Engagement in Political Process

Engagement in the political process is expected to be ethical. Political plans should create an ethical infrastructure within the plan. This ethical infrastructure should ensure that there is a system of checks and balances that occur with the execution of each political strategy. This promotes integrity, transparency, and accountability within the political process of policymaking. This means that the ethical decision-making process should be executed when discerning among political strategies selected. However, prior to the working of the political action plan, the individuals involved in the decision making and implementation of political strategies must identify and clearly understand their values and guiding ethical principles.

Government Employees and Ethics

Government employees and elected officials are expected to engage in ethical behavior and conduct the affairs of their offices in an ethical manner. Government employees, regardless of the branch of government (executive, legislative, or judicial) should hold their positions of public trust in high regard. The American people have a right to expect that all government employees will be loyal to the Constitution (or state constitutions or city charters), laws, regulations, ethical principles, and codes of ethics. **Boxes 16-2** and **16-3** provide codes of ethical conduct for lobbying and government service.

BOX 16-2   CODE OF LOBBYING ETHICS

Lobbyists are expected to demonstrate the highest ethical conduct during lobbying efforts. The American League of Lobbyists provides the following code of ethics for independent lobbyists. This code of ethics can provide a framework for all individuals engaged in lobbying activities. The American League of Lobbyist Code of Ethics is summarized below:

- Honesty and integrity
  - Truthful in communicating with public officials.
  - Provide accurate and factual information.
  - Ensure that new accurate and updated information is provided if any information that was provided becomes inaccurate.
- Compliance with applicable laws, regulations, and rules
  - Be familiar with laws, regulations, and rules.
  - Do not cause self or public officer to violate any law, regulation, or rule.
- Professionalism
  - Act in a fair and professional manner.
  - Acquire knowledge of legislative and governmental processes.
  - Represent clients in a competent and professional manner.
  - Engage in continuing education to understand legislative and governmental processes.
  - Treat others with respect and civility.
- Conflicts of interest
  - Do not engage in representation that creates conflicts of interest without all parties involved having full disclosure through an informed consent process.
  - Avoid advocating a position while representing another client on the same issue with a conflicting position.
  - Obtain consent from a client if representation of one client on an issue may have a significant adverse impact on another client's interest.
  - Disclose all potential conflicts to current and prospective clients and disclose methods to resolve conflicts of interest with all parties.
  - Inform all clients when receiving a direct or indirect referral or consulting fee from the lobbyist in connection with the client's work.

(continues)

BOX 16-2   CODE OF LOBBYING ETHICS (CONTINUED)

- Due diligence and best efforts
  - Devote adequate time, attention, and resources to lobbying efforts.
  - Exercise loyalty.
  - Keep client informed regarding your work activities on their behalf.
- Compensation and engagement terms
  - Retain clients using a written agreement specifying the terms and conditions of the agreement.
  - Cite basis for compensation, fees, and other expenditures in which compensation is required.
- Confidentiality
  - Do not disclose confidential and privileged information without the client's expressed consent.
  - Do not use confidential information against the interest of any other parties.
- Public education
  - Ensure the public understands and appreciates the nature, legitimacy, and necessity of lobbying.
- Duty to governmental institutions
  - Respect all governmental institutions.
  - Do not undermine public confidence and trust in the democratic governmental process.
  - Do not act in any manner that demonstrates disrespect for governmental institutions.

Data from American League of Lobbyists. (2010). *Code of ethics*. Retrieved on March 12, 2017 from http://doa.alaska.gov/apoc/pdf/LobbyistCodeOfEthics.pdf

---

BOX 16-3   UNITED STATES GOVERNMENT SERVICE CODE OF ETHICS

Any person in government service should:

I. Put loyalty to the highest moral principles above loyalty to persons, party, or government department.

II. Uphold the Constitution, laws, and legal regulations of the United States and of all governments therein and never be a party to their evasion.

III. Give a full day's labor for a full day's pay; giving to the performance of his duties his earnest effort and best thought.

BOX 16-3   UNITED STATES GOVERNMENT SERVICE CODE OF ETHICS (CONTINUED)

   IV. Seek to find and employ more efficient and economical ways of getting tasks accomplished.

    V. Never discriminate unfairly by the dispensing of special favors or privileges to anyone, whether for remuneration or not; and never accept, for himself or his family, favors or benefits under circumstances which might be construed by reasonable persons as influencing the performance of his governmental duties.

   VI. Make no private promises of any kind binding upon the duties of office, since the government employee has no private word which can be binding on public duty.

  VII. Engage in no business with the government, either directly or indirectly, which is inconsistent with the conscientious performance of his governmental duties.

VIII. Never use any information coming to him confidentially in the performance of governmental duties as a means for making private profit.

   IX. Expose corruption wherever discovered.

    X. Uphold these principles, ever conscious that public office is a public trust.

From H.R. Doc. No. 64-103 (1958).

In 1989, President George H. W. Bush issued Executive Order 12674 (which was then modified in 1990 by Executive Order 12731), which outlined general principles broadly defining the obligation of public service. Two core concepts provided the basis for these principles:

- Employees shall not use their public office for private gain.
- Employees shall act impartially and not give preferential treatment to any private organization or individual.

In addition, these executive orders strongly encouraged that employees avoid any action that would create the appearance of violating the law or ethical standards. President Bush was striving to generate public confidence and trust in the integrity of government operations and programs. Other recommended cautions to not misuse a position in the executive branch of government consisted of:

- Employees are not to use their position, title, or any authority associated with their office to coerce or induce a benefit for self, family, or friends.
- Employees are not to use or allow the improper use of nonpublic information to advance the private interest of themselves or their acquaintances.

- Use government property only for authorized purposes.
- Employees may not misuse official paid time.

Similarly, on January 21, 2009, President Barack Obama issued an Executive Order 134900, titled Ethics Commitments for Executive Branch Personnel. This executive order required appointees to sign an Ethics Pledge confirming their commitment to abide by the provisions of ethical behavior set forth by President Obama in the Executive Order. Further details of this Executive Order can be reviewed at https://www.justice.gov/jmd/ethics-pledge-executive-order-13490. Consistent with his predecessors, President Donald J. Trump issued an executive order on January 28, 2017, titled Ethics Commitments by Executive Branch Appointees. Further information can be reviewed on President Trump's executive order at https://www.whitehouse.gov/the-press-office/2017/01/28/executive-order-ethics-commitments-executive-branch-appointees. These executive orders are an indication of the ethical behavior expected of government appointees and personnel within the executive branch of government.

A great concern in relation to the ethical behavior of governmental employees involves financial conflicts of interest. The following strategies are suggested to avoid potential financial conflicts of interest:

- Recusals—Do not participate in any matter that poses a conflict of interest.
- Waivers—Secure a waiver from the appropriate authorized official.
- Divestiture—Sell or separate legally from any property or financial interest that may appear to be a financial conflict of interest.
  A "certificate of divestiture" may be required from the appropriate authorized official.
- Trusts—Develop trusts in accordance with the Internal Revenue Code.

Governmental employees are encouraged to build public trust through the creation of transparent activities. Transparency is a key leadership strategy for building trust within organizations and among constituents. The following are recommendations to facilitate the development of transparency and to ultimately build trust:

- Communicate in a meaningful, purposive, unpretentious, and clear manner presenting factual information with full disclosure.
- Provide access to information within a public arena. This information can be limited to the internal citizens of an organization.
- Publicize areas of responsibility and accountability among the administrative team.
- Reveal information regarding yourself that is pertinent to your position and activities.

- Disclose any apparent, potential, or actual conflicts of interest.
- Limit interlinking of personal and professional relationships; if they are present, ensure that the exact nature of the relationship is known.
- Encourage open meetings, publicize closed "executive" sessions prior to the meetings.
- Publicize meeting agendas.
- Have an open-door policy.
- Have open meetings with no agenda and encourage open questions and dialogue.
- Publicize strategic vision, mission, and strategic plans. Consider posting action plans of the strategic plan.
- Provide access to outcome and other evaluation data.
- Ensure that the fiscal management has an open process that provides individuals with access to the organization's financial data.

Transparency and accountability best practices are critical to ensuring ethical policymaking. The Transparency and Accountability Initiative (TAI) has developed a compilation of best practices to promote transparency, accountability, and civic engagement across public sectors. The TAI is a donor collaborative organization that aims to expand the impact, scale, and coordination of funding and activity in the areas of transparency and accountability as a nonpartisan organization (Transparency and Accountability Initiative, 2010). The following is a brief summary of best practices identified by the TAI:

- Aid transparency
  - Publish information on all donors and the manner in which financial aid flows; includes both donors and recipients.
- Asset disclosure
  - Disclose all personal assets and sources of income.
- Budgets
  - Publish budgets, increase access to budget reports.
- Campaign finance
  - Complete transparency in political party and campaign contributions; disclose financial campaign contributions from all domestic and international interest groups and countries.
- Climate finance
  - Developed countries want to ensure their funds are used efficiently and effectively.
  - Developing countries want to know that committed funds will actually materialize from developed countries.

- Fisheries
  - Publish details and provide information about activities that impact the degradation of marine ecosystems.
- Financial sector reform
  - Conduct annual reviews of foreign politically exposed persons as part of a risk assessment; conduct accounting and forensic activities to impact the nexus of corruption, economic development and money laundering within the financial system.
- Forestry
  - Codify consultation protocols for interest groups in forestry matters; permit independent assessments of transparency in the forest and related sectors; adopt a natural resources charter to ensure best practices.
- Electricity
  - Develop long-term power development plans, national power plans, and integrated resource plans to forecast the amount of electrical power needed.
- Environment
  - Empower communities, individuals, and civil society organizations to participate in policy decision-making processes to ensure the safeguarding of the environment; environmental reports should be publicly available; air and water quality data should be publicly available.
- Extractive industries (oil, gas, and mining)
  - Public has a right to know what is being done with the country's natural resources; engage public in decision making regarding the production, importation, and exportation of extractive resources; public should be informed regarding revenue generation using extractive resources.
- Open government data
  - Government-produced data should be open and available to the public; establish open access standards for government data and metadata.
- Procurement
  - Procurement of government assets should be transparent, procurement rules and procedures and use of technology for information dissemination should be disclosed.
- Right to information
  - Right to information should be considered an intrinsic part of the right to freedom of expression; right to information should be

considered a human/civil right; provide access to all information held by public authorities.
- Service delivery
    - Government should make key information on basic services, entitlements, budgets, and performance accessible to all people, to include funds spent on education, health, and water (Transparency and Accountability Initiative, 2010).*

Conflict of Interest

Transparency is one means to avoid conflicts of interest. A conflict of interest occurs when an individual has a conflict between personal or private interest and the responsibilities associated with his position of authority. Conflicts of interest do not only pertain to financial benefits. Conflict of interest does not always have to be actual with tangible outcomes but can exist if others perceive that there is a conflict of interest. There are several types of conflicts of interest: objective, subjective, potential, actual, or apparent. An objective conflict of interest involves a financial relationship. A subjective conflict of interest is based on emotional ties or a relationship. A potential conflict of interest occurs when an individual has an interest that may influence his judgment and decisions in the future. An actual conflict of interest occurs when an individual has an interest that impacts her judgment and engaged in an activity that is directly related to the area of the conflict. An apparent conflict of interest occurs when there is no actual conflict of interest but other persons looking at the situation perceive that there is an actual conflict of interest (Velasquez, 2012). An individual's employment position, profession, and personal obligations and responsibilities influence conflicts of interest.

Regardless of the type of conflict, engagement in a conflict of interest activity is considered unethical behavior. The best strategy regarding conflicts of interest is to prevent or avoid an actual or perceived conflict of interest. The following measures are recommended to avoid conflict of interest:

- Maintain role clarity.
- Act in accordance with rules and regulations.
- Follow the letter and intent or spirit of the policy.

---

* Reproduced from Transparency and Accountability Initiative. (2010). *Opening government: A guide to best practice in transparency, accountability, and civic engagement across the public sector.* Retrieved on March 12, 2017 from http://www.transparency-initiative .org/uncategorized/1741/open-government-guide/.

- Recognize potential conflicts of interest early.
- Identify primary and secondary constituents of a potential conflict of interest.
- Examine and reflect on any potential conflict of interest.
- Review policies governing potential conflicts of interest.
- Discuss potential conflicts of interest with individuals whose span of authority encompasses the area of potential conflict.
- Secure an opinion regarding the potential conflict of interest prior to engaging in an activity that may be determined to be a conflict of interest.

Policy Research Ethical Principles

The conduct of policy research should produce a substantial social benefit to be considered ethical. The ethical principles guiding policy research have been discussed throughout this chapter. The Belmont Report written by the National Commission for the Protection of Human Subjects of Biomedical and Behavioral Research (1979) describes three guiding ethical principles for policy research as respect for persons, beneficence, and justice. These three guiding ethical principles form the basis for acceptable ethical research principles. **Box 16-4** outlines common ethical principles for the conduct of policy research based on these three guiding principles.

BOX 16-4   POLICY RESEARCH ETHICAL PRINCIPLES

- Minimize the risk of harm.
- Obtain informed consent.
- Protect anonymity and confidentiality.
- Avoid deceptive or coercive practices.
- Provide the right to withdraw from the study without harm, permit voluntary withdrawal.
- Avoid conflicts of interest or partiality.
- Investigator is responsible for ensuring safety of research subject.
- Ensure data remain private.
- Research subject should demonstrate an understanding and competence for informed consent to occur.
- Avoid exculpatory language that waives any legal rights or removes sponsor's liability.

Summary Points

- The public expects accountability in all aspects of governmental relations.
- Ethics is defined as the study of the nature and justification of principles that guide individuals to act in a moral manner that is consistent with society's customs, values, beliefs, and norms.
- Professional ethics "seek out the values and standards that have been developed by practitioners and leaders of a given profession over a long period of time and . . . identify those values that seem most salient and inherent" to the professional discipline. (Callahan & Jennings, 2002, p. 172).
- Applied ethics adopts a point of view that promotes practical application in real-world ethical issues.
- Deontology states that an action's moral rightness or wrongness depends on the action itself and the motivation behind the action.
- The utilitarian framework proposes that the most ethical action is that which results in the greatest good for the largest number of individuals.
- The most common principles encountered in ethics are beneficence, nonmaleficence, justice, and autonomy.
- Beneficence consists of weighing the benefits of an action against the risks or costs to the individual, group, or community involved.
- Nonmaleficence is the ethical principle of "doing no harm."
- Justice is the principle of being fair and equitable.
- The principle of autonomy provides individuals with the right to make free, uncoerced, and informed decisions.
- The value clarification process promotes clarity regarding an individual's personal and professional values that form the foundation for their thoughts and actions in relation to policy and politics.
- The value clarification process promotes self-reflection to identify an individual's values and value system.
- Ethical decision-making processes facilitate the selection of an ethical resolution by outlining the steps that promote an understanding of the ethical dilemma and the preferred resolution.
- Transparency is a strategy to avoid conflicts of interest and promote trust.
- Research ethical principles are respect for persons, beneficence, and justice.

References

American League of Lobbyists. (2010). *Code of ethics.* Retrieved on March 12, 2017, from http://doa.alaska
.gov/apoc/pdf/LobbyistCodeOfEthics.pdf

Beauchamp, T. L., & Childress, J. F. (2012). *Principles of biomedical ethics* (7th ed.). New York, NY: Oxford
University Press.

Callahan, D., & Jennings, B. (2002). Ethics and public health: Forging a strong relationship. *American
Journal of Public Health, 92*(2), 169–176.

Coletta, S. (1978). Value clarification in nursing: Why? *American Journal of Nursing, 78*(12), 2057.

H.R. Doc. No. 64-103 (1958).

Josephson Institute of Ethics. (1999). *Five steps of principled reasoning.* Retrieved on March 12, 2017, from
https://ethicsalarms.com/rule-book/ethical-decision-making-tools/

National Commission for the Protection of Human Subjects of Biomedical and Behavioral Research. (1979).
The Belmont Report. Retrieved on March 12, 2017, from https://www.hhs.gov/ohrp/regulations-and-policy
/belmont-report/

Porche, D. (2003). *Public and community health nursing practice: A population-based approach.* Thousand
Oaks, CA: Sage Publications.

Raths, L., Harmin, M., & Simon, S. (1966). *Values and teaching.* Columbus, OH: Charles E. Merrill.

Raths, L., Harmin, M., & Simon, S. (1978). *Values and teaching* (2nd ed.). Columbus, OH: Charles E. Merrill.

Transparency and Accountability Initiative. (2010). *Opening government: A guide to best practice in
transparency, accountability, and civic engagement across the public sector.* Retrieved on March 12, 2017,
from http://www.transparency-initiative.org/wp-content/uploads/2011/07/Opening-Government3.pdf

Velasquez, M. G. (2012). *Business ethics: Concepts and cases* (7th ed.). Essex, England: Pearson Education
Limited.

Policy Institutes

Policy institutes are organizations that engage in a variety of policy activities that impact the policymaking process, policy analysis, policy research, or policy evaluation. Policy institutes are generally nonprofit and nonpartisan. Some policy institute organizations have a membership base. A policy institute with a membership base may also serve as a special interest group. Policy institutes may have resources (human, physical, or fiscal) that can be mobilized to engage in political activities to influence the policymaking process. Each policy institute has its own policy agenda. Policy institutes influence policy through conducting policy analysis and evaluating existing policies. These policy institutes typically have a repertoire of information regarding the issues on their policy agenda. Therefore, policy institutes serve a critical role as an information source for policy agendas, policy analysis, and policy evaluation. In addition, the policy institute can be mobilized to politically influence the policymaking process. Familiarity with policy institutes is encouraged. The following is a partial list of well-known policy institutes. See Appendix C for more information on policy resources.

American Association of Retired Persons (AARP) Public Policy Institute

The American Association of Retired Persons (AARP) Public Policy Institute is a component of the national organization American Association of Retired Persons. AARP is a nonprofit, nonpartisan membership-based organization that provides assistance to persons 50 years of age and older to improve their quality of life. Topics of interest for the AARP Public Policy Institute include consumer protection (financial services, financial literacy, fraud and deception, energy and public utilities, telecommunications, advance planning, and legal rights), economic security (Social Security, pensions and retirement savings, income and assets, tax and budget, work and retirement, low-income programs), health care (Medicare, Medicaid, health costs, health coverage and insurance, health quality, patient safety, access to care, health behaviors, prescription drugs, healthcare workforce, and nursing), livable communities (housing and transportation), and long-term care issues (assisted living, caregiving, home health, community-based care, long-term care insurance, nursing homes). AARP Public Policy Institute activities include program development, policy research, educational conferences, production of surveys, development of educational media and information to inform the public, and generation of policy reports.

American Enterprise Institute for Public Policy Research

The American Enterprise Institute for Public Policy Research is a private, nonpartisan, not-for-profit organization dedicated to research and education on government, politics, economics, and social welfare issues. This institute engages in policy research, open debate, and reasoned argument regarding the institute's primary areas of interest. Research is conducted in seven primary areas: economic policy studies, foreign and defense policy studies, health care, education, politics and public opinion, poverty studies, and society and culture. A host of experts, scholars, officers, and fellows conduct the activities of this institute.

Aspen Institute

The Aspen Institute's mission is to foster values-based leadership and to promote a neutral and balanced venue for nonpartisan discussion and acting on critical issues. Activities of the Aspen Institute include but are not limited to conducting seminars; sponsoring leadership programs; youth and engagement programs; engaging nonpartisan forums for policy analysis; consensus building and problem solving in relation to policy issues; fostering international partnerships to address global challenges; and sponsoring public conferences to share ideas and engage in debate. The Aspen Institute strives to create an enlightened population regarding critical issues.

Brookings Institution

The Brookings Institution is a nonprofit public policy organization. The mission of the Brookings Institution is to conduct in-depth independent research that leads to new ideas for solving problems facing society at the local, national, and global levels. The Brookings Institute supports independence and integrity policies, diversity and inclusion, and policy on public health service. The goals are to strengthen the American democracy; foster economic and social welfare; promote security and opportunity for all Americans; and secure an open, safe, prosperous, and cooperative international system. Members of the Brookings Institution write books, papers, articles, and opinion pieces, and testify before congressional committees on various issues.

Cato Institute

The Cato Institute is a nonprofit public policy research foundation. This institute functions as a policy think tank. The Cato Institute focuses on increasing the understanding of public policies with the premise of limited government, free markets, individual liberty, and peace. The Institute originates, advocates, promotes, and disseminates policy proposals for a free, open, and civil society in the United States and the world. The work of the Cato Institute is achieved through several centers and projects: constitutional studies, educational freedom, global liberty and prosperity, representative government, monetary and financial alternatives, trade policy studies, and study of science.

Center for Responsive Politics

The Center for Responsive Politics is a nonpartisan, independent nonprofit organization. The center focuses on tracking of financing of U.S. politics and its resultant effect on elections and public policy. Researchers conduct studies on congressional and political trends. The center also focuses on the specific areas of campaign finance, government ethics, political foundations, public policy, the media and Congress, and the inner workings of Congress.

Claremont Institute for Economic Policy Studies

The Claremont Institute for Economic Policy Studies conducts policy research and analysis on domestic and international economic policy issues. This institute exists in partnership with Claremont Graduate University. Major research focus areas include energy and environmental policy, government growth, central bank independence, inflation and economic growth, monetary policies in emerging markets, political business cycles, and political economy of international trade policies.

The Commonwealth Fund

The Commonwealth Fund is a private foundation. The specific aims of the Commonwealth Fund are to promote a high-performing healthcare system to achieve the primary outcomes of better access, improved quality, and greater efficiency. The Commonwealth Fund focuses on the most vulnerable members of society such as low-income, uninsured, and minority Americans; young children; and elderly adults. The Commonwealth Fund's current issues are health system cost, Medicare, Affordable Care Act repeal debate, high-need and high-cost patients, vulnerable populations, state health policy, and Affordable Care Act reforms. The Commonwealth Fund engages in policy research, produces reports, and funds grants.

Economic Policy Institute

The Economic Policy Institute is a nonprofit think tank organization that promotes discussion about economic policy. The mission of the Economic Policy Institute is to inform and empower individuals to seek solutions that ensure broadly shared prosperity and opportunity. This organization focuses on the economic issues that impact both low- and middle-income workers. The Economic Policy Institute engages in policy research, policy analysis, community outreach, and education. The economic issues of focus include but are not limited to budget, taxes, and public investment; economic growth; education; green economics; health; immigration; inequality and poverty; jobs and unemployment; minimum wage; race and ethnicity; raising American's pay; regulation; retirement; trade and globalization; unions and labor standards; and wages, incomes, and wealth. The products of the Economic Policy Institute consist of books, studies, issue briefs, education materials, conferences and seminars, technical support, local activism, and testimony.

The Educational Policy Institute

The Educational Policy Institute's mission is to expand educational opportunities for low-income and historically underrepresented students. The Educational Policy Institute engages in policy research and analysis. A goal of the Educational Policy Institute is to generate policy research and analysis that increases the number of students prepared for, enrolled in, and completing postsecondary educational programs. The competencies of this institute are program evaluation, policy analysis, professional development, research design and management, and data services. Research areas of the institute are early childhood, students with disabilities, teacher preparation and development, early intervention and outreach, student graduation and retention, student aid, access and affordability, retention and success, quality measurement in higher education, and university rankings.

Fairness and Accuracy in Reporting

Fairness and Accuracy in Reporting is a national media watch group organization. This organization attempts to review the accuracy of media reports. The desire is to invigorate the First Amendment by advocating for greater diversity in the press and scrutinizing media practices that marginalize public interest, minority and dissenting viewpoints. Fairness and Accuracy in Reporting produces a magazine, newsletter, and a nationally syndicated weekly radio program.

Hudson Institute

The Hudson Institute is a nonpartisan conservative policy research organization that conducts innovative research and policy analysis. Hudson Institute's desire is to guide public policymakers and global leaders in government and business to formulate policy. The focus of the Hudson Institute studies include defense, international relations, economics, health care, technology, culture, and law. The activities of the Hudson Institute are producing policy publications, sponsoring conferences, and publishing policy recommendations. The current research agenda for the Hudson Institute includes economics, health care, human rights, national security, culture and social policy, energy and environmental policy, government and politics, international relations, legal affairs and criminal justice, and technology and applied science. The Hudson Institute's policy centers include economics of the Internet, trends in Islamist ideology, religious freedom, global prosperity, initiative on future innovation, obesity solutions, Bradley Center for Philanthropy and Civic Renewal, American seapower, substance abuse, Kleptocracy Initiative, and political studies.

Institute for Higher Education Policy (IHEP)

The Institute for Higher Education Policy (IHEP) is an independent, nonpartisan, nonprofit organization focused on access and success in postsecondary education around the world. IHEP engages in research and innovative program development as a means to inform policymakers' decision-making processes and shape public policy. IHEP supports economic and social development through policy initiatives in postsecondary education. The vision of IHEP is a world in which all people achieve their full potential by participating and succeeding in postsecondary education. The four policy priorities are access and success, affordability and finance, accountability and transparency, and critical communities and institutions. IHEP serves as a nonpartisan global research and policy center for government agencies, higher education organizations, philanthropic foundations, and other organizations with an interest in postsecondary education access and success. The activities of IHEP include policy research, policy analysis, composing professional reports and briefings, and program evaluation.

Institute for Philosophy and Public Policy

The Institute for Philosophy and Public Policy investigates the conceptual and ethical aspects of public policy formulation and debate. The institute provides expertise on the normative dimension of public policy. The institute explores the philosophical issues that influence constituents and policymakers. Areas of pressing policy work for the institute consist of climate change, environmental sustainability, bioethics and emerging technologies, international development, peace and conflict, and global demands for justice.

Justice Policy Institute

The Justice Policy Institute is a national nonprofit organization that changes the conversation around justice reform and advances policies that promote well-being and justice for all people and communities by reducing our reliance on incarceration. The mission of the Justice Policy Institute is to promote effective solutions to societal problems and to end society's reliance on incarceration of prisoners by promoting fair and effective policies. The Justice Policy Institute engages in developing policy briefs, policy reports, and research projects; strategic communications and media advocacy; providing technical assistance and consultation; providing training on research and communications; and rapid response initiatives relating to emerging issues of incarceration.

Kaiser Family Foundation

The Kaiser Family Foundation is a nonprofit, private foundation. This foundation focuses on major national healthcare issues in the United States and the country's role in impacting global health policy. The Kaiser Family Foundation serves as an information source that provides facts and information to inform policy analysis and policy research. This foundation serves as the "go to" organization for policy information. The foundation produces its own journalism and communication programs in partnership with major news organizations.

Kettering Foundation

The Kettering Foundation is a nonprofit research organization rooted in cooperative research. The Kettering Foundation conducts research in the areas of community, governing, politics, and education. A special focus area of the Kettering Foundation is deliberative democracy. Kettering promotes a robust democracy that consist of citizens, communities, institutions, democratic practices, and problems behind the problems.

National Institute for Public Policy

The National Institute for Public Policy is a nonprofit public education organization. This institute's policy agenda focuses on U.S. foreign defense policies and international policy issues. Areas of specific focus for this institute are international security issues; proliferation of missiles and weapons of mass destruction; effectiveness of post–Cold War deterrence theory; measures to delay and counter the proliferation of weapons of mass destruction and missile delivery systems; North Atlantic Treaty Organization (NATO); U.S.–Russian political and military relations; evolution of arms control regimes; future of U.S. strategic forces and role of nuclear weapons; roles and missions of the U.S. intelligence community; role of air power; role of ballistic missile defense; emerging transnational threats; and space power and policy studies.

Rand Corporation

The Rand Corporation is a nonprofit, independent, institution focused on improving policy and policy decision making through the conducting of policy research and policy analysis. The following issues are of primary importance to the Rand Corporation: health, education, national security, international affairs, law and business, and the environment. The core research areas of the Rand Corporation are children and families, education and the arts, energy and environment, health and health care, infrastructure and transportation, international affairs, law and business, national security, population and aging, public safety, science and technology, and terrorism and homeland security.

Robert Wood Johnson Foundation

The Robert Wood Johnson Foundation strives to improve the health and health care of all Americans. The targeted focus areas are health leadership, health systems, healthy communities, and healthy children and healthy weight. This is accomplished through grants and grant programs, research evaluation, and learning, and building a culture of health.

The Rockefeller Foundation

The Rockefeller Foundation provides funding to support the goal of improving the well-being of humanity through smart globalization and global impact. A goal of of the foundation is to build greater resilience and advance more inclusive economies. The Rockefeller Foundation seeks to nurture innovation; pioneer new fields; expand access to and improve distribution of resources; empower beneficiaries; and to generate a sustainable impact on individuals, institutions, and communities. The names of the initiatives include resilient cities 100, alliance for a green revolution in Africa, Asian cities climate change resilience network, bus rapid transit, centennial, digital jobs Africa, disease surveillance networks, fresh water, global resilience partnerships, health of informal workers, innovation, innovative finance, mission-related investing, natural disaster resilience competition, New Orleans, New York City cultural innovation, oceans and fisheries, planetary health, program-related investments, rebuild by design, smart power for rural development, social impact bonds, transforming health systems, U.S. youth employment, and yieldwise food waste.

Schneider Institutes for Health Policy

The Schneider Institutes for Health Policy is a group of policy research institutes within Brandeis University's Heller School of Social Policy and Management. The mission of the Schneider Institutes for Health Policy is to conduct health services research and engage in policy efforts focusing on healthcare financing and service delivery; the relationship between health services, behavior and socioeconomic characteristics; and the connection between health status and individual and societal well-being. The institute conducts domestic and international research in the areas of financing, organization, value, high-cost and high risk populations, and health technologies. This work is done through institutes of behavioral health, healthcare systems, and global health and development.

Urban Institute

The Urban Institute's mission is to open minds, shape decisions, and offer solutions through economic and social policy research. The Urban Institute engages in policy analysis, program evaluation, and informing community development. The focus of the Urban Institute is to improve social, civic, and economic well-being. The mission of the Urban Institute is to gather data, conduct research, evaluate programs, conduct policy analysis, offer international technical assistance, and educate Americans regarding social and economic issues. The Urban Institute has eleven policy centers: international development and governance; labor, human services, and population; nonprofits and philanthropy; health policy; housing finance; income and benefits; justice; metropolitan housing and communities; policy advisory; statistical methods; and Urban-Brooking Tax. These centers have several cross-center initiatives—education and training, inequality and mobility, kids, low-income working families, neighborhoods and youth development, opportunity and ownership, performance measurement and management, immigrants and immigration, programs on retirement, social determinants of health, state and local finance, tax policy and charities, and Washington DC research initiatives.

Summary Points

- Policy institutes engage in activities such as policymaking, policy analysis, policy evaluation, and policy research.
- Policy institutes each have a focus area of interest.
- Policy institutes may be membership based, and/or have a group of experts and scholars who conduct the activities of the policy institute.
- The products of policy institutes include books, reports, briefs, testimony, educational materials, conferences, and seminars.

Bibliography

Almanac of Policy Issues. (2005). *Major public policy organizations*. Retrieved from http://www.policyalmanac .org/directory/General-Organizations.shtml

Boris, E. T., & Steuerle, C. E. (2016). *Nonprofits and government: Collaboration and conflict* (3rd ed.). Lanham, MD: Rowman & Littlefield Publishers.

Presidential and Congressional Political Party Leadership

	Presidential Leadership			Congressional Leadership	
Time Period	President	Political Party	Congress	Majority Party	Minority Party
1789–1797	George Washington	Independent	1st (1789–1791)	Pro-administration	Anti-administration
			2nd (1791–1793)	Pro-administration	Anti-administration
			3rd (1793–1795)	Pro-administration	Anti-administration
			4th (1795–1797)	Federalist	Republican
1797–1801	John Adams	Federalist	5th (1797–1799)	Federalist	Republican
			6th (1799–1801)	Federalist	Republican
1801–1809	Thomas Jefferson	Democratic-Republican	7th (1801–1803)	Republican	Federalist
			8th (1803–1805)	Republican	Federalist
			9th (1805–1807)	Republican	Federalist
			10th (1807–1809)	Republican	Federalist
1809–1817	James Madison	Democratic-Republican	11th (1809–1811)	Republican	Federalist
			12th (1811–1813)	Republican	Federalist
			13th (1813–1815)	Republican	Federalist
			14th (1815–1817)	Republican	Federalist
1817–1825	James Monroe	Democratic-Republican	15th (1817–1819)	Republican	Federalist
			16th (1819–1821)	Republican	Federalist
			17th (1821–1823)	Republican	Federalist
			18th (1823–1825)	Republican	Federalist
1825–1829	John Q. Adams	Democratic-Republican National Republican	19th (1825–1827)	Jacksonian	Adams
			20th (1827–1829)	Jacksonian	Adams

Years	President	President's Party	Congress		
1829–1837	Andrew Jackson	Democratic	21st (1829–1831)	Jacksonian	Anti-Jackson
			22nd (1831–1833)	Jacksonian	Anti-Jackson
			23rd (1833–1835)	Anti-Jackson	Jackson
			24th (1835–1837)	Jacksonian	Anti-Jackson
1837–1841	Martin Van Buren	Democratic	25th (1837–1839)	Democratic	Whig
			26th (1839–1841)	Democratic	Whig
1841–1841	William H. Harrison	Whig	27th (1841–1843)	Whig	Democratic
1841–1845	John Tyler	Whig (1841–1841) Independent (1841–1845)	28th (1841–1845)	Whig	Democratic
1845–1849	James K. Polk	Democratic	29th (1845–1847)	Democratic	Whig
			30th (1847–1849)	Democratic	Whig
1849–1850	Zachary Taylor	Whig	31st (1849–1851)	Democratic	Whig
1850–1853	Millard Fillmore	Whig	32nd (1851–1853)	Democratic	Whig
1853–1857	Franklin Pierce	Democratic	33rd (1853–1855)	Democratic	Whig
			34th (1855–1857)	Democratic	Opposition
1857–1861	James Buchanan	Democratic	35th (1857–1859)	Democratic	Republican
			36th (1859–1861)	Democratic	Republican
1861–1865	Abraham Lincoln	Republican National Union	37th (1861–1863)	Republican	Democratic
			38th (1863–1865)	Republican	Democratic

(continues)

PRESIDENTIAL LEADERSHIP			CONGRESSIONAL LEADERSHIP		
TIME PERIOD	PRESIDENT	POLITICAL PARTY	CONGRESS	MAJORITY PARTY	MINORITY PARTY
1865–1869	Andrew Johnson	Democratic National Union and Independent	39th (1865–1867)	Republican	Democratic
			40th (1867–1869)	Republican	Democratic
1869–1877	Ulysses S. Grant	Republican	41st (1869–1871)	Republican	Democratic
			42nd (1871–1873)	Republican	Democratic
			43rd (1873–1875)	Republican	Democratic
			44th (1875–1877)	Republican	Democratic
1877–1881	Rutherford B. Hayes	Republican	45th (1877–1879)	Republican	Democratic
			46th (1879–1881)	Democratic	Republican
1881–1881	James A. Garfield	Republican	47th (1881–1883)	Republican	Democratic
1881–1885	Chester A. Arthur	Republican	48th (1883–1885)	Republican	Democratic
1885–1889	Grover Cleveland	Democratic	49th (1885–1887)	Republican	Democratic
			50th (1887–1889)	Republican	Democratic
1889–1893	Benjamin Harrison	Republican	51st (1889–1891)	Republican	Democratic
			52nd (1891–1893)	Republican	Democratic
1893–1897	Grover Cleveland	Democratic	53rd (1893–1895)	Democratic	Republican
			54th (1895–1897)	Republican	Democratic
1897–1901	William McKinley	Republican	55th (1897–1899)	Republican	Democratic
			56th (1899–1901)	Republican	Democratic

Years	President	President's Party	Congress		
1901–1909	Theodore Roosevelt	Republican	57th (1901–1903)	Republican	Democratic
			58th (1903–1905)	Republican	Democratic
			59th (1905–1907)	Republican	Democratic
			60th (1907–1909)	Republican	Democratic
1909–1913	William H. Taft	Republican	61st (1909–1911)	Republican	Democratic
			62nd (1911–1913)	Republican	Democratic
1913–1921	Woodrow Wilson	Democratic	63rd (1913–1915)	Democratic	Republican
			64th (1915–1917)	Democratic	Republican
			65th (1917–1919)	Democratic	Republican
			66th (1919–1921)	Republican	Democratic
1921–1923	Warren G. Harding	Republican	67th (1921–1923)	Republican	Democratic
1923–1929	Calvin Coolidge	Republican	68th (1923–1925)	Republican	Democratic
			69th (1925–1927)	Republican	Democratic
			70th (1927–1929)	Republican	Democratic
1929–1933	Herbert Hoover	Republican	71st (1929–1931)	Republican	Democratic
			72nd (1931–1933)	Republican	Democratic
1933–1945	Franklin D. Roosevelt	Democratic	73rd (1933–1935)	Democratic	Republican
			74th (1935–1937)	Democratic	Republican
			75th (1937–1939)	Democratic	Republican
			76th (1939–1941)	Democratic	Republican
			77th (1941–1943)	Democratic	Republican
			78th (1943–1945)	Democratic	Republican

(continues)

PRESIDENTIAL LEADERSHIP			CONGRESSIONAL LEADERSHIP		
TIME PERIOD	PRESIDENT	POLITICAL PARTY	CONGRESS	MAJORITY PARTY	MINORITY PARTY
1945–1953	Harry S. Truman	Democratic	79th (1945–1947)	Democratic	Republican
			80th (1947–1949)	Republican	Democratic
			81st (1949–1951)	Democratic	Republican
			82nd (1951–1953)	Democratic	Republican
1953–1961	Dwight D. Eisenhower	Republican	83rd (1953–1955)	Republican	Democratic
			84th (1955–1957)	Democratic	Republican
			85th (1957–1959)	Democratic	Republican
			86th (1959–1961)	Democratic	Republican
1961–1963	John F. Kennedy	Democratic	87th (1961–1963)	Democratic	Republican
1963–1969	Lyndon B. Johnson	Democratic	88th (1963–1965)	Democratic	Republican
			89th (1965–1967)	Democratic	Republican
			90th (1967–1969)	Democratic	Republican
1969–1974	Richard Nixon	Republican	91st (1969–1971)	Democratic	Republican
			92nd (1971–1973)	Democratic	Republican
			93rd (1973–1975)	Democratic	Republican
1974–1977	Gerald Ford	Republican	94th (1975–1977)	Democratic	Republican
1977–1981	Jimmy Carter	Democratic	95th (1977–1979)	Democratic	Republican
			96th (1979–1981)	Democratic	Republican
1981–1989	Ronald Reagan	Republican	97th (1981–1983)	Republican	Democratic
			98th (1983–1985)	Republican	Democratic
			99th (1985–1987)	Republican	Democratic
			100th (1987–1989)	Democratic	Republican

Term	President	President's Party	Congress		
1989–1993	George H. W. Bush	Republican	101st (1989–1991)	Democratic	Republican
			102nd (1991–1993)	Democratic	Republican
1993–2001	Bill Clinton	Democratic	103rd (1993–1995)	Democratic	Republican
			104th (1995–1997)	Republican	Democratic
			105th (1997–1999)	Republican	Democratic
			106th (1999–2001)	Republican	Democratic
2001–2009	George W. Bush	Republican	107th (2001–2003)	Democratic, then Republican	Republican, then Democratic
			108th (2003–2005)	Republican, then Democratic	Democratic, then Republican
			109th (2005–2007)	Democratic, then Republican	Republican, then Democratic
			110th (2007–2009)	Republican	Democratic
2009–2016	Barack Obama	Democratic	111th (2009–2011)	Republican	Democratic
			112th (2011–2013)	Republican	Democratic
			113th (2013–2015)	Democratic	Democratic
			114th (2015–2017)	Democratic	Republican
2017–2020	Donald Trump	Republican	115th (2017–2020)	Republican	Democratic

Note: Presidency is defined as a consecutive time in office. Congress is defined as the time in which the House of Representatives get a new term of office.

List of Public Laws*

Congress of the Confederation

1. Northwest Ordinance of 1784
2. Land Ordinance of 1785

1st U.S. Congress

1. Act to regulate time and manner of administering certain oaths
2. Hamilton Tariff
3. Judiciary Act of 1789
4. Census of 1790
5. Naturalization Act of 1790
6. Patent Act
7. Southwest Ordinance
8. Copyright Act of 1790
9. Residence Act
10. Indian Intercourse Act of 1790
11. First Bank of the United States
12. Whiskey Act

2nd U.S. Congress

1. Postal Service Act
2. Coinage Act of 1792
3. First Militia Act of 1792
4. Second Militia Act of 1792

*The public laws list is not comprehensive. Public and private public laws can be located and accessed through the Office of the Federal Register online at https://www.ofr.gov/Catalog.aspx#FederalLaws.

5. Fugitive Slave Law of 1793
6. Judiciary Act of 1793 (including Anti-Injunction Act)

3rd U.S. Congress

1. Naval Act of 1794
2. Naturalization Act of 1795

4th U.S. Congress

1. Treaty of Madrid

5th U.S. Congress

1. The U.S. Department of the Navy was established
2. Alien and Sedition Acts to establish a uniform rule of naturalization (Naturalization Act of 1798)
3. The Marine Corps was established
4. Alien and Sedition Acts for the punishment of certain crimes against the United States (Sedition Acts)

6th U.S. Congress

1. Judiciary Act of 1801
2. District of Columbia Organic Act of 1801

7th U.S. Congress

1. Judiciary Act of 1802
2. Enabling Act of 1802

8th U.S. Congress

1. Louisiana Purchase

9th U.S. Congress

10th U.S. Congress

1. Embargo Act of 1807

11th U.S. Congress

1. Macon's Bill Number 2

12th U.S. Congress

1. Declaration of War on Great Britain

13th U.S. Congress

    1. Treaty of Ghent

14th U.S. Congress

    1. Second Bank of the United States

15th U.S. Congress

    1. Flag Act of 1818
    2. Navigation Act of 1818

16th U.S. Congress

    1. Land Act of 1820

17th U.S. Congress

18th U.S. Congress

    1. Tariff of 1824

19th U.S. Congress

    1. Treaty of Washington

20th U.S. Congress

    1. Tariff of Abominations

21st U.S. Congress

    1. Indian Removal Act

22nd U.S. Congress

    1. Tariff of 1832
    2. Compromise Tariff (Tariff of 1833)
    3. Force Bill

23rd U.S. Congress

24th U.S. Congress

25th U.S. Congress

26th U.S. Congress

27th U.S. Congress

1. Bankruptcy Act of 1841
2. Preemption Act of 1841
3. Tariff of 1842 ("Black Tariff")

28th U.S. Congress

29th U.S. Congress

1. District of Columbia retrocession
2. Walker tariff

30th U.S. Congress

1. Coinage Act of 1849

31st U.S. Congress

1. Fugitive Slave Act
2. Donation Land Claim Act

32nd U.S. Congress

33rd U.S. Congress

1. Kansas-Nebraska Act

34th U.S. Congress

1. Guano Islands Act

35th U.S. Congress

36th U.S. Congress

1. Morrill Tariff

37th U.S. Congress

1. Revenue Act of 1861
2. Confiscation Act of 1861
3. Legal Tender Act of 1862
4. Homestead Act
5. Morrill Anti-Bigamy Act
6. Revenue Act of 1862
7. Pacific Railway Act

8. Morrill Land Grant Colleges Act
9. Militia Act
10. National Banking Act
11. False Claims Act
12. Enrollment Act

38th U.S. Congress

1. Coinage Act of 1864

39th U.S. Congress

1. Civil Rights Act of 1866
2. Judicial Circuits Act
3. Reconstruction Act
4. Tenure of Office Act

40th U.S. Congress

1. Reconstruction Acts

41st U.S. Congress

1. Judiciary Act of 1869 (Circuit Judges Act of 1869)
2. Force Act of 1870
3. Naturalization Act of 1870
4. District of Columbia Organic Act of 1871

42nd U.S. Congress

1. Ku Klux Act (Civil Rights Act of 1871, Ku Klux Klan Act)
2. Yellowstone Act
3. General Mining Act of 1872
4. Amnesty Act
5. Practice Conformity Act (precursor to the Rules Enabling Act)
6. Coinage Act of 1873
7. Timber Culture Act

43rd U.S. Congress

1. Civil Rights Act of 1875

44th U.S. Congress

1. Desert Land Act

45th U.S. Congress

1. Bland-Allison Act (Coinage Act [Silver Dollar])
2. National Quarantine Act
3. Timber and Stone Act

46th U.S. Congress

47th U.S. Congress

1. Chinese Exclusion Act
2. Pendleton Civil Service Reform Act

48th U.S. Congress

49th U.S. Congress

1. Interstate Commerce Act
2. Indian General Allotment Act (Dawes Act)
3. Hatch Act of 1887
4. Tucker Act
5. Edmunds-Tucker Act

50th U.S. Congress

1. Enabling Act of 1889

51st U.S. Congress

1. Sherman Antitrust Act
2. Sherman Silver Purchase Act
3. Morrill Land Grant College Act of 1890
4. McKinley Tariff
5. Forest Reserve Act of 1891
6. Land Revision Act of 1891

52nd U.S. Congress

1. Geary Act (amended the Chinese Exclusion Act)

53rd U.S. Congress

1. Wilson-Gorman Tariff Act
2. Maguire Act of 1895

54th U.S. Congress

55th U.S. Congress

1. Dingley Tariff (amended the Wilson-Gorman Tariff Act)
2. Bankruptcy Act of 1898
3. Newlands Resolution, No. 55
4. Rivers and Harbors Act of 1899

56th U.S. Congress

1. Gold Standard Act
2. Foraker Act (Puerto Rico Civil Code)
3. Anarchist Exclusion Act

57th U.S. Congress

1. Newlands Reclamation Act (National Irrigation Act, Reclamation Act)
2. Isthmian Canal Act (Panama Canal)
3. Militia Act of 1903 (Dick Act)

58th U.S. Congress

1. Kinkaid Act

59th U.S. Congress

1. Federal Employers' Liability Act
2. American Antiquities Act (National Monument Act)
3. Pure Food and Drug Act
4. Meat Inspection Act

60th U.S. Congress

1. Aldrich-Vreeland Act

61st U.S. Congress

1. Payne-Aldrich Tariff Act

62nd U.S. Congress

1. Lloyd-LaFollette Act

63rd U.S. Congress

1. Revenue Act of 1913 (including Underwood Tariff)
2. Federal Reserve Act

3. Federal Trade Commission Act
4. Clayton Antitrust Act
5. Harrison Narcotics Tax Act

64th U.S. Congress

1. Federal Farm Loan Act
2. National Park Service Act
3. Keating-Owen Child Labor Act of 1916
4. Revenue Act of 1916
5. Stock-Raising Homestead Act
6. Immigration Act of 1917 (Barred Zone Act)
7. Smith-Hughes Vocational Education Act
8. Flood Control Act of 1917

65th U.S. Congress

1. 1st Liberty Loan Act
2. Enemy Vessel Confiscation Joint Resolution
3. 1st Army Appropriations Act of 1917
4. Selective Service Act of 1917
5. 2nd Army Appropriations Act of 1917
6. Search Warrant Act of 1917
7. Emergency Shipping Fund Act of 1917
8. Espionage Act of 1917
9. River and Harbors Act of 1917
10. Priority of Shipments Act of 1917
11. Obstruction of Interstate Commerce Act of 1917
12. Food and Fuel Control Act (Lever Act)
13. Grain Standards Act of 1917
14. 2nd Liberty Loan Act
15. Aircraft Board Act of 1917
16. War Revenue Act of 1917
17. Repatriation Act of 1917
18. Explosives Act of 1917
19. International Emergency Economic Powers Act (Trading with the Enemy Act)
20. War Risk Insurance Act of 1917

21. Smoot Amendment
22. Federal Possession and Control Act
23. Revenue Act of 1918
24. Soldiers' and Sailors' Civil Relief Act
25. Standard Time Act (Calder Act)
26. Daylight Savings Act (Borland-Calder Act)
27. Federal Control Act of 1918
28. 3rd Liberty Loan Act
29. War Finance Corporation Act
30. American Forces Abroad Indemnity Act
31. Destruction of War Materials Act
32. Alien Naturalization Act
33. Housing for War Needs Act
34. Departmental Reorganization Act (Overman Act)
35. Passport Control Act
36. Entry and Departure Controls Act
37. Veterans Rehabilitation Act (Smith-Sears Act)
38. Industrial Aid Act (Fess Act)
39. Migratory Bird Treaty Act of 1918
40. Army Appropriations Act of 1918
41. 4th Liberty Loan Act
42. Public Health and Research Act of 1918 (Chamberlain-Kahn Act)
43. Charter Rate and Requisition Act of 1918
44. River and Harbors Act of 1918
45. Immigration Act of October 16, 1918 (Dillingham-Hardwick Act)
46. Corrupt Practices Act of 1918 (Gerry Act)
47. National Bank Consolidation Act of 1918
48. War-Time Prohibition Act
49. Revenue Act of 1919
50. Child Labor Act of 1919
51. Grand Canyon Park Act of 1919
52. Acadia National Park Act of 1919
53. River and Harbors Act of 1919
54. War Minerals Relief Act of 1919 (Dent Act)
55. Hospitalization Act of 1919
56. War Risk Insurance Act of 1919

57. 5th Liberty Loan Act
58. Wheat Price Guarantee Act (Lever Act)

66th U.S. Congress

1. National Prohibition Act (Volstead Act)
2. Mineral Leasing Act

67th U.S. Congress

1. Emergency Quota Act (Johnson Quota Act)
2. Emergency Tariff of 1921
3. Future Trading Act
4. Revenue Act of 1921
5. Fordney-McCumber tariff
6. Grain Futures Act
7. Cable Act (Married Women's Citizenship Act)

68th U.S. Congress

1. World War Adjusted Compensation Act (Bonus Bill)
2. Immigration Act of 1924 (Johnson-Reed Act)
3. Indian Citizenship Act of 1924 (Snyder Act)
4. Revenue Act of 1924 (Mellon tax bill)

69th U.S. Congress

1. Revenue Act of 1926

70th U.S. Congress

1. Settlement of War Claims Act
2. Flood Control Act of 1928 (Jones-Reid Act)
3. Merchant Marine Act of 1928 (Jones-White Act)
4. Forest Research Act (McSweeney-McNary Act)
5. Revenue Act of 1928
6. Boulder Canyon Project Act (Hoover Dam)
7. Color of Title Act
8. Migratory Bird Conservation Act (Norbeck-Anderson Act)
9. Increased Penalties Act (Jones-Stalker Act)

71st U.S. Congress

1. Migratory Bird Conservation Act
2. Agriculture Marketing Act

3. Reapportionment Act of 1929
4. Hawley-Smoot Tariff (including Plant Patent Act)

72nd U.S. Congress

1. Reconstruction Finance Corporation Act
2. Revenue Act of 1932
3. Federal Home Loan Bank Act
4. Buy American Act

73rd U.S. Congress

1. Emergency Banking Relief Act
2. Economy Act
3. Civilian Conservation Corps Reforestation Relief Act
4. Federal Emergency Relief Act
5. Agricultural Adjustment Act
6. Securities Act
7. Home Owners' Loan Corporation
8. Glass-Steagall Act (Banking Act of 1933)
9. National Industrial Recovery Act
10. Farm Credit Administration
11. Tydings-McDuffie Act (Philippine Independence Act)
12. Johnson Act
13. Securities Exchange Act
14. Reciprocal Tariff Act
15. Indian Reorganization Act
16. Rules Enabling Act
17. Communications Act of 1934
18. National Archives Act
19. Federal Credit Union Act
20. National Firearms Act of 1934
21. National Housing Act (including Federal National Mortgage Association Charter Act/Fannie Mae)

74th U.S. Congress

1. Soil Conservation and Domestic Allotment Act
2. National Labor Relations Act (Wagner Act)
3. Motor Carrier Act (renamed part II of the Interstate Commerce Act)
4. Social Security Act (including Aid to Dependent Children, Old Age Pension Act)

5. Public Utility Act (including: Public Utility Holding Company Act of 1935, Federal Power Act)
6. Revenue Act of 1935
7. Neutrality Act of 1935
8. Neutrality Act of 1936
9. Rural Electrification Act
10. Commodities Exchange Act
11. Flood Control Act of 1936
12. Merchant Marine Act
13. Walsh-Healey Public Contracts Act

75th U.S. Congress

1. Agricultural Marketing Agreement Act
2. Marijuana Tax Act
3. National Cancer Institute Act
4. 1937: Neutrality Acts of 1937
5. Foreign Agents Registration Act
6. Natural Gas Act
7. Civil Aeronautics Act
8. Fair Labor Standards Act
9. Federal Food, Drug, and Cosmetic Act

76th U.S. Congress

1. Reorganization Act of 1939
2. Hatch Act of 1939 (Hatch Political Activity Act, An Act to Prevent Pernicious Political Activities)
3. Neutrality Act of 1939 (Cash and Carry Act)
4. Investment Company Act of 1940
5. Investment Advisers Act of 1940
6. Alien Registration Act (Smith Act)
7. Selective Training and Service Act of 1940
8. Investment Company Act of 1940

77th U.S. Congress

1. Lend Lease Act
2. Flood Control Act of 1941
3. Emergency Price Control Act

78th U.S. Congress

1. Magnuson Act (Chinese Exclusion Repeal Act of 1943)
2. Mustering-out Payment Act
3. Servicemen's Readjustment Act of 1944 (G.I. Bill)
4. Veterans' Preference Act
5. Public Health Service Act
6. Pick-Sloan Flood Control Act

79th U.S. Congress

1. Export-Import Bank Act of 1945
2. United Nations Participation Act
3. War Brides Act
4. Rescission Act of 1946
5. Employment Act
6. Federal Airport Act
7. Richard B. Russell National School Lunch Act
8. Administrative Procedure Act
9. Hobbs Anti-Racketeering Act
10. Lanham Trademark Act of 1946
11. United States Atomic Energy Act of 1946
12. Legislative Reorganization Act of 1946
13. Federal Tort Claims Act
14. Federal Regulation of Lobbying Act of 1946
15. Foreign Service Act
16. Hospital Survey and Construction Act (Hill-Burton Act)
17. Farmers Home Administration Act

80th U.S. Congress

1. National Security Act of 1947
2. Mineral Leasing Act for Acquired Lands
3. United States Information and Educational Exchange Act
4. Foreign Assistance Act (Marshall Plan)
5. Greek-Turkish Assistance Act of 1948
6. Civil Air Patrol Act
7. Presidential Succession Act
8. Federal Water Pollution Control Act
9. War Claims Act of 1948

81st U.S. Congress

1. Central Intelligence Agency Act
2. Uniform Code of Military Justice
3. National Science Foundation Act
4. McCarran Internal Security Act
5. Federal Civil Defense Act of 1950

82nd U.S. Congress

1. Mutual Security Act
2. Immigration and Nationality Act (McCarran-Walter Act)
3. Veterans' Readjustment Assistance Act
4. Federal Coal Mine Safety Act Amendments of 1952

83rd U.S. Congress

1. Small Business Act
2. Refugee Relief Act
3. Outer Continental Shelf Lands Act
4. Federal National Mortgage Association Charter Act
5. Multiple Mineral Development Act
6. Internal Revenue Code of 1954
7. Federal Unemployment Tax Act
8. National Firearms Act
9. Communist Control Act of 1954

84th U.S. Congress

1. Flood Control and Coastal Emergency Act
2. Air Pollution Control Act
3. Poliomyelitis Vaccination Assistance Act
4. Health Research Facilities Act
5. Federal-Aid Highway Act of 1956 (National Interstate and Defense Highways Act)

85th U.S. Congress

1. Airways Modernization Act
2. Price-Anderson Nuclear Industries Indemnity Act
3. Civil Rights Act of 1957
4. National Aeronautics and Space Act
5. Transportation Act of 1958

6. Federal Aviation Act
7. Military Construction Appropriation Act (Advanced Research Projects Agency)
8. National Defense Education Act
9. Department of Defense Reorganization Act

86th U.S. Congress

1. Admission of Hawaii Act
2. Airport Construction Act
3. Landrum-Griffin Act
4. Civil Rights Act of 1960
5. Social Security Amendments (Kerr-Mill aid)
6. Flood Control Act of 1960

87th U.S. Congress

1. Area Redevelopment Act
2. Foreign Assistance Act of 1961
3. Interstate Wire Act of 1961
4. Mutual Educational and Cultural Exchange Act of 1961
5. Peace Corps Act of 1961
6. Arms Control and Disarmament Act
7. Community Health Services and Facilities Act
8. Manpower Development and Training Act
9. Migration and Refugee Assistance Act
10. Communications Satellite Act of 1962
11. Trade Expansion Act
12. Bribery Act
13. Vaccination Assistance Act
14. Rivers and Harbors Act of 1962

88th U.S. Congress

1. Equal Pay Act
2. Community Mental Health Centers Act (including Mental Retardation Facilities Construction Act)
3. Clean Air Act
4. Civil Rights Act of 1964
5. Urban Mass Transportation Act of 1964 (Federal Transit Act)
6. Economic Opportunity Act of 1964

7. Food Stamp Act of 1964
8. Wilderness Act
9. Land and Water Conservation Act
10. Nurse Training Act

89th U.S. Congress

1. Elementary and Secondary Education Act
2. Federal Cigarette Labeling and Advertising Act
3. Social Security Act of 1965 (including Medicaid and Medicare)
4. Voting Rights Act
5. Housing and Urban Development Act of 1965
6. Public Works and Economic Development Act of 1965
7. National Foundation on the Arts and the Humanities Act
8. Immigration and Nationality Act of 1965
9. Heart Disease, Cancer, and Stroke Amendments
10. Motor Vehicle Air Pollution Control Act (including Solid Waste Disposal Act)
11. Highway Beautification Act
12. Higher Education Act
13. Vocational Rehabilitation Act Amendments
14. Uniform Time Act
15. Freedom of Information Act
16. National Traffic and Motor Vehicle Safety Act
17. National Historic Preservation Act
18. National Wildlife Refuge System Administration Act
19. Department of Transportation Act
20. Cuban Adjustment Act
21. Comprehensive Health, Planning, and Service Act

90th U.S. Congress

1. Supplemental Defense Appropriations Act
2. Public Broadcasting Act
3. Age Discrimination in Employment Act
4. National Park Foundation Act
5. Bilingual Education Act
6. Civil Rights Act of 1968
7. Consumer Credit Protection Act
8. Omnibus Crime Control and Safe Streets Act of 1968

9. Uniform Monday Holiday Act
10. Aircraft Noise Abatement Act
11. Architectural Barriers Act of 1968
12. Wild and Scenic Rivers Act
13. National Trails System Act
14. Gun Control Act of 1968

91st U.S. Congress

1. Federal Coal Mine Health and Safety Act
2. Truth in Lending Act
3. National Environmental Policy Act
4. Airport and Airway Development Act
5. District of Columbia Delegate Act
6. Organized Crime Control Act (including the Racketeer Influenced and Corrupt Organizations Act [RICO])
7. Bank Secrecy Act
8. Controlled Substances Act
9. Postal Reorganization Act (United States Postal Service)
10. Urban Mass Transportation Act of 1970
11. Rail Passenger Service Act (Amtrak)
12. Family Planning Services and Population Research Act of 1970
13. Plant Variety Protection Act
14. Occupational Safety and Health Act (OSHA)
15. Clean Air Act Extension
16. Housing and Urban Development Act of 1970 (including National Urban Policy and New Community Development Act of 1970)
17. Lead-Based Paint Poisoning Prevention Act
18. Economic Stabilization Act
19. Environmental Quality Improvement Act

92nd U.S. Congress

1. Alaska Native Claims Settlement Act
2. National Cancer Act
3. Federal Election Campaign Act
4. Equal Employment Opportunity Act
5. Title IX Amendment of the Higher Education Act
6. Federal Advisory Committee Act
7. Federal Water Pollution Control Amendments of 1972

8. Marine Mammal Protection Act
9. Marine Protection, Research and Sanctuaries Act
10. Consumer Product Safety Act
11. Noise Control Act
12. Coastal Zone Management Act

93rd U.S. Congress

1. Federal Aid Highway Act of 1973
2. Rehabilitation Act
3. Domestic Volunteer Services Act of 1973 (VISTA)
4. Amtrak Improvement Act
5. War Powers Resolution
6. District of Columbia Home Rule Act
7. Comprehensive Employment and Training Act
8. Endangered Species Act
9. Water Resources Development Act of 1974
10. Disaster Relief Act of 1974
11. Research on Aging Act
12. Congressional Budget and Impoundment Control Act of 1974
13. Legal Services Corporation Act
14. Family Educational Rights and Privacy Act
15. Employee Retirement Income Security Act (ERISA)
16. Juvenile Justice and Delinquency Prevention Act of 1974
17. National Mass Transportation Assistance Act
18. Vietnam Era Veterans' Readjustment Assistance Act
19. Safe Drinking Water Act
20. Privacy Act of 1974
21. Trade Act of 1974
22. Federal Noxious Weed Act of 1974
23. Hazardous Materials Transportation Act
24. National Health Planning and Resources Development Act

94th U.S. Congress

1. Revenue Adjustment Act (Earned Income Tax Credit)
2. Individuals with Disabilities Education Act
3. Railroad Revitalization and Regulatory Reform Act
4. Government in the Sunshine Act

5. Hart-Scott-Rodino Antitrust Improvements Act
6. Toxic Substances Control Act
7. Overhaul of vocational education programs
8. Copyright Act of 1976
9. Federal Land Policy and Management Act
10. Resource Conservation and Recovery Act
11. Water Resources Development Act of 1976
12. National Forest Management Act

95th U.S. Congress

1. Surface Mining Control and Reclamation Act
2. Community Reinvestment Act
3. Unlawful Corporate Payments Act of 1977 (including Foreign Corrupt Practices Act)
4. Clean Water Act
5. International Emergency Economic Powers Act
6. Department of Energy Organization Act
7. Nuclear Non-Proliferation Act
8. Civil Service Reform Act
9. Drug Abuse Prevention, Treatment, and Rehabilitation Act
10. Airline Deregulation Act
11. Foreign Intelligence Surveillance Act
12. Ethics in Government Act
13. Humphrey-Hawkins Full Employment Act
14. Pregnancy Discrimination Act
15. Contract Disputes Act
16. Bankruptcy Act of 1978
17. Public Utility Regulatory Policies Act
18. National Energy Conservation Policy Act

96th U.S. Congress

1. Panama Canal Act of 1979
2. Department of Education Organization Act
3. Refugee Act
4. Regulatory Flexibility Act
5. Fish and Wildlife Conservation Act of 1980
6. Alaska National Interest Lands Conservation Act

7. Comprehensive Environmental Response, Compensation, and Liability Act (CERCLA or Superfund)
8. Paperwork Reduction Act of 1980

97th U.S. Congress

1. Economic Recovery Tax Act (ERTA or Kemp-Roth Tax Cut)
2. Omnibus Budget Reconciliation Act of 1981
3. Bus Regulatory Reform Act
4. Job Training Partnership Act
5. Garn-St. Germain Depository Institutions Act
6. Surface Transportation Assistance Act
7. Nuclear Waste Policy Act

98th U.S. Congress

1. Voting Accessibility for the Elderly and Handicapped Act
2. Comprehensive Crime Control Act

99th U.S. Congress

1. Balanced Budget and Emergency Deficit Control Act of 1985 (Gramm-Rudman-Hollings Balanced Budget Act)
2. Gold Bullion Coin Act of 1985
3. Consolidated Omnibus Budget Reconciliation Act of 1985 (COBRA) (including Emergency Medical Treatment and Active Labor Act)
4. Goldwater-Nichols Act of 1986 (Defense Reorganization)
5. Comprehensive Anti-Apartheid Act
6. Immigration Reform and Control Act of 1986 (Simpson-Mazzoli Act)
7. Emergency Planning and Community Right-to-Know Act (title III)
8. Electronic Communications Privacy Act of 1986
9. Tax Reform Act of 1986
10. Anti-Drug Abuse Act
11. Age Discrimination in Employment Act
12. Water Resources Development Act of 1986

100th U.S. Congress

1. Surface Transportation and Uniform Relocation Assistance Act
2. Malcolm Baldrige National Quality Improvement Act of 1987
3. Balanced Budget and Emergency Deficit Control Reaffirmation Act of 1987 (Gramm-Rudman-Hollings Balanced Budget Act)
4. Agricultural Credit Act of 1987

5. Computer Security Act of 1987
6. Medicare Catastrophic Coverage Act
7. Civil Liberties Act
8. Family Support Act
9. Indian Gaming Regulatory Act
10. Department of Veterans Affairs Act
11. Water Resources Development Act of 1988
12. Anti-Drug Abuse Act of 1988 (including Child Protection and Obscenity Enforcement Act, Alcoholic Beverage Labeling Act)

101st U.S. Congress

1. Whistleblower Protection Act
2. Water Resources Development Act 1990
3. Flag Protection Act of 1989
4. Americans with Disabilities Act
5. Omnibus Budget Reconciliation Act of 1990 (including Human Genome Project funding)
6. Water Resources Development Act of 1990
7. Administrative Dispute Resolution Act
8. Native American Graves Protection and Repatriation Act
9. Negotiated Rulemaking Act
10. Immigration Act of 1990
11. Judicial Improvements Act of 1990 (including Visual Artists Rights Act)

102nd U.S. Congress

1. Civil Rights Act of 1991
2. High Performance Computing and Communication Act of 1991
3. Intermodal Surface Transportation Efficiency Act
4. Chinese Student Protection Act of 1992
5. Weapons of Mass Destruction Control Act
6. Water Resources Development Act of 1992

103rd U.S. Congress

1. Family and Medical Leave Act
2. National Voter Registration Act of 1993
3. Omnibus Budget Reconciliation Act of 1993
4. Religious Freedom Restoration Act

5. Brady Handgun Violence Prevention Act (Brady Bill)
6. National Defense Authorization Act for Fiscal Year 1994 (including "Don't Ask, Don't Tell")
7. North American Free Trade Agreement Implementation Act
8. Freedom of Access to Clinic Entrances Act
9. Violent Crime Control and Law Enforcement Act (including the Violence Against Women Act)

104th U.S. Congress

1. Congressional Accountability Act
2. National Highway Designation Act
3. Lobbying Disclosure Act
4. Private Securities Litigation Reform Act
5. Telecommunications Act of 1996 (including the Communications Decency Act)
6. Cuban Liberty and Democratic Solidarity (Libertad) Act of 1996 (Helms-Burton Act)
7. Line Item Veto Act
8. Antiterrorism and Effective Death Penalty Act
9. Taxpayer Bill of Rights 2
10. National Gambling Impact Study Commission Act
11. Small Business Job Protection Act
12. Health Insurance Portability and Accountability Act (HIPAA)
13. Personal Responsibility and Work Opportunity Act (Welfare Reform Act)
14. Defense of Marriage Act
15. Domestic Violence Offender Gun Ban
16. Emerson Good Samaritan Food Donation Act
17. Water Resources Development Act of 1996

105th U.S. Congress

1. Balanced Budget Act of 1997
2. Taxpayer Relief Act of 1997
3. Transportation Equity Act for the 21st Century
4. Taxpayer Bill of Rights III
5. Workforce Investment Act
6. Child Online Privacy Protection Act

7. Sonny Bono Copyright Term Extension Act
8. Digital Millennium Copyright Act (including Online Copyright Infringement Liability Limitation Act)
9. Iraq Liberation Act

106th U.S. Congress

1. Emergency Supplemental Appropriations Act (Kosovo operations)
2. Water Resources Development Act of 1999
3. Gramm-Leach-Bliley Financial Services Modernization Act
4. American Inventors Protection Act (including Anticybersquatting Consumer Protection Act)
5. Iran Nonproliferation Act of 2000
6. Wendell H. Ford Aviation Investment and Reform Act for the 21st Century
7. African Growth and Opportunity Act
8. Electronic Signatures in Global and National Commerce Act
9. Oceans Act
10. Religious Land Use and Institutionalized Persons Act
11. Children's Health Act
12. Robert T. Stafford Disaster Relief and Emergency Assistance Act
13. Water Resources Development Act of 2000
14. Commodity Futures Modernization Act of 2000 (as part of the Consolidated Appropriations Act, 2001)

107th U.S. Congress

1. Economic Growth and Tax Relief Reconciliation Act
2. Uniting and Strengthening America by Providing Appropriate Tools Required to Intercept and Obstruct Terrorism (USA PATRIOT) Act
3. No Child Left Behind Act
4. Small Business Liability Relief and Brownfields Revitalization Act
5. Job Creation and Worker Assistance Act
6. Bipartisan Campaign Reform Act (McCain-Feingold)
7. Farm Security and Rural Investment Act of 2002
8. Sarbanes-Oxley Act
9. Trade Act of 2002
10. Authorization for Use of Military Force Against Iraq
11. Sudan Peace Act

12. Help America Vote Act
13. Homeland Security Act
14. E-Government Act of 2002

108th U.S. Congress

1. Do-Not-Call Implementation Act of 2003
2. PROTECT (Prosecutorial Remedies and Other Tools to end the Exploitation of Children Today) Act (including Illicit Drug Anti-Proliferation Act)
3. Jobs and Growth Tax Relief Reconciliation Act of 2003
4. Prison Rape Elimination Act of 2003
5. Partial-Birth Abortion Ban Act
6. Medicare Prescription Drug, Improvement, and Modernization Act
7. Fair and Accurate Credit Transactions Act
8. Syria Accountability and Lebanese Sovereignty Restoration Act
9. CAN-SPAM Act
10. Unborn Victims of Violence Act (Laci and Conner's Law)
11. Bunning-Bereuter-Blumenauer Flood Insurance Reform Act
12. GAO Human Capital Reform Act of 2004
13. Global Anti-Semitism Review Act
14. North Korean Human Rights Act of 2004
15. Belarus Democracy Act of 2004
16. Intelligence Reform and Terrorism Prevention Act

109th U.S. Congress

1. Class Action Fairness Act of 2005
2. Bankruptcy Abuse Prevention and Consumer Protection Act
3. Family Entertainment and Copyright Act
4. Dominican Republic-Central America-United States Free Trade Agreement Implementation Act (CAFTA Implementation Act)
5. Energy Policy Act of 2005
6. Transportation Equity Act of 2005
7. Protection of Lawful Commerce in Arms Act
8. Caribbean National Forest Act of 2005
9. Department of Defense Appropriations Act (including McCain Detainee Amendment)
10. Deficit Reduction Act of 2005 (including Federal Deposit Insurance Reform Act)

11. Tax Increase Prevention and Reconciliation Act of 2005
12. Respect for America's Fallen Heroes Act
13. Adam Walsh Child Protection and Safety Act
14. Federal Funding Accountability and Transparency Act of 2006
15. Safe Port Act (including Unlawful Internet Gambling Enforcement Act of 2006)
16. Military Commissions Act of 2006
17. Secure Fence Act of 2006
18. Combating Autism Act
19. Tax Relief and Health Act of 2006

110th U.S. Congress

1. House Page Board Revision Act of 2007
2. U.S. Troop Readiness, Veterans' Care, Katrina Recovery, and Iraq Accountability Appropriations Act of 2007
3. Preserving United States Attorney Independence Act of 2007 (including Fair Minimum Wage Act of 2007)
4. Foreign Investment and National Security Act of 2007
5. Implementing Recommendations of the 9/11 Commission Act of 2007
6. Protect America Act of 2007
7. Honest Leadership and Open Government Act
8. Water Resources Development Act of 2007
9. Energy Independence and Security Act of 2007
10. Economic Stimulus Act of 2008
11. Genetic Information Nondiscrimination Act
12. Food and Energy Security Act of 2007 (2007 Farm Bill)
13. Supplemental Appropriations Act of 2008 (including Post-9/11 Veterans Educational Assistance Act of 2008/G.I. Bill 2008)
14. FISA Amendments Act of 2008
15. Housing and Economic Recovery Act of 2008
16. Emergency Economic Stabilization Act of 2008

111th U.S. Congress

1. Lilly Ledbetter Fair Pay Act of 2009
2. Children's Health Insurance Program Reauthorization Act (SCHIP)
3. American Recovery and Reinvestment Act of 2009 (ARRA)
4. Omnibus Appropriations Act of 2009

5. Omnibus Public Land Management Act
6. Edward M. Kennedy Serve America Act
7. Fraud Enforcement and Recovery Act of 2009 (FERA)
8. Helping Families Save Their Homes Act of 2009
9. Weapon Systems Acquisition Reform Act of 2009
10. Family Smoking Prevention and Tobacco Control Act
11. Supplemental Appropriations Act of 2009
12. National Defense Authorization Act for Fiscal Year 2010, including the Matthew Shepard and James Byrd, Jr. Hate Crimes Prevention Act
13. Worker, Homeownership, and Business Assistance Act
14. Statutory Pay-As-You-Go Act
15. Patient Protection and Affordable Care Act

112th U.S. Congress

1. PATRIOT Sunsets Extension Act of 2011
2. Airport and Airway Extension Act of 2011
3. Restoring GI Bill Fairness Act of 2011
4. Combating Autism Reauthorization Act of 2011
5. Child and Family Services Improvement and Innovation Act
6. Kate Puzey Peace Corps Volunteer Protection Act of 2011
7. Federal Courts Jurisdiction and Venue Clarification Act of 2011
8. Fallen Heroes of 9/11 Act
9. Belarus Democracy and Human Rights Act of 2011
10. Risk-Based Security Screening for Members of the Armed Forces Act
11. Border Tunnel Prevention Act of 2012
12. Food and Drug Administration Safety and Innovation Act
13. Veteran Skills to Jobs Act
14. Pilot's Bill of Rights
15. Sequestration Transparency Act of 2012
16. Iran Threat Reduction and Syria Human Rights Act of 2012
17. Child Protection Act of 2012
18. Hatch Act Modernization Act of 2012
19. Theft of Trade Secrets Clarification Act of 2012
20. Drywall Safety Act of 2012
21. Foreign and Economic Espionage Penalty Enhancement Act of 2012
22. Protect Our Kids Act of 2012
23. Jumpstart Our Business Startups Act

113th U.S. Congress

1. Intelligence Authorization Act for Fiscal Year 2014
2. Workforce Innovation and Opportunity Act
3. Veterinary Medicine Mobility Act of 2014
4. Unlocking Consumer Choice and Wireless Competition Act
5. Veterans Access, Choice, and Accountability Act of 2014
6. Improving Trauma Care Act of 2014
7. Victims of Child Abuse Act Reauthorization Act of 2013
8. Preventing Sex Trafficking and Strengthening Families Act
9. Improving Medicare Post-Acute Care Transformation Act of 2014 (IMPACT Act of 2014)
10. Child Care and Development Block Grant Act of 2014
11. Sunscreen Innovation Act
12. Traumatic Brain Injury Reauthorization Act of 2014
13. Enhance Labeling, Accessing, and Branding of Electronic Licenses Act of 2014 (E-LABEL Act)
14. Digital Accountability and Transparency Act of 2014 (DATA Act)
15. Kilah Davenport Child Protection Act of 2013
16. Water Resources Reform and Development Act of 2014
17. Reliable Home Heating Act
18. Presidential Appointment Efficiency and Streamlining Act of 2011
19. Pesticide Registration Improvement Extension Act of 2012
20. FDA User Fee Corrections Act 2012
21. Government Charge Card Abuse Prevention Act of 2012
22. Hazardous Waste Electronic Manifest Establishment Act
23. Whistleblower Protection Enhancement Act of 2012
24. Violence Against Women Reauthorization Act of 2013
25. Pandemic and All Hazards Preparedness Reauthorization Act of 2013
26. Freedom to Fish Act
27. Pay Our Military Act
28. School Access to Emergency Epinephrine Act
29. HIV Organ Policy Equity Act
30. Drug Quality and Security Act Compounding Quality Act
31. Community Fire Safety Act of 2013
32. Accuracy for Adoptees Act
33. Poison Center Network Act

34. Agricultural Act of 2014
35. Homeowner Flood Insurance Affordability Act of 2014
36. Protecting Access to Medicare Act of 2014
37. Gabriella Miller Kids First Research Act
38. Death in Custody Reporting Act of 2013
39. Cybersecurity Workforce Assessment Act
40. American Savings Promotion Act
41. Veterans Traumatic Brain Injury Care Improvement Act of 2014
42. Propane Education and Research Enhancement Act of 2014
43. United States Anti-Doping Agency Reauthorization Act

114th U.S. Congress

1. Clay Hunt Suicide Prevention for American Veterans Act (Clay Hunt SAV Act)
2. Slain Officer Family Support Act of 2015
3. Medicare Access and CHIP Reauthorization Act of 2015
4. Energy Efficiency Improvement Act of 2015
5. Justice for Victims of Trafficking Act of 2015
6. Girls Count Act of 2015
7. Steve Gleason Act of 2015
8. Need-Based Educational Aid Act of 2015
9. Drinking Water Protection Act
10. STEM Education Act of 2015
11. Ensuring Access to Clinical Trials Act of 2015
12. Adoptive Family Relief Act
13. Wounded Warriors Federal Leave Act of 2015
14. Protecting Our Infants Act of 2015
15. Every Student Succeeds Act
16. Improving Access to Emergency Psychiatric Care Act
17. Stem Cell Therapeutic and Research Reauthorization Act of 2015
18. Emergency Information Improvement Act of 2015
19. Patient Access and Medicare Protection Act
20. Child Nicotine Poisoning Prevention Act of 2015
21. Integrated Public Alert and Warning System Modernization Act of 2015
22. Transnational Drug Trafficking Act of 2015
23. Native American Children's Safety Act

24. Recovering Missing Children Act
25. Female Veteran Suicide Prevention Act
26. Global Food Security Act of 2016
27. Comprehensive Addiction and Recovery Act of 2016

Policy Resources and Websites

Governmental Agencies, Centers, Policy Institutes, and Publications

Administration for Children and Families: http://www.acf.hhs.gov

Administration on Aging (AoA): http://www.aoa.gov

Agency for HealthCare Research and Quality (AHRQ): http://www.ahrq.gov

American Health Care Association: www.ahcancal.org

American Hospital Association: www.aha.org

American Medical Association: https://www.ama-assn.org

American Society of Law, Medicine, and Ethics (ASLME): http://www
.aslme.org

Annie E. Casey Foundation: www.aecf.org

Bureau of Labor Statistics: http://www.bls.gov

Capital Hill Blue: www.capitolhillblue.com

Centers for Disease Control and Prevention (CDC): http://www.cdc.gov

Centers for Medicare and Medicaid Services: http://www.cms.gov

Child Welfare Information Gateway: https://www.childwelfare.gov

Chronic Disease Prevention and Health Promotion (of the CDC):
http://www.cdc.gov/chronicdisease

ClinicalTrials.gov: http://clinicaltrials.gov

Department of Health & Human Services: http://www.hhs.gov

Department of Veterans Affairs, health care section: http://www1.va.gov
/health

Education Commission of the States: www.ecs.org

FedStats: https://fedstats.sites.usa.gov

Government Accountability Office (GAO): http://www.gao.gov

Global Health Center (of the CDC): http://www.cdc.gov/globalhealth

Health Resources and Services Administration (HRSA): http://www.hrsa.gov

Healthcare.gov: https://www.healthcare.gov

Healthy People 2020: http://www.healthypeople.gov

Huffington Post: http://www.huffingtonpost.com

Modern Healthcare: www.modernhealthcare.com

National Academy for State Health Policy: www.nashp.org

National Cancer Institute: http://www.cancer.gov

National Center for Complementary and Alternative Medicine (NCCAM): http://www.nccam.nih.gov

National Center for Environmental Health (NCEH) (of the CDC): http://www.cdc.gov/nceh

National Center for Health Statistics (of the CDC): http://www.cdc.gov/nchs

National Center for Injury Prevention and Control (of the CDC): http://www.cdc.gov/ncipc/ncipchm.htm

The National Center for Preparedness, Detection, and Control of Infectious Diseases (NCPDCID) (of the CDC): http://www.cdc.gov/ncpdcid

National Guideline Clearinghouse (of the AHRQ): http://www.guideline.gov

National Health Law Program (NheLP): http://www.healthlaw.org

National Human Genome Institute: www.genome.gov

National Institute for Occupational Safety and Health (NIOSH) (of the CDC): http://www.cdc.gov/niosh

National Institutes of Health (NIH): http://www.nih.gov

National Library of Medicine (of the NIH): http://www.nlm.nih.gov

Occupational Safety & Health Administration (OSHA): http://osha.gov

Office of Disease Prevention and Health Promotion (ODPHP): http://www.healthfinder.gov

Policy Archive: www.policyarchive.org

Political Wire: https://politicalwire.com

Rand Corporation's Health Care Organization and Administration: www.rand.org

Real Clear Politics: www.realclearpolitics.com

Senate Journal: www.memory.loc.gov/ammem/amlaw/lwsj.html

State Children's Health Insurance Program (SCHIP), FirstStep program: http://www.cms.gov/apps/firststep/content/schip-qas.html

U.S. Census Bureau: www.census.gov

U.S. Congressional Budget Office (CBO): http://www.cbo.gov

U.S. Department of Health and Human Services: www.hhs.gov

U.S. Department of Labor: www.dol.gov

U.S. Food and Drug Administration (FDA): http://www.fda.gov

The Washington Monthly: www.washingtonmonthly.org

Associations and Professional Organizations

The Alliance: http://www.the-alliance.org

American Academy of Family Physicians: http://familydoctor.org/online/famdocen/home.html

American Association of Colleges of Nursing: www.aacn.nche.edu

American Association of Nurse Attorneys: http://www.taana.org

American Bar Association, health law section: http://www.abanet.org/health/home.html

American College of Healthcare Executives: www.ache.org

American Association of Retired Persons (AARP): http://www.aarp.org/health

American Board of Medical Specialties (ABMS), CertiFACTS: http://www.certifacts.org

American Cancer Society: http://www.cancer.org

American College of Preventive Medicine (ACPM): http://www.acpm.org

American Health Care Association (AHCA): http://www.ahcancal.org

American Health Lawyers Association: http://www.healthlawyers.org

American Heart Association (AHA): http://www.heart.org

American Lung Association: http://www.lungusa.org

American Medical Association (AMA): http://www.ama-assn.org

American Public Health Association (APHA): http://www.apha.org

America's Health Insurance Plans (AHIP): http://www.ahip.org

Annals of Long Term Care (American Geriatrics Society): http://www.annalsoflongtermcare.com

The Commonwealth Fund: http://www.commonwealthfund.org

Families USA: http://www.familiesusa.org

HealthCareCoach.com (National Health Law Program): http://www.healthcarecoach.com

Health Care Jobs Career Center: http://www.healthcarejobs.org

Joint Commission, accreditation programs section: http://www.jointcommission.org/AccreditationPrograms

Kaiser Family Foundation: http://www.kff.org

Long Term Care Provider.com: http://www.longtermcareprovider.com

Mayo Clinic: http://www.mayoclinic.com

Medscape: http://www.medscape.com

Modern Healthcare: http://www.modernhealthcare.com

MultiMedia HealthCare (MMHC): http://www.mmhc.com

National Alliance for Caregiving: http://www.caregiving.org

National Alliance on Mental Illness (NAMI): http://www.nami.org

National Association for Home Care & Hospice: http://www.nahc.org

National Association of County and City Health Officials (NACCHO): http://www.naccho.org

National Center for Assisted Living (NCAL): http://www.ahcancal.org/ncal

National Committee for Quality Assurance (NCQA): http://www.ncqa.org

National Council on Aging (NCOA): http://www.ncoa.org

The Rand Corporation: http://www.rand.org

Utilization Review Accreditation Commission (URAC): http://www.urac.org

World Health Organization: www.who.int

Policy and Politics Journals

Administration and Policy in Mental Health and Mental Health Service
  Research
American Journal of Political Science
American Political Science Review
American Politics Journal
American Politics Research
Applied Health Economics and Health Policy
Clinical Governance
Comparative Political Studies
Comparative Politics
Democratization
Economic Analysis and Policy
Environmental Politics
Ethics and Global Politics
Foreign Affairs
Foreign Policy
Foreign Policy Analysis
Forum for Health Economics and Policy
Global Governance
Global Policy
Governance
Government and Opposition
Health Affairs
Health Economics, Policy, and Law
Health Policy
Health Policy and Planning

Health Policy and Technology
Health Research Policy and Systems
Healthcare Policy
International Journal of E-Politics
International Journal of Equity in Health
International Journal of Politics, Culture, and Society
The International Journal of Sociology and Social Policy
International Political Science Review
International Politics
Journal of Cancer Policy
Journal of Democracy
Journal of Drug Policy Analysis
Journal of Economic Policy Reform
Journal of Gender Law and Policy
Journal of Health Care Law and Policy
Journal of Health Economics
Journal of Health Politics
Journal of Health Politics, Policy, and Law
Journal of Health Services Research and Policy
Journal of Information Technology and Politics
Journal of International Aging, Law, and Policy
Journal of Law and Politics
Journal of Law, Economics, and Policy
Journal of Legislation and Public Policy
Journal of Mental Health Policy and Economics
Journal of Policy Analysis and Management
Journal of Policy History
Journal of Political Economy
Journal of Political Science, Government, and Politics
Journal of Politics
Journal of Politics and Law
Journal of Politics and Society
Journal of Public Health Policy
Journal of Public Policy and Marketing
Journal of Race, Ethnicity, and Politics
Journal of Theoretical Politics
Journal of Women, Politics, & Policy

Muckraker: Journal of the Center for Investigative Reporting
Legislative Studies Quarterly
Nations and Nationalism
New Political Economy
Perspectives on Politics
Policy and Internet
Policy and Practice in Health and Safety
Policy, Politics, and Nursing Practice
Policy Studies Journal
Political Behavior
Political Psychology
The Political Quarterly
Political Research Quarterly
Political Science
Political Science and Politics
Political Science Quarterly
Political Science and Research Methods
Politics and Gender
Politics & Religion
Politics and Society
Presidential Studies Quarterly
Public Citizen
Public Opinion Quarterly
Quarterly Journal of Political Science
Research and Politics
Social Science Quarterly
Social Theory and Practice
Whittier Law Review
World Medical and Health Policy
World Policy Journal
World Politics

Executive Department Functions

EXECUTIVE DEPARTMENT	FUNCTIONS
Department of Agriculture	• Administers programs to help American farmers • Ensures food safety • Works to expand international markets for U.S. agricultural products • Provides food assistance and nutrition education • Protects natural resources • Fosters rural communities
Department of Commerce	• Promotes American businesses both in the United States and internationally • Collects economic and demographic data to measure the well-being of the U.S. economy • Promotes U.S. exports • Enforces international trade agreements • Regulates the export of sensitive goods and technologies • Issues patents and trademarks • Works with businesses, universities, communities, and workers to promote job creation, economic growth, sustainable development, and improved standards of living for Americans

(continues)

© Orhan Cam/Shutterstock

EXECUTIVE DEPARTMENT	FUNCTIONS
Department of Defense	• Provides the military forces needed to deter war and to protect the U.S. security interest • Major forces are the Army, Navy, Marine Corps, and Air Force
Department of Education	• Establishes policy for, administers, and coordinates federal education assistance • Executes U.S. education policies • Promote student achievement and preparation for global competitiveness • Foster educational excellence and ensuring equal access
Department of Energy	• Advances the national, economic and energy security of the United States • Implements policies on nuclear power, fossil fuels, and alternative energy sources • Promotes scientific and technological innovation in all energy sectors • Responsible charged for the environmental cleanup of the national nuclear weapons complex • Formulation and implementation of the National Energy Policy (NEP). NEP includes impacts of high energy prices; protecting America's environment; increasing energy conservation and efficiency; increasing domestic energy supplies; increasing America's use of renewable and alternative energy; America's energy infrastructure; and enhancing national energy security and international relations)

EXECUTIVE DEPARTMENT	FUNCTIONS
Department of Health and Human Services	• Promotes patient safety and healthcare quality in healthcare settings and by healthcare providers, by assuring the safety, effectiveness, quality, and security of foods, drugs, vaccines, and medical devices • Eliminates disparities in health, as well as healthcare access and quality, and protects vulnerable individuals and communities from poor health, public health, and human services outcomes • Conducts health, public health, and social science research • Uses health technology to improve the quality of care and use HHS data to drive innovative solutions to health, public health, and human services challenges • Promotes improvements in maternal and infant health; the safety, well-being, and healthy development of children and youth; and the youth's successful transition to adulthood • Promotes economic and social well-being for individuals, families, and communities • Promotes health promotion through wellness efforts across the life span • Prevents and manages the impact of infectious diseases/communicable and chronic diseases and conditions on the population's health • Disaster preparation that provides comprehensive responses to health, safety, and security threats, foreign and domestic, whether natural or human-made

(continues)

EXECUTIVE DEPARTMENT	FUNCTIONS
Department of Homeland Security	• Guards against terrorism • Secure U.S. borders • Enforce U.S. immigration laws • Improve U.S. readiness for, response to, and recovery from disasters • Provides employers with current and effective resources to maintain a legal workforce • Assist in disaster preparation • Promotes partnerships at the local, tribal, state, federal, and international levels • Deployment of science and technology
Department of Housing and Urban Development	• Manages federal programs to meet U.S. housing needs • Fosters increased homeownership • Supports community development • Increases access to affordable housing free from discrimination • Enforces federal housing laws
Department of Interior	• Manages and sustains U.S. lands, water, wildlife, and energy resources • Honors U.S. commitments and responsibilities to tribal nations • Protects fish and wildlife • Preserves our parks and historic lands
Department of Justice	• Represents U.S. citizens by enforcing laws of public interest in the public interest • Protects against criminal activity • Operations are performed by various agencies—Federal Bureau of Investigations (FBI), Drug Enforcement Administration (DEA), Immigration and Naturalization Service (INS), Bureau of Prisons (BOP), and U.S. Marshals Service (USMS)

EXECUTIVE DEPARTMENT	FUNCTIONS
Department of Labor	• Administers federal labor laws pertaining to workers' rights to safe and have healthful working conditions, minimum hourly wage and overtime pay, freedom from employment discrimination, unemployment insurance and other income support programs
Department of State	• Promote diplomacy of the federal government • Manages matters of foreign affairs with other nations and international bodies • Prepare strategic assessments
Department of Transportation	• Maintain and develop the U.S. transportation systems and infrastructure to include roads, airlines, and railways • Conducts planning that supports the movement of Americans by cars, trucks, trains, ships, and planes • Provides funding to improve the means of transport that Americans use • Regulates commercial airlines and airports to promote the industry and ensure the safety of passengers
Department of Treasury	• Manages federal finances • Pays all U.S. bills • Collects taxes, duties, and monies paid to and due to the United States • Currency and coinage production • Manages government accounts • Manages public debt • Supervises national banks and thrift institutions • Advises on domestic and international financial, monetary, economic, trade, and tax policy • Enforce federal finance and tax laws • Investigate and prosecute tax evaders, counterfeiters, and forgers

(continues)

EXECUTIVE DEPARTMENT	FUNCTIONS
Department of Veterans Affairs	• Provides vital services to U.S. veterans to include health care and veteran benefit services (veteran's compensation, veterans pension, survivor's benefits, rehabilitation and employment assistance, education assistance, home loan guaranties, and life insurance) • Provides burial and memorial benefits for veterans to include interment, headstones and markers, and presidential memorial certificates • Operates national cemeteries in the United States and Puerto Rico

Index

NOTE: Page numbers followed by *b*, *f* and *t* denotes box, figure and tables respectively.